D1379700

THERLE HUGHES

COLLECTING SMALL DECORATIVE ANTIQUES

BOOKPLAN

First published in one volume 1966

This edition published 1966 by
Lutterworth Press, London for
Bookplan

MADE AND PRINTED IN GREAT BRITAIN BY
WILLIAM CLOWES AND SONS, LIMITED, LONDON AND BECCLES

SMALL DECORATIVE ANTIQUES

THERLE HUGHES

SMALL DECORATIVE ANTIQUES

BOOKPLAN

First Published 1959
Second Impression 1960

CONTENTS

PLATES

Between pages 128 and 129

Plate

Plate

Plate

Plate

conscious penwork (*Victoria and Albert Museum*); locket profile signed J. Miers; the Duchess of Atholl by John Miers; by C. C. Rosenberg, painted on convex glass; by J. Gapp (*collection of Mrs. W. E. Hopley*); the Duke of Sussex painted on card, by W. Mason

29. Late Georgian pedlar doll (*Victoria and Albert Museum*)
30. Early dolls: a painted wooden doll of about 1690, a doll of the 1700s, *and* a magnificent Mrs. Candour doll (*all Victoria and Albert Museum*); a doll of carved and painted wood, 1760 (*London Museum*)
31. Nineteenth-century dolls: mid-Victorian doll dressed in costume of about 1875; doll of the 1830s; elaborate court dress on a typical early Victorian doll (*all Victoria and Albert Museum*)
32. The poet Christopher Anstey painted by William Hoare, showing a doll and an inkstand (*National Portrait Gallery*)
33. A fine dresser forms the ideal background to an array of pewter (*S. W. Wolsey*)
34. Pewter: spoons of the fifteenth and sixteenth centuries; wine-measure with a double-volute thumbpiece; trumpet-base candlestick; candlestick with a heavy salt-cellar base; tankard decorated with joggled work; a group of two measures and two tankards (*all Victoria and Albert Museum*)
35. Kitchen garden ceramics: group of Wedgwood's green-glaze ware; group of Chelsea fruits and vegetables (*Christie, Manson & Woods, Ltd.*)
36. Kitchen garden ceramics: Worcester leaf with pictorial ornament, greenish-glazed Staffordshire stoneware leaf, Longton Hall melon, *and* a cauliflower tea-pot (*all Victoria and Albert Museum*); melon in Leeds cream-coloured earthenware painted with flowers (*Leeds City Art Gallery*); a Chelsea sunflower (*Christie, Manson & Woods Ltd.*)
37. Georgian dessert glasses (*Delomosne & Son*)
38. Dessert glasses showing the typical small feet and the wide range in bowl design (*Delomosne & Son*)
39. Brass candlesticks: a specimen of about 1680; late seventeenth-century stick with a slide to adjust the height of the candle; late seventeenth-century pillar candlestick; two early eighteenth-century specimens; one of the late eighteenth century and three of the early nineteeth century (*all Victoria and Albert Museum*)
40. Porcelain candlesticks: three Bow flower-encrusted candlesticks (*Christie, Manson & Woods Ltd.*); Derby shepherd group (*collection of Mr. W. W. Fox*); Chelsea-Derby figure supported by a flowery "tree-stump" (*Delomosne & Son*)

DRAWINGS

INTRODUCTION

THIS book has accumulated itself over the years, chapter by chapter as my interests have led me. I cannot remember when the first of its subjects captured my imagination nor envisage any end to my questings. By writing I have been compelled to turn fascinating speculation into verified fact, but always the driving force has been a basic delight in the decorative value of the articles I have examined or acquired.

Age may provoke admiration and long use may in itself induce a mellow grace, but to me mere "earliness" is never enough. Even rarity offers satisfaction only when some morsel of long-forgotten fashions can be identified and acclaimed. The antiques that can hold me entranced are in themselves delightful to possess, to look at and live with on the close terms necessitated by the conditions of modern home-making. The joy is that able design, fine materials and trustworthy craftsmanship have tended to outlast their shoddier contemporaries. Many small antiques of great decorative value are still to be found, and the pleasures of the search are only equalled by the pleasures of piecing together the background details that explain their existence.

Others, I know, share this sheer, indescribable delight in seeing and handling something lovely, something that others before us have loved and appreciated too. We go hopefully into every junk shop, lumber room, auction sale, and when we find antiques to our liking it is with a peculiarly vivid sense of contact with the people who made and used them. To such collectors as to myself the real stuff of history is to be found in old letters, household books and inventories, in wills and advertisements, even in patent specifications, and the following pages are greatly enriched by such documents. Our historical figures are the gossipy commentators on their times and fashions, and these too I have consulted, as old friends.

One result of such interests, of course, is that we do find "bargains". We know what to look for and what to reject. And that, inevitably, makes us feel justified in redoubling our search. But who cares when at every turn we may find so much to charm and challenge, so much to enrich and decorate our glossy existence of today.

Chapter One

CHINA TEA-POTS AND COFFEE-POTS

SEVEN o'clock on a black December evening almost two hundred years ago, the ritual of four o'clock dinner accomplished, fires settled into a comfortable blaze, soft fingers of candlelight fondling furniture and ornaments, a gracious, peaceful, intimate time of day. . . . And at the "Queen's House", as in a humble cottage, the lady of the house would open the tea canister and ladle the leaves into the tea-pot, and her husband would bear the cups of tea to their honoured guests. George III had been twelve years king of England before he and Queen Charlotte introduced any greater formality to their enjoyment of this homely ritual. Then, on December 26, 1772, their visitor the Duchess of Newcastle noted a change. On this occasion, she recorded, "two Pages of the Backstairs enter'd each with a Cup of Tea with creampot &c." for "each of their Majestys".

Even so the charm of the homely scene was retained: the partaking of tea was a pleasure deeply rooted in the daily life of the eighteenth century, for king and commoner, for the lady of title and for the maid she hired at "five guineas a year and tea twice daily". The tea itself, admittedly, was of corresponding quality, varying from the most delicately aromatic green tea to the commoner's heavy black. Much was smuggled, and much more was adulterated with ash tree leaves, gathered on such a scale that outcry was raised, not at the spoilt tea, but at the havoc in the woodlands.

There was a difference, too, in the vessels that constituted the tea equipage of the eighteenth century, but

Fig. 1.

here is a point of advantage to the present-day collector. Costly porcelains never wholly ousted peasant potteries, and however rare or however everyday the ware might be, the winter firelight would fling its warm glow around much the same design of pot, ostensibly derived from Chinese tea-ware but really speaking the universal language of ceramic craftsmanship.

Today's collector may gather together a small group of tea-pots that will show the main changes in design down the years and in the materials that give them their individuality. Always the craftsman had to provide his pot with the structural strength to meet the constant impact of boiling water: globe and melon forms in countless variants have the lasting grace of sound design, the ribbed melon of the silversmith proving equally successful for the potter, and as satisfying to our eye to-day. But such a group will show how the potter acknowledged other passing whims introduced by the silversmith.

The melon and pear shapes in fashion from the 1680s to 1750 were succeeded and accompanied by early Georgian pyramidal designs on octagonal bases. The early eighteenth-century bullet pot developed in the mid-century into the inverted pear shape, wide above and narrowing down to a moulded foot. By the mid-century the width from spout tip to handle was often greater than the vessel's height. The lid had lost its early high dome, and the spout tip might acknowledge the current craze for naively realistic bird and animal heads.

All too soon, however, came the more staid designs to suit Adamesque surroundings: oval or cylindrical pots with straight sides, straight tapering spouts, and flat bases fitting accompanying trays or stands. The vertical in-and-out shapings, making such pots serpentine in plan, came in the 1780s. These might supply necessary strength to the silversmith's thin metal but remained better suited to silverware, whereas the rounded rectangles typical of the following years have a friendly capacious line about them, too buxom for silver but splendid in cottage wares.

There was indeed a factual increase in size. The precious early tea had been too costly for pots of more than 1 pint capacity. The cheaper teas that a determined public had managed to win by 1785 created a demand for 1½-pint vessels, and in about 1800 came the familiar quart size, in designs that were soon so varied and undisciplined and lavishly adorned as to defy classification but delight us to-day with their sheer magnificence. The most massive include china versions of the silversmiths' "revived rococo" of the 1820s, with an ornate scrollwork foot replacing the loose tray or stand of the 1800s.

Such a collection of pots may show, for instance, how the early potter perched the lid precariously on the rim of the round or pear-shaped body. His first effort to improve matters was merely a chain from handle to lid and from lid to spout. But soon came the lid opening encircled with a vertical collar to receive a similar deep flange on the lid. This looked better when the collar was raised and made more shapely with an undulating edge, so that the lid fitted snugly into a recess, giving the pot its characteristic upswept line of Regency days. A sliding lid was then an alternative.

Another early problem to the potter was the spout. Eighteenth-century porcelains and most earthenwares fared badly in everyday use. One way of protecting the spout was a silver tip: so many were presented for hall-marking that the silversmiths' assay list for 1777 specifically included them. Queen Charlotte herself ordered Wedgwood to supply a "Silver-Spout Tea-pot" in 1795.

Perhaps the most intriguing quest today, however, is for tea-pots representing the different ceramic wares in and out of fashion between the 1680s and 1860s. The first tea-pots of all, of course, were as Chinese as the tea itself, but by 1684 John Dwight of Fulham was already copying the famous impervious hard-fired Ching stoneware, miscalled red porcelain. By 1690 the Dutch silversmith-potters John Philip and David Elers were giving a metallic gloss to their now-famous little red tea-pots by polishing them on the lathe. The Elers ornamented their pots with applied pads of clay impressed with designs in relief. The pots were all circular, and lighter in colour than the other unglazed red stoneware tea-pots made until as late as the 1820s and all, to collectors, given the Elers' name.

Salt-glazed stoneware came in the 1730s, drab-colour, brown and then white. Relief ornament in pipe clay appears on these, but their original gilding has left few traces. The body of the pot is globular, but handle and spout are in the virile shapes of knotted branch and gnarled stump of crab-apple tree generally known as crabstock, and the lid has a looped twig handle.

Altogether more adventurous styles remain to us from around the mid-century, when pots might be formed by shaping in moulds instead of by throwing on the wheel. Everything was possible then as a tea-pot design, from cottage to kneeling camel, although the clear-cut ornament associated with stoneware, worked in relief in all-over patterns, was still bounded by the silversmiths' limitations. Evidence of the first plunge into the joys of colour appears on "scratch blue" stoneware tea-pots with incised blue lines. Fleeting unfired colours and gilding were followed from the 1750s by fired enamel colours in Chinese designs.

Pots in earthenware show a similar course of development, including ornament with white reliefs from the 1720s. Technically we may note that there was an important change in about 1750 away from the old form of glazing, which involved scattering powdered lead on the unfired clay. The new method consisted of dipping once-fired ware into a liquid white lead glaze and refiring it—at shocking hazard to the health of the men who did it.

Some of the most satisfactory among the mould-shaped pots in earthenware are in the greenish-greyish-brownish marbled effects known as agate ware, composed of clays in different colours blended and cut and blended and cut again until suitably streaked and mottled. This process dates from about 1730 onwards. It made the clays so stiff and unresilient that they had to be pressed into the moulds. They were finished by lathe turning, and only slight breaks in the marbling betray the joints. This is solid agate ware, as distinct from the marbled effects achieved on plain pottery with colour blendings and combings not very different from the paper marbler's technique.

The most famous among early Georgian earthenware pots, however, have blotchy patches of different-coloured glazes, and were known as tortoiseshell ware throughout a period that delighted in reproducing these mottlings in many media, their resemblance to the shell often extremely remote. Nowadays such tea-pots are attributed almost invariably to Whieldon. In Chapter 15 more detailed consideration is given to the "Whieldon" pots modelled as cauliflowers, pineapples, melons and the like, in surprisingly lifelike greens and yellows.

Stonewares and earthenwares have never gone out of fashion, but the 1740s saw the production of porcelain tea ware at Chelsea and Bow. Here for once it was Staffordshire that gave the porcelain men the lead, the salt-glaze moulded tea-pots in figure forms reappearing in Chelsea ware, such as the famous Chinaman with his wide-spreading conical hat for a lid, and a bird in his arms with open beak for a spout.

Collectors are justifiably ecstatic about the lovely soft-paste porcelains, but to their owners they must have been heartbreakingly fragile. Undoubtedly some of the fireside talk of the 1750s was about the soapstone porcelain especially associated with the tea ware of Worcester, proof against boiling water and decked out in wonderful blues and greens, purple and scarlet and gold, in the fashionable Japanese patterns. Worcester collectors note that rolled handles were succeeded by designs flat on the outer surface of the curve and rounded on the inside, followed towards the 1780s by small scroll handles.

The current classical mood was reflected in Worcester's pots from 1783, and the decorators of their panels of pictorial ornament developed a characteristic technique in their precise painting of landscapes, figures and so on. Less expensive tea-pots show flowers painted or transfer-printed in blue.

The most ornamental rivals dating to the late eighteenth century are tea-pots in the fine earthenware known as creamware. These were made by many potters and at their best are shapely and attractive. There are the Leeds pots, for instance, that we expect to find with openwork twisted handles secured by substantial flower motifs at the ends. These cannot, in fact, be regarded as exclusive to the famous Leeds pottery that today is a special darling among collectors.

These pots often follow porcelain designs—and, more remotely, silver—such as the cylindrical body with a flat base and an accompanying tray. But more generally creamware pots are round and either painted in blue, transfer-printed—also, of course, a one-colour process—or sparsely painted in a more colourful range of enamels.

Wedgwood made fine pots in his queen's ware and in the whiter ware he called pearl ware, with a hint of pearly lustre about it that was lost when other potters developed it, although they retained the popular name. But today Wedgwood himself is associated more particularly with tea services in velvety unglazed jasper wares bearing impeccable classical ornament in white relief, and with the black basaltes that were imitated equally profitably by many firms in the periods 1780–1820 and 1850–75.

Lustre-decorated tea-pots date from 1810 onwards and are a study all their own. Even a version of the creamy imitation of marble known as parian ware appears in mid-nineteenth-century tea-pots made by Copeland, Coalport,

Minton and others, but this is domestic parian, not the statuary ware with its easily sullied bloom. Earthenwares never went out of fashion, of course. The brown "Rockingham glaze" is with us to this day, still appreciated aesthetically for its lovely "bloom" and gastronomically for making really good tea. This glaze was developed in the early 1790s at Rockingham in Yorkshire and the ware was known at the time as Rockingham china. The lead glaze was heavily stained with pure oxide of manganese, producing a purple brown, lighter on the neck of a tea-pot and darker at the foot because it tended to run during the firing process.

Hard porcelain, too, may be found in Regency style, from New Hall. But the ceramic triumph for early nineteenth-century tea ware was the development of bone china, launched by Josiah Spode in the 1790s, white and translucent like earlier porcelains yet comparatively sturdy and cheap. The earliest bone china pots are oval, flat-based, with deep lid recesses, but specimens from the Regency may be round-bodied with foot rings, and with high scalloped capes surrounding their lid recesses. These pots demonstrate the period's horror of blank white spaces, whether by their expensively lavish painting and gilding or by their simpler all-over blue transfer work. All too soon, however, Regency elegance was lost in Victorian grandeur, and potters followed silversmiths into complexities of relief work including much meaningless gilded scrolling.

All have their place in the collector's cabinet, and among them those particularly appealing diminutive pots now generally regarded as children's toys but more probably intended as receptacles for gifts of costly tea. And no cabinet can be regarded as complete until it includes that curiosity among tea-pots the Cadogan pot, the vessel that mysteriously lacks any lid opening and, equally surprising to the uninitiated, has to be filled upside down.

"Tea at three-halfpence a serving, coffee at twopence...." Some of us can still remember such days. But the context of the particular announcement I am quoting shows that the cup was a handleless "dish", the tea "green", the coffee black and spiced perhaps with mustard—and a labourer's wage the shilling a day of Queen Anne's reign. By then coffee had become firmly established in England, after its stormy introduction in the previous century, and its ritual dominated by one of the most handsome pieces of tableware ever devised. In silver and porcelain and throughout the whole range of imitative wares the coffee-pot retained an elegance and individuality that have made it the pride of numberless collectors.

Coffee houses had been opened in Oxford by 1650 and in London by 1652, and tokens from some of these establishments preserved in Guildhall Museum indicate that many early coffee-pots were of the Turkish-ewer pattern with narrow-waisted bulbous bodies and curving spouts. But these, it appears, were all imported. All too soon the coffee houses began to lose their first sparkle of wit in a deterioration that led eventually to the tavern atmosphere of a Rowlandson caricature. But long before then, even by the beginning of the eighteenth century, English craftsmen had found the perfect shapes and proportions for presenting coffee as a gracious detail in the ritual of entertaining at home.

"Blacke as soote and tasting not much unlike it", as George Sandys described the Turkish drink in 1610, coffee at its most elegant was first presented in tiny cups of Oriental porcelain, poured into silver or silver-gilt saucers and placed on mats of gold-fringed silk. The less affluent merely used small bowls. But as early as 1672 it was noted that the "smell and taste of the Mock China Bowl" affected the coffee's flavour; presumably these were cups of tin-glazed delftware, English or Dutch. It is not surprising, therefore, to find silver predominant in the early service of coffee, and the changing designs chosen by the silversmith are important to the ceramic collector, for china coffee-pots never broke free as tea-pots did to establish their separate individuality.

The earliest existing specimens, in silver of the 1680s, are in the lantern shape with a handle at right angles to the spout, noted in K'ang-hsi porcelain, with tall unwaisted body narrowing to the top where the line is continued in the high cone lid. Soon, however, even in silver the design became less austere, and early eighteenth-century work shows the lid in a double or treble dome, the base enriched with wide moulding, and the spout in the graceful swan-neck curve.

The aggressive style of the 1730s ideally suited the coffee-pot, flat lidded, straight sided and with bold castings to ornament the spout, now diametrically opposite the handle socket. By the 1740s body, spout and lid might all be cast in a welter of surface ornament, flowers, birds, or scrollwork, hand finished with chasing. The ultimate for the collector of this style is the spout in an eagle's head. By the late 1730s some pots had incurving bases mounted on deep, spreading foot-rims, but in the eagle decade there might be three feet instead of a rim, in claw-and-ball shape, or sometimes scrolls or dolphins.

All this is important because it shows the collector what the potter was attempting to reproduce and rival. Probably the earliest ceramic pots were in brown salt-glazed stoneware, followed by the dense, hard, red stoneware now known as Elers ware. These pots were selling for twelve to twenty-four shillings each in the early eighteenth century and were made until the 1760s. They copy silver models with applied ornament still determined by the relief effects possible in metal, and occasionally, like silver, showing traces of gilding.

Silver again sets the style for the pot's most adventurous shapes in Staffordshire salt-glazed white stoneware. This was made in the 1720s, shaped on the wheel, but is more usually represented in collections of coffee-pots by specimens of the 1740s when the method was to shape them in moulds. Some are lantern form, some eight-sided and tapering, some moulded in relief with double-headed eagles, animals or flowers. All manner of silver fantasies were imitated with snake's head spouts and dolphin feet, and sometimes the silversmith's faceted spouts. After about 1750 came enamel colours on this ware, often in the Chinese range of red, pink, blue, purple, green, brown, yellow and opaque white.

Colour employed with the greatest distinction is

Fig. 2

associated, of course, with coffee-pots in the less sturdy eighteenth-century porcelain. The copper coffee-pot on a stand and spirit lamp that may now take pride of place in a collection of bygones was frequently regarded in the mid-eighteenth century as a kitchen vessel, kept in the background on formal occasions so that its coffee could be transferred to a pot of glowing porcelain.

The ornament of these porcelain pots delights us more than their outlines. Pear-shaped body and flattened loop handle constitute the accepted form, still 6 inches or less in height in the mid-eighteenth century. Hard porcelain from China was an exquisite extravagance from the late seventeenth century, and some English pots were made by Bristol and New Hall, but English-made coffee-pots were mostly in soft porcelains of Chelsea, Bow, Longton Hall, Worcester, Derby, Lowestoft, made between the 1740s and the early nineteenth century, lovely, fragile, and now rare indeed. It is interesting to note that the pot of the 1780s is somewhat taller, probably because by then the frugal or the over-indulgent were adding chicory to make the coffee go further. William Littler of Longton Hall is associated with some pots in a deep blue glaze, painted with flowers and foliage in thick white enamel touched with black and gold.

Coffee-pots in less extravagant earthenware were never more

delightful than in the third quarter of the eighteenth century. Some that remain, like contemporaneous tea-pots, are in the mottled manganese lead glazes known as tortoise-shell ware. Some have the tea-pot's fashionable twiggy crabstock handle, and are smothered in fruiting vines, shaped in relief and picked out in gold. There are cauliflowers and pineapples, too, with relief mouldings and coloured glazes dating from about 1760 onwards and described in Chapter 15.

Once lead-glazed, cream-coloured earthenwares became established in the 1770s, however, the trend was away from naturalistic forms. Instead, surfaces are smooth, outlines conventional, and patterns the routine painted and printed ornament of Staffordshire, Leeds, Liverpool, Bristol, Sunderland and elsewhere. Few examples are marked. Transfer-printing is found in black and in rare eighteenth-century examples in red or purple, applied over the glaze. Graceful interlaced handles may be found, occasionally and triumphantly, and a highly domed lid topped perhaps by a squirrel or a flower, the whole vessel being as much as 11 inches high. Fine white pearl-ware pots painted in underglaze blue may date to the 1780s, while printing in underglaze blue dates more especially from about 1820 onwards.

The Wedgwood firm made notable coffee-pots for seventy or eighty years in black basaltes ornamented with low relief work and the pleasantly unemphatic, intricate line-work known as engine turning. In coloured jasper wares the coffee-pots bear the familiar white relief decorations. But Wedgwood had many imitators and it is a mistake to credit a Wedgwood origin to any unmarked coffee-pot of these types. We may find more frequently that the stoneware has been surface-coated with a coloured jasper dip, blue, sage green, or straw-yellow. Henry Palmer, William Adams, John Turner, Elijah Mayer and William Baddeley made and marked jasper ware in the late eighteenth century, but it must be remembered that fine stoneware coffee-pots continued in production until the 1850s.

By then the tough, more or less translucent bone china, felspar china, semi-opaque china and similar strong substitutes for porcelain had been added to the range of materials for painted and transfer-printed coffee-pots, some with the early right-angled spout and handle arrangement. Many appear in the familiar eighteenth-century outlines, but others are vertically fluted and baluster shaped, on deep foot rims. They include the squat coffee biggin, fitted with a wire strainer or a fabric bag.

Even before 1800 men were discovering that boiling was altogether too fierce a treatment for exquisite coffee. First filtration in the early 1800s, then percolation, was substituted. The first pumping percolator, using steam pressure to raise the water, was invented as late as 1819, a hundred and sixty-two years after the first English coffee advertiser had observed that the drink "quickneth the Spirits, maketh the heart lightsom".

Chapter Two

SCENT BOTTLES

SCENT and the love of it are as ancient as history. Old household books lead you endlessly between still-room and herb garden, between flower knots and linen closet. Home-prepared waters, essences and sweet vinegars vied with pomanders and pouncet boxes, aromatic oranges and exotic-sounding goa stones in overcoming the discomfort of ill-odours and danger of lurking pestilence. Aromatic vinegars were especially valued. One favourite was concocted of lavender flowers and the tops of sweet rosemary, sage, mint, garlic, bitter wormwood and repellently pungent rue, with calamus, cinnamon, clove and nutmeg.

Today we may leave the chemistry to specialists and collect the tiny vessels that once contained such prophylactics. Just to handle such a vessel, Chelsea figure or sparkling rococo enamel, Bristol-blue glass or Wedgwood jasper-ware, is to appreciate the encouragement and support it must have diffused in jolting coach, stuffy playhouse or thronged market square. The term scent bottle is comparatively new and formal: the smelling bottle was something to be handled, to be carried on the chatelaine or in the reticule, companionable and wholly personal.

Even by Elizabethan days little chain "flagon bracelets" were worn, specifically for carrying such smelling bottles; in Victorian days the chain was around the waist but still its purpose might be to carry a tiny smelling bottle of gold.

Collectors find that most of their specimens date from the second half of the eighteenth century onwards. Previously it had been something of a problem to make a wholly suitable vessel at a popular price. Gorgeous little pieces, of course, were fashioned in gold and in gold-mounted natural stones, such as agate and the crystal known as Bristol stone, and by about the beginning of the nineteenth century Derbyshire blue-john in glowing amethyst-and-honey colours was used for egg-shaped hand-cooler smelling bottles. But late in the eighteenth century such books on perfumes as *The Temple of Flora* still tended to base their scents on powder, that could be stored in bags of leather to preserve the precious sweetness of civet and ambergris and musk.

Silver "casting bottles" for sprinkling perfume about the house were introduced in the mid-sixteenth century. One is mentioned in the Earl of Northampton's household inventory of 1614, among a list of gorgeous dress and jewellery and furnishings in which even the many "sweet-bags" or flower sachets are detailed in all their embroidered loveliness. Yet even here there is no reference to a smelling bottle. Occasionally, too, silver scent flasks of the seventeenth century are to be found, simple bottles with small domed caps and square shoulders and perhaps slight flower engraving. There were light soda-glass bottles in plenty, of course, and they kept their contents fresh and sweet, but they were disastrously fragile so that they had to be covered with wicker or leather: the Howard household accounts make several references to such bottles, as in 1633: "I glass bottell covered with leather, to put orenge flower water in, xviijd"—the flower water, of course, being home prepared, from flowers gathered two hours before sunrise.

Pottery smelling bottles are completely and delightfully of the exciting, experimental eighteenth century. A pottery smelling bottle needed to be strongly glazed. Cracks and crizzling soon wasted a concentrated essence. Hence the early Georgian development of bottles in salt-glazed stoneware, the white ware known at the time as flint ware to distinguish it from common brown stoneware, and ornamented with incised lines in the 1730s and 1740s. Before 1750 there were bottles in agate ware too, as small as an inch in diameter, in marble effects created by mingling variously tinted clays. You can detect how moulds were used to shape the difficult, almost non-plastic clay mixture that baulked at the potter's wheel. A yellowish galena glaze was used at first, but after the mid-1750s the glaze was clear, and by the 1760s might even be tinted slightly blue, the more nearly to resemble real agate.

These were plainly unsophisticated, however. The sparkle of gaiety came with the arrival of soft paste porcelain at Chelsea. Even by the early 1750s, which Chelsea collectors know as the periods of the raised anchor and red anchor marks, this French-inspired firm was producing charming, whimsical little figure bottles, though still simple and in subdued colours. These include models of nuns and monks, and of birds with their heads forming the stoppers. The collector today watches for other early designs too, such as bottles with faceted sides in imitation of glass, and the smoothly plain pear shapes carefully painted with flowers or river scenes. In December 1754 and again in April 1755 auctions of Chelsea wares included many smelling bottles, the sale announcements indicating clearly enough that they were highly prized little luxuries "mounted in Gold and ornamented with stones of several sorts as rubies, diamonds, etc."

One guide in recognising the early Chelsea bottle is the depth of the hollow in its base: the purpose was to mount this with a lid and make a patch box. In later Chelsea bottles, produced at the period when the firm's mark was a gold anchor, the base is shallower. Colours are richer too and there may be gilded detail. This was the period that produced such familiar little charmers as the boy holding a goat beside a stump bearing grapes and vine leaves. Sometimes this has a bunch of grapes as a stopper, but there is no rule as to any detail, or even as to colour or the lack of it. And this was but one design among myriads. A few, but only a few, such as the famous harlequins, were Dresden imitations. Later figures avoided the indignity of having their heads removed as the bottle stoppers, other details in the design being put to this use.

Every design has its own individuality. However trivial it may be, it escapes the vapid "prettiness" of later would-be imitators. It is easy to go on and on about Chelsea smelling bottles—about a fox and hound from the Aesop fable, a boy with a bird cage, a triple bottle formed of a group of three hens, a stick of asparagus, a bouquet of rosebuds with an étui in its stem, or a group composed with cheerful inconsequence of a nymph, a cupid, a dog, a clock and a flower bouquet. There are lovely, lively birds for the finding, and really feline cats, elaborate dovecotes. . . . But it must be stressed that you will almost certainly search in vain for a *genuine* specimen bearing any Chelsea mark.

The finishing touch was a case of shagreen. This was the work of men specialising in shagreen and fish-skin products, such as John Folgham, whose trade card dated 1760 makes special reference to the requirements of smelling bottles.

For all their variety of mood and elaboration these smelling bottles tended to conform to the same flattened pear outline, and this was even more marked among the other main styles manufactured in gay abundance during the third quarter of the eighteenth century. Among these the collector delights particularly in the South Staffordshire enamels that still tend to be labelled Battersea in many curio shops. Dainty as porcelain yet extremely sturdy, at their best these are among the most delightful minor products of their period. They were handsome little substitutes for Chelsea work, and a marked similarity of pattern is apparent, even to the sentiments in more or less inaccurate French sometimes incorporated in a design.

I have handled and browsed over hundreds, including the fabulous collections of Queen Mary and the Hon. Mrs. Ionides, and still I find it hard to imagine how their inventors ever conceived the idea of making such fragile-looking morsels by enclosing a strong core of copper with a smooth, glossy covering of opaque enamel. This was fixed to the copper by intense heat and painted by hand like porcelain in coloured enamels too, so that even the ornament would be made permanent in the firing oven. In many the small pictures are painted over transfer prints for greater speed, but then even the renowned Battersea enamels factory was developed precisely because of the wonderful possibilities suggested by this revolutionary technique. In the best South Staffordshire enamel scent bottles the hand colouring is so good and the gilt metal mounts so dainty that you have very much the sense of those individual miniatures, gold mounted and jewel encrusted, that had long been the privilege of the wealthy few.

Some bottles carry tiny copies of popular prints showing contemporary beauties. It is a prize indeed to find a reproduction of Houston's engraving from Mercier's "Night", or "Taste" in Houston's series of Senses. Less exciting bottles have flower posies or small figure scenes suggesting contented idleness. Bright raised gilding in all manner of rococo scrolls and flourishes gives a gay trimming to the white or coloured neck of the bottle, and in good work the mount is extremely delicate. A poor mount and carelessly speedy dabs of hand colouring betray the late and excessively cheap smelling bottle, but these, thank goodness, are less common than the horrid little snuff boxes that bring discredit to the craft. Most usually the paintings appear on the sides of a flattened pear-shape bottle, but I suppose every collector hopes to find the bottle shaped as two billing doves with a twining ribbon in their beaks bearing the donor's off-French sentiments.

In the 1760s there was another rival to soft porcelain, fragile too but manufactured with far fewer wasters. This was the opaque white glass known at the time as enamel glass. Such bottles, made at Bristol and Warrington by the 1760s—experimentally at Bristol in the 1750s—are a dense white, smooth and soft to the touch, no more translucent than oriental porcelain and looking indeed far more like porcelain than glass. The soft surfaces became sadly scratched and blackened in use, however, which is the greater pity, for this brittle but particularly appealing glass was splendidly decorated in brilliant colours, mainly with flowers or birds or little figures, robust and not too painstakingly oriental. The stopper may be of glass, ground to fit tightly and protected by a cap of silver or gilt metal. Occasionally a bottle has retained its protective case: you may even have the supreme good fortune to find a set of three in a case of openwork gilt metal scarcely more than 2 inches tall.

Only Bristol and Warrington, it seems, made this enamel

glass, but smelling bottles in a somewhat inferior milk white glass were made in many places. In these the opacity was achieved with arsenic instead of tin oxide. They can be recognised by their ruddy opalescent glow against the light, indeed by the mid-nineteenth century the ware had become known as opaline glass. The same dainty tricks of ornament that succeeded on enamelled bottles are to be found for the searching. Some are especially appealing for the inclusion among their ornament of a name and date, obviously applied at the order of the purchaser in somewhat amateurish penmanship—wonderful for those of us with sentimental imaginations.

Bristol glass to most of us, of course, means blue glass—none too accurately, for it was the blue cobalt preparations to colour the glass that were the monopoly, and Bristol-blue glass was made in many places and qualities. Here again it is possible to recognise the same flower and bird ornament associated with the 1760s and 1770s, and to contrast it with the more formal cutting and faceting on the flask shapes of the century's end.

Smelling bottles in the velvety-opaque blue or green of jasper ware suggest yet another specialist—and plentiful—field for a collector who enjoys their graceful vestal virgins and fat roguish cherubs. Today those Sacrifices to Hymen and Conquering Heroes, intensely white against their matt backgrounds, seem to express to perfection the mood of the later eighteenth century that introduced them on Wedgwood's jasper ware. But a serious collector has to be on guard against reproductions.

Clear-glass scent bottles can be formed into a sparkling and abundantly varied collection. This may include, for example, bottles painted in white in the style, though probably not from the brush, of the Newcastle Beilbys of the 1760s, but will be dominated by the brilliant cut glass work that came at the end of the eighteenth century, the finely moulded glass of the late 1820s and the coloured glass, often dubbed Regency, in lovely tones of ruby, green, amber, of the 1840s and after. Gold-mounted in a limitless array of shapes, these bottles continued popular far through the nineteenth century.

Nailsea has acquired a reputation for making all the splotched and swirling coloured specimens (see Chapter 7), including tiny named and dated bottles and amusing shapes. I am quite certainly prejudiced when I prefer my own small bellows specimens—imitations of the dressing-table bellows of hair-powder days—which are now clear glass with scarcely a hint of the gilding that once transformed them.

Cut glass, of course, has its own chronological record for those who aim at a representative collection or merely wish to identify a shilling "find". Clear-glass smelling bottles have come to us, I feel, from matronly dressing-tables, from the rich quiet where even the tallest- and smallest-footed vessels could take their ease. The main point to recognise, however, is that until about 1790 the glass was suitable only for cutting in low relief, for the shallow slices and facets that please the fingers. The eye-dazzling brilliance of deep cutting really began about 1790 and was the rage of, say, 1805 to 1830. A bottle with a gold stopper might have a hinged outer cover, so that bottle and cover could be cut all over with deep, prickly diamonds.

Fig. 3. Cut glass: top left is harnessed with silver.

One sparklingly brilliant glass style must have special mention. In 1819 Apsley Pellatt devised a way of mounting little moulded busts and figures in slight relief within the very fabric of his glass vessels. Such a silver "sulphide" held suspended in the clear-glass face of a scent bottle might be set off by deeply cut faceting, the whole effect being chaste and charming. Contrasts of clear and frosted glass were elaborated around the mid-nineteenth century.

For today's collector much depends on the quality of a glass bottle's mount. Gold hall-marking may aid in dating and it must be remembered that all hall-marked gold was of at least eighteen carat until 1796. The glass bottles

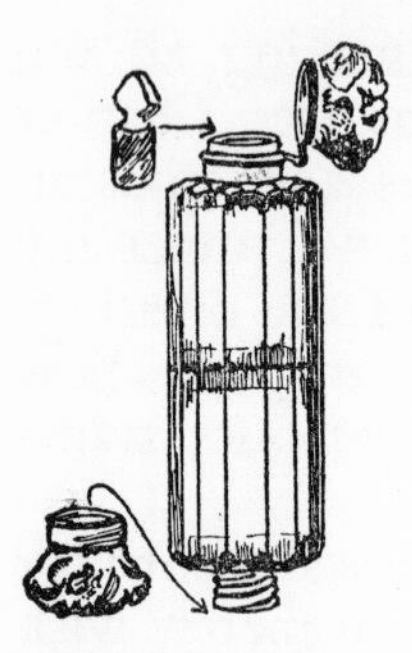

Fig. 4. Two-part bottle in clear coloured glass.

themselves were inexpensive trifles. In 1829 the wholesale price of even the best flint-glass moulded perfume bottles was but two shillings a pound weight, or three farthings each, and smelling bottles intended for cutting were about twopence-farthing each. By the third quarter of the century the Rotherham Glass Works listed "smelling bottles various" at seven shillings a gross; its perfumery bottles included squares, ovals with long and globe necks, panelled squares, Oxford lavenders and conical octagons.

One later nineteenth-century design that catches the eye in many a window of collectors' trifles is the double bottle with a cap at each end, one half intended for one of the new "artificial" perfumes, the other for aromatic vinegar. In a rich shade of ruby glass, with neatly-finished mounts, this can be a handsome little piece, well able to outlast that short-lived rival the vinaigrette.

Chapter Three

MOTHER OF PEARL

EVERY century, almost every generation, rediscovers the delicate soap-bubble loveliness of mother of pearl, and recalls that its opalescence bears the magic name of orient. A hundred years ago there were mother of pearl tea caddies and innumerable card cases; two hundred years ago foiled and fretted pearl sticks to the most magnificent mid-Georgian fans; three hundred years ago pearl inlay mellowing the pomp of late Stuart furniture. Yet another hundred years before that the first Elizabethans riveted mosaics of shell over their silverware, and mounted whole shells of pearly nautilus to form some of the most decorative vessels ever devised. Long centuries earlier still, mother of pearl was a favourite ornament among ancient Egyptians, and some fragments of inlay still exist that have been dated to about 4500 B.C.

Yet mother of pearl is merely the innermost lining to various shells, conch-shaped and bivalve, that include the most familiar pearl oysters. The play of colour results from the way its structure is built up. The nacreous surface is formed gradually of thin, tiny laminae overlapping each other. These are microscopically crinkled and so nearly transparent that underlying layers, more or less in prism forms, contribute to the total iridescence. The waves of light are reflected back from different levels, and the minute prisms separate them into the unexpected glints and gleams of vivid rainbow colours, so that mother of pearl may seem to resemble opal, or even black opal, rather than the crustacean-formed pearl that in fact is chemically identical.

If at present the shell contributes little beyond what are

still the most attractive small buttons, certainly it appears due for a revival. Meanwhile some of the previous centuries' delights are becoming popular. These, fortunately, are still to be found in every shop window of curios, and can be cleaned and cajoled into forming a collection of the most splendid yet ethereal cloud-castle beauty. Such a collection may illustrate the changing tones of the nacre favoured by earlier generations, as new pearling regions were developed, but even when our purchases are financially restricted to the nineteenth century we can occasionally light upon one of the century's "Tudor" reproductions, its pearl no less radiant for being given the more adept handling of Victorian tools and experience.

Some of the most iridescent, slightly roseate pearl comes from the pearl oyster *margaritifera margaritifera* of the Indian and Pacific Oceans; spectacular dark greenish shades are found in Polynesian waters, and the most consistently silvery white dates from the great mid-nineteenth-century development of Australian pearling. But reds and yellows, purples and browns, coppery greens and steely blues extend the colour range.

Collectors group and date their finds according to the way the craftsmen have treated and applied the shell. Loveliest perhaps but obviously rare is the extravagantly radiant nautilus shell, more resplendent than any of the bivalves and presented whole, in its satisfying snail curves, as a drinking cup, harnessed with gilded silver. But far more mother of pearl was applied in small pieces, whether as "scales" riveted to metal, as solid articles engraved or fret-cut, or as glued-on enrichment to wood. In each of these applications the craftsmen gradually became more expert and much early Victorian mother of pearl is superb in its kind.

The shell obviously caught the imaginative fancy of early Elizabethans but they were puzzled how best to display it. The spectacularly magnificent nautilus shell cup could never be more than an extravagant rarity. The shell lining was revealed by the difficult process of chipping and filing away the tough outer casings, at grave hazard to the radiant pearly nacre. Then this was engraved with such obvious delights as scaly sea monsters, and the whole difficult shape given a gorgeous mount of gilded silver, with Neptune, perhaps, as the stem and a mother of pearl shelled turtle as the base.

From our point of view, however, it might almost be better to consider these Tudor-Stuart nautilus cups among the major triumphs for the collectors of Victorian mother of pearl, since reproductions far outnumber the rare originals and are easily differentiated by their silver hall-marks.

In any case these rarities can never be more than a digression. Elizabethan and early Stuart craftsmen were mainly concerned with pieces of shell selected for their brilliant iridescence rather than for shape or size, and these they handled less imaginatively and less surely. Their method was to cut and file the pieces into small scales and rivet these closely all over vessels of silver or hammered latten to form an outer sheath of colour and rigidity to goblet or dish or ewer.

This was slow, careful work, for the scales were easily cracked and each had to be shaped individually to fit the curve in the vessel that it was to cover. For each scale two small rivets were soldered to the metal vessel, affecting only the outside, so that it remained watertight; and finally the scales were fixed, and polished till they glowed.

A box in this mosaic work was assayed by the London Goldsmiths' Company in 1566, and ten years later one was presented to Queen Elizabeth as a container for "some litell beare glasses", itself protected by an outer box "of crimson silke embroudered with golde and silver". When romantic Victorians rediscovered mother of pearl they delighted in reproductions of the Tudor and Stuart scale work too. A really lovely little vessel of the period is the small mother of pearl tazza with an oval bowl of the riveted shell on a baluster-shaped stem of rock crystal and a gilded silver foot.

The Victorians, however, could call on the great Australian resources, producing pearl from the giant *margaritifera maximus*, often a foot across, although this member of the oyster family tends to show the yellow tones around the edge of the shell that fashion has always ruled out. The scales were often prepared in Italy, by grinding rather than the old hand-filing: they are thicker and larger than the early work and far less lustrous. Each is attached by a single rivet to a base that may be merely of a silver-toned nickel alloy. Tudor and Stuart vessels were reproduced for the 1851 Exhibition, but even by 1864 the British Association was reporting that they were "now out of fashion".

Pearl knife handles continued the craft of riveting pearl scales—the cutler's term to this day—to a metal base, blade and handle being a single piece of steel in Anne's reign. In some the pearl is set into a ground of chiselled steel. By 1720 the knife in pistol shape had become established. Silver-bladed pearl-handled folding knives have been noted hall-marked from the 1770s, always the aim being to produce a tool free of the base metal that would spoil the flavour of the fruit. In these even the blade may be engraved on both sides. Paper knives, of course, were much more simply cut entirely from mother of pearl, as noted in Brookes *Gazetteer* in 1802. Early Victorian records of Sheffield cutlers show considerable use of shell as an alternative to ivory, bone and horn for dessert knives and forks, and for hafts rather than scales.

Indeed mother of pearl handles never lost their value while ladies regarded voluminous dress as imperative and cool hands as more important than comfort. We find them on parasols, for instance, called "parasol hooks", and on some of the most carefully fashioned gilt metal clasps that were made in their millions for carrying small bunches of flowers and were popular with young Victorians as posy holders (see page 92).

By early Georgian days shells of all kinds were much sought after as we see in all kinds of ornamental craftsmanship of the period. Even the practical Mrs. Delany could write exultantly when a sea captain promised to bring her rarities for her cabinet "from Guinea, Jamaica, etc.", for all the world was still marvellous. Mother of pearl, as shell at its most exquisite, ranked with ivory, amber, tortoiseshell and jet for amateur handicrafts, at a period when those who could afford the costly lathes created decorative turnery requiring considerable skill and infinite patience. Mrs. Delany shared this hobby with the Duchess of Portland. One of her letters, written in 1755, refers to a lustre they had been making to ornament a craze of that period, a "Gothic cell". "It is as beautiful and elegant as *amber*, *ivory*, *jet*, *mother of pearl* and such hands could make it."

Throughout the eighteenth century, too, the pearl was fashioned less elaborately into counters for the lady of leisure who preferred cards to turnery, and, like Jane Austen's Lydia, could talk incessantly "of the fish she had lost and the fish she had won". Counters, round, square, oblong and fish-shaped, engraved or decorated in extremely shallow relief and with reserves for their owners' monograms, were in use from as early as the 1690s. Lady Grisell Baillie bought three dozen pearl fish for eighteen shillings and three dozen counters for twelve shillings in 1716. Wolverhampton shell workers made countless thousands engraved on both sides and with no duplicates in a set. Many others found today are Oriental. The fish were associated especially with the game of quadrille that was taking the place of ombre by the 1720s, and were important enough to be illustrated intriguingly on jewellers' trade cards. Counters, round and rectangular, may be found too in mid-nineteenth-century games compendiums, but these tend to be less elaborately engraved.

Those early Georgians had more spectacular mother of pearl treasures, however. The giant *margaritifera maxima* shell was already arriving from the Malay Archipelago, silvery white and less convex than other oyster shells. Some lovely pieces were carved and pierced with flowers and foliage surrounding figures cut in three-dimensional relief, and presented as plaques or mounted as box lids. But very many more, and some roseate conch shells too, were cut into fan sticks. The size of the shell recommended it for this purpose, though the long flat strips were expensive, and in some instances we find that a piece has been increased in length by splicing under the paper fan mount. Cutting, piercing, carving and gilding of fan sticks became important and highly skilled crafts, executed to elaborate perfection by the famous lock-case workers of Wolverhampton, for instance, with their century-long traditions of designing, engraving, fine carving and gilding. Some date to as early as the 1740s.

A fan in perfect condition will be found to have a set of sixteen or eighteen sticks between a pair of more solid and especially handsome guards. When open these overlapping sticks display an intricate, balanced pattern, frequently pictorial and, from early in George III's reign, enriched with gold or silver. Both sides of every stick are ornamented. This is altogether richer, more three-dimensional carved work than the ornament on fan sticks of ivory and frequently guards of the gilded pearl, immensely decorative, protect and enrich ivory sticks. France did some of this work too, but England led.

Almost as exacting to construct was the snuff box or bonbonnière of shell mounted in gilded silver. Only the base is flat: the sides and lid are in the elaborate bombé curves beloved of the French cabinet maker, so that panels of shell had to be selected to match in double or treble curves. The lid is richly carved all over or fashioned from a complete half-shell and may be mounted inside with a miniature portrait on ivory, sure indication of a valued possession. A delight of these boxes is that the interior possesses the same pearly beauty as the exterior, since the shell pieces constitute the box, with the metal restricted to narrow edge-mounts and corner strips.

Less ambitiously, the pearly shell was fixed with adhesive on to wood in squares and diamond-shaped pieces, filed and scraped flat and cut to uniformity around metal templates. These pieces, closely fitted together, transformed tea chests, jewel cases and other boxes, rubbed to glowing brilliance with pumice stone and putty powder followed by buffing with rotten stone. Mid-nineteenth-century boxes—jewel caskets, and even writing cases—may be found, shell mounted and set with garnets.

Every collector seeks a little tea caddy of the late eighteenth or early nineteenth century. They were exhibited in 1851 and still made in the 1860s, and sell today for perhaps five or ten guineas. A specimen all in white pearl of matching quality and with pearl veneer on its loose lids is quite likely to be earlier—say pre-1840.

From the late 1830s the trade in mother of pearl increased, with considerable use of the beautiful Sulu oyster shell. At this time the pearl was shaped on horizontal grinding wheels instead of being filed. Even the waste was saved: powdered, mixed with lemon juice, filtered and bottled, it was sold as a beauty wash, assuredly promising a pearly complexion if not positive iridescence.

Many treasures remain to remind us of that rich period, from wide bands of inlay on workboxes of rosewood to the exquisitely cut scissor-handles, silk winders and needlecases within (Plate 26). In 1868 £60,000 was paid in London for 200 tons of mother of pearl. Card cases were made with the pearl glued to entirely hidden cores of boxwood, lined with red velvet—and infuriatingly just too slim for cigarettes. These are frequently found in good condition for a guinea or less. Some of the most attractive are in the early design with a slide-off lid so perfectly fitting that it requires no fastening, and a later design opening like a book.

They were fashionable for half a century from the early 1830s but by the 1840s the most usual design had a lid that hinged across the narrow width of the box. This has proved too fragile to be much use today. Every part, even the edges, was in the pearly shell, and the rims bordered with smooth strips of ivory. Some are wholly delightful in their parquetry patterns of shell, making the most of colour contrasts with lines and panels in blue-green tones or, at their finest, depending on the subtle contrast achieved wholly in light-toned shell. Some show individual pieces of the shell engraved, or even inset with mother of pearl motifs in another tone, or carved in deep relief; others give the shell a rich frame of contrasting tortoiseshell. The fragments of shell may be cut so small and arranged so close and neat that more than seven hundred are required to cover a slender little case. Usually there is a silver or silvery metal shield for the owner's name, crest or monogram, or a less conspicuous strip of metal on the top edge.

Collectors soon find further evidence of the nineteenth-century imagination—in panels of mother of pearl perhaps, where pictorial work in translucent paints is lit with the underlying radiance (Plate 26). There are wafer boxes for the finding still, and mother of pearl beads, and most companionable little night-lights, where the candle glimmers behind small mother of pearl windows, like moonlight through cirrus cloud.

Chapter Four

MINIATURE TOYS

SCISSORS, thimble, bodkin, all the details of a sewing outfit nestling in the red velvet lining of a hazel nut. . . . Few toys surely could be so irresistible. But then their owner, Queen Mary, took delight in collecting exquisite miniature trifles, and toys, all toys, are quite illogically captivating, most of all when they are replicas of the small things that fill our childhood memory-pictures of home.

In earlier centuries distinction was made between toys and children's playthings, but today even the cheap little dolls' house furnishings of yesterday are collected, and deservedly so, for their contribution to social history, for the skill in their making, or just for their evocative charm.

For hundreds of years miniatures have been collected. Their story ranges from Egyptian kitchen bronzes less than two inches long, and the medieval pottery and pewter wares dug up under the City of London, through the rich glories of post-Restoration silver to such recent exotics as, say, a Fabergé sedan chair in gold and enamel, its furnishings mother of pearl, its windows engraved rock crystal, its height 1⅝ inches. And for the many of us who can only dream of such exquisites there are many delights that still sell for shillings rather than pounds.

Victoria beguiled her lonely childhood with spectacularly lavish dolls' house elegancies, and was fourteen years old before she would relinquish such treasures as an ivory bookcase complete with the minute printed books, a diminutive golden harp, or an ivory woman at her spinning wheel. Her small contemporaries enjoyed all manner of similar delicate nonsense, only too liable to be claimed for adult pleasure as mantelshelf ornaments. In china, in metals, in variegated woods and in clear and coloured glass, nineteenth-century pieces tend to form the basis of most minor collections today, from fish kettles to grand pianos, naive, absurd, entrancing.

In silver, fortunately, the furnishings of Lilliput have always been valuable enough to be preserved. Some of the earliest were Dutch, but English hall-marks prove that they were made here continuously for a century from the late 1660s. Goldsmiths might announce themselves as jewellers and toymen. Some, such as John Sotro in 1750, specified that they made toys for children. A maker to watch for, at least in millionaire collections, is George Middleton, working in the Strand from 1692 until about 1745. His work is considered the most perfect of all. Augustin Courtauld, of St. Martin's Lane, produced even more numerous if somewhat less exquisite miniatures, and comparable work came from Isaac Malyn of Gutter Lane, and John Clifton of Foster Lane, both working in the early 1700s.

Furniture, firedogs, grates and fenders, salvers and candlesticks, toilet sets and table baskets, present a perfect miniature reflection of the wealthy, silver-flaunting household in flamboyant late Stuart days. Even the men and women, cavaliers, beggars, their horses and carriages, parrots and lapdogs were fashioned in silver toys. Tiny toilet sets are superb treasures, complete with silver framed mirrors and receptacles for trinkets, soap, unguents and the rest. But scarcely less beguiling is, say, a frying pan complete with fish, or even a mid-eighteenth-century kettle by John Medleycott, perhaps, with exaggerated handle, bird-head spout and all the rococo ornament of a full-size contemporary. Every detail of the tea equipage, the very placing of the snuffers in their dish, had to conform to the fashion and customs of the moment, and be hall-marked to set that moment in its place in history.

Until 1739 the full hall-marks including a date letter were required, but then the law was changed and such small and fragile pieces escaped this useful disfigurement: hence the lamentably numerous modern reproductions, bearing only so-called makers' marks, accepted as eighteenth-century originals.

There was some notably delicate work in the nineteenth century too, but so light and frail that late Stuart creations have outlasted it. John Greenwell in the mid-nineteenth century boasted of a silver tea-pot, coffee-pot and tea-kettle that together weighed only two drachms, one scruple.

Real antique silver toys are costly little things, but they repay close scrutiny, for they established the traditions maintained by toys in other materials. Sheffield plate, for instance, was fashioned into the most genteel of neo-classical tea services when tea-urns were still regarded as articles of beauty.

The influence of house-proud Netherlanders is clear in much of this work, but some of our most delectable items are leisure trivia, the silver augmented perhaps by ivory, mother of pearl and other pleasant materials. These include sets of chessmen, cards and dominoes, and the tiny cup-and-ball toys which too often are credited to Oriental genius instead of the English turners who have been making them since the seventeenth century.

Pewter newly burnished was nearly as bright as silver itself. Flatware until towards the end of the eighteenth century was made from hammered plate, and the hammer marks are still discernible on these early toys. Other pewter toys were turned or cast, but the latter in their abundance are mainly associated with the nineteenth century, products especially of a London trade. One Victorian toymaker alone fashioned a ton of pewter a month into tea, coffee and dinner sets, most especially into 23-piece tea sets, the metal obtained by melting down earlier ware. A girl worker could turn out 2,500 small tea cups a day, or three a minute, shaped in a four-piece mould. In 1877 *Chambers's Journal* cited one factory where two and a half million pewter articles were made yearly.

Coppersmiths' vessels may be found today, too, to bring the loveliest note of colour to doll's kitchen or collector's cabinet. Until late in the nineteenth century they were produced by the traditional methods of full-scale work for the specialist in miniatures was slow to become established; and when he did he worked in sheet brass too. One copper toymaker interviewed in *Hogg's Instructor* in 1852 explained that a copper tea-kettle was made from no fewer than sixteen pieces. He made 5,000 of them a year "all fit to boil in", and yet they were sold in the shops for sixpence. Kettles, coffee-pots, coal scuttles, warming pans and brass scales, he claimed, were "always in continuous production".

Less common today are the toys in japanned tinplate, richly and gaily painted. These were made in Wolverhampton from the 1790s. At one time they must have glowed like tiny jewels in numberless crowded dolls' establishments, for buyers from all over the country attended Wolverhampton's annual eight-day toy fair. As in the sturdy workaday japanning of real dining room and parlour (see Chapter Nine), the toys were in vivid colours with painted ornament. Plain kitchen tinplate appeared too, in tiny spice boxes, colanders, frying pans, whole sets of utensils in tinned iron plate that even won a medal at the Great Exhibition as popular chimney ornaments.

Toy glass understandably has seldom lasted. It appears to have been made by little one-man establishments for more than half a century before it was gradually developed commercially, the first maker on record being a woman in Greenwich in the late seventeenth century. A hundred years later several firms were advertising glass toys.

Most of the ware was in England's speciality—rich, clear flint-glass. Once in a way, however, we may see a tiny Regency tea-set in gilded Bristol-blue glass from such a centre of the glass trade as Warrington. Around the end of the eighteenth century the blue in toy glass was a disappointing tint: war conditions put the colour in short supply and dolls were the first to suffer. Another delight is a set in semi-opaque striped glass. These, too, are "Nailsea" only in name, and most often come from Birmingham.

This city made a speciality of glass toys, advertising "glass toys for young ladies". It was certainly producing them by 1765 when John Peploe advertised for his runaway apprentice. In 1816 there were ten makers of glass toys on the city's lists, and in 1829 there were twelve. In work dating to the mid-nineteenth century the range is quite astonishing, the colours are radiant and the ornament includes cutting.

These certainly are toys for young ladies and not for porcelain-fingered dolls—little triumphs of patient labour such as liqueur glasses, pale blue, cut with hunting scenes, and vases of flowers beneath clear glass domes for mantel ornaments. The Verreville Glasshouse, Glasgow, was selling toy glasses at four shillings a pound in 1811, and English glassmen the same for half the price by 1829.

Early earthenware was too coarse and too fragile for much miniature work, but Staffordshire salt-glazed stoneware, clear-cut, delicate but tough, is a noteworthy eighteenth-century addition; some pieces with raised decoration have been attributed to the 1720s, and more was made from the 1740s with the ornament achieved by shaping in moulds. Inevitably this off-white ware has been copied and faked.

Earthenware attained some standing among dolls when Thomas Whieldon made minute tea-sets in his various colour-blending wares such as agate-ware, and his creamy earthenware with the so-called tortoiseshell glazes. There are the nicest of homely handle-less cups and huge deep saucers for drinking tea from in days when people as well as dolls were permitted this indulgence. Some of the most attractive are three-inch globular tea-pots with crabstock spouts and handles, but many of these are nearer to four inches tall, too large for the perfectionist, though pretty enough little bits of nonsense when handle and spout are well shaped and a cord has preserved the lid.

While tea was expensive such a pot was a perfect receptacle for a small gift. An occasional specimen with applied ornament in white glaze has been attributed as early eighteenth-century Astbury work. By the end of that century there was Staffordshire blue for the dolls' dresser, painted with Chinese patterns or transfer printed, and more colourful painted wares. Dinner sets are comparatively rare and were made only after about 1820, but what an array such a service may be, with its soup tureens and sauce tureens, and their covers and stands, with entrée dishes, salad bowl, shell dish and other serving dishes, and all its plates for soup, meat, pudding and cheese. Davenport made and marked such sets, patterned, for instance, with pendant flowers and a star border. Wedgwood marked toy earthenware tea sets and even little watering cans and flower pots. Queen Charlotte ordered two toy tea sets in 1795. Slipware and other earthenware cradles are sometimes encountered, their outlines representing either wood or osier work. Just as those 3-inch tea-pots conveyed presents of costly tea, so these cradles were obvious receptacles for mother-and-baby congratulations.

When English potters of the 1740s attempted the graces of porcelain the small intricacies of toys appeared to be appropriate trials of their skill. So aristocratic dolls might be served from sauceboats bearing the early Bow mark of Thomas Frye, and take tea from the soapstone porcelain of Dr. Wall's Worcester. Underglaze blue in Oriental patterns may be found decorating a set by Worcester or by Caughley, containing tea-pot and coffee-pot, milk jug, hot water jug, covered sugar bowl, tea canister, strainer and six coffee cups, six tea bowls and six saucers. Even the Worcester "leaves" for pickles are to be found in miniature. Lowestoft made tea sets painted with Chinese landscapes and figures and miniature sets of vases and beakers. Such a set, or garniture, with Chinese ornament and delicate borders in sepia and black and gold, is a wonderful centrepiece for a collector today. So is a piece of Swansea miniature ware, such as a cup and saucer, though this was obviously intended for a china cabinet.

Mugs and jugs are among the most likely finds in bone china, with lustre ornament perhaps, or a japan pattern by Derby's Stevenson and Hancock or one of the Worcester firms. Spode's ledgers and pattern books record a wide range of "toy sets" in bone china beginning in about 1800 —such things as pot pourri baskets with perforated covers, double-handled vases in Oriental ornament, and the water-cans that have so conspicuously outlasted the rest of the paraphernalia connected with the potted plants of the period. I have in mind especially a Spode miniature candlestick, fluted, leaf-shaped dish, all flower-encrusted and even the nozzle a tulip. Grainger, Lee of Worcester made candlesticks and extinguishers too.

Genuine flower-encrusted work is so lovely it deserves a chapter to itself, but may be mentioned here in connection with teapots by Rockingham, brilliantly coloured and gilded, their flower ornament in full relief yet their height a mere 2½ inches. Coalport's particularly fresh, gay flower-heads are to be found in miniature, too, on a 2-inch tea-pot, for instance, with a fruit handle to the lid, or a flower-decked basket. Genuine tiny cottage pastille burners are still rarer but even more desirable, and were made, for example, by Rockingham and Grainger, Lee and Company.

By the mid-nineteenth century such bone china potters as G. F. Bowers of Tunstall were making best-selling watering cans in green and gold, and tea cups and saucers in mazarine and gold. Queen Victoria's dolls' tea ware included a big bone china set transfer-printed in red with Adam Buck's beguiling scenes of mother and child. Another set bears hand-painted landscapes very much in the grandest late Georgian manner, but the coffee-pot is scarcely 2½ inches high.

Bone china, the spectacularly successful "porcelain" of the nineteenth century, is deservedly popular with today's collector, and still surprisingly inexpensive when we are content with individual pieces rather than complete sets and do not insist on manufacturers' marks. The range of toys goes far beyond dolls' equipment. There are all manner of figures, their fairy quality infinitely intensified by their minuteness. Some collectors specialise in toy animals, not only the famous Rockingham poodles but canaries, hares, cats. Derby made sheep 2 inches high among applied flowers; these of the Worcester firm of Chamberlain have black eyes and feet and gilded horns. Some are in the mid-nineteenth-century's marble-textured parian ware. These are more homely if less realistic than some of their rich relations, such as Queen Alexandra's gold-whiskered chalcedony dormouse with green sapphire eyes, from Fabergé.

Miniature furniture is another quest on its own, from the most common inlaid tables and fitted workboxes to the comely little pieces of the mid-nineteenth century white-wood toymaker who made "nothing beyond a penny in sawed and planed pinewood . . . penny dressers with drawers . . . penny bedsteads".

There is a tendency, perhaps, to credit too many of these small pieces with a more serious purpose than the pleasure of the eighteenth-century toy collector or the nineteenth-century doll. A few may be 'prentice pieces or even samples for country customers, but the majority of these tiny antiques show disproportionate design and coarse detail even when much time and patience must have gone into the fitting of drawers and the rest. The difference is as great as between, say, a miniature Chamberlain Worcester cabinet cup perfectly painted with a willow warbler or a view of Malvern, and a doll's tea-set daubed with a few gay flowers.

Finely upholstered morsels of dolls' house luxury were available in abundance in the later nineteenth century, and the *Daily Telegraph* in 1875 declared that a "wagon load of such articles could be obtained from Houndsditch in half an hour". Souvenir trifles of the various naturally coloured woods of Tunbridge ware are often charming in miniature too. There are pincushion tables turned in stickwork, for instance, the pins inserted round the circular rim. Here again reproductions are plentiful. Even modern desks, games tables, polescreens and grandfather clocks are a delight to toy with, provided only that they have not caught you unsuspecting.

Perfect setting for such toys is a dolls' house of the period. Early baby houses, to give them their older name, are rare indeed, individually architect-designed, and constructed and furnished by cabinet-makers, silversmiths, coppersmiths, tinsmiths and pewterers. They were rarely sold in the shops until after 1750, although single rooms known as Nuremberg kitchens were imported from the 1660s, bristling with brass cooking pots, copper warming pans, pewter jelly moulds and every conceivable culinary tool.

Most fascinating are some of the home-made houses, following an example of amateur hobby work set by the Prince of Wales himself in 1750 when he was reported to be "building baby houses at Kew". By the early nineteenth century there were even kitchen dolls whose skirts opened cupboardwise to reveal suitably papered rooms with shelves and hooks for all manner of pots and pans. There were shops too, of course, with great possibilities in the way of miniature wares. "Mr. Spratt" the grocer offered a wonderful range of treasures to Queen Victoria's children in their Swiss cottage at Osborne, and would assuredly astonish our supermarket children of today.

Chapter Five

INKSTANDS

OLD manuscripts are often infuriating treasure, but the array of tools that created those blotchy, spidery effusions are pleasure unalloyed. The inkstand in all its gracious grandeur was an eighteenth-century development. It was entirely in keeping with the literate, self-expressive mood of its time, and elegantly remote from the plain little writing trays and boxes that had served on earlier desks under the name of standishes.

Henry VIII owned a "standysshe with a lyon thereuppon", but probably the earliest silver specimen still in existence is a small tray hall-marked for 1630. This has a cylindrical quill holder at each end linked by the rod that supports its semi-circular handle. Inkpot, pounce dredger and wafer box complete its outfit. The tray design was developed, enriched, translated into various decorative media but never outmoded. In the gorgeous silver of post-Restoration England it was described by Hulme as "a place for ink, sand box, taperstick, and a long box in which to lay wax, pens, and knife; all fixt together".

At this time an alternative was the oblong box with a hinged lid over the ink, pounce and wafers, and a drawer below for quills and knife. By the early years of the eighteenth century this had developed into the double-lidded box with a hinge running down its length between the lids and serving both. One lid covers the ink, pounce and wafers at the front; the other covers a long narrow compartment for quills. In silver these continued until the 1830s, and I have seen them too in pewter. The more important style, however, was always the open tray.

By the end of the seventeenth century this had settled into the general design we associate with the word inkstand, a shallow tray on four feet serving as an attractive platform for harmonising ink and pounce vessels, and other equipment dependent upon individual choice. There might be depressions in the tray or a low raised moulding to keep the vessels in position, forerunner of more elaborate guards. Such a tray may be dated by its hall-marks if they are not rubbed into obscurity, but anyway its period may be indicated clearly enough by the style of rim and foot, so that we avoid the obvious dangers of ill-associated tray and equipment. The future George II when Prince of Wales possessed one of the earliest recorded as an inkstand: before the end of the century it had become the customary gift of appreciation among members of the royal family, suitably engraved with coronet and cypher.

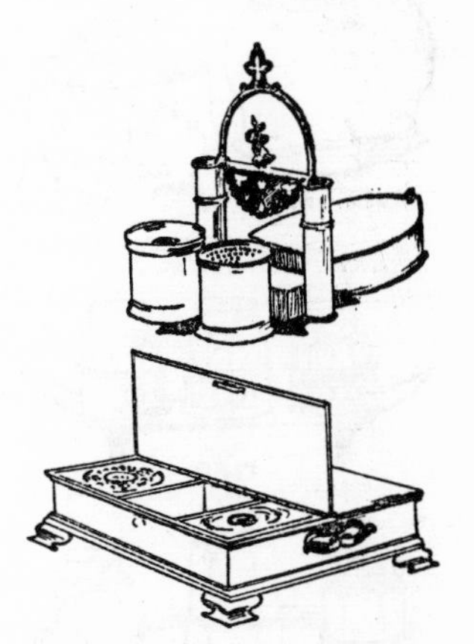

Fig. 5. Standish and writing box: Charles I and George I.

Trays dating to the early years of the eighteenth century are straight-edged, plainly and deeply dished, with bullet feet. Early Georgian specimens are shallower, their ends bowed perhaps and their rims reeded, until rococo ideas were developed on silver in the 1740s, expressed in more elaborate rims and particularly trim-looking scrolled or knurled feet. The dished channel along the front or rear of the tray—or both—was introduced in about 1750 to hold such items as the penknife, its blade sheathed in carved ivory to match its handle.

The major changes in silverware that marked the 1770s become clear-cut and understandable when we attempt to classify and group-date such substantial working ornaments as inkstands. Some merely reflect the neo-classic vogue for oval and canoe-shaped vessels in smooth uninterrupted curves with wide swing handles, but others mark the rise of the factory silversmith determined to produce a good-looking, even handsome, display of paraphernalia at a reasonable price. The successful design may be compared with the silver cruet tray of its period, the vessels for ink and pounce and quills fitting into sockets built of light silver wire.

Even the vessels themselves succeed in looking magnificent while remaining comparatively inexpensive by the substitution of silver-mounted glass for silver. Early glass ink bottles and matching pounce pots are cylindrical, their bodies ground with vertical flutes, their shoulders cut with facets. For the stand of the 1790s we look for square flint-glass containers, with flat shoulders and shallow cutting on their sides. Deep diamond cutting belongs to the Regency set or later, and urn shapes with round feet to the 1820s.

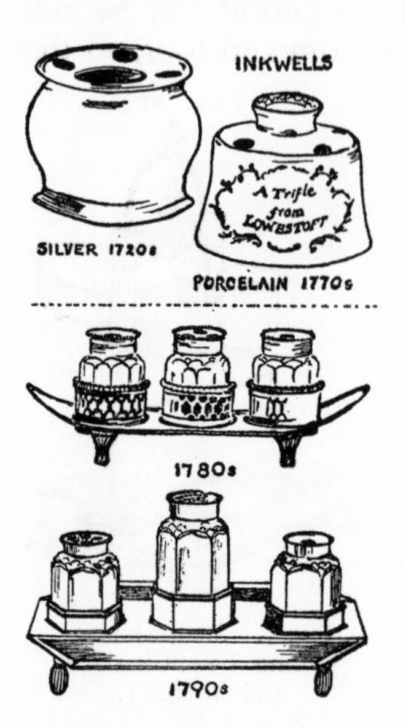

Fig. 6. Inkwells and factory-styled inkstands.

The master silversmith's tray continued a sumptuous affair, however, more splendid than ever in Regency years and flamboyant by the 1820s, with wide moulded rims around the top and base of the tray, tall sockets for the silver-mounted vessels, and heavy lion feet. The culminating glory is the silver-gilt ambassador's inkstand of the 1830s, copied widely in finely finished bronze and less expensive brass. The tray serves as the top of a box containing a deep drawer and mounted on elaborate feet. Pounce pot, pen-holder and wafer box are forgotten, and the tray displays two handsome covered inkpots flanking a group of statuary.

Early writing equipment may be found in still simpler form in less expensive materials. In pewter, for instance, low, plain circular inkpots were made in the sixteenth century, and by the seventeenth century the base was a tray, and the hinged lid had acquired a couple of holes as quill rests. This is the vessel sometimes known as a loggerhead. By the eighteenth century the trays and their vessels were following silver designs, even to the late eighteenth-century lion feet.

More remarkable, however, is the parallel development of intensely colourful ceramic inkstands, first in eighteenth-century porcelain and then in nineteenth-century bone china, supplemented by the jaspers and basaltes of Wedgwood and his rivals. It is hard to imagine today that such inkstands were really used, but they must have been appealing when set off by the feminine furniture of their heyday, with its shell-shaped inlays and beribboned trophies in marquetry and paint. Such inkstands, obviously, were selected less for service than for their design and decoration, their rich colours and superb gilding. But here, as in silver, each changing detail in their equipment brings a reminder of a lost ritual belonging to times when letter-writing was not only an art but a craft.

The Chinese had a long history of ceramic writing caskets and were followed by the Continental porcelain makers, such as Dresden, Sèvres and Nymphenburg. Dresden in particular produced elaborate writing table sets including bells, taper holders and extinguishers, vases for spills and pencils, even paperweights. Both French and German factories made figure inkstands, ranging from milkmaids with ink in their yoked buckets to frolicking Chinese boys. English inkstands are more formal, never letting the ornament overwhelm the design, but they are essentially gay and charming.

Almost from its beginning the English porcelain factory at Bow made porcelain inkpots, but these are comparatively simple souvenirs displaying the factory's name of New Canton and the year of manufacture, 1750 or 1751. The first English porcelain inkstands in their full elaboration date to the 1760s, when Chelsea repeatedly and justifiably pronounced them elegant. For about four guineas, then, one could buy a Chelsea inkstand, its scroll-edged platform bearing a covered pen tray, tall lidded ink and pounce pots and a central taper holder. The pen tray lid handle may be a tiny figure such as a flower-garlanded lamb, and surface ornament may include gilded insects and scrolls on a richly coloured ground, leaving white reserves for full-colour painting of Chelsea's famous exotic birds.

Intense mazarine blue combined with gold appears to have been one of the most popular colour bases in both porcelain and bone china inkstands, with green and gold as an alternative. Worcester work has been noted with a pale pink background, but it was common sense to avoid pale shades, even for use with some of the milder and more fleeting inks of their day.

Much of our pleasure in an antique inkstand lies in its equipment. If this is correct, if it belongs to the stand, it is fairly certain to be of attractive proportions and good design. But the finer points cannot be enjoyed unless the purpose of each detail is appreciated. The preparation of the pen itself required a razor-sharp penknife on the tray to point and slit the barrel of a quill taken from a goose or raven wing. Such a pen has never been bettered.

With the ink of Georgian days, however, its flowing grace might be short-lived. This ink was bought as powder or block, prepared with water and stirred up each day before use, and it was essential to drain and clean the pen afterwards. Hence the introduction of the quill cleaner, filled with lead shot. It was customary for this vessel to match the ink and pounce pots. On the silver inkstand all began as plain heavy based cylinders or hexagonal shapes, but by the 1730s urn and pear outlines were coming into fashion, the moulding on rim and foot matching that applied to the rim of the tray. The quill cleaner then would be a wide-footed urn or pear shape too, with spreading gadrooned lip. Then in the 1760s the vessel was developed into a quill holder as well and soon there might be a pair on the tray, each with three or four holes in the lid for inserting quills when not in use. Those projecting feathers easily caught in voluminous clothing, however, and we look in the well-made inkstand for deep sockets to keep the pen-holders safely.

On the porcelain tray the quill cleaner often forms part of the inkpot, the inkwell being enclosed in an outer casing partly filled with the lead shot. Four or five holes in its rim permit pens to be inserted for cleaning and storing, the weight of the shot being important in keeping the quills from causing disaster. Only when steel nibs replaced the quill pens did Victorian bazaars blossom with pen wipers.

The other eighteenth-century essential on the inkstand tray was the pounce pot, and not, as so often asserted, as a forerunner of blotting paper. The unglazed writing paper absorbed the ink too quickly and thoroughly to require blotting. Only in the early nineteenth century came the joy of penmanship on highly glazed paper. Eighteenth-century "pounce" was required when the writer made a mistake and erased it with considerable labour and that essential penknife. Subsequent writing on the roughened paper would tend to blotch unless the erasure were rubbed with the fine powder, preferably with an agate burnisher selected from among the rulers, real lead pencils, wax and seals that might fill the pen-tray.

One cause of confusion, perhaps, over the uses of pounce and sand lies in the fact that parchment required entirely different treatment. The parchment's oily surface had to be rubbed with gum sandarac powder tied in a bag to make it fit for ink, while it was ancient custom to spread sand or "dust" over the newly written page.

The pounce itself consisted of powdered gum sandarac, and acquired its common name because it was scattered from a pounced or perforated pot. Incidentally even the holes changed from period to period in the metal pounce pot's concave lid, decorative saw-cut crosses replacing the plain holes in the 1730s, and these being followed by the curved patterns of the 1760s. Occasionally pounce went by the misleading shortened name of sand. Real sand, "lily white sand", to cast over the slow-drying ink on glossy paper, came into general demand along with mechanically callendered notepaper in the 1790s. Really highly glazed paper dates from the 1820s, and commercially produced blotting paper later still. When the ink was dry the paper was funnelled to pour the sand back into its caster, which had comparatively large perforations to receive it. Early nineteenth-century inkstands are sometimes found equipped with both pounce and sand vessels.

To avoid the calamity of spilled pounce the pot on a porcelain inkstand is often found without a loose lid. This can be filled through a hole in the base sealed with a cork.

Next the writer seeks upon an inkstand for the wherewithal to seal a letter. With no envelopes available, every eighteenth-century writer knew exactly how to fold the paper to hide all writing. Unimportant notes were given the flimsy security of wafers. These adhesive discs, about the size of a shilling, were made of flour mixed with gum or gelatine and tinted red (black for mourning). Charles I issued a licence for the monopoly of making them in 1635 when they were selling at a hundred a penny. In the eighteenth century the price was about six times as great. Their use accounts for the frequent inclusion of a small lidded wafer box on an inkstand.

When machine-gummed envelopes became common in the 1840s the wafer box was used for stamps, then scissor-cut from the sheet. But always the more fastidious preferred to seal their letters with wax. Hence the slim little taperstick that gives the finishing touch of grace to many inkstands. This was still a valuable part of the Victorian inkstand, flanked by two inkpots for red ink and black.

One other detail is more especially a feature of the silver and later eighteenth-century Sheffield plate inkstand, although noted also in porcelain. This is the hand bell, which would ensure the prompt arrival of a servant to despatch the letter. Here again we look for the details of design and ornament, such as matching rim or stem motifs that indicate an original fitment. The early Georgian bell is delightful, with spreading rim and baluster handle. After about 1745 the bell might cover the wafer box.

Those who are surprised at the fine quality of porcelain inkstands—magnificence is the word they often suggest—must remember that such creations had to compete with silver trays elaborately equipped. Even the possible monotony of colour in silver work was overcome either by gilding or by the introduction of intense blue glass vessels, silver mounted and displayed to perfection through the little fret-cut galleries that held them in position. Wedgwood, it seems, was one of the few who sought to compete with the silversmiths for representation on the gentleman's desk, producing black basaltes stands in the heavy Egyptian manner of the 1800s.

Silver found its most obvious rival, of course, in Sheffield plate, just as porcelain met competition in the painted enamels of South Staffordshire and Birmingham. These enamels date to the later eighteenth century, but often now are attributed to the Battersea establishment of 1753–56. A glance is enough to distinguish these from porcelain, but their wonderfully durable enamelled surfaces are as daintily painted, the ornament often including a waterside or pastoral scene on the tray. Inkstands in Chamberlain's Worcester ware have been noted with similar painting, some bearing local views, and there must have been a considerable souvenir trade in minor writing equipment.

We still occasionally find a pleasant little eighteenth-century pot, less than 3 inches high, for ink or pounce, flower painted in underglaze blue and announcing itself as "A Trifle from Lowestoft". There are flowery inkpots in the hard paste porcelains of Bristol and Plymouth too, shaped as slightly waisted cylinders and dating to the 1770s; Worcester at this period made a squatly cylindrical design in scale blue, the moveable ink vessel surrounded by an outer lid with five pen apertures.

Josiah Spode and other leading bone china potters of the early nineteenth century were quick to value this rich scale blue background. In one Spode design the three small wells on the tray are painted with roses visible only when the ink and sand vessels are moved for use. Spode made letter racks in the same mood. The quality of some of this flower painting is comparable with that of Nantgarw, inspired by the famous William Billingsley. One Nantgarw design consists of a pair of cornucopias flanking a taper holder. The Bramelds at Rockingham experimented with metal ink vases on some china stands, their covers of china in the lavish gilded Rockingham manner.

The flower-encrusted work of Rockingham's rival Coalport—Colebrookdale to its contemporaries—appears on some of the loveliest early nineteenth-century inkstands, with individually created blooms in full relief wreathing the inkpots and trimming their lids and trays. Even when ornament is restricted to surface painting, a Coalport inkstand may have its vessels shaped as opening flower buds, as unashamedly pretty as the flanking candlesticks, in similar flower-petal mood.

Chapter Six

BIRD PRINTS AND FLOWER PRINTS

WAS it by drawing owls and cockatoos that Edward Lear caught the essence of his *Book of Nonsense* humour? He was but one of many early nineteenth-century recorders of the birds in private aviaries, but unquestionably a most sensitive, appreciative artist. His work for famous ornithologists, and his own book of hand-coloured lithographs on the parrot family, confirm this, but then he belonged to a group of artists that have always tended to express delight in their work. That surely is why today old bird prints make such companionable decorations for the collector. Spectacular or perky, flamboyant or domesticated, all these finches and grebes, bee-eaters and humming birds and the rest are displayed with a zest that suggests they were delineated just for the joy of it. Some of their artists—the mid-eighteenth-century Peter Mazell for instance—surely sometimes laughed outright.

No apology is needed for falling under the spell of these old prints. Just because they were made primarily for use rather than for decoration, and printed with the plain directness of engraving or lithograph, they often catch the very spirit and character of the birds portrayed. Grouped on a screen or individually framed to flank a passage or stairway, they can prove endlessly decorative and refreshing. Moreover, as pictures go, many are cheap. They are not so easy to procure as flower prints, perhaps, and may often cost two or three pounds, but only a few such as an Audubon aquatint are likely to be much more than ten pounds.

Those spectacular life-size gannets and terns and all the

other restless, raucous, exciting prints by J. J. L. Audubon were issued in fewer than two hundred sets in the original edition. For the rest of us there are many less exclusive prints to be found that for delicate draughtsmanship and lively colour are any print lover's delight.

As a nation of garden and country lovers we have always been intensely aware of the bird life around us. Not more than about a hundred species of land birds and about another hundred sea or water varieties play anything like an important part in this wild life, but, as the notable modern ornithologist James Fisher has said, these are perhaps "the most written of, the most poeticised, the most sung of, dreamed of, listened to, observed, protected, loved birds in the world". For some two hundred and fifty years they have also been drawn, engraved on wood and on metal, aquatinted, lithographed and chromolithographed and even, by 1868, reproduced in hand-coloured photographs, with an unsentimental, fact-seeking objectivity in line with the bird observations of our own century.

By the third quarter of the seventeenth century the curious exaggerations of the now extinct great auk were being recorded by Daniel King, and W. Faithorne was engraving stiff little birds, such as a swallow perched improbably on a leafy bough, for Willughby's *Ornithologia*, 1676, now regarded as the first standard text book on the subject. After them came an ever increasing abundance of bird delineators. Style, medium, method of approach varied with period and individual choice but today's collector is still enticed less by the age of a print, or the fame of its artist, than by the lively appeal of its subject. Instinctively we reject the routine depiction of a stuffed bird in favour of the poised grace or apt gracelessness of the true portrait.

Tyro collectors of old prints have always to start by acquiring at least some idea of the range of work to look for, remembering that almost all their prints will have been originally in book form so that they must peer closely to read the name of either the original artist or the copyist. The abbreviation *del.* or *delin.* after a name, short for *delineavit* or *delineaverunt*, indicates the artist or artists who drew the original and is usually found under the print at the left; *sc.* or *sculp.*, short for *sculpsit* or *sculpserunt*, indicates the engraver or engravers, usually found under the print on the right. *Lith.* or *lit.* denotes the lithographer, either the draughtsman or the printer of the lithograph, though frequently, of course, a single name followed by the phrase *del. et lith.* avoids any doubt.

Copper plate line engraving, virile if uncompromising, is to be found in the majority of eighteenth-century bird prints. But Faithorne himself and a minority of his successors used wood engraving to achieve more softly feathered effects. We look to Thomas Bewick (1753–1828) for the most notable wood engravings, his homely puffins and coaltits and the rest being portrayed with exceptional delicacy of plumage by his frequent introduction of white lines on black, in reverse of the usual black outlines. This indeed was his main contribution to the revival of wood engraving. Alexander Fussell as draughtsman and John Thompson as engraver also produced naturalistic birds in wood engraving: in their work as in Bewick's only the backgrounds were slightly tinged with sentimentality.

A greater range of tone gradations could be achieved from the late 1770s with aquatinting, although as far as bird prints are concerned the only notable exponents worked for Audubon. The artist covers his metal plate with a protective resin substance and so works on this that when he applies aquafortis the acid affects the metal to precisely the degree he requires, a difficult process but producing mellow effects impossible with line engraving. The richness and three-dimensional clarity of this technique ideally suited the dramatic style of Audubon's huge drawings.

When lithography was more or less accidentally discovered late in the eighteenth century, however—it was patented in 1798—the process had such obvious advantages for cheap reproduction that it dominated bird illustration as soon as the patent expired. Even Audubon's work was reissued, tamed and lessened, by this method. The process consists of drawing rather than engraving and makes fewer technical demands upon its user than either engraving or aquatinting. We find considerable numbers of nineteenth-century lithographed bird prints today, good and bad, but even the good, such as those made by Mrs. Gould of her famous husband's early work, lack the brilliance of earlier engravings. The plumage is exquisitely soft, admittedly, but we look in vain for the beady eye, the brittle leg and claw that declare the master at this work.

Colour, of course, is the final contribution to the beauty of a bird print. Copper engravings were hand-coloured throughout most of the eighteenth and early nineteenth centuries. Only study of authenticated museum specimens can help the beginner to avoid the old print recently coloured and to recognise the vivid masculine depths of the old colours, those eighteenth-century struggles to achieve reliable orange tones, those satin-surfaced yellows and sunless greens and that superb gentian blue.

Even far into the nineteenth century hand colouring continued, for chromolithography was an elaborate process involving a different stone for every colour printed. A small amount of very fine colour printing was achieved in France early in the century, touched up by hand, notably in part of *Les Pigeons* by Antoinette Krip. But virtually all colour was hand-applied until chromolithography was improved by Hullmandel in about 1820, bringing strident tones as harsh as the voices of the parrot breeds it so ably reproduced.

The use of these technical processes for producing bird prints in quantity means that collectors must frequently scan a print not for one name but for two. The original artist, even the most widely known by name such as John James Laforest Audubon and John Gould, usually prepared only the original drawing or sketch for his artist-technicians.

Audubon (1785–1851) was more thorough than most, for as well as penetrating wild Indian country and virgin swamp for twenty-five years to make water colour records for his *Birds of America* (published 1827–38), he himself prepared the written manuscript for the accompanying book, and came to England to arrange their reproduction and publication. But even he depended entirely on others, and in particular the Englishmen Robert Havell father and son, for the magnificent full-scale aquatints—1,065 life-size birds—that gave life to his peculiarly vivid, angular, sometimes angry looking birds, wild birds to the feather tip. To Robert Havell, perhaps, should go credit for the delicacy of the feathers, the sense of rounded life in the bird's glossy plumage, but to Audubon the keenly observed "movement" expressed in the whole design of each print.

In the same way John Gould (1804–81) issued enormous numbers of bird studies—birds of the Himalayas, of Europe, of Australia, of Great Britain, forty-three huge volumes. But the completed pictures were prepared by others, mainly William Hart or the more expert Joseph Wolf, from his graceful, often charmingly natural and carefully exact drawings. He spent two years in Australia and added three hundred birds to their recorded list. But with a Gould print we look at once for the name of his draughtsman-lithographer. His wife, E. Gould, did some of the best work, and for a while he had the notable services of Edward Lear, but on his work as on that of his contemporaries we note particularly the names of Hart, H. C. Richter, the fine draughtsman Wolf and the prolific John Gerard Keulemans.

Such men are the most welcome contributors to a small collection of bird prints, although the specially fortunate collector may occasionally find an eighteenth-century specimen: a coloured engraving by Peter Mazell from the famous Thomas Pennant's *British Zoology* (published 1761–1766), perhaps, or even a rare engraving hand-signed in ink by William Hayes and Gabriel Smith (published 1771–5) or, rarer still, a hand drawing, hand painted, by William Lewin (published 1789–94) who made every one of the three hundred and twenty-four plates that went into each of the sixty copies of his *Birds of Great Britain*.

The nineteenth century, however, was the period in which prints appeared in quantity. Moreover, although earlier work has its own naive appeal we have to admit that it tended often to be dull. Such early artists as the seventeenth-century Mark Catesby perched their birds in unimaginative similarity on the kind of twigs associated with taxidermy.

Eleazar Albin and his daughter, working 1713–59, produced the earliest hand-coloured copper plate book of British birds, their *Song Birds*, 1737, which was reissued and much pirated. George Edwards, too, produced equally laboured engravings in the mid-eighteenth century that were regarded nevertheless as the most important of their day and printed in French as well as English. The saving grace of all these prints is their honest purposefulness, with no nonsense about feathered friends and the like. Even in the most sentimental years of the nineteenth century such an approach to the subject was comparatively rare and technical advances in ornithological knowledge and in reproduction methods give these fine nineteenth century artists and craftsmen—and their birds—a far greater freedom.

Even for learning bird recognition they are often more helpful than more modern photography, which is precisely the praise their creators would have sought. Looking at those exact and vigorous bird records of past centuries it is difficult to recollect how recently men argued that the cuckoo wintered in a fallen tree-trunk, or was transformed into a fox.

Flower prints have an even longer and fuller history than bird prints. They are easier to obtain and often remarkably cheap. Even the seventeenth century can be represented in a collection of prints costing no more than a few shillings each, if the work of the more renowned artists is omitted. Always there is the chance of an Ehret, say, or a Sydenham Edwards, in a junk shop's sixpenny tray, but even flower prints are not always what they seem and an old print originally issued in black and white is often ruined by modern colouring.

Those who take the hobby seriously can familiarise themselves with the names and dates of leading artists and engravers and study their styles and contemporary colours in books and museums. It is fascinating to trace the development of various reproduction methods, as the stiff woodcuts of the sixteenth and early seventeenth centuries gave way to the more subtle techniques of metal engraving and etching—occasionally stipple—which reached their prime in the eighteenth century, followed by the nineteenth century's wood engraving, fairly rare lithography, and steel engraving.

By no means all the names to be found are English. Old prints are as international as the lilies and irises and auriculas they perpetuate. The old botanists and herbalists in Germany, Italy and France sought the same "curious" plants and required the same assistance in identifying them. Even in such famous sixteenth-century books as Turner's *New Herbal* and John Gerard's *Herball* the woodcuts were generally taken from much-copied Continental sources. Spontaneity was sacrificed, of course: those early woodcuts are hard and monotonous; but the puny daffodil and straggling pea are unmistakably of their period. For generations Gerard's *Herball* (1597) and Parkinson's *Paradisus* (1629) ranked as the finest herbals, but early woodblock flower prints are largely Continental.

By the early eighteenth century, however, metal engraving for English flower prints had come into its own—a process of cutting lines into metal instead of laboriously cutting away the background as had been required for the woodcut. In the 1720s there was even an attempt to print flower illustrations by a three-colour process invented by Christopher Le Blon. John Martyn's *Historia Plantarum Rariorum* (1728–36) showing plants in the Chelsea Physic Garden, is a source of such prints from lovely drawings by Jacob van Huysum. These are now highly valued, but are not very attractive, though they were touched up with water colour.

Far more decorative are such hand-coloured products as the famous *Twelve Months of Flowers* (1730) by Robert Furber, "a gardiner over against the Hyde Park Gate at Kensington" (Plate 14). This sumptuous volume is really the first English illustrated seed catalogue, the flowers characteristic of each month, "coloured to life", being grouped in a bowl and numbered for identification in a list below. Collectors must beware of the pirated versions of these prints, and even of Furber's own reduced versions issued in 1742, poorly engraved and wretchedly coloured.

Most of the famous eighteenth-century flower illustrators, however, are associated with the work that appeared after Charles Linnaeus had issued his new principle of plant classification that turned the botanical world upside down. There was Georg Ehret of Heidelberg (1708–70), for instance, who spent much of his life in England, producing superbly rich, vigorous plant paintings and sometimes himself making the engravings for the printed reproductions, as in his most famous *Plantae et Papilliones Rariores* (1748–59). There were the splendid German draughtsmen Ferdinand and Francis Bauer, of whom Francis (1758–1840) became permanent draughtsman to Kew Gardens, remaining at the work for fifty years while his brother travelled the world to record new species.

Yet another foreigner whose work shares the same international language was Pierre-Joseph Redouté (1759–1840), a Belgian who spent most of his life in France and was also among those attracted to England by the rare plants at Kew. Redouté's work must be seen by those who seek standards to aid their own less expensive choice. But there is much attractive work by Englishmen, too. By John Edwards, for example, whose beautifully composed, simply executed designs appeared in his own *British Herbal* (1770) and *A Collection of Flowers drawn after Nature and disposed in an Ornamental and Picturesque Manner*. He is not to be confused with Sydenham Edwards who drew many of the flower designs in early issues of the *Botanical Magazine*, founded in 1787.

These prints are greatly enriched by their meticulous colour work, the same care being given to a wealth of colours on a passion flower and the minor touches on, say, a mignonette. Occasionally a flower, such as a rose, is effectively printed in red or brown instead of black, but the final charm still depends on the hand painting given to each separate print—and each issue of the magazine sold several thousand copies. James Sowerby, whose name appears as "*del et sculp*" on a number of the early prints in this first botanical periodical, may be found again associated with very many more drawings in the thirty-six-volume

English Botany (1790–1814), his originals now preserved in the Natural History Museum.

By this time women, too, were contributing to the rich store of flower illustrations. The work of the little-known late eighteenth-century Philippa Crabtree is exquisite. Mary Lawrence's work, drawn, etched and published by herself, is better known, but decorative rather than exact. That most famous flower enthusiast Mrs. Mary Delany is only indirectly associated with flower prints, although remembered for flower embroideries and for her volumes of "paper flowers", an extraordinarily successful collection suggesting pressed flowers that have kept their full colour and freshness. In reality these are composed of coloured papers cut with extreme delicacy, every leaf-frond, every stamen meticulously cut and pasted in position, yet avoiding the obvious dangers of fussiness and prettiness.

During the nineteenth century Mrs. Edward Bury of Liverpool, Mrs. Withers "flower painter in ordinary to Queen Adelaide", Mrs. Clara Pope and others continued the work. By then, however, flowers were pouring into Britain from the four corners of the world, and the publications ranged from specialised studies of heaths, camellias, roses and the like to prints of flower groups such as Ackermann's *Series of Thirty Studies from Nature* (1812) to aid young ladies at their fashionable hobby of flower painting. The most gloriously extravagant publication dating to this period is *The Temple of Flora*, published by Robert John Thornton as part of a larger work issued in parts between 1799 and 1807. Here such artists as Peter Henderson, Philip Reinagle and Sydenham Edwards have set wonderful flowers growing hugely, almost overpoweringly, out of "natural" backgrounds. These settings may be wildly inaccurate but contribute much to the presentation. Thus a study of *Mimosa Grandiflora* includes not only Jamaican mountains and humming birds but also, in Thornton's own words, "one of the aborigines struck with amazement at the peculiarities of the plant" (Plate 13). Inevitably the cost of producing a work of this magnificence was ruinous.

It is impossible to detail all the noteworthy botanical artists of this period—men such as Peter Taylor, William

King, Frederick Nodder, Botanic Painter to Queen Charlotte, George Loddiges, William Baxter, Robert Sweet, Benjamin Maund. One of the rare English botanical illustrators in stipple engraving was William Hooker, pupil of Francis Bauer and official artist to the Horticultural Society in the early nineteenth century, but now associated with a particularly strident green.

Lithography, another process found comparatively seldom in flower prints, was used with distinction by Walter Hood Fitch who was associated with the *Botanical Magazine* between 1834 and 1877. Nearly 10,000 published drawings by Fitch have been recorded. Wood engraving, as distinct from woodcuts and cheaper than metal engraving, was developed for flower illustration as well as for birds in the late eighteenth century by Thomas Bewick and became popular in the 1830s.

By then books teaching the art of flower illustration were popular, and here again is an opportunity to discover work by well-known artists who had pupils to instruct, such as James Sowerby, Peter Henderson and Mrs. Withers. In a minor way, too, an early nineteenth-century botanical copy book by Patrick Syme, for example, or Edward Pretty or George Brookshaw, offers interesting sidelights on a fascinating craft.

Chapter Seven

NAILSEA GLASS

HEAT a rod of glass and it can be spun into cobweb threads; inflate it like a balloon on the end of a blow pipe; cut it with shears and join it again invisibly; deck its surface with glass of many colours, in trails and loops and frilly crimpings, and the glass will fuse but the patterns show fresh and clear. Glass, surely, is the most nearly magical of craftsmen's materials, but magic is notoriously liable to be shattered into nothingness.

The old itinerant glass spinner could quickly attract a fascinated crowd to his little roadside table, and the ruffianly glass-blowers of Bristol or Nailsea or Newcastle found a ready market for their gay caricatures of small everyday necessities, but since it was so fragile such nonsense had, above all, to be cheap. Those who collect coloured glass curios today seldom realise how importantly this factor affected their whole story, since now they are the more highly admired, and priced, for the fragility of their mocking at sober usefulness.

Those with a liking for gaily-coloured absurdities among their glasses find a wide range of subjects, from gigantic tobacco pipes to melodious coaching horns. There are walking sticks with threads of colour spiralling inside the glass from handle to ferrule. There are reflecting witch or watch balls, and those glass rolling pins that may be regarded indeed as more use than ornament. There are glass hats for toothpicks and coloured flasks obviously made for the toilet table.

The toasting fork in green or blue glass was probably intended for use, and certainly glass bells must have been meant to declare their rich voice. It is even possible sometimes to drink from the ugly glass boots that some collectors now try to associate with the "boot" caricatures of the hated Marquis of Bute, but these are often trick glasses to turn the drink into a drenching. Jugs, mugs, tumblers, jars and serving bottles, however, form the basis of most collections.

Nailsea, a few miles from Bristol, has given its name to so much of this work that today all coloured glass tends to be so classified, and the scrupulous collector has to apply the term to a style rather than a source. Sunderland, Newcastle, Stourbridge, Warrington, Wrockwardine Wood in Shropshire, Alloa in Scotland, all had their glasshouses, and all had obvious markets for curios if only they could make them cheap enough, and colourful.

Glass bells, for example, 9 to 18 inches tall, have been made in many colour combinations, some with colour-twist handles, at Newcastle, Stourbridge and Warrington and even by John Davenport of Longport, Staffordshire, who is better remembered today for his pottery than for his coloured glass. The bell clapper is in clear flint-glass but dome and handle may be in a wide range of shades, such as blue with pale yellow, green with opaque white, red with a colour-twist, or red striped in white with opalescent blue. Sometimes a bell is effectively all white, ribbed perhaps or with the contrast of a clear handle; sometimes the handle is moulded as an opaque-white hand.

As early as 1738 when Prince Frederick and Princess Augusta visited Bristol the pompous procession of city companies was headed by glass-makers equipped with swords, sceptres and trumpets of glass, and when Newcastle, like Bristol, had its annual procession of glassmen, "some carried a glass bell which they rang lustily". This procession must have been a splendid event, with the men and youths tricked out in all manner of sparkling cut and coloured glass, glass feathers in their hats, chains of many coloured glass lustres about their necks, and staffs displaying their specialities. However, Nailsea remains the name, and its neighbourhood perhaps the most dangerous for those who may be caught by tame modern copies of these guileless curios.

The story of this coloured glass begins in the bottle factories where brownish-green glass was blown into bottle moulds for West Country cider. Excise duties made clear flint-glass a luxury domestic ware—the tax had risen to sixpence per pound weight by 1815. But dusky "black" bottle glass was lightly taxed, and it was easy enough to make mugs and jugs and other minor hollow-ware by inflating the glass into open-topped moulds and finishing it with hand tools. The genius was the man who first thought of turning back to primitive ornament, quick, cheap and satisfying, with specks and loops and spiralling whorls of milky white.

After about 1800 pale green bottle glass might be used, decked over the surface with white "crackling" or trailing notched ornament, and threads of colour appeared, although the real delight in whirling lines of colour came with the use of translucent glass, when flasks and other vessels acquired a Maypole liveliness.

Meantime, the major development, under stress of heavy taxing, was the colouring of low-taxed pale green bottle glass in many semi-opaque shades of blue, green, amber and red which could be made more decorative with the simplest of flecks, stripes, mottlings and quillings in white and pink and blue.

Even at the time some excise officials probably suspected what was really happening, and in 1851 the experts who judged the glass at the Great Exhibition shrewdly observed that the low-taxed bottle glass had appeared remarkably fine in quality when fashioned into "toys" and domestic ware. But by then, of course, the duty had been lifted and glass-men had turned to far more ambitious coloured glass objects, such as millefiori work for desk and dressing table. The old, almost childish style was largely lost, with its homely designs and obvious ornament.

Some of the earliest specimens for the collector, then, are those in brownish-green bottle glass, casually sprinkled with flecks—white usually, but occasionally in striking tones of red or yellow and perceptibly raised above the smooth surface of the glass. Modern copies lack the tiny thread-like cracks on the flecks that tell of many long years of ever-changing atmospheric conditions. Jugs, tumblers, sealed and dated serving bottles, mugs and rolling pins are among possible discoveries.

Flasks include the twin or gimmel design, often speckled in pink and white and mounted on a crimped or petal foot. This was really two bottles fused together, and was often sold containing toilet water, although the earliest were probably cruets. The hair-powdering bellows suggested another shape for a toilet table flask sold by the perfumer. A giant made in the mid-nineteenth century may be 12 inches or more in height on its stemmed foot, made in clear flint-glass and trimmed with red and white loops and frillings, with an applied monogram in gold, or an enamel-painted posy, or the Prince of Wales's feathers after the birth of the future Edward VII in 1841. This would hold perfumed water slowly evaporating to scent the room.

Always, as I have stressed, the glass-men's need was for speedy ways of achieving conspicuous ornament, and they succeeded even when producing such distinctive effects as the raised vertical lines of quilling that stripe many flasks. Here the method was to arrange rods or "quills" of coloured glass around the inner surface of the mould that was used to shape the glass vessel. When a blob of hot glass on the end of the blowing iron was put into the mould the quills adhered to it. The vessel, shaped by the mould, was then blown to the required size, tooled around the neck, and sometimes twisted, quills and all, to achieve a spiral effect.

Small hats, 2 or 2½ inches tall, were easily shaped in clear or coloured glass, and were convenient holders for tooth-picks. The high crown and narrow brim usually resemble the late Georgian and early Victorian beaver hat, and there may be a pattern impressed on the top of the crown.

Some candlesticks have survived, in the sea-green or coloured bottle glass. These are hollow from socket to base, so simply made by shaping glass tubes that they may be credited with unduly early origin. Coaching horns, too, are sometimes found, nearly 4 feet long, in blue and amber glass, perhaps spirally ribbed. Yellow specimens were made around 1850, the colour intended to suggest burnished brass. They have been copied, but not apparently the design with the tube curved into three loops. These horns, and glass bugles, too, can be coaxed into voice by the knowledgeable, but were primarily tavern ornaments to be hung on the wall, along with a white striped riding crop perhaps, or a big tobacco pipe.

These pipes are interesting, as apparently they were intended at first merely as ornament for tobacconists' shops, but by 1820 people were buying them for their homes. In consequence many have survived, for even the damp fustiness of a little-used parlour could not dull or damage them. They have small bowls like those of the clay pipes that get dug up in the garden, and solid stems with spiralling threads of colour or opaque white enamel, and they range in length from 10 to 25 inches, with an occasional monster

Fig. 7. Hunting horn.

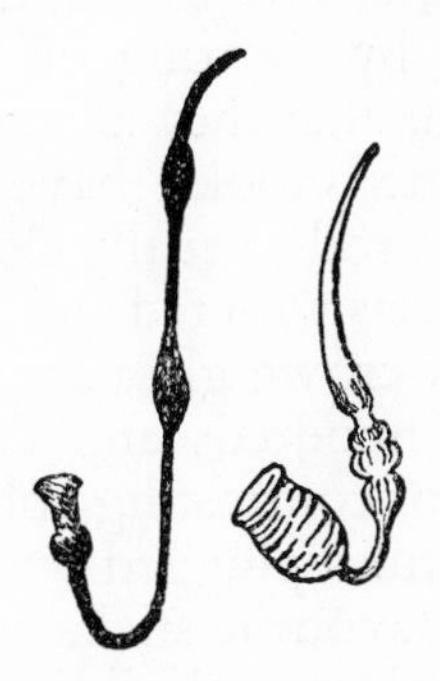

Fig. 8. Tobacco pipes, early and later.

more than a yard long. They lack the affluent air of the later pipes made from high-quality pot metal from the mid-1840s, with bowls following the designs of contemporaneous new-fangled briar pipes, and long slender mouth pieces.

Some of these later pipes have solid stems with swellings, known as knops, containing bright bubbles of air. Blown hollow pipes are found too, also in the coloured flint-glass tax-released and developed from 1845.

Spiralling threads of colour are to be found, too, in glass poignards, and in walking sticks, but here again there is a wide choice for those who have the experience or flair to distinguish the real country fairing from the many modern pretences. The typical poignard has blue guards, green grip and transparent pommel above its clear colour-twist blade. There are handsomely hilted adaptations of ceremonial dress swords, also, 3 to 4 feet long, with triangular blades, and square blades in blue glass tipped horrifically with red. The ceremonial mace, too, may be mentioned here, with a colour-twist staff bearing a hollow crown-shaped head, although some of the earliest are in Bristol-blue, their ornament painted in enamel and gold.

Walking sticks, of course, are innumerable. Early specimens are carefully tapered at the ferrule end. These are in the pale green bottle glass, sometimes twisted. The cylindrical rod shape in clear or coloured glass is later work, the end merely rounded off with a tool. Indeed, most shepherds' crooks found today appear to have been finished merely by shearing off the glass with a cold iron, which suggests that they all came from a single source. The most elaborate crooks have ribbed handles and twisted or writhen rods, usually clear with a core of amber or in white lace effects with red and blue ribbons. Some hollow "canes" of clear crown glass are still filled with their original sweets—tiny hundreds and thousands arranged in 2-inch wide bands of contrasting colours. They have knob handles and the ferrules plugged with cork.

The favourite sticks with spirals of coloured glass threads or spiral enamel ribbon throughout their length may be classed as early or late. At first the coloured spiral caused a slight ridge on the surface of the glass. This is not found on a flint-glass rod, fairly certainly dating after 1845. Some sticks have their threads of colour spiralled down the outside of the glass, masking any imperfections.

Glass rolling pins were remarkably popular among seamen and their families. Here, too, the earliest are in ordinary dusky bottle glass: filled with salt they were hung near the fire and involved in the small rituals and old wives' tales associated with this valuable commodity, increasingly taxed between 1694 and 1829 and vitally important for preserving fish and other winter supplies.

Flecked, and later striped and streaked, they were known as Bristol rollers, but in early work they were bottles rather than pastry-makers, for they tapered slightly from the centre to each end, until someone realised that the cold glass, heavy with salt, made a fine rolling pin.

The design persisted and we find them blown in the somewhat later clearer bottle glass, measuring 15 inches long by 2 inches in diameter, precisely the size to hold a pound of tea, and making an attractive looking gift, in the Regency years, in purple, blue, mottled or striped glass. Still fashionable in the 1820s, they were filled with comfits for selling as gaudy little fairings. These were painted and inscribed in gold and coloured enamels, but as lucky mascots for the cottage wall and no longer seriously involved in sailor superstitions. The open end, fitted with a ground-in ball-headed stopper, at once distinguishes the filled roller from the solid-knobbed, wholly ornamental style that followed.

The ornament itself is notably varied for such a prosaic basis and to some extent indicates a roller's source. As well as the white flecked variety in dark bottle glass they are frequently found in opaque white and only less commonly in clear deep blue—"Bristol-blue" since for a time Bristol had the monopoly of the German smalt that gave glass its finest colour, and supplied it to glass-makers up and down the country. Amber and green rollers are found, too, but the opaque white proved ideal for the most widespread painted and transfer-printed ornament, such as simple wishes of good luck and naive verses that have made them more famous than their simple originators could ever have dreamed. There may be all manner of pictorial work, especially ships and flowers with such words as

> When far at sea remember me
> And bear me in your mind.
> Let all the world say what they will
> Speak of me as you find.

This confirms the theory that many were given to sailors as well as by them, and this is borne out, too, by a typical advertisement for "Sailor's Charm, Glass Rolling-Pins for hanging in a Ship's Cabin, white, decorated in colours with ships, motto and inscription. 14¾ inches long."

The Bristol-blue makes a splendid ground for such ornament in colour and gold but has proved irresistible to the faker. Opaque white rollers were made at Sunderland, ornamented at first in well-fired enamel colours but later in oil colours only lightly fired and soon wearing off. By 1845 transfer-printed ornament was usual, and at Alloa in Scotland too. Sunderland produced other rollers in pale bottle green and marbled red and white, and in the 1840s made a speciality of ornament in closely-spaced dots, to depict a paddle steamer, perhaps, or a view of the Sunderland Bridge. Wrockwardine Wood in Shropshire made rollers in striped glass in two or more colours and the Birmingham-Stourbridge area made uncountable thousands in plain colours.

The repeal of the glass tax in 1845 meant that the rolling pin could be of solid, heavily leaded flint-glass, with plain knobs. Bacchus and Company of Birmingham even thought them worth showing at the 1851 Exhibition, and Nailsea is known to have been making them as late as 1865.

At best the rolling pin is a tiresome shape. One alternative for the cottage parlour was the witch or watch or wish ball. The silvered globes of innumerable Dutch paintings soon tarnished, but by the late years of the seventeenth century glass-blowers were making clear glass globular vessels for holy water and eventually, like the rolling pin, these were reduced to the status of luck-bringers, made in Nailsea's thick dark bottle glass and then in green or blue, with the wealth of ornament associated with other Nailsea work.

Some balls in dark glass are flecked and spotted. In coloured glass they are inscribed with Scriptural texts in gold. Many of the best have threads of coloured glass arranged on their spherical surface in a series of loops. The loops had to be arranged on the ball of glass when it was partly blown so that they merged a little into the glass when it was fully expanded. Sometimes the threads are spiralled on to the ball; sometimes the whole design is enclosed in an outer layer of clear or coloured-clear glass so that the pattern appears in the thickness of the glass.

Even these balls eventually were given transfer-picture

ornament, applied to the interior and made more conspicuous by a background of opaque white marbled in vivid colours. Many, like late rolling pins, have no opening. In dark green glass they are still in production for fishermen's net floats—a delight to find on a storm-cluttered beach. But today even the name is challenged, and lucky-mascot usage has suggested wish ball as an alternative to the more sombre witch or watch ball, with its suggestion that not only every detail of its surroundings but even a glimpse of the future might be perceived in its dark distorted mirror.

A word to be avoided these days by tyro-collectors is friggers. At one time all intriguing Nailsea glass curios were credited to experimental apprentices and off-duty glass-men working for their own pleasure or profit. This theory simply does not take into account the working conditions around 1800. A twelve-hour day six days a week left the men little enough enthusiasm for extra hours in the intense heat and straining gloom of the glasshouse, and in any case until 1845 the severe tax on glass made every fragment valuable to the glasshouse owners. Probably the makers of spun glass ornaments inadvertently prompted the story.

Spun glass is altogether different from the creations usually classed as Nailsea. As early as 1696 a Mr. Grillet (name and date suggest that he was a Huguenot refugee) at the sign of the Castle in St. Martin's Lane "who lately wrought and spun glass publick" advertised in the *Post Man* that he would make "whatever can be desired or thought on either in Glas or Enamelled". This was, indeed, a style of work that called for showmanship as well as skill. In his diary the first Earl of Egmont, August 10, 1738, describes how he "went to Greenwich to show my daughter Helena and niece Dering, together with Lady Bland's children, the manner of blowing glass into the shape of men, beasts, etc.", and a few lines further on he refers, too, to "the gentlewoman who blew glass". Occasional writers of the early nineteenth century could still describe such street corner scenes, as the man set up his little table and heated and shaped his coloured rods of

Fig. 9.
Jacob's ladder,
spun glass.

glass. These were so light as almost to defy the tax-man, but even so it is thought that the most elaborate work was achieved after 1845.

The results, obviously, may be entirely individualistic, but not much remains apart from unwelcome modern work. The Victoria and Albert Museum possesses an enchanting spun glass ship in blue and clear glass (Plate 17), and a fountain of clear glass with vividly coloured glass birds, their long tails gossamer-fine. A slightly more likely find today is a pair of Jacob's ladders, consisting of openwork diminishing spirals of glass, slightly suggesting coil springs, that can be twisted into each other and, with much greater skill, disentangled again.

So much craftsmanship is to be found among old coloured glass that it is sad to have to end on a note of caution, but as long ago as 1911 Mr. St. George Gray in *The Connoisseur* announced that such delightful articles "specially prepared for the unwary collector, are already on the market".

Chapter Eight

VICTORIAN JEWELLERY

GREAT-GRANDMOTHER'S jewel box is being ransacked for collectable Victoriana. The sumptuous brooches studded with diamonds and dangling with pearls may have gone years ago, along with the massive carbuncles inset with jewels and the necklets of delicate gold filigree. But now the search is for the little locket great-grandfather bought for her engraved in flat-stitch with two hearts linked by forget-me-not flowers, the sentimental ring whose stones—ruby, emerald, garnet, amethyst, ruby, diamond—spell Regard, and the great black snowflakes of jet with which she participated in royal bereavement. Maybe we shall find some of the "Runic" bracelets and "Etruscan" ear-rings that rivalled the "Elizabethan" enamelled gold in satisfying her cravings for romantic antiquity, or those sentimental hair brooches which critics in the early 1870s still thought would "doubtless always be in demand".

A spray of diamond flowers that can be taken to pieces and transformed into stomacher, head-dress, brooches and bracelet holds the very spirit of the eager, demonstrative Victorian epoch in its fiery glitter. Other products of the period were largely controlled by considerations of utility and durability, but Victorian jewellery was all unequivocal pleasure, and never more extravagantly indulged. Only the purist today concedes that jewellery during this century lost its aesthetic standards, and degenerated into imitative craftsmanship serving mankind's love of dressing up.

The diamonds might be paste, the "Whitby jet" might be the black glass marketed by the ingenious Mr. Whiteby, just as the gold settings might be imitated by the machine-stamped gilt-metal toys that brought Birmingham world renown. Today's collectors of Victorian jewellery can find their specimens among gold tiaras tipped and pointed with diamonds and pearls till their outlines suggest their original owners' carriage-drive gates, or among lockets complete with photographic miniatures of the Prince and Princess of Wales that sold wholesale in 1863 for a halfpenny.

Today's prices are still governed by the quality of stones and settings; but the jewellery craft must be distinguished from the gilt-toy trade. Among the jewellery a fine specimen is highly valuable, but among the trinkets that closely shadowed or reflected its style we can still find lockets for a guinea, brooches and hair ornaments for a little more or a cut steel chatelaine for five shillings, that recreate equally perfectly the atmosphere of nineteenth-century pleasure. In jewellery as in furniture this was a century of sets and suites: a full matching parure is every collector's goal.

Victorian jewellery may be found in "classic" mood or "Gothic", "Egyptian" or "Elizabethan", "Renaissance" or "Runic". Quotation marks are unavoidable. The period's styles were wholly compounded of earlier fashions, and yet wholly recognisable because, as commentators at the time proudly stressed, the old designs were adapted—improved—not slavishly copied. The alternative praise for a design was "original, yet perfectly scientific". Whatever the classification, however, the atmosphere is as much a part of the nineteenth century as the wide swirling crinoline—rich crowded ornament, often finely designed and magnificently executed, swinging and glittering to the wearer's exultant step.

Indeed the main criticism is that of all the Victorian's vaunted art-manufactures: restlessness. The very abundance of the decoration results in a lack of effective contrasts. But jewellery, more than most articles, can rejoice in a plum-cake richness, in great carbuncles stuffed with brilliants, and in innumerable pearls.

As a brief outline of fashion trends, the 1830s to 1850s have left us much sentimental and romantic jewellery.

Among the romantic may be mentioned the countless serpent rings and bracelets and the bird's-nest-and-serpent brooch motif, the elaborate knot and tassel designs derived from French activity in Algeria in the 1840s—popular again in the 1860s—and the tartans of the 1850s. Sentiment finds expression in the period's memorial work, hair jewellery, idealised portrait cameos. There is much naive naturalistic work, too—tree-stumps, ivy leaves, sprays of glowing red currants, even exquisite flower brooches in pearly lustred Belleek porcelain, and the carved ivory effects of porcelain parian ware.

We find the last considerable use of delicate seed pearls and pavé work in tiny turquoises, and the triumph of coral, and the hardest, most enduringly sharp-edged Whitby jet. The mid-century love of contrasting polished and oxydised metal surfaces was echoed in the association of polished and unpolished jet, or opaque enamels and gold, and of brilliants with pearls. Pearls are found close-packed around sapphire and ruby; they point the tiara's tracery; individual pearls in fantastic heart shapes are linked by golden true-love knots.

Fig. 10. "Tasselled ribbon" bangle.

The same romantic mood has left us many pseudo-medieval and Celtic notions. As early as 1839 the *World of Fashion* declared "the forms of our *bijoux* are now entirely borrowed from the style of the Middle Ages". But the full flowering of Etruscan-Greek enthusiasm contributes especially to mid-Victorian jewellery. This was a period of rich colour and swagger in clothes, and its jewellery is bright with enamelled gold and brilliant jewels. There is much in this period to compare with the 1600s, even to the crude delight in jewel insects. But this period's jewellery witnesses, too, the gradual fading of that colour towards the 1880s, in favour of silver, ivory, more jet and the promotion of the diamond that resulted from its discovery in South Africa in 1867. Already the tendency was to cheapen jewellery's settings and mounts by impersonal factory processes, and in consequence there was a corresponding tendency for the jewels themselves to become infinitely more important.

From the late Victorian period, 1880 to 1901, remain the amber necklaces of the early 1880s, when little else was permitted by the rising aesthetes, much use of polished stones *en cabochon* instead of glittering facets, and narrow rings and bracelets that give full emphasis to the jewels themselves. This is the period of excessively naturalistic horseshoe "novelties", of small, insignificant "lace brooches" to dot the dress, scarf, even the bonnet strings, but of little inspiration beyond traditional elegance.

Memorial jewellery is one of the more interesting early Victorian fashions that lost favour later in the century, although black enamel and jet continued throughout the queen's widowhood in such associated work as the brooch with star, cross, anchor and heart symbolising faith, hope and charity. Some collectors concentrate on memorial pieces, but most usually the Victorian work forms only the slightly pompous finale to a collection that starts with the delicate pictorial work of the 1790s. "Charlotte at the tomb of Werther" from Goethe's famous novel appeared in every decorative medium: in early Victorian days the figure was still to be observed in flowing robes and more or less grief-stricken pose, prostrate at the urn-topped tomb among the weeping willows. This was a favourite on pointed oval medallions, pearl rimmed, on rings and black velvet wrist bands.

Many memorial pieces include the deceased's initials, worked out in gold, for example, laid over a plait of hair and set into frame of garnets, for a buckle to mount on black velvet, or around a heavy ring of gold-rimmed black enamel. Rings usually contain dates and inscriptions on the inner side. I have mentioned the finest silhouette specimens in Chapter Twelve. The black enamel on rings and brooches is often a setting for flower designs in gold and pearls, though forget-me-nots are virtually impossible to reproduce in this way, or for the long-rayed star that persisted into late Victorian days.

Hair is found, not only as a curl at the back of a locket

as it was for the rest of the century, but variously coiled and plaited into the decorative symmetry of loops, circles and quatrefoils, and even worked into such motifs as weeping willow trees with trunks of pearls. Lockets were soon ousted by the high-necked fashions of early Victorian days but reappeared in the 1860s, and these are the ones we most often find, large enough to hold tiny photographs.

Hair work is another expression of early Victorian sentiment, perfectly described in the often-quoted, irresistible passage from the English fashion journal *La Belle Assemblée*, 1858: "Our artist converts the relic into an ornament for all times and places—expands it into a broad ribbon as a bracelet and fastens it with a forget-me-not in turquoises and brilliants, weaves it into chains for the neck, the flaçon, or the fan; makes it into a medallion of leaves and flowers; and of these last the most beautiful specimens I have seen have been formed of the saintly white hair of age. This he converts into orange-flowers, white roses, chrysanthemums and, most charming of all, clusters of lily of the valley." It is scarcely surprising that aesthetes of the eighties had small use for the "beloved tress" or "precious curl".

For the early Victorian many of the most becoming mementoes were of jet, some real English jet, some of softer quality from Spain and Turkey early in the century, or English-made imitations in the sixties and later, made from metal-mounted glass, sharply facet-cut. Jet brooches decorated with flowers of pearl tears are often backed with receptacles for pictures or hair, so that we open them with a certain diffidence. But the really impressive pieces are the ear-rings and bracelets whose long black splinters supply a dangling, glittering accompaniment to their wearer's every movement, as if in macabre delight.

Some cameo jewellery may be regarded as memorial work, although the heads delicately cut in bas relief are idealised portraits if not wholly pseudo-classic. Classic design in England is associated with Regency days, but it was not until the second half of the century that many jewellers attempted the more ambitious pieces such as bracelets engraved with scenes from classic legend. Cameos cut in onyx were revived: the famous Sir Matthew Digby Wyatt designed such jewellery in contrast to the medieval style adopted by A. W. Pugin. But most of the early Victorian cameos found today are of shell, and here again is a subject that is often sought.

Cameos are as old as civilisation itself, and were being faked even in Renaissance days. Periods of great national advance have always been associated with a renewed desire for the unchanging, idealised grace of classic art. This the cameo offered to perfection, and never more effectively than when carved in vari-coloured shell, pink, tawny-orange, maroon and black, so that profiles and even whole figures carved in the shell's whiter opaque outer layers are shadowed in somewhat deeper tones and silhouetted against more vividly coloured backgrounds.

The flaring sleeves of the 1830s brought a universal need for shawls and cloaks that long outlasted the return to slim shoulders in the 1840s, and called for cameo fasteners. This was a great time for jewellery—diadems, combs and pins for the hair, necklaces, ear-rings, bracelets, rings, brooches, waist buckles. Cameos are found as brooches, pendants and chain-linked necklaces. There are even fashionably dangling ear-rings, and cameos carved with associated subjects decorate the nineteenth century's version of the chatelaine.

At least as early as about 1820 Italians were again carving shell cameos, and although English cutters were late in establishing themselves England was the great distributing centre, supplying all Europe with shells for the craft throughout this prolific period between, say, 1820 and 1870. Itinerant carvers of these cameos toured the country offering likenesses that were portraits of Apollo and Venus and Juno rather than men and women, but were at least more detailed than the silhouette which was its alternative, more durable than wax and sanctioned by public opinion as in ancient and therefore impeccable taste.

Mounted in nine carat gold a head might cost £1 to £5, a large brooch perhaps £3, a necklace, brooch and ear-rings set twenty guineas. This may be perhaps a quarter of their present price, although more recent specimens may be obtained for a pound or two, not to mention fakes in plastic.

The shell's strata imposed very narrow limits, calling for extremely delicate cutting to make the most of light and shade and graceful contour. After about 1860 the cutting tended to deteriorate until by the 1870s the vogue had largely passed. One deceit we may find from this period is the shell cameo carving mounted on agate and appearing at a glance to be wholly of the stone. There was a revival in the late 1880s sponsored by Princess Louise, Marchioness of Lorne, resulting in many of the tiny specimens found today for rings, buttons, cuff-links and ear-rings, even album and cabinet mounts.

There are no stylistic changes to aid the collector in dating, but hall-marks on the mounts are sometimes helpful. The same classic perfection was the ideal throughout this period, as during Renaissance days. How fully England had absorbed this mood may be judged by the fact that the shell cameos shown at the 1851 Exhibition by the well-known Italian Saulini were largely copied from the work of the English sculptor Gibson.

Gold mounts suit the warm tones of the shell; in cheaper work golden-coloured pinchbeck may be found, but not silver. Strangely, the colder glint of cut steel was approved with the shell, perhaps because of its long association with austere cameos of jasper ware.

Cut steel jewellery is another later eighteenth-century triumph that lost its importance in mid-Victorian days but is collected today even in its final phase. It was at its best, cool and remote, in the hot golden blaze of candles that lit the mid-Georgian ballroom. It is scarcely surprising, though gratifying, that for once the French seized upon the quiet elegance of this English fashion, and took some of their inspiration from the ethereal steel creations of an Englishman, John Worralow. Today's collection may include brooches and necklets, buckles and buttons, and all the jingling equipment of the seal-hung chatelaine. In the best eighteenth-century work the wrought steel faceted gems were hand-forged and claw-mounted. But the well-known Birmingham manufacturer Matthew Boulton devised more quickly assembled steel ornament, produced in factory abundance between 1765 and 1795 and again between about 1815 and the 1830s. It is this that is most widely collected today, with the steel facet-cut "gem" heads riveted to cast mounts of solid steel—or screwed, in the ornament made at Woodstock, Oxfordshire, to allow easy cleaning and reburnishing.

The long hours spent grinding and polishing the facets still kept prices high, however—140 guineas for a gross of steel buttons—and some deterioration in quality was

Fig. 11. Steel facets, 1790s and 1850s, including detail from chatelaine.

Fig. 12. Mid-19th-century chatelaine with étui, etc.

inevitable in the cut-price scramble that followed. In the early nineteenth century there was a revival of faceted, studded work, even lighter in weight than before and including many shimmering strings of small facet-cut beads, some knitted into the long money bags with slit openings secured by sliding rings often called stocking purses.

There are steel gems mounted on the sticks of early nineteenth-century ivory fans, and shallow boxes, the ivory set with the facets and bearing marked Wedgwood jasper cameos. By no means all jasper cameos are Wedgwood work. Sunderland produced many inferior steel mounted cameos between 1815 and 1830. But the real deterioration dates to the early 1840s. There was another revival then in keeping with the romantic mood. But the steel ornament was formed by stamping facets and other motifs *en bloc* with their mounts, and this meant that all sense of "gems" was lost.

Tortoiseshell hair combs were made, studded with steel facets, and the re-established chatelaine which at its best may prove to be in the earlier faceted style, praised at the time for the fact that none of it was stamped, and composed of about a dozen pieces including étui, key, tablets, almanack and the rest. Occasionally a pocket book reticule turns up as a perfect sample of its period, bearing a range of stamped

Fig. 13. The royal Tara-brooch found near Drogheda: a copy shown at the Great Exhibition, 1851.

Fig. 14. Posy holders: (*r.*) cap on stem removed to release feet.

steel enrichment, steel spangles, a steel filigree clasp, often in an urn motif, and steel chains for carrying it.

The romantic mood prompted other pseudo-medieval and "Runic" jewellery. There were adaptations of the Irish Tara brooch, for example, an eleventh- or twelfth-century bronze found near Drogheda in 1850 and copied ater in cheap Birmingham work. There were plainly circular brooches, too, thickly covered with low relief ornament and praised for their "remote, sober dignity". Scottish granite may be found mounted in silver in plain designs such as four-petal flowers, and amber bracelets and Scotch pebble (agate) brooches and bracelets continue the style with interlacing patterns, attractively solid after the tinsel glitter of gilt-toy work, and well suited to heavy plaids. Close gold chains were approved for Runic pendants. Other romantics were equally well satisfied by an "Elizabethan" gem setting of enamelled gold, acclaimed at the time as the Holbein setting, green, blue, turquoise and white.

Somewhat later came the revival of the rococo style with its asymmetrical forms, and the open setting for stones that entirely ousted the old close setting. We are often reminded of the small black and white cuts filling in the blank spaces in books and magazines of the day. The period's love of naturalistic flower copies, too, could never be lost for long, and resulted in some sprays with similar associations, as well as such monumental specimens as the bouquet of diamonds that could be separated into seven brooches, and which even the 1851 Exhibition adjudicators praised "but for its weight".

The majority of Victorian jewellery found today, however, may be classed as traditional, the pendants and brooches, stomachers and ear-rings, combs and diadems showing formal, symmetrical arrangements of stones and precious metal. Amethyst, aquamarine, turquoise, garnet, topaz were endlessly popular. The jewellery tends to assume either a daisy design or a more or less heart-shaped outline, frequently culminating in a pendant drop.

Although we associate these years with thickly clustered jewels, the desire to fill every fraction of the surface with decorative detail was often equally well satisfied by the use of that peculiarly Victorian delight, metal filigree. In fine quality work this is of gold, the whole piece of jewellery built up entirely by hand from delicate gold wires with superb effect. But here again Birmingham gilt-toy manufacturers produced admirable substitutes for a cheaper market. Even posy holders are found in the filigree.

Posy holders are to be found in simple vase shapes and various styles of cornucopia, in silver and in gilt-metal, and with handles of porcelain, amber, agate and mother of pearl. Among the most ingenious is the handle composed of three pieces of metal around a central spring so that when released the stem becomes a tripod stand which its owner can put down without damaging the flowers.

Indeed Victorian dress might often appear too comprehensive in itself to leave much opportunity for jewellery other than carried accessories, or the popular brooch securing a band of velvet around the neck. Even bracelets had frequently to be worn over the cuffs of long sleeves, which accounts for their general style as broad solid bands, smooth edged and beautifully close-hinged. It is understandable that late in the century there was a general desire for rich, uncluttered jewels, although Victoria's reign is recognised today as a notable era for gold. This was used with alloys such as silver and zinc as well as copper to achieve whitish and greenish tones, or "coloured" by dipping in an acid mixture that removed all alloy from its surface and left it with a delicate bloom. And for the cheaper market there was always the gilt-metal imitation, so thinly electro-plated with gold that the fifteen or thirty shilling gold locket of fashion could be copied to sell for a penny.

Chapter Nine

JAPANNED WARE

OF all the past centuries' wildly abused terms it would be hard to find one applied more indiscriminately or improbably than japan ware. This is understandable enough, of course, when viewed in its seventeenth-century setting, as the lacquers from China, Japan, India or other outlandish heathen parts were brought to England by the East India Company to dazzle and amaze our Stuart forefathers. But the term is so vague that some enthusiasts today prefer to speak of *tôle peinte*, not only for French specimens but even for the most unequivocably English products of the craftsmen known at the time simply as japanners.

This at least distinguishes the most important craft of japanned ironware from the various styles, professional and amateur, of late Stuart and Georgian japanning on wood, some of it no more than varnish paint; and the more closely allied craft of japanning on paper ware and papier mâché in the late eighteenth and early nineteenth centuries.

There was never any amateur nonsense about japanned iron, which at the height of its popularity was put to work in every genteel drawing room in England, and which was exported in all its fiery brilliance both to the wintry gloom of Russia and Norway and to sun-drenched, colour-draining South America and Spain.

Today when we chance upon a genuine specimen, see it take possession of a room and instantly relegate its surroundings to the status of a setting for its extravagant brilliance, it is difficult for us to regard it as a factory product. Yet there lay the secret of the ware's huge success. Skilled artists might devise some of the ornament, but they depended upon the brilliant copyist technique of factory workers, and they in turn depended on the japanners who prepared the ware for its decoration, till the varnish was hardened through and through by long bakings in the japanners' oven, and gleamed with the limpid glow rubbed into the surface by women's and children's hands, dipped in cold water, hour after hour through the long factory day.

Even in these sophisticated times there is something almost startling in the fact that so much flame-bright colour could be thrust into the heart of a charcoal fire and no harm be done to the sealing wax reds, mustard yellows, full sapphire blues and thick chocolate browns. But its decorative appeal is only one aspect of this ware. A persistent searcher can still assemble inexpensively a small display from a very considerable range of pieces that are as usable as they are handsome. What is more, they usually prove to be in the plain, functional outlines we live with today: the hard core of metal responded best to such forthright handling, and the surface ornament offered decoration enough and to spare.

Among collectable items may be found tall urns in scarlet and gold, yellow candlesticks, tea caddies and boxes enriched with gold and greens and blues, tea kettles and water holders, plate-warming cabinets and braziers, pierced fruit baskets, wall sconces and similar household equipment. In style, they will range through mid-eighteenth-century-rococo and Chinese fantasy, the chaste classicism of Adam's day, the solemn pomp of the Regency, and the inexpensive geometrical forms of the late 1820s. In colour, they will include such grounds as crimson and scarlet, yellow, bluish green and the highly prized full blue, blotchy representations of tortoiseshell, rich brown and the now rare cream.

The fine varnish of the real Pontypool and Usk wares gives a glowing translucency to the crimson, a golden tint to the solid chocolate brown. This quality is the test of the genuine ware, made in and not merely named after Pontypool or nearby Usk, before coloured grounds were largely ousted in the 1820s.

The ware goes back even to the seventeenth century but the quality was poor then. Success came when the invention of smoothly rolled and tin-plated sheet iron was combined by William Allgood with the development of a hard-glazed, heat-resistant varnish. The Pontypool method of tinning the iron before japanning it has much to do with its lustrous tone. Fixed upon the tinned iron by as many as twelve or sixteen stovings—the final one for as long as three or four weeks on the finest ware—this varnish presents a smooth surface, thick and velvety, ideally suited to painted decoration.

Allgood thereupon founded the Pontypool Japan Works, combining the fantasy of Oriental lacquer designs with a unique durability that won his ware rapid and widespread popularity. Before 1750 similar work was being carried out on a large scale by John Baskerville in Birmingham, but the extensive South Staffordshire japanning industry, making the "fancy Pontipool goods" now widely collected, began in Wolverhampton in 1770.

Towards the end of the eighteenth century the ground colours became more numerous, including, for instance, orange and grey, all rendered richly mellow by the stoving process. In Bristol, the firm of J. Bartlett and Sons developed a fine green japan as a background for Oriental themes in gold. The use of colour to replace and augment the gold in the painted decoration was a tricky complication requiring a separate firing for each tone, and was long confined to Birmingham and Wolverhampton. In France the craft was eventually established by the Martin brothers who obtained the monopoly.

On early Pontypool ware the sparse gilding and simple border decorations of widely spaced, die-punched perforations are often set off by the "tortoiseshell" ground that became as characteristic of Pontypool japanning as the butterfly motif that brought these japanners their nickname of butterflies. The current vogue for tortoiseshell effects was met by splashing the background with circles of gold or silver and then covering the whole surface with a layer of yellow or crimson japan.

Tea canisters were made and candlesticks, and small

comb trays with bevelled sides and mitred corners. But the spectacular heat resistance of Pontypool japanning from about 1760 gave special prominence to the development of a wide range of charcoal burning articles. Tea and coffee urns turn up from time to time, kettle and charcoal brazier sets, and smokers' charcoal equipment. Tea and coffee pots in large numbers follow the lines of contemporaneous silver plate. Moulded metal mounts came into use from about 1800. You find them introduced not only for curving urn shapes but for bases, finials, lids and handles. Bases and lion-head ornaments might be cast in lead, the latter often gilded; lathe-finished acorn finials and lion-head ring handles are often in brass.

From such early stock patterns as the familiar vermicular lines known as the Stormont, the wares had advanced before the end of the eighteenth century to border patterns of filigree delicacy around elaborate central motifs varying from the most fantastic to the strictly topographical. Some consist merely of simple star designs, but there is an endless variety of elaborate flowers and scrolls, re-emerging today as fresh as a Victorian posy. These are seen in all their variety of design and treatment in any representative collection of japanned trays—picture trays as they are usually called today.

Pontypool became particularly celebrated for its "hand tea tables" or "voiders", as trays might still be called in Chippendale's day, popularised by the introduction of porcelain and pottery tea equipages. Even by the 1730s the rich splendour of japanning appeared on a few Allgood trays and on very many more after 1748 from John Baskerville of Birmingham. At first all the trays were of iron, but in 1772 Henry Clay invented a heat-resistant papier mâché, and thereafter "paper trays" and iron trays demonstrated the same changes and chances of fashion in a display of uninhibited colour and ornament.

Those with a critical eye for construction may note how the metal trays were first folded and riveted at the corners, but later were cut and brazed. Circular trays were being hand hammered from thinly rolled iron plate by the mid-eighteenth century; oval trays with plain turn-up rims date from about 1800, and the scalloped and gadrooned rims from 1805.

During the Regency every well-equipped drawing room had its set of picture trays and in the following years a considerable range of shapes was defined, including the straight-sided "sandwich" with flat-topped, almost vertical rim, and the oval "Windsor" or "kidney" shape. There are the "gothic" patterns, too, king, queen and sandwich gothic, all with gadrooned edges. Round trays with scallop edges are "Victorian", dating from 1845 onwards. Many of these edges and rims are delicately ornamented, with weeping willow, perhaps, or a vine pattern traced in gold leaf filigree—never gold paint. But from about 1830 speedier formal patterns of circles replaced the livelier work. Formalised flowers appeared again, in the best-selling Brown's border of about 1848, and heather borders arrived in the 1850s.

Often a tray has rim and panel margins covered by a single wide pattern as a frame to the plain tray centre and its burden of tea urn or porcelain. But many other trays, surely, were never intended for any more serious burden than a handful of visiting cards. These are the picture trays that collectors most cherish. Some bear reproductions of paintings specially commissioned from leading artists, or of famous paintings that were unprotected by copyright laws until 1842. Edward Bird, R.A., was once a tray painter, his subjects developing from Gainsborough beauties to scenes from Shakespeare.

Other trays bear scriptural and historical scenes, romantic views and endless little glimpses of a country life that was already tinged with nostalgia—a spanking mail coach, wheels a-twinkle, huntsmen roaring over wintry fields, or overdressed cottage children. An obscure William Davis painted many of the rustic scenes often attributed to George Morland. But many other collectable trays bear more fantastic ornaments, crude enough in colour and line but decorative in their riot of birds and fountains, of flowers and fruit and butterflies. Here too gold is an alternative to oil colours and may even underlie and enrich the brilliant colours of a flower petal or butterfly wing.

In the last twenty years of the eighteenth century many trays were ornamented with flowers and foliage in gold and these were followed by a flood of vivid colour during the Regency years with more or less conventionalised asters and chrysanthemums, bright and huge, spreading to the very edges of the tray. Stalks are gold, leaves in yellow tones or the greenish yellow bronze that came in about 1815.

Bronze decoration really dates from the 1812 invention of Thomas Hubball. For the next twenty years all sorts of pictorial work, even landscapes, appeared on trays depicted in powdered gold, silver, copper, brass, zinc and so on, applied over size with cotton swabs. Bronze and colours appeared together in the 1830s—bronzes for the background landscape, perhaps, and bright oil colours for a bouquet of flowers and a gaudy bird. But bronzes at their most ambitious were introduced by the Walton firm of Wolverhampton in 1844, with such subjects as church interiors showing sunlight streaming through stained glass gothic windows.

Surprisingly few japanned trays follow Oriental designs, though Joseph Booth, working for Jennens and Bettridge of Birmingham, introduced a formal willow pattern widely copied elsewhere and leading to other templed, pagoda-studded scenes. But by the 1830s more naturalistic flowers were flourishing all over the house and many a tray painter specialised in flowers, even to the extent that to this day the collector may associate tulips with Luke Amner, verbenas with William Bourne, lilies of the valley with George Jackson, and fronds of fern with David Sargent. George Neville in 1831 was the first to paint flowers on the black backgrounds now most generally associated with japanned work: formerly Staffordshire had used pale tinted backgrounds and even Pontypool had experimented no further than bright vermilions and purples behind their flowers.

Even before Victorian days, however, the scope of tray ornament was astonishing, quality ranging from landscapes, painted between 1827 and 1832, by George Wallis, later a keeper at the South Kensington Museum, the lively coaching scenes of Robert Noyes and the scriptural subjects of Joseph Barney to the cheap transfer-printed work devised in 1834 by Gerard Barber of Bilston. In the years that followed came such impressive best-sellers as the Bengal tiger leaping on its prey, exported in tens of thousands a year, and the persian carpet patterns introduced by John Hinks in 1855.

Always it is worth searching for a name on the back of a japanned tray. The important Birmingham firm of Jennens and Bettridge painted their names on some early trays: after 1842 until they closed in 1861 their address was "London and Birmingham", and after 1851 they sometimes added a crown and the words "Makers to the Queen". Like most other major firms, too, they might mark a tray with the diamond-shaped registration device used between 1842 and 1883 to safeguard a design from pirate copyists. Frederick Walton and Company of Wolverhampton employed six hundred people working almost wholly on trays, sometimes marked. But there were many others. Alderman and Illidge, for example, and Shoolbred and Loveridge, and Edward Perry, to mention but a few. There are, of course, reproductions, too, but even if their painting deceives the eye their surface undulations are unlikely to cheat a wary finger that knows the superb texture required of tray japanners upwards of a century ago.

Chapter Ten

HANDKERCHIEFS

HANDKERCHIEFS have been prized mementoes ever since the first young cavalier decked his hat with his sweetheart's token—just a few square inches of fabric tasselled at the corners. Their everyday status in this country, their humdrum duty role, is of comparatively recent date, but today's handkerchief collector recalls enviously that Henry VIII, for example, had "handkerchefs of Holland frynged with Venice gold, and redd and white silk", and Queen Elizabeth I did not disdain to accept a New Year's gift of "six fair handkercheves wrought with silk and gold".

The story of such decorative handkerchiefs goes back to the early fourteenth century when they were of embroidered linen, some even set with jewels, and for a century or more were entirely covered with ornament. Today some collectors seek only the loveliest examples of embroidery and lace down the centuries; others delight in handkerchiefs associated with celebrities; others again are fascinated by the comments on social history contained in many a printed pictorial specimen, or specialise in the colourful bandanna types of the early nineteenth century. As with all delicate fabrics, there are few survivors among the earliest specimens, but from the later eighteenth century onwards the various styles can still be represented in a collection of peculiarly personal little reminders of past times and customs.

Anne Boleyn's trousseau included four dozen handkerchiefs, but while less exalted women possessed a surprising wealth of other kerchiefs, foresleeves, cuffs, aprons and the like, they seldom owned even one handkerchief worth including in the will or inventory that tells us it ever existed. This is not, of course, conclusive evidence of their absence. It is only by chance that we know, for example, that Edward IV had five dozen "handcoverchiefs", noted among his personal wardrobe merely because Alice Shaplter was once paid for making and washing them.

In any case, Elizabeth I's addiction to exquisite Continental specimens soon led to an increasing demand for delicate squares of cambric and other linens. These might be plain or edged with Flanders lace. Some were ornamented with gold thread, and others picot-edged, often further enriched with loveliest of all Venetian needlepoint lace insertions. Some bore embroidery massive enough to suggest carving in ivory. Even people of yeoman standing might now include them in their wills and inventories, such as farmer Henry Fissher of Kendal who left "collars, ruffs and handkertchefs" valued at fifteen shillings.

"Put thy hande-kercher at thy girdle", was Hollyband's advice in 1593, and the continuance of this ancient custom is witnessed, for example, by the tomb brasses that contribute to our knowledge of the minor customs taken for granted in their own day and all too seldom put into words. For instance, Peter Best who died at Merstham, Surrey, in 1585 is shown with a large handkerchief tied to his girdle. Before the end of the century English ladies were making and ornamenting their own. Fringes, picots and other knotwork were developed as well as dainty embroidery in running stitch and other line and filling work that were the period's pride on delicate fabrics.

By the beginning of the seventeenth century many Englishwomen were edging them with needlepoint and bobbin lace. Even a plain handkerchief of cambric might cost over a shilling, and a 12-inch square sold for nine or ten shillings when worked in the exquisite lace-like patterns created at this period in the white cut-and-drawn-thread embroidery that was stronger but scarcely less elaborate than lace and was known as cut-work.

It is typical of the period that the Howard family at Naworth in the early seventeenth century frequently bought ribbon and lengths of lace from travelling pedlars "at the gate", but handkerchiefs were made at home. The household accounts record, for instance, in 1623 "3 yardes of Scott's cloth for handkerchers for my Lord, 7s. 6d.; one ell of holin [holland] for handkerchiefes 7s. 6d.; 2 yardes of Lace for my Ladye's handkercheefs, 2s. 6d."

The love tokens of the seventeenth century were in cambric or the gauzy muslin known as tiffany and carried all manner of embroidery, inadequately noted as "names and true-love knots" by Bacon in 1604. Stow's *Annals*, 1580, call them "little handkerchiefs of about three to four inches square, wrought round about and with a button at each corner". The corner "buttons" or tassels might be cut short suggesting acorns: they were in sufficient demand to be hawked in the streets. Many were in expensive passementerie work, imported from the Continent until this was forbidden in 1672 and thereafter smuggled.

This was the period when handkerchief edgings might form part of matching sets with collars and cuffs, given honoured place in boxes ornamented with marquetry work in similar lacy designs. A lace handkerchief was an expensive dress accessory, valuable enough for its "loss"—cautious term for pickpocket theft—to be advertised in the press. . . . "Lost, six handkerchers wrapt up in brown paper, two laced, one point laced, set on tiffany . . .' as advertised in the *Intelligencer*, 1665. The *London Gazette*, 1672, detailed the loss of "a lawn handkercher, laced round with fine point lace, about four fingers broad, marked with an R in red silk".

French manners continued to set the fashion, but by then the old French name *mouchoir*, like the early English handcoverchief, had largely given place to the term handkerchief or handkercher. "Pocket" as a prefix arrived with the fashion for carrying an inconspicuous little duty handkerchief in addition to the decorative dress specimen late in Charles II's reign, but the term was comparatively rare until the 1860s. Evelyn and his daughter in the satire *Mundus Muliebris* included "pocket mouchous" in a fashionable lady's trousseau—"a dozen lac'd, a dozen plain".

By then late Stuart ladies had many other accessories to display their dainty Peter Lely fingers, and magnificent lace handkerchiefs gave place to jewelled snuff boxes, scent bottles and painted fans.

Until Georgian days dress handkerchiefs were carried only by privileged people and on ceremonial occasions, at festivities and when dancing. But 12-inch and 18-inch squares came in with the Hanoverians, and by the mid-eighteenth century many a lady was flaunting a dress handkerchief 24 inches or more across, yet a dainty wispy article nonetheless. This might be in the finest tiffany or in the "cobweb lace" that Mrs. Delany noted as an important dress accessory when, rather acidly, describing the famous Lady Coventry in 1754. A magnificent handkerchief was an indispensable costume detail for the tragedienne throughout much of the eighteenth century.

At the same time the popularity of snuff ensured the widespread use of more serviceable handkerchiefs to dust the clothing. The lady carried hers in a linen bag between her petticoats sewn to tapes from her waist, but men's coat-tails began to be fitted with handkerchief pockets, to the delight of the nimble pickpocket. Snuff handkerchiefs are collectors' items in themselves, the various faint aromas lingering in their brownish folds, and they are considered separately at the end of this chapter.

Nineteenth-century dress handkerchiefs are likely to figure largely in a collection, and how lovely many of them are. This century witnessed their return to the status of fashion plate details after more than a century's omission. They were carried conspicuously throughout a period which still expected women to toy with some decorative and expressive trifle.

The Empress Josephine is credited with renewing the French vogue for purely decorative dress handkerchiefs deeply bordered with lace, and the style reached England in about 1815. The somewhat large, plain handkerchief suited to the Regency's Grecian fashions soon gave place, like the dress it served, to less voluminous but more richly elaborate designs, adorned with embroidery and lace. According to ecstatic gossip writers the lady of fashion now carried in her gloved finger tips a handkerchief "like a delicate bas relief sculptured by the finger of a fairy".

This was the period when every toilette had its own special handkerchief, and good salesmanship ensured that there were different styles for morning, noon and evening, for walking, theatre visits, the privacy of the boudoir, even specially for visits of charity. Inevitably special handkerchiefs were embroidered to suit every kind of anniversary—and to delight the modern collector. Nothing was too ambitious for their decoration, from such betrothal motifs as hearts and lovebirds to representations of the potter's willow pattern. Lovely shadow work was popular, achieved by working light filling stitches on the wrong side of the gauzy fabric, but we find a wonderful range of stitches and lace fillings.

Smaller and daintier than ever before, the early Victorian handkerchief became so lavishly enriched with all manner of embroidery and lace that only a small central circle remained plain. Only men's handkerchiefs changed little, and still customarily were coloured rather than white.

Patterns for women's handkerchiefs formed the unambitious theme of endless special features in women's magazines and must have fostered much amateur work. But the period witnessed, too, a bewildering amount and variety of commercial white embroidery, some of it immensely elaborate and decorative. This, like lace and tambour stitching on machine-made net, was worked by country girls no longer able to make a living at the old cottage craft of spinning and glad to earn even sixpence a week. This embroidery must be distinguished, too, by the handkerchief collector from the machine work that gradually followed the 1834 invention of an embroidery machine.

As for all the fascinating styles of lace on old handkerchiefs, these are a life-long study in themselves, and a considerable guide to dating. The collector must know the various kinds being produced down the centuries, wholly hand-made or applied to machine-made net or, by the 1840s, perhaps entirely machine made. *Lace* by Mrs. Bury Palliser is still the invaluable classic on the subject, although she has been imitated closely.

In addition to the varied Continental work much bobbin

lace was produced in Devonshire and the Midland lace centres. In the nineteenth century the well-known Honiton sprigs were being sewn on to machine-made net, replacing the earlier bobbin-made net, and later in this century there was some use of Honiton tape lace with brides instead of a mesh ground.

The Midland counties made some bobbin lace for handkerchiefs influenced by Lille and Mechlin, with attractively dainty fillings and wide flat gimp outlines. Their so-called Maltese lace may be dated after about 1850. Lace-like embroidery was worked delightfully in the Isle of Wight, and the famous Irish Carrickmacross appliqué embroidery was developed around the mid-century, the pattern cut from cambric, applied to net and given needle-point lace fillings. Already by then all kinds of lace could be machine woven.

Once the sewing machine was developed the least ambitious of nineteenth-century handkerchiefs might be machine hemmed: formerly the cheaper handkerchiefs had lacked this nicety. Contrary to popular belief, the sewing machine was an English invention, and lockstitch machine sewing was produced by 1851. By the second half of the century the range of women's decorative handkerchiefs had become limitless. Cambric and lawn, tucked and hem-stitched, embroidered and lace edged, they varied in quality from the simplest with a machine-worked border to such exquisite elaborations as drawn-thread work, hand-stitched crests and monograms, and superbly delicate floral embroidery.

Meanwhile, snuff handkerchiefs had become part of a stylised ritual as early as the end of the seventeenth century. Williamite London, led by Beau Nash, soon twinkled with jewelled snuff-boxes and fluttered with billowy lawn handkerchiefs 18 to 24 inches square. This was a period of high soap taxes and no great reputation for snowy linen, and obviously the dusty powdered tobacco leaf called for coloured fabric to protect the neck-cloth and dust the fingers.

Women such as Lady Grisell Baillie were for ever buying what her early accounts described as snuff-napkins and after about 1702 as snuff handkerchiefs. Some were for show—"gold and white" for ten shillings, for example—but others were certainly for use, such as cost fourteen shillings the half-dozen in 1717. Jonathan Swift described himself to Stella as "a mighty handkerchief-monger" with an abundance of snuff handkerchiefs.

One attempt to minimise the ugly snuff stains was to dye the handkerchiefs light brown, but those we look for today disguised the blemishes with an abundance of pattern, just as potters hid the flaws in their plates. Eighteenth-century England was renowned for colourful, slow wood-block printing, each colour separately applied, and those shrewd calico printers found handkerchiefs an ideal way of testing the appeal of new patterns. Throughout much of the century attempts were made to help the declining wool trade by restricting the use of cotton materials but even the Act of 1720 permitted the continued manufacture of plain blue cotton handkerchiefs for snuff.

Silk squares were made for those who could afford them, imported from the East, or English-made after 1721. But today our most exciting finds are among the pictorial prints made with copper plates. These offer glimpses of the interests and pleasures of the late eighteenth and early nineteenth centuries and some are quite astonishing in their detail, dotted with small figures expressing themselves in long balloons full of words as if even handkerchiefs could not escape their period's verbosity.

The best I have ever seen, perhaps, is a product of the early 1800s and offers a scene of A.D. 2000. This has armed soldiers descending by wings from air balloons and the "steam guards" on parade. One character is taking an air trip to Dublin and back to get an appetite for breakfast, and the scene is dominated by a Sky High Inn on a tall pedestal, and a row of buildings moving along on wheels, not altogether remote from caravans. The motive power is still steam, the air travel by balloon, but the "ludicrous" fantasy reaches uncomfortably near reality.

Pictorial printing on textiles with engraved copper plates was introduced in the early 1750s, twenty years earlier than in France where, nevertheless, it was hailed as a great discovery and developed a reputation better deserved perhaps by English work. The process produced only a one-colour design but this could be supplemented by applying patches of colour from wood blocks.

The earliest of these printed snuff handkerchiefs are in silk, and in the fabric of linen warp and cotton weft that complied with the law forbidding all-cotton textiles. It was impossible to obtain really clear-cut printed outlines until the relaxation of the law in 1774, however, and the development of Arkwright's power loom. The calicos then became so smooth, even and fine textured that the smallest printed exclamation mark can be distinguished.

Even then the direct copper plate printing was restricted in the eighteenth century to black, purple and light brown. Dyes of other colours could only be fixed to textiles by the ancient resist and mordant processes. Red could be used by about 1800 and blue and green a few years later. For technical reasons concerning the quality of the copper plates the shadow work in these pictorial prints lost its clarity at the beginning of the Regency and therefore from about 1815 we find handkerchief evidence that this was overcome by stippled shadows—attractive for their more roundly three-dimensional effects.

That was only one of the problems to be overcome, however. Taxes for the maker and printer of calico were a heavy and increasing burden between 1774 and 1831 when their repeal resulted in vast numbers of inexpensive cotton snuff handkerchiefs. A single steam-driven roller printing machine could then print 9,000 one-colour handkerchiefs a day, although silk squares at this period were still printed in hand-presses.

Here then is where the social historian gets busy. Like fans, ceramics and painted enamels, these handkerchiefs set on record in crude but elaborate detail their views and opinions of people, events and political controversies, they plug popular songs, extol famous buildings and scatter hearts and lovebirds and amatory couplets on what were known as flirting squares. Maps, calendars, Masonic insignia, bugle call instructions and army signalling are for the finding, along with a host of commemorative souvenirs, for the coronations of all monarchs from George IV, for the jubilees of George III and Victoria, for Wellington's funeral in 1855. As on wall plaque and lustre jug the Sunderland or Wear Bridge was recorded, as early as 1796 and as late as the 1870s.

Dickens refers more than once to "moral handkerchiefs", and in particular to "The Beggar's Petition" observed by Sam Weller in the linen-drapers' shops, and applied to his tears by diminutive Master Belling in *Nicholas Nickleby*. This particular handkerchief shows a lame beggar talking to a lady and her son, surrounded by the popular poem by the Rev. Thomas Moss who died in 1808.

Artists were commissioned by the printers to engrave suitable pictures, but until 1842 there was nothing to prevent other printers from instantly pirating the results. The Registration of Designs Act in 1842 checked this, making it possible to protect a design for three years and from our point of view this has the advantage of dating many designs for us. A small diamond-shaped device in the design can be interpreted to give the date of its registration at the Patent Office. This useful practice continued until 1883.

Sometimes, too, we find engravers' signatures, such as that of Robert Cruikshank, brother of George, on "The Glorious Reform in Parliament", a design celebrating the abolition of the excise tax that was popular enough to be printed on silk and linen and calico. Between 1831 and 1900 propaganda snuff handkerchiefs abounded, early examples 24 inches square selling for fourpence and free of newspaper duty. Always, too, there were souvenir handkerchiefs, such as one displaying the Royal Exchange and commemorating Queen Victoria's opening of it in 1844.

All this was one-colour printing unless over-coloured with wood block printing, but occasionally a silk snuff handkerchief appears with hand-tinting. Three printers won gold medals at the Great Exhibition for their handkerchiefs, and thereafter put their names to their work—David Evans & Co., London, Mary Ann Littler, Merton Abbey, and Welch Margetson & Co., London.

All too soon, however, snuff handkerchiefs lost their

public as the snuff-box gave place to the wooden tobacco pipe. Printers in the 1870s did try to save the declining trade, using recently invented synthetic dyes, but soon the printed handkerchief was no more than a decorative souvenir of Boer war battle or Victorian jubilee, a propaganda gift, or a child's nursery rhyme plaything.

It is easy to be carried away by so many intriguing prints, and well, perhaps, to remember that really the great majority of the eighteenth century's snuff handkerchiefs and many of the nineteenth century were just cotton squares dyed with madder or indigo in bright, commonplace patterns. These are in four standard sizes, 21, 24½, 28 and 31½ inches square. The printer-dyer put a pattern into his fabric by using either a resist or a mordant on selected areas before dipping it in the dye. Stencils or blocks or even hand-painting could be used for this preliminary but obviously patterns had to be reasonably simple. The great advantage was that the process dodged the heavy taxes, and by the early nineteenth century advances in technique meant that variety of pattern could be endless, if unexciting.

Big bandanna handkerchiefs, invented in 1792 by James Bayley of Shoreditch, brought those untaxed snuff handkerchiefs to their most elaborate and collectable best. But once the tax was lifted from the printed handkerchief few other patterns were required, save the red spotted handkerchief of our grandmothers' nursery tales, for Peter Rabbit and Benjamin Bunny.

Chapter Eleven

COMPENDIUMS

QUEEN ELIZABETH I in 1562 had her beauty flattered and her journeys made a little less arduous by a New Year gift from Sir John Alee of a richly-fitted toilet case. This carved oak coffer, painted and gilded, was set out with steel mirrors and combs and the perforated silver balls of perfume known as pomanders. But it would have seemed a simple affair to succeeding generations, as "elegancies for presentation" became more and more elaborately true to their Victorian name of "lady's companion".

The very word compendium suggests something of the cluttered, trivial existence of even the would-be serious-minded Victorian lady. Yet now, within a hundred years of their heyday, these most revealing historic documents of domesticity are fast disappearing. Already an eighteenth-century specimen with authentic fittings is something of a rarity, and even a Victorian one of any quality may cost several pounds. For such a sum, however, the collector may be buying the very thoughts of its original owner, the curious mixture of elaborately businesslike "receipts" for cooking and curing and naively romantic lore from current periodicals tucked away in the semi-secret recesses that never, surely, were quite secret enough for real privacy.

The peculiar appeal of such compendiums lies, of course, in the fact that they were, generally speaking, the most intimate private possessions of their owners through centuries when valuables of any kind tended to be a constant problem. Even at home the bedchamber might be open to callers and servants at most hours of the day, and for the traveller the burden of possessions increased a hundredfold.

Compendium makers acknowledged that men and women appreciated some degree of comfort even on a coach journey, and today we can find designs that aimed to meet their every need, for the toilet, for valuables, for desk work, embroidery, refreshments, medicaments, games. What is more, these relics display that brilliance of craftsmanship demanded for luxury goods in days when the normal receptacle for almost anything was some shape and size of box.

Katherine of Aragon owned a "cofar having four tilles [box-like drawers] therein, the forefront of every one of them gilte", and the Victoria and Albert Museum, London, contains a fitted box of wood covered in leather with the heraldic badges of Katherine and Henry VIII among extremely ornate decoration in paint and gold. This box has lidded compartments in the upper section and a fall-front allowing access to three small drawers below, and measures 16 by 11½ by 9 inches.

By Elizabethan days the gallery of the London Royal Exchange glittered with the stalls of the milliners and haberdashers, whose imported "small wares" included toilet cabinets with bottles of perfume, combs and mirrors, fitted chests to hold medicaments and cases for the needlewoman. In 1614 the Earl of Northampton owned eight "cabinets" such as a "desque with a cabonett therein of crimson velvet laced with gold and silver lace", but this is only what we might expect, since his carefully inventoried possessions are almost breathtaking for their numerous forerunners of later fashions and their sumptuous quality.

With the rise in coach travel came the great seventeenth-century development. By then the shallow desk was a possible alternative to the box design. At first the lid hinged at the back, with a chain to check its opening, but soon it proved more convenient to hinge it at the front and use the open lid as a rest for papers or book, with the contents accessible. In the bun-footed late seventeenth-century desk, covered with velvet, perhaps, and edged with silver galon, these consist merely of toilet bottles, a tray of sewing needs and corner vessels at the front for ink and pounce. But later designs include drawers and pigeon holes around a central recess where any thief would look for a secret compartment.

The design now especially associated with the seventeenth century, however, is the cabinet-compendium covered with pictorial beadwork or the raised embroidery that Victorians knew as stump work. To many a mid-seventeenth-century girl this light-hearted work, exquisitely stitched, completed her apprenticeship to the needle, following laborious samplers in colours and white-work. These panels are mounted on all sides of a wooden cabinet. Some are worked in flat, all-covering tent stitch, suggesting tapestry and equally well suited to pictorial work, but more are in a wide range of stitches, embroidered on the narrow white satin then in vogue. This was the delight of needlewomen as its rich quality did not need to be hidden: they could lavish all their enthusiasm on the small figures and pictorial settings associated with this slightly absurd work. Often some of the main, lightly padded figures have been created separately, their dress daintily worked in the style of the 1660s with minute lace stitches that even a slightly tawdry excess of trimmings cannot seriously mar.

So popular has this style of cabinet-compendium become, both antique and reproduction, that it is easy to forget how many more of these early compendiums were wholly professional work. In these the wooden frames may be covered with leather or shagreen or veneers of wood parquetry, cornered in gilded brasswork. Some are veneered in tortoiseshell on a red or yellow ground edged with ivory and later even inlaid with ivory butterflies, shells or cherub heads.

The general design of these caskets or cabinet-compendiums is familiar, the rising lid releasing either a fall-down front or two doors covering small drawers. The uppermost section is often compartmented for silver vials of perfume and toilet waters and sometimes for ink, arranged around a small central well that may be walled with pieces of then still-novel looking glass and floored with a hand-coloured print. There may be a looking glass in the lid, a fashion that was taken for granted in compendiums by the nineteenth century when it was perfectly angled to reflect not the face but the jewelled fingers.

The drawers are probably intended for jewellery and

letter writing equipment, the padded linings of silk taffeta or velvet contributing to the safety of the contents if not to the spaciousness of the cabinet. If it was intended as a traveller's set it may have holes arranged in the sides so that long screws could secure it to the floor of a jolting coach. There may be a secret compartment, too, a small niche for coins or letters revealed when pressure on the right spot releases a spring.

It was in the following century, however, that a more imaginative compendium came into its own, encouraged if not inspired by imports from Japan. This may be divided into various deep and shallow compartments holding stoppered bottles, velvet-lined trays cut with shallow recesses for the scissors, snuff-spoon and toilet essentials, and lidded boxes for powder and patches.

For the tedious business of a coach journey, of course, this had to be supplemented by further stout, well-padded boxes. One would be for a tea-pot and its accompaniments, perhaps in porcelain: as late as 1850 we find a morocco-cased travelling tea equipage for two advertised at £4. 10s. 0d.

Another would be for silver-mounted bottles and drinking vessels, a rigid, well-padded wooden box with a heavy little drawer near the base for spice and sugar. Even here the workmanship has to suggest an air of luxury: the bottles may be gilded or engraved with flower motifs to match those on a small tumbler and a wide-footed, stemmed drinking glass. As for games compendiums, they have never really gone out of favour, with the folding chess board in the lid over a tray of chessmen, draughts and dominoes, and a lower drawer for cards and games counters. Some sets in the nineteenth century catered for more than thirty games: Tunbridge ware makers such as Fenner, Hollamby and Russell produced work that is particularly pleasant to handle.

The perfectly fitted parquetry of Tunbridge ware was but one among many coverings for the compendium. Case making was a specialist trade, advertised on trade cards in the eighteenth century. In Sir Ambrose Heal's collection of such cards several designs are illustrated on John Folgham's card, issued from "opposite the Castle Inn, Wood Street,

London". He was an expert in shagreen ware, and in dog-fish skin stained green and blue. One of his boxes is shown divided into compartments, four with stoppered bottles, two with trays recessed for scissors and other accessories.

In the late eighteenth century, however, the long-popular shagreen was ousted by more adventurous treatments. Here was the perfect setting for figure-painted satinwood, for example, a wood used in solid and veneer but showing comparatively little grain in the variety used before about 1795. We may find a compendium in lemon wood bearing a coloured stippled engraving, or in a cheaper wood painted all over in white or the honey colour of satin-wood or in tinted chestnut or the greenish-coloured sycamore known as harewood. Etched ivory, and ivory-mounted ebony may be noted, and gemstone enrichment of the compendium jewel-case.

Evelyn's *Fop Dictionary* in 1690 refers to a "casette of silver filigree" but the filigree we search for today as compendium ornament is the eighteenth-century amateur work in parchment, vellum or stiff paper known to every lady from Mrs. Delany to Jane Austen as rolled paper work. This was a minor art between 1660 and about 1715, as escapist as raised embroidery, but more that remains is associated with another wave of popularity between 1775 and about 1810. Then ladies of leisure might receive professional instruction in how to roll the narrow strips of paper and edge-glue them to a background of paper or silk-covered wood. Glass might protect the elaborate small patterns thus created which in their creamy natural colour suggest fine chip carving or even ivory but more often are coloured or resemble wire filigree in gold. Princess Elizabeth in 1791 was supplied with a "box made for filigree work with ebony moulding [around the shallow recesses for the filigree ornament], lock and key, lined inside and outside".

It is not so easy, perhaps, to understand the craze for another compendium ornament, an enthusiasm of the 1800s that caught fire again briefly in mid-Victorian days, for covering the deal frame of the compendium box with a parquetry of split straws, stained in bright colours, glued in close-packed formations to produce patterns geometrical, floral, even pictorial. Today in work of the earlier period the outside of the compendium may be faded and dull, but the colours gleam brightly on interior drawer fronts and compartment lids, and in the major pictorial effects lining the lid and the central well of the box.

This work is associated with the austerities of the Napoleonic wars if not in fact always attributable to French prisoners of war. But indeed it is easy to imagine a laborious, time-squandering attempt to create in close-laid straws the vivid diagonal striped effects of costly French veneered furniture.

Tunbridge ware is too important a craft to be described adequately in this survey. Its makers were producing games outfits before the end of the seventeenth century, and every kind of fitted box may be found in the veneers of natural coloured woods that were their fame. Eighteenth-century and Regency compendiums may be veneered in the shaded cube patterns and deep vandykes inspired, I suspect, by centuries of backgammon "tables". These are more pleasing, perhaps, than the minute pictorial Tunbridge mosaics that followed though these had a great appeal with their pictorial presentation of local "sights" while early Victorian needlewomen were delighting in similar square mosaic effects in their cross-stitch embroideries.

The lock fitment is often a guide in dating a compendium. Box locks with link plates and inlaid keyhole escutcheons date from the 1780s onwards. Early plates and escutcheons were hand-sawn from the plate; later they were cast and finally might be stamped. Japanned cabinets and caskets called for particularly elaborate mountings in the Oriental manner. In the same way the handles may be scrutinised for changes in technique. The showy mid-eighteenth century's rococo designs were followed by the simple circles and ellipses of the neo-classical mood, the back plates cast until the late 1770s and then perhaps stamped in relief patterns. After about 1790 came the familiar lion heads holding rings, in heavy cast work, and substantial flower wreaths.

The metal work on a Regency specimen may be an impressive small reminder of one of the few occasions when this country tolerated elaborate metal inlay on its domestic furniture. A box may be covered with red leather, for example, as a setting for brass claw feet, lion-and-ring handles judged for quality by the way the mouth grips the ring, and a brass name plate and key escutcheon.

Many elaborate, heavy mounts, too florid for eighteenth-century rococo, date to the last days of the Georgians. But the Victorians, with their romantic delight in the styles of earlier centuries, offer a profusion of mounts that defy classification, although almost always they are distinguishable at a glance from the early medieval, Elizabethan and similarly favoured originals. The determined romantic could stow her multitude of small necessities in a magnificent box-shaped compendium of fragrant cedar of Lebanon, with heavy silver mounts, or of ancient yew wood fitted with ebony and massively clamped with exterior mounts in pseudo-Gothic frets of antique bronze or the nickel alloy known as German silver enriched with gilt pins.

Stained maple and sycamore veneers offered greyish panels for oil paintings preserved with clear varnish, and further alternatives ranged from the gaiety of closely patterned, shell-glinting papier mâché to the lasting graciousness of rosewood inlaid with brass or mother of pearl. Tortoiseshell inset with mother of pearl has a delicacy all its own.

In design it is interesting to note occasionally the same tendency found in massive Victorian furniture, with elaboration of crest and base out of all proportion to the useful body of the cabinet-compendium. However, the flattish box shape remains the most usual design to find today, on small feet, perhaps, and with lifting handles at the ends, but no longer requiring a strut to supplement the hinges on the lifting lid. Often an elaborate example contains an upper tray fitted for the toilet that lifts out to give access to sewing needs. An adjustable swing mirror fits inside the lid and drawers below include a folding desk equipped for writing.

When the designer has really given his imagination full play, however, we find the "carriage basket" with dressing case fittings of mirror and brushes, jewellery and toilet compartments supplemented by a vast array of possible requirements. These may include glass and cutlery, sandwich case and liqueur bottle, every detail for writing, from patent ink to paper knife, secret drawers for cash and diary, equipment for sewing, netting, crochet, even for sketching the scenery if ever the other supplies allow for such a leisurely pursuit. An elegant final thought is the inclusion of a musical box in the base: Queen Adelaide's lady of the bedchamber, Emma Countess Brownlow, had such a musical compendium enriched with alabaster and ormolu in 1830 (Plate 25).

Every detail of the craftsmanship stands up to close examination in a compendium of the quality worth collecting. Drawers open at a touch and every fitting really fits perfectly, but what especially pleases the modern eye is the care lavished on such details as the lining to the lid—in silk perhaps and gold-stamped leather, or satin printed with an engraving such as a favourite of mine of Britannia receiving Commerce, who unblushingly brings tribute from the Far East. A detail to hope for in a Victorian specimen is a long bolt in the wooden frame-work that can be pulled out only when the lid is open, to release a spring that pushes out a drawer from the side of the box.

The equipment should be of comparable quality, provided only that it is the same that first graced the box, and graced is surely the appropriate word. In early compendiums silver was the rule, except where cutting edges and piercing points called for steel. Some of the old steel work is a connoisseur's delight, too, hand-wrought, hand-carved and decorated throughout the eighteenth century. The green-stained ivory handles of the mid-eighteenth century were later rivalled by mother of pearl, tortoiseshell, ebony, bronze, cornelian, even the marbles of Derbyshire.

Equipment for the needlewoman is often worth special scrutiny, with small scissors that have no rivals today, needlecases and thimbles in all manner of materials and pincushions to stir any collector's enthusiasm. We have but to look at the Maltese crosses and snowflake shapes of the winders for skeined silks to assess the quality of some of these boxes. The quantity of such fitments, too, is sometimes astonishing. They date from days when scissors were considered by the set and needles required boxes and books and glass vessels and emery bags. They may include pencils and dividers and measures, stilettos and tatting shuttles. Always, too, there must be button hooks, and corkscrews for scent bottles, and elaborate writing equipment, and sets of brushes for the hair, for cloth, for velvet. . . . Indeed the manufacturers' temptation, in those highly competitive days, was to prepare so fully for every possible eventuality that the box had to be transformed into a piece of furniture, mounted on a somewhat whimsically "feminine" castor-footed tripod, handsome in the manner of its day, but lacking the persuasive charm of the "lady's companion".

Chapter Twelve

SILHOUETTES

WOMEN worked, children played and warriors prepared for battle 5000 years ago in ancient Egypt, and have left their shadows on tomb and mummy case. Georgian England took many liberties with the ideas and ideals of ancient civilisations in the name of the classical revival, but we can rejoice today that it set the seal of high fashion on the minor art of shadow work. Those of us who are lucky enough to acquire some of these "profile shades" are constantly aware of their vivid witness to the manners and modes of that period. But we keep and treasure them simply because they are entrancing.

Napoleon gave silhouettes of himself to favoured generals—black profiles backed with gilded tinsel. George III and Queen Charlotte posed for innumerable profile painters and "scissor artists", their own daughter Princess Elizabeth among them. The rounded baby features of the toddler Victoria were copied in twenty seconds with "common scissors" and "without drawing or machine" by the boy prodigy Master Hubard, scarcely ten years older than England's future queen.

Such patronage assured the enthusiastic support of the populace. Everyone who was anyone had a profile cut or painted, but the joy of this fashion was that for once innumerable nobodies could do the same. Even pompous costume was immaterial, and the great Charles of Bath himself stressed that his patrons were under no necessity to have their hair dressed. For some seventy or eighty years from about 1780 the profile shade was the most popular style of "likeness" this country had ever known.

To their purchasers these black profiles were first and foremost valued not for beauty but for accurate recording of facts. They constituted the first cheap method, essentially modern and practical, of presenting vividly and with reasonable permanency the characters, or at least the facial characteristics, of family, friends, celebrities. Comparatively few could afford even one oil portrait, painted miniature or model in wax, and in any case in unskilful hands these were wooden and weary-looking. The profilist could boast of his speed and the truth of his likeness, simplifying and thus illuminating the personality behind the pose. With the aid of an impressive "machine" even the itinerant fairground cutter could produce a passable likeness and any number of copies.

For the first time ordinary folk could secure a record of the solemn little face of a favourite son, chubby cheeks half hidden in high white collar, or the gay curls and tip-tilted nose of a village belle, all secret exultation at this depiction of her precious ribbons and bows. Here was portraiture as cheap and vivid as the promenade snapshot of today—and unfortunately as frequently anonymous.

If our collection has to be assembled as a minor hobby, each specimen costing shillings rather than pounds, we can seldom hope for signed work or the utterly desirable framed examples. Nevertheless, some museum study of the acknowledged masters can quickly establish standards of craftsmanship and indicate the range of techniques dismissed only by the uninterested as haphazard scissorwork, or Thackeray's "sticking plaster portraits". And always there is the real possibility of lighting upon a specimen which is precisely as it was when handed to its purchaser, the back of the original frame still pasted with the artist's self-laudatory label.

The price of such a specimen depends upon the fame of the profilist: an early "Leeds label" Miers is a costly treasure, and even a labelled specimen of his later period in London may cost ten pounds or more. On the other hand profiles in contemporaneous frames but by unknown or unrecognised artists and of unknown subjects may be almost as finely executed and can be bought for as many shillings. I am proud of boasting myself of my own labelled pair by the royalty-patronised Charles Christian Rosenberg (1745–1844) painted on the inside of convex glass and secured a few years ago for ten shillings.

Even at the time these shades were collected—and created—by innumerable amateurs. It was an era that loved quick and easy handicrafts, and anyone could trace a shadow outline, though the coiffures and hats of the late eighteenth century necessitated huge sheets of paper, and practitioners had to be cautioned to use the comparatively steady flame of a wax candle. Such an outline sufficiently reduced by mechanical means acquired a piquancy which makes it as appealing now as to the girl who first received it for her album.

Today's collector derives the most enjoyment from silhouettes if they are viewed with a similar catholicity of taste. It is necessary to recognise the rival merits of those who boasted of free-hand work, whether with brush or with scissors, and those who stressed the accuracy of the likenesses ensured by their "machines". We must approve the original classic simplicity of the profile in unrelieved black and the gaudier adventures into coloured detail. There is a wealth of variety even in nineteenth-century work, such as the characterful poses of Edouart's full-length portraits, however weak the lines of hand and foot, as well as in such earlier treasures as Mrs. Isabella Beetham's fashion records and the fascinating conversation pieces of Francis Torond.

Such references indicate something of the range of style to be looked for among silhouettes. There is a similar range of technique. Untrained amateurs and third-rate professionals alike produced so many cut outlines in and after the 1820s that it is necessary to stress the alternative methods, all of which are now more highly prized. Cut work prompted the other more subtle methods, but even here it is important to distinguish between the common scissor-cuts and the delicate knife-cut vellum.

Mrs. Pyburg cut profiles of William III and Mary, Swift's verse of the 1740s refers to the girlish pastime, with scissors and paper and silk, and George I's associates made him laugh uproariously by cutting caricatures of English courtiers. But the real vogue began in the 1770s, and its most coveted prizes are the painted shades of the "classic" late eighteenth century up to about 1810. The profilist was then most closely associated with the miniature artist, and was governed by the period's appreciation of gracious line and its detestation of fussy ornament. Indian ink or a soot mixture was used, intensely black, painted on plaster, ivory, vellum, card or glass.

The most perfect craftsman, perhaps, was John Miers (1758–1821). He frequently painted in black on card or on solid white composition medallions, his profiles clear and full of character and exquisitely set off by evanescent effects of hair and headdress. Typical is his masterly portrayal of Mrs. Siddons, her long nose and determined mouth in clear black profile but with gossamer-delicate veiling and curls to soften the outline of the head.

Miers's labels stressed that in his "peculiarly Striking and Elegant likenesses" the "forcible animation is retained to the minutest size for setting in Rings, Lockets, Bracelets, etc." Miers began and did his loveliest work in Leeds where his father was a painter of heraldic coach panels. But he moved to London in 1788, as profile painter and jeweller. Every collector's dream is to acquire a piece of silhouette jewellery with the delicate profile on its flake of ivory signed J. Miers under the bust.

Equally wonderful to acquire, perhaps, would be a conversation piece painted by the Huguenot refugee who worked under the name of Francis Torond (1743–1812). Torond began as a miniaturist in Bath but became so successful as a profile painter in London after 1784 that he employed several assistants. In Indian ink on card he painted delicious story-telling scenes, perfect to the last curve of his favourite Gothic-Chippendale chairs—too perfect to escape many modern copyists. William Wellings and J. A. Schmetterling were other creators of such shadow tableaux.

Rosenberg and Charles were also among the many who practised in Bath, and here again there is particularly delightful work for the finding, as they often used the technique of painting on the inside of an oval glass measuring about 2½ by 3 inches. Charles claimed this as his invention and charged as much as a guinea for a profile on glass or ivory, intensely black but with details of hair and lace delicately translucent. Full length was a guinea. On paper a profile was 3s. 6d., raised to 6s. when "elegantly framed".

Some profiles on glass were backed with white card or plaster; others with gold or silver tinsel, popular in Germany. But in some of the loveliest the profile inside the curved glass stood away from the flat white background, as in my Rosenberg couple, so that the facial outlines were softened by the shadow they cast on the flat white behind. Others such as H. Gibbs of Bristol and Chelsea backed their painted profiles with wax so closely that some have thought they were painted on the wax itself.

Mrs. Isabella Beetham, of Fleet Street, London, sometimes painted her dress-conscious little figures on the glass with wax or composition to "protect" them, rather disastrously since it has tended to crack. Fortunately, however, this versatile lady painted also on plaster and ivory. She cut silhouettes from paper, too, then mounted them on card so that she could soften their outlines with brushwork. The delicacy of her detail must be recognised as a signature for she rarely signed her name.

William Holland painted profiles in Dublin from 1774 to 1786, the few signed specimens being painted on glass backed with silk. He used his own water-colour composition which he declared was better than the usual water colour on plaster or oil colour on glass. Rosenberg, too, boasted of the pigment he used on convex glass, claiming that it would not fade. Rosenberg came to England as a bright young page to Princess Charlotte in 1761 and basked in George III's patronage, eventually retiring from Court to work in Bath and charging from 7s. 6d. to one guinea for a minute sitting. His silhouettes included brushwork on plain glass backed with pink (now faded) card to suggest marble, and minute work for locket, ring and snuffbox.

Rosenberg used intensely black pigment and still achieved the painter's subtle tenderness of outline. But for dramatic effect no method compared with the profile cut from black paper and mounted on card. This work lent itself especially to the inevitable infant prodigies of the art. There was Frederick Frith of Dover for example, and William Hubard of Whitchurch, Shropshire. Hubard (1807–62) is interesting because he was a real portrait painter despite the sideshow atmosphere of his publicity, and because something of his life is known, including its sudden ending in America, when he was preparing shells for the Confederate army.

Hubard first caught the shadow of a boring preacher in church when he was seven years old, but grew up to be a fairly considerable master of his long-bladed scissors. In the blare of publicity that surrounded his "Hubard Gallery" the emphasis was upon his originality and skill in free-hand cutting—no drawing, no machine—years before Edouart claimed invention of this technique, and in his late work he achieved a vivid sense of movement and delightful touches of humour.

He was in Ireland in 1821, received recognition from Glasgow Philosophical Society in 1823, toured America, then opened his Gallery in London in 1829, returning to America in 1834. His work is always labelled. Early specimens may be embossed on the mount "Cut with Scissors by Master Hubard without Drawing or Machine" and the later London work was embossed "Taken at the Hubard Gallery". He cut his portraits two at once, giving one as part of the price of admission (50 cents in New York, 1s. in London) and either selling the other or putting it into his Gallery display.

Lavish bronzing of various qualities increased the price. This was added after the silhouette had been pasted on card, so that solidity of outline was combined with subtler detail, and he might touch in gauzy aprons and caps with white. But this was a great period for scrapbooks, and very many Hubard shades were intended to compete with such examples of amateur talent as Princess Elizabeth's famous but somewhat jerky cherubs and romping toddlers. Hubard cut pictorial scenes such as Oxford High with its steeples and students, and even Epsom races with two hundred or more tiny figures, down to the small chimney-sweep pickpocket. Some had background trees cut in gold paper. But eventually what emerged was Hubard the portrait painter.

Inevitably once cutting of scrapbook standard became acceptable the shadow men lost their early status. Results could sell so cheaply, the outlay was so small and the work so speedy and spectacular that in the early nineteenth century they were tending to be associated with fairground sideshows. There was J. Gapp in his booth on Brighton chain pier, for instance, and Dempsey of Liverpool, attracting emigrants with offers of a likeness for 3d., bronzed 6d. and coloured 18d., and reminding them of the cheap new penny post for distributing such mementoes.

The indefatigable August Edouart entered the craft unwillingly in 1825, as a descent in the social scale from the heights of fashioning portraits in human hair. Between 1825 and 1860 he cut about a quarter of a million silhouettes, and soon rose above the "Shilling Business" as he called it to charge 2s. for a profile bust and 5s. or more for his most usual full-length, with helpful extras for a pet horse, dog or cat in the picture. Some were set against hasty pictorial backgrounds or even lithographs.

Today one of the charms of these silhouettes is their rapid free-hand liveliness. But at the time what was wanted was accuracy, and many took a pride in the machines that ensured an outline mechanically exact, no matter how lacking in spontaneous expression. As early as 1775 Mrs. Sarah Harrington toured the country making her machine-guided cut-outs which she advertised as "the most striking likenesses at 2s. 6d. each". She made a feature of white silhouettes on black silk. But it was after 1820 that the silhouette machine became widely established and the art collapsed into a small mechanical operation.

Some of these machines merely ensured an undistorted outline to the shadow cast and drawn in, slightly larger than life, behind the sitter's profile. Another mechanical aid then reduced this outline to the required size. An alternative device reduced the actual shadow, and yet another contained an arm that passed over the sitter's features while a second arm recorded them on paper. By 1806 Charles Schmalcalder of London had patented a machine that also cut the silhouette and the lapse of this patent in 1820 resulted in widespread use. In 1811 E. W. Foster had a machine for etching the silhouette on a copper plate to ensure any number of identical copies.

The real disaster to the silhouette, however, was not, I suspect, the machine which then appeared wholly admirable, but the use of colour. Even in the last years of the eighteenth century W. Spornberg made startling strident use of bright brick red pigment, before he hastened away to America to ensure that his bones would rest in the land of his dreams. He painted in black inside convex glass but only outlined the profile and features and details of hair and clothes, surrounding all this with a solid black background. Then, from behind, he introduced red pigment so that his portraits —profiles is an inadequate term—appear in the red against black surroundings.

Most eighteenth-century profile painters, of course, would have scorned the tricks that followed later. Miers and Field work may be pencilled with bronze paint: John Field (1771–1844) applied it with great delicacy, but the perfection of simplicity was lost. And more was to come. Hamlet of Bath, painting on flat or convex glass from about 1780 to 1815, may be noted introducing touches of colour to his expensive guinea and half-guinea profiles—often full-length figures which required a full three minutes of astonishingly concentrated work.

Then came W. Phelps of Drury Lane, one of the first to use bright greens and blues for his ladies' dresses, and colour under the shading of their hair. Next it was brown profiles instead of black, and rusty red heightened with gold by the long-lived Edward Foster of Derby (1762–1864). But the great vogue for colour work began among the early 19th-century military and naval officers. Buncombe in the Isle of Wight—another victim of the modern copyist —produced magnificent small portraits. Indeed the only discordant note among all the splendour is the strange little eyeless blackamoor face with the aristocratic features that peeps out from so much finery.

Edouart decried the childish taste in his *Treatise on Silhouette Likenesses*, 1835, writing of "harlequinades" with their gold hair, coral earrings, blue necklaces and white frills. Yet today even coloured backgrounds—scarlet, blue, yellow—are rare and sought after, and still rarer and more prized are shockingly decadent little silhouettes with gummed-on fabric for their trimmings.

From such absurdities it is pleasant to turn to the silhouette at its most exquisite and unspoiled, in the precious work of the profile jeweller. John Miers is especially associated with this work, to which alone he often signed his name. Some tiny Miers silhouettes were mounted on cream satin or green velvet in small red leather cases. His rings are plainly oval, with convex glass over the silhouette. The signature Miers and Field is that of his son when associated with Miers's assistant John Field for about ten years from 1821, and is found on the more elaborate jewellery of its period.

Rosenberg was another contributor to this delicate ornament, as were J. Smith of Edinburgh, who also worked in hair and pearl, and Paskin of Colchester and W. F. Godfrey. Bracelets of agate and garnet were gold-mounted with tiny silhouettes in their clasps and there were brooches and scarf pins too as well as the more obvious lockets and rings. Memorial rings are especially rare and sought after. Simple gold mounts were most usual for silhouette jewellery but some were set in pearls and a few of the many boxes for snuff and patches and playing cards carry silhouettes mounted in enamel.

Small circular silhouettes to go in the backs of watches are rare and collectable, too, dating to the 1840s. The profile may be cut within a perforated border or painted within a border unadventurously printed. Indeed the value of silhouette ornament has been recognised down the ages, ever since stylised figures adorned Etruscan vases. John Field advertised book frontispieces and while silhouettes were in vogue George III himself appeared on Worcester porcelain, and Apsley Pellatt made a feature of little "clay" silhouettes buried in the clear glass of bottle and paper-weight.

Plate 1

Tea-pots at their most elegant, in fine translucent porcelains. The bone china specimens at the top are typical of the best Rockingham and Spode. The Rockingham (*left*) is ornamented in the firm's intensely rich gold, including a delightful gold crown for a finial. The Spode has the deservedly famous japan pattern in deep velvety blue, vivid brick red and green, all lit with gilded detail. In the centre the pot with the wolf and the lamb suggests a particularly fascinating quest—for china bearing Aesop fable illustrations, which can be pursued in tea-ware, dessert sets, candlesticks and so on. On the right, also early nineteenth century, is work from Baxter's famous London china-enamelling workshop, about 1810, in blue and gold on Caughley porcelain. At the bottom is porcelain of about 1770. The Bristol specimen on the left has a blue ground veined to suggest marble with white reserves painted in full colour and bordered in gold. The "Dr. Wall" Worcester in the familiar ribbed design has panels of scale blue and delicate flower painting.

Plate 2

Tea-pots in more homely wares. (*Top left*) Staffordshire salt-glazed stoneware moulded all over to suggest basket ware and coloured pink. The fruit and foliage are enamelled in green, pink, yellow and red. 4¾ inches high. About 1760. (*Top right*) Leeds cream-coloured earthenware with crabstock handle and spout and blue decoration painted under the glaze. Late eighteenth century. (*Centre left*) Familiar Wedgwood jasper ware, the "Domestic Employment" motif designed by Lady Templetown appearing in white relief on a blue ground. 10 inches high. 1785. (*Centre right*) An early specimen in drab-coloured Staffordshire salt-glazed stoneware, the clear-cut decoration achieved by applying—sprigging—reliefs stamped in white clay. This has traces of oil gilding. 4 inches high. About 1740. (*Bottom left*) The fine stoneware known as Egyptian black shaped into an austere cylindrical pot giving full value to the restrained engine turning. Impressed Spode. Early nineteenth century. (*Bottom right*) Salt-glazed stoneware mould-shaped and incised with "scratch blue" ornament of birds and formal flowers. 5½ inches high. About 1740.

Plate 3

Coffee-pots. (*Upper left*) A crude interpretation of silver elegance in Staffordshire salt-glazed white stoneware ornamented in pink, green, blue and brownish red. 9½ inches high. About 1765. (*Upper right*) Porcelain from Longton Hall in the most familiar style of pear-shaped body and flat loop handle attractively enriched with enamel colours and gilding. Early 1750s. (*Lower left*) Wedgwood cream-coloured earthenware in the shell-edge shape with double-twist handle and flower lid-finial. 9 inches high. Late eighteenth century. (*Lower right*) Worcester porcelain painted and gilded in the familiar meticulous manner and topped with a tulip bud finial. Made between 1765 and 1775.

Plate 4
Scent bottles at their loveliest. (*Upper left*) Bristol-blue glass naively gilded in the manner of the 1760s–70s and topped with a gilded silver stopper. (*Upper right*) A silvery cameo portrait of George IV framed in brilliant cut-glass by the renowned Apsley Pellatt. The fine diamond-cutting on the mouth rim is a rare feature. (*Lower left*) Three eighteenth-century examples. The striated agate is mounted in gold, its base forming a patch box. The Harlequin is Chelsea porcelain: later figures avoided the indignity of having their heads removed as stoppers. (*Lower right*) Chelsea specimen of a girl with grapes, 3½ inches high. The stopper is above the girl's head and is made an interesting feature with a pigeon pecking fruit. About 1760.

Plate 5

Scent bottles. All the upper row are of glass. (*Upper left*) In the Nailsea manner, clear with opaque stripes, made individual by the date trailed over the surface in ruby glass: on the other side are the initials I M. (*Upper centre*) Bristol-blue glass of about 1820, pleasant to handle with panels of cut ornament and daintily gilded. (*Upper right*) Individual naming is a charming feature of many scent bottles made in the white opaque glass that would be taken at a glance as porcelain. Dated 1780. (*Lower left*) English painted enamel work at its best. A South Staffordshire specimen painted in full colour from a print of the period and surrounded by raised scrolling lightly gilded. (*Lower centre*) Wedgwood, showing the meticulously perfect background detail that could be achieved in jasper ware. 1785–6. (*Lower right*) Glass mounted with a Wedgwood jasper, white on black, from a design by Lady Templetown. 1785.

Plate 6
Contrast in the handling of mother of pearl. In the paper-mounted fan the matching pairs of sticks, delicately fret-cut, form a balanced, intricate design. This dates to the first half of the nineteenth century. Below, in the late Elizabethan casket, small scales of pearl are mounted in gilded silver, depending for effect entirely upon the colour and lustre of the shell and, originally, the careful shaping and fitting of the scales. This elegant small vessel is less than $3\frac{1}{2}$ inches high.

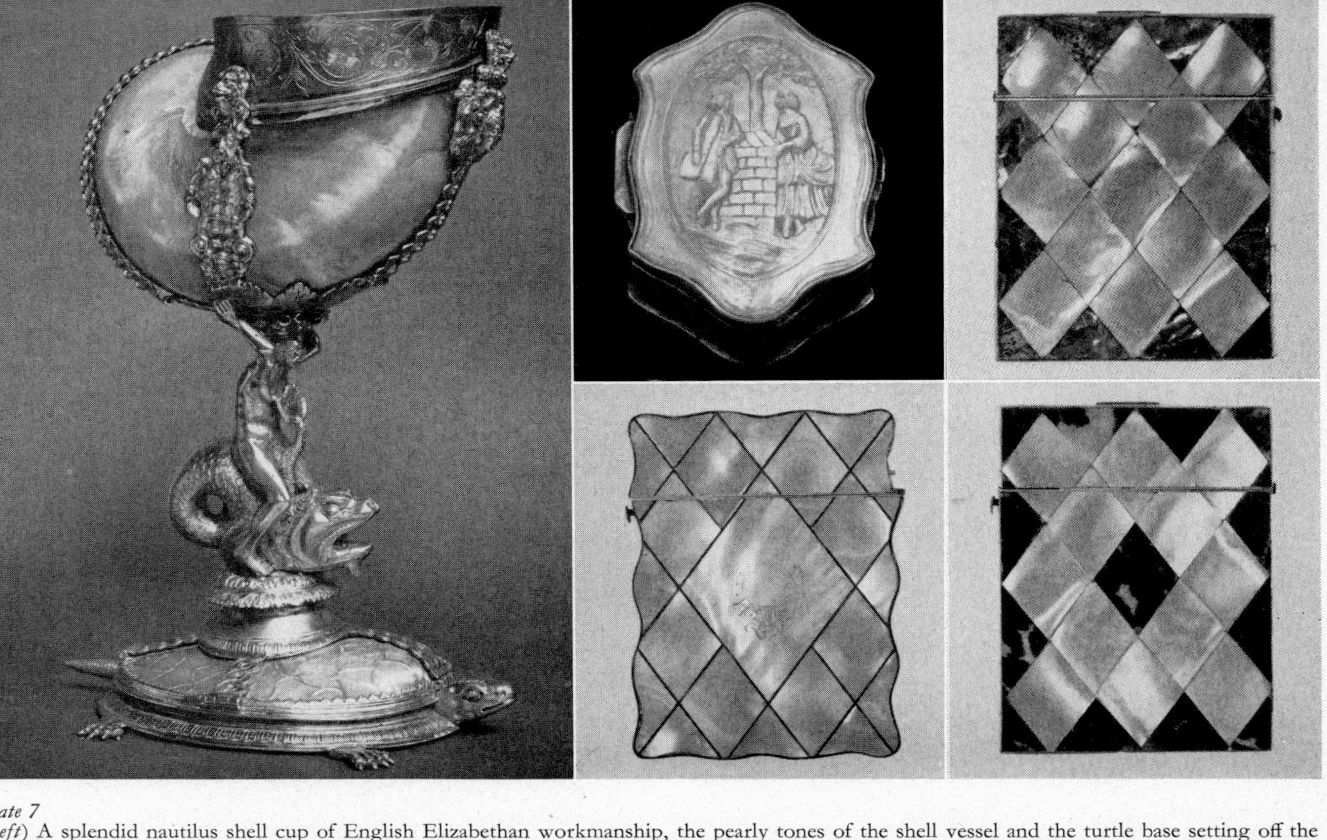

Plate 7
(*Left*) A splendid nautilus shell cup of English Elizabethan workmanship, the pearly tones of the shell vessel and the turtle base setting off the elaborate figure work in gilded silver. (*Upper centre*) In this eighteenth-century snuff-box the mother of pearl is delicately carved in low relief with the typical pastoral figures of its day and mounted in silver. (*Upper right and lower centre and right*) Card cases showing typical nineteenth-century use of the shell, and still inexpensive today. Those on the right introduce contrasts of dark mother of pearl (*above*) and tortoiseshell. The light pearl case is engraved; the others have small strips of silver at the top for initials.

Plate 8
A kitchen in miniature to warm any doll's heart. Every detail is worthy of scrutiny, from the glass and pottery on the dresser to the Staffordshire blue platter on the wall and the "Dutch oven" below it for cooking in front of the fire.

Plate 9a
Miniature silver from a notable collection at the Victoria and Albert Museum, London. Such toys were for adult enjoyment, and one expects to find every detail in proportion and the finish impeccable. The candlestick on the left in the middle row is one of a pair hall-marked for 1694–5 and made by George Middleton.

Plate 9b
Miniature china made for the collector's cabinet. The tiny tea-pot, milk jug and covered sugar bowl with their china tray are notably near in design to a Swansea porcelain cabaret set of the Regency period, with the soft richness of the highly skilled ceramic decorator if not quite the perfection of Swansea's William Billingsley. There are no marks, but a probable source is Coalport.

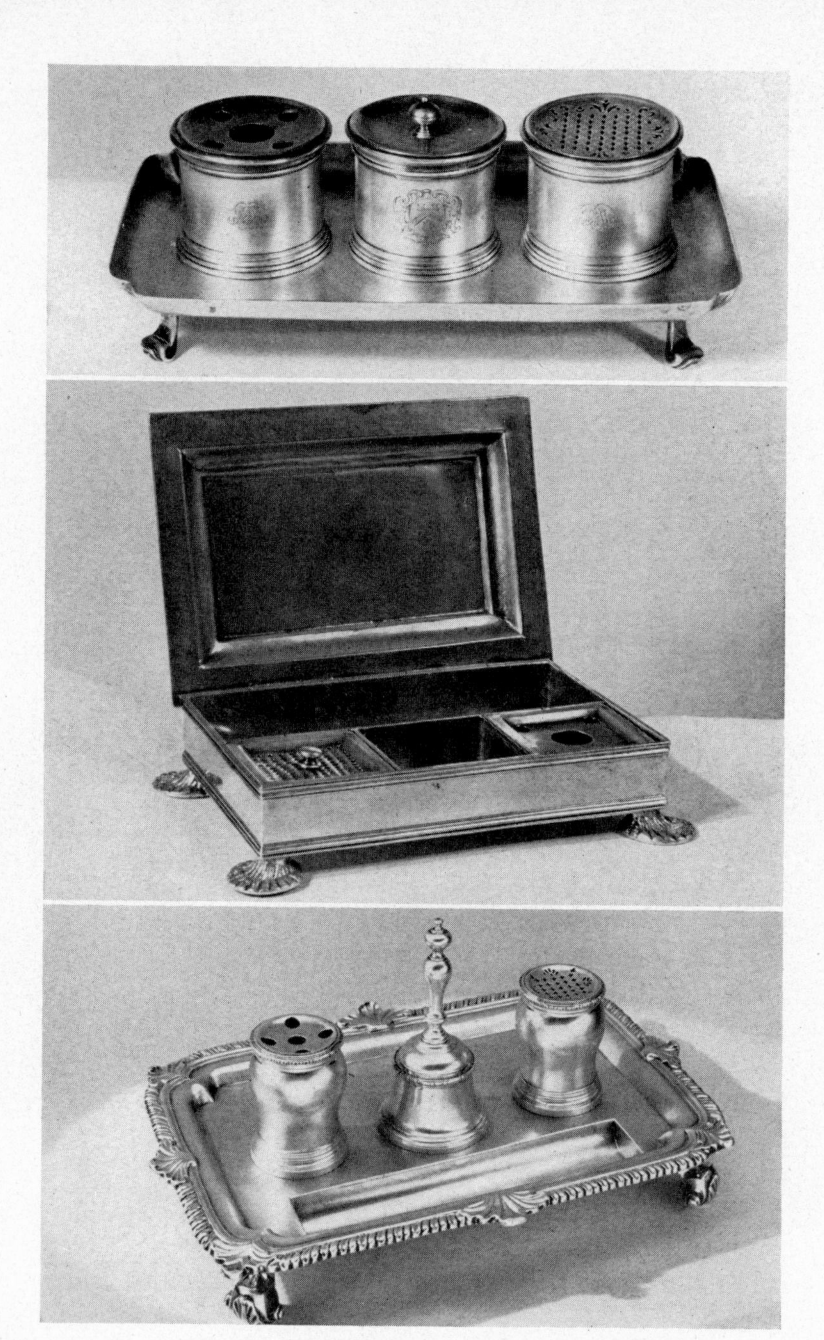

Plate 10
Silver inkstands. (*Top*) By Paul de Lamerie in pleasantly austere mood. The vessels are for ink, wafers and pounce respectively. 1734. (*Centre*) The lidded fore-runner of the inkstand, an attractively solid silver pen-and-ink box by George Garthorne, with the London hall-mark for 1676. (*Bottom*) A more ornate tray of 1745, each piece hall-marked and with unmistakably matching ornament, including the delightful bell—important points for a cautious collector. By Robert Innes of London.

Plate 11
Inkstands. (*Upper left*) A magnificent George IV specimen with cut-glass vessels and a candlestick and extinguisher for sealing. By John Angell, 1823. (*Upper right*) A mid-eighteenth-century specimen with its tray recessed for ink and pounce vessels. The central urn for shot covers a wafer recess. By George Methuen, 1751. (*Lower left*) The long rectangular lines of the 1800s expressed in 204 ounces of silver by John Parker, 1802. (*Lower right*) Neatly elaborate foot-design and urn-shaped vessels typical of the 1770s. This was made by John Parker and Edward Wakelin, London, 1771, and originally belonged to Horace Walpole.

Plate 12

China inkstands. (*Upper left*) Far too lovely for the stains of pen and ink, in Coalport's delectable flower-encrusted manner. (*Upper right*) Rockingham, marked with the griffin in puce and measuring $15\frac{1}{4} \times 12$ inches. The pierced trellis border is richly gilded and the birds are in green, mauve, red and pale yellow. (*Lower left*) Unmarked but probably Coalport with flower-encrusted candlestick and rose finials to the inkpots. (*Lower right*) Derby of the 1820s decorated in richly coloured imitation of the Japanese Imari work. There is a recess at the front for pens.

Plate 13a
Flower prints. (*Left*) A graceful study of the dwarf double poppy drawn and engraved by John Edwards from his heavily-titled *Collection of Flowers drawn after Nature and disposed in an Ornamental and Picturesque Manner* (1783). (*Right*) One of the impressive illustrations to Thornton's *Temple of Flora* (1799) painted by Reinagle and engraved by Stadler. The flower is *mimosa grandiflora*—large-flowering sensitive plant—here shown complete with humming birds and astonished Jamaican.

Plate 13b
(*Left*) An early Victorian group of compositae individually delightful but expressing the period's restless dislike of blank spaces. Drawn by Henry N. Humphreys for Mrs. Loudon's *British Wild Flowers* (1845). (*Right*) A wonderful study in textures that makes most other flower prints appear amateur work. The rose La Duchesse d'Orleans painted by Pierre-Joseph Redouté and superbly engraved by Langlow for Redouté's work *Les Roses* (1824).

Plate 14
A flower print of exceptional magnificence justified by its purpose. This is from *Twelve Months of Flowers*, by Robert Furber (1730), which was in effect the first English seed catalogue. The illustration represents March and lists 34 spring flowers including maple and larch trees, all numbered under the blooms and named in the key below, such as No. 1, Royal Widow auricula and No. 4, High Admiral anemone. This bears the names of Ptr. Gassteels as designer and H. Fletcher as engraver and is "from the Collection of Robt. Furber Gardiner at Kensington."

Plate 15
Bird prints. (*Upper left*) The mid-eighteenth century's delight in the marvels of nature expressed in George Edwards' lively yellow water wagtail from his *Gleanings of Natural History* (1756). The sharp outlines of the copper plate are softened with hand colouring. Typically, Edwards also includes "the walking leaf" on his print and a stone from the Giant's Causeway. (*Upper right*) An early hand-coloured, copper-plate print by Eleazar Albin dated 1736. Here there is still virtually no association between bird and setting, not even in the grip of its claws, but the clarity of the engraving is attractive. (*Lower left*) Whip-poor-Will, an Audubon study, showing the angular vigour he loved, but here reproduced in a later, lithographed form lacking the three-dimensional dramatic effect of the earlier aquatints. (*Lower right*) Edward Lear's immensely alive study of Baudin's cockatoo, which he drew and lithographed for his *Illustrations of the Family Psittacidae or Parrots*, to show lithography at its best.

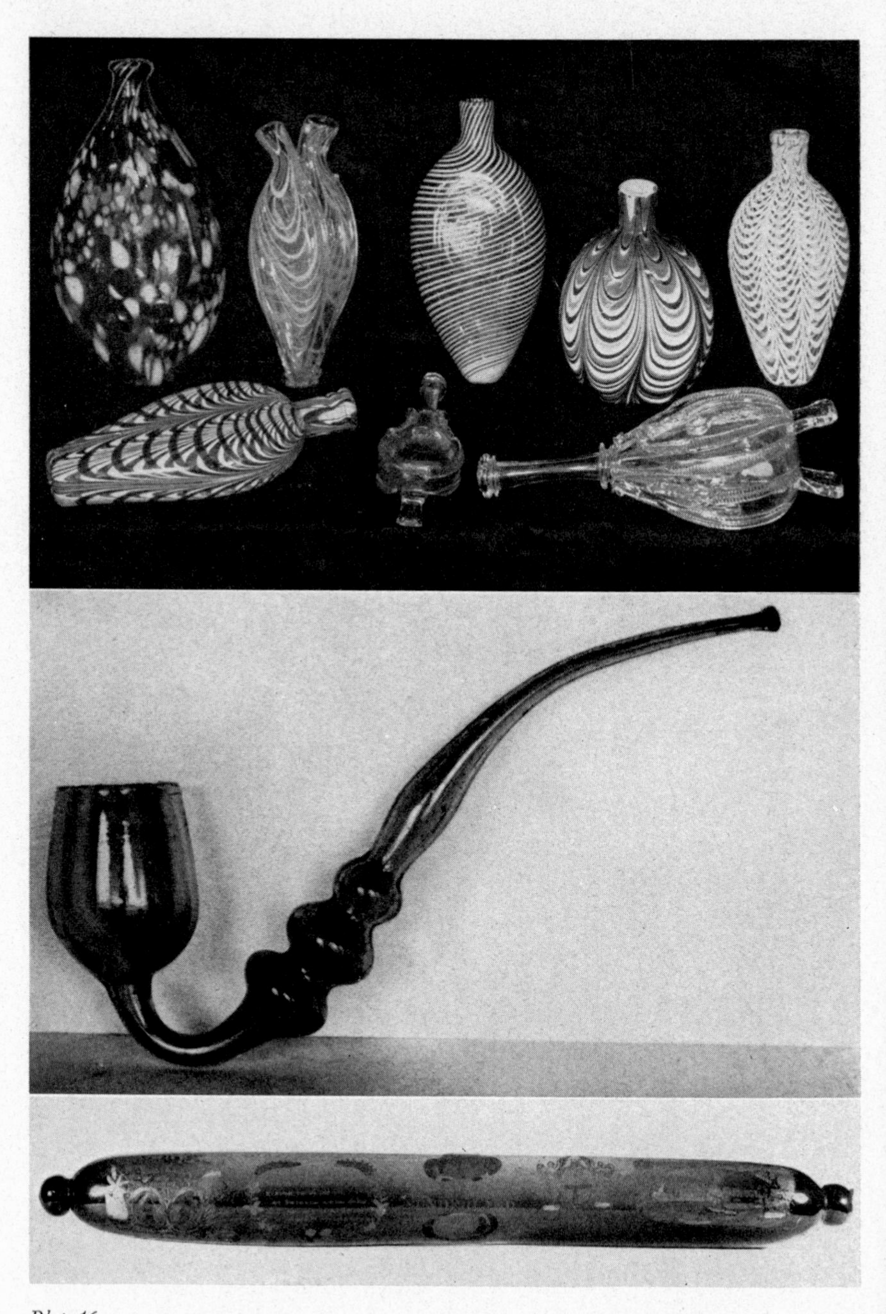

Plate 16
Nailsea glass. (*Top*) Flasks mottled, quilled and striped. In the back row is one of the two-part or gimmel design, and in front are two bellows flasks. (*Centre*) Hollow-stemmed pipe of lovely clear blue glass. Early nineteenth century. (*Bottom*) Rolling-pin plainly knobbed for hanging on the wall to display a variety of ornament including a view of the famous bridge and the words "A PRESENT FROM SUNDERLAND."

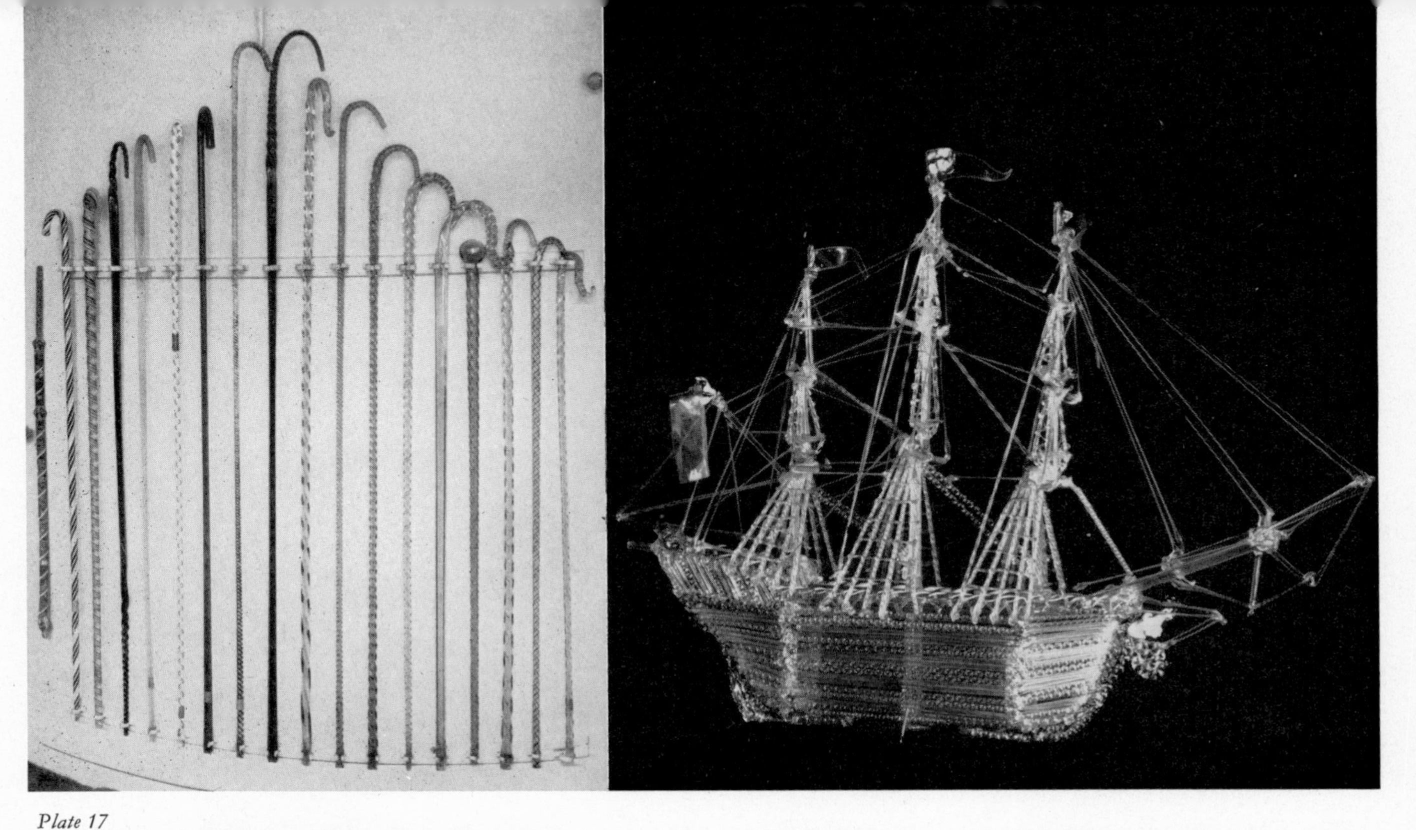

Plate 17

(*Left*) Glass walking-sticks which the craftsmen have made remarkably straight and even in spite of a fascinating variety of spiral treatments, colour and pattern being introduced inside the glass and over its surface. (*Right*) A superb little model of a ship made and rigged in spun glass, partly in blue glass and partly in clear. This is 8 inches long and 6 inches high. Mid-nineteenth century.

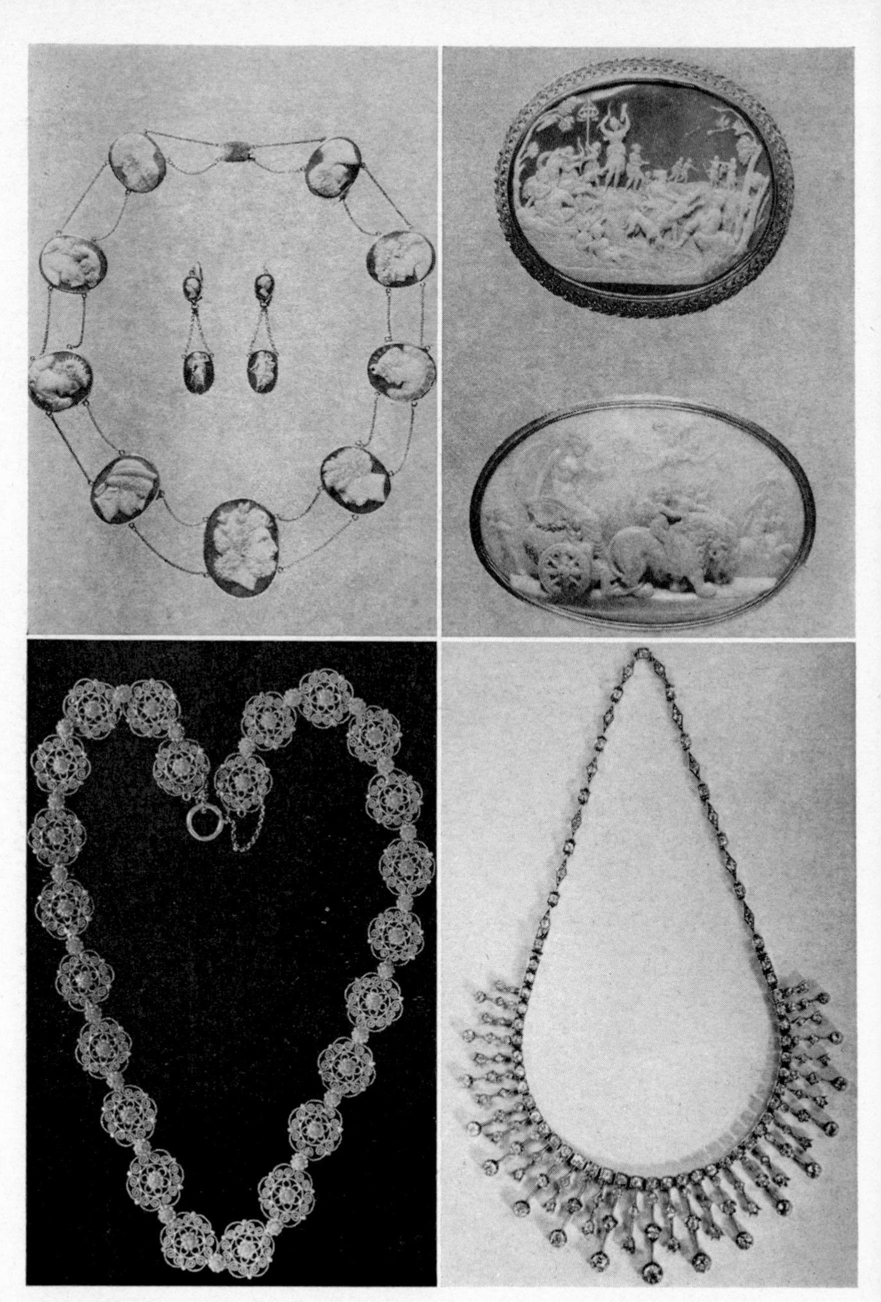

Plate 18
Victorian jewellery. (*Upper left and right*) Shell cameo work. The necklace is notable for the perfect balance of the design, and has pendant ear-rings to complete the ensemble. The brooches show the wealth of detail that could be achieved by skilful cutting in very low relief, the lower one particularly effective in its use of three strata. The upper specimen has its original gold frame. (*Lower left*) Gold filigree at its best, the fine gold wire in twisted-rope outline being delicately and exactly shaped to form a particularly graceful necklace. (*Lower right*) A brilliant late nineteenth-century necklace, the diamonds set in silver backed with gold: the longer drops end in large brilliant-cut diamonds and the shorter ones between in bell-flower outlines.

Plate 19
Victorian jewellery showing the period's delight in substantial outlines and massed detail expressed in markedly different media. (*Upper left*) My most dignified great-aunt's favourite everyday wear and typical of much heavy work of later Victorian days, this set—locket, ear-rings and bracelet—are solidly mounted with smoothly-rounded amethysts, their rich purple tones contrasting with the deep gold shade of their settings. (*Upper right*) Carbuncles and pearls high-lighting a brooch in which the pavé effect is achieved not with gems but with gold filigree. (*Lower left*) Pearls from British rivers were once of considerable importance. In this mid-Victorian necklace the delicate outlines are cut in eleven pieces of mother of pearl and the tiny Scottish pearls threaded and bound over this firm foundation. (*Lower right*) Impressive flower spray brooch of the second quarter of the nineteenth century. The flowers and leaves are diamonds set in gold, the stalks are green enamel and the berries are pearls.

Plate 20
Early Victorian jewellery typical of the best naturalistic work, sparkling with diamonds set in gold. The butterfly is greatly enhanced by the outlines in crimson enamel. The bee is in the same mood, glittering with diamonds, and may be dated to about 1840. The spray of oak and ivy is a lovely piece, in a simple, well-balanced design. The rose-cut diamond flower at its simplest and most impressive—a scabious perhaps—is from a mid-nineteenth-century set.

Plate 21
Japanned ware from the renowned Allgood factory at Pontypool. The urn-shaped covered vase has lion mask and ring handles. Its glossy black japanning is painted with sprays of conventional flowers and butterflies in gold, silver and red. The chamber candlestick is crimson with silver flower ornament. The pleasantly proportioned coffee-pot has ambitious painting with buildings and a river scene; the lid is hinged. Beside it is a Levno coffee urn heated by a charcoal brazier in the perforated box underneath. Chinese figures in gold decorate the black japanning.

Plate 22

Japanned iron picture trays. (*Top left*) "Windsor" shape finely painted with fruit at the Old Hall Works, Wolverhampton, in about 1847. (*Top right*) This oval tray has hand grips in the rim. The rustic scene in Morland style was perhaps painted by William Davis of the Old Hall Works. (*Centre left*) The "king gothic" shape with a bronzed border framing the oil painting of a lively river scene. (*Centre right*) This tray has a gold ground border of the type shaped by the earliest Naismyth press, acquired by Walton and Company, Wolverhampton. (*Bottom left*) One of a pair of huntsman trays from a long series issued by Alderman and Illidge, Wolverhampton. (*Bottom right*) Tray painting at its most elaborate in a land and sea battle scene 30 × 21½ inches.

Plate 23
Printed handkerchiefs. (*Left*) A detailed, carefully printed view of "The Procession after claiming the Gammon of Bacon at the Monastry [sic] of Great Dunmow in Essex". The border is printed with the "Form of Oath" for couples to swear to qualify for the bacon. Second half of the eighteenth century. (*Right*) The design of this specimen was registered at the Patent Office to protect it from copyists. This was one of many humorous designs envisaging ludicrous situations in a preposterous "1981", such as women in the armed forces, in law and politics, in the police and on the railways, while men are reduced to window cleaning and domestic chores.

Plate 24a
Handkerchiefs at their most ornate, intended as delicate ornament. These were formerly in Queen Mary's Collection. (*Left*) Dainty as a snowflake, this specimen is in Carrickmacross appliqué, the cambric cut out and sewn on to net with such care for arrangement and stitch that it suggests the perfection of lace and indeed includes rudimentary needlepoint fillings. (*Right*) a monogrammed handkerchief that once belonged to Queen Alexandra, ornamented with lace and embroidery yet retaining its air of gossamer delicacy.

Plate 24b
(*Left*) The daintiness of flower embroidery and the elaboration of the border are typical of much fine white embroidery of the early nineteenth century, highly professional work by skilled craftswomen. 18 inches square. (*Right*) An exquisite specimen once possessed by that perfectionist collector of handkerchiefs, Queen Elizabeth I.

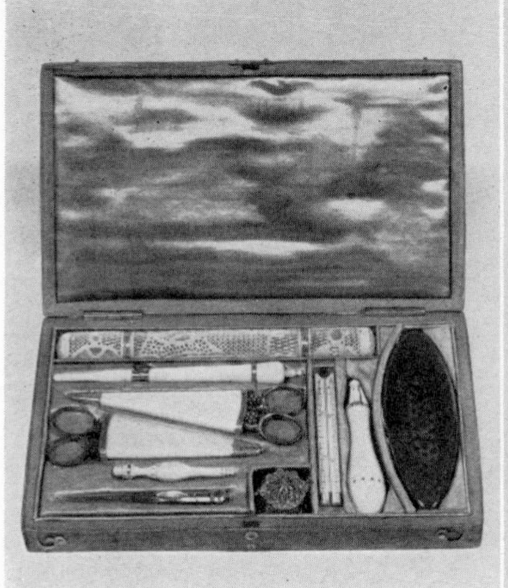

Plate 25a
Compendiums. (*Left*) A slim box covered with shagreen, fitted for needlework, tatting, etc. This forms part of a set of three which together take the place of a fitted cabinet. (*Right*) An embroidered casket of the type associated with the second half of the seventeenth century. This is dated 1657. The lid gives access to a compartmented tray with a central well and the doors at the front open to their full extent disclosing drawers for jewellery. This example is worked in the earlier style of flat, all-covering tent-stitch embroidery in contrast to the bolder raised work on a base of white satin equally popular on these caskets and giving them their Victorian name of stump-work cabinets. The background detail of disproportionate animals and insects is typical of both. The basic framework of wood is almost entirely hidden, outside and in.

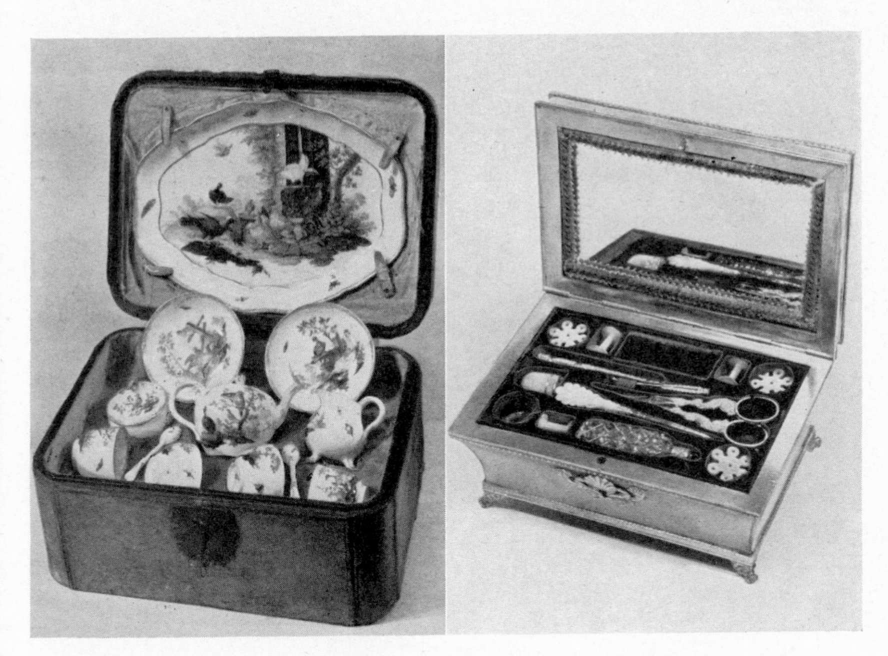

Plate 25b
(*Left*) Compendiums of varying complexity were devised for the coach traveller, plain outside but often delightful within. This eighteenth-century set includes full equipment for tea, even to the porcelain tray to hold it all. (*Right*) An elegant work-box of the 1830s that originally belonged to Emma, Countess Brownlow (1791–1872). This is of alabaster with ormolu mounts. In addition to its attractive equipment this has a musical box in the base.

Plate 26

Four beautifully made compendiums of the nineteenth century, the upper left and the two below presented to the Bethnal Green Museum by Queen Mary. (*Upper left*) Rosewood inlaid with pearl, with red leatherwork stamped in gold and fittings of cut steel. (*Upper right*) Satinwood with carved and fret-cut pearl fittings. (*Lower left*) Cabinet compendium, the panels painted in transparent colours over mother of pearl. (*Lower right*) Tooled leather of about 1865, with fittings of pearl-mounted steel.

Plate 27
Silhouette conversation pieces. (*Above*) Vivid likenesses set in a particularly attractive story-telling scene recorded by the brilliant French refugee silhouettist who worked under the name of Francis Torond (1743–1812). This birthday party scene is in indian ink on paper. The oval under the scene is Torond's label, announcing that he would take likenesses singly and in groups, with drawing and painting lessons as a sideline. (*Below*) Signed and dated by the London profilist William Wellings, 1782, and full of interesting contemporary detail.

Plate 28

Silhouettes, all valued primarily at the time as records of likenesses. (*Upper row, left to right*) Cut by Master William Hubard, with his typical use of bronzing; painted inside convex glass, showing one of the later eighteenth century's freak coiffures; fashion-conscious penwork by Mrs. Isabella Beetham; locket profile signed J. Miers, showing the diaphanous delicacy of his style. (*Lower row, left to right*) By John Miers, the Duchess of Atholl in a contemporaneous frame of pressed brass; by C. C. Rosenberg, painted on convex glass; by J. Gapp; by W. Mason, the Duke of Sussex painted on card.

Plate 29
Delightful late Georgian pedlar man, finely dressed and firmly mounted on a block covered with marbled paper. His wares are mainly ornamental—gloves, beads, feathers, stocking purses and the like—more desirable to the collector than the mixed collection more often found today.

Plate 30
Early dolls, setting high standards for today's collector. (*Upper left*) A painted wooden doll, the costume suggesting a date of about 1690, contemporaneous with the carved walnut chair. (*Upper right*) A doll of the 1700s showing the well-modelled face and the poorly-made arms typical of its period. 22 inches high. (*Lower left*) A doll of carved and painted wood, once handsome and elegantly dressed and equipped with jointed arms and legs. This was a family treasure since 1760 until given to the London Museum. (*Lower right*) 2 feet 9 inches of late eighteenth-century elegance on a doll magnificently wigged and gowned to represent Mrs. Candour from R. B. Sheridan's *The School for Scandal*, a play first produced at Drury Lane in 1777.

Plate 31
(*Upper left*) The starry eyes and tiny mouth of the mid-Victorian doll. This specimen is 19¾ inches tall. The confusion of clothes represents outdoor costume of about 1875. (*Upper right*) An attractive doll of the 1830s despite the cracks of age in the modelled and tinted wax of her head and shoulders and the weak treatment of hands and feet. (*Below*) Elaborate court dress on a typical early Victorian doll. Here the arms and hands are carefully, plumply modelled. 21 inches high.

Plate 32

The poet Christopher Anstey (1724–1805) painted by William Hoare. A glimpse of a late eighteenth-century doll with fantastic feathered and beaded headdress, hard-worn features and typically unattractive hands, and really being used as a plaything. (See Chapter 13.) The inkstand has high, perforated rims, with vessels for ink, shot and pounce and a tray for pen-knife and other accessories. The poet's quill pen would rest in the five-holed vessel for shot. (See Chapter 5.)

Plate 33
A fine dresser forms the ideal background to an array of pewter. As well as the flatware, specimens here displayed include a caster (*top shelf*), and a tea canister, funnels and an inkstand. When plates so arranged were in constant use it was customary to show their undersides, as these would not be defaced with knife scratches and other wear marks.

Plate 34
Pewter at its best. (*Upper row*) The spoons are of the fifteenth and sixteenth centuries, their handles known as: slipped-in-the-stalk, maidenhead, writhen ball, ribbed ball, notched and lion sejant. The 4-inch wine measure has a double-volute thumbpiece; mid-eighteenth century. The trumpet-base candlestick is of the late seventeenth century. (*Lower row*) the seventeenth-century candlestick has a heavy salt-cellar base. The tankard, about 1695, is decorated with joggled work. In the group, the measures (*left and centre*) are Scottish, 1690–1720 and about 1720, and the tankards (*upper centre and right*) are about 1720 and of the late seventeenth century.

Plate 35
Kitchen garden ceramics. (*Upper group*) Wedgwood's green-glaze ware. The fir cone custard cup and the frond-and-leaf dish are from patterns designed in 1770 and the vine-and-strawberry dessert plate follows a design dating back to 1759 when the ware was invented. (*Lower group*) Fascinating Chelsea fruits and vegetables. Their scale may be gauged from the apple which is 3½ inches long. The cos lettuce dish and cover rest on a stand of overlapping leaves. Below are a bundle of asparagus and a cauliflower.

Plate 36

The upper leaf is from Worcester, about 1760, pictorial ornament introduced on a "scroll of paper". The lower leaf is greenish-glazed Staffordshire stoneware of about the same date. The upper melon is particularly attractive in its design and its green and yellow and purple colouring. It has a stand of lettuce leaves. Longton Hall porcelain, about 1775. The lower melon is in Leeds cream-coloured earthenware painted with flowers. The cauliflower tea-pot is $4\frac{1}{2}$ inches high with a handle of overlapping leaves and a small cauliflower lid finial. About 1760. Lower

Plate 37
Georgian dessert glasses of the third quarter of the eighteenth century. (*Top row*) Sweetmeat glasses with blown bowls. The stems are: silesian with knops containing air "tears"; short baluster; opaque white twist on domed and folded foot. (*Centre row*) Two sweetmeat glasses with silesian stems and domed and folded feet flanking a sillabub glass and a two-handled custard glass. (*Bottom row*) Sweetmeat glasses with shallow-cut bowls and scalloped rims; two have faceted stems.

Plate 38

Dessert glasses showing the typical small feet and some indication of the wide range in bowl design. (*Top row, left to right*) Double ogee bowl and baluster stem; rare design with baluster stem and folded foot; bowl with "dog's tooth" edge and silesian stem on domed foot; wide flanged bowl 6 inches across on silesian stem. (*Middle row*) Three glasses with light-catching moulded hammering and one engraved. The lid is a rarity and the looped rim a feature to seek. (*Bottom row*) Three examples of shallow cutting and scalloped rims. (*Left*) The waisted ogee bowl has shallow diamond cutting, on an eight-sided silesian stem and high-moulded foot. (*Centre*) Sliced cutting on the bowl is echoed by facet cutting on the knopped stem which has an eight-sided domed foot. (*Right*) Cup-shaped bowl on a hollow stem cut with hollow diamonds.

Plate 39a

Brass candlesticks. (*Extreme left*) An attractive little specimen of about 1680, the socket and stem turned from two castings and the base an additional, solid casting. (*Left centre*) Late seventeenth-century stick with a slide to adjust the height of the candle. The upper section was cast solid and drilled in the lathe, the greasepan shaped from the hammered brass plate known as latten and the foot cast solid and lathe-turned. (*Centre*) Late seventeenth-century pillar candlestick made from latten showing the period's typical use of light-catching ornament. (*Right*) Two early eighteenth-century specimens made when design was at its happiest. In each the socket and stem are cast as two hollow vertical sections brazed together and the foot cast separately and attached.

Plate 39b

A tall, slender late eighteenth-century brass candlestick surrounded by early nineteenth-century specimens. All are made by casting socket and stem in one hollow piece and attaching a separate, hollow foot. The difference in manufacturing method prevents any confusion in dating despite the nineteenth century's delight in reintroducing pleasant old designs.

Plate 40
(*Upper group*) Bow candlesticks in the perfect eighteenth-century manner never quite recaptured in the nineteenth century although the flower encrustations are comparatively simple. (*Lower left*) The jaunty shepherd with his pipe and dog were unfailing favourites with the porcelain makers. This group is from Derby. (*Lower right*) Dainty Chelsea-Derby figure supported by the flowery "tree-stump" that holds the candlestick, one of the most satisfactory designs for a porcelain candlestick.

Plate 41

(*Top row*) Porcelain candlesticks in magnificent Chelsea-Derby and Chelsea work, the essentially substantial scrolling bases transformed into charming features of the designs. Every detail of the Chelsea group (*right*) repays close scrutiny. (*Centre row*) The two flower-encrusted bone china candlesticks of the early nineteenth century are unmarked but suggest Coalport work. The austere corinthian column, 10 inches high, is in Leeds cream-coloured earthenware. The rustic "Summer" candlestick is in Wedgwood jasper, the figure and the twining ivy in white against a background of sage green. (*Bottom row*) The pottery group in the Walton style of the early nineteenth century is best classed as a chimney ornament. Great numbers were made for extremely cheap sale which could be used for toothpicks, spills, flowers, candles as required. The chamber candlestick is typical of Coalport, the flower-strewn dish centred with a socket of blue convolvulus.

Plate 42a
Ceramic wall plaques. (*Left*) Adam and Eve on a specimen bearing the date 1674. This crude but striking style associated with the slipware bearing the name Thomas Toft would make conspicuous wall ornament even high on a dresser or cupboard top. (*Right*) Mellow English delftware of the late seventeenth century made in Bristol and painted in a design typical of its period. This has the "blue dash" border that has given the popular name to such work, quick brush strokes achieving a suggestion of twisted rope.

Plate 42b
(*Left*) Kneller's portrait of Queen Anne reduced to the simple outlines of a popular memento. Portrait and leafy frame are of English delftware (tin enamelled earthenware) made in Bristol in the first half of the eighteenth century. This measures $9 \times 7\frac{1}{4}$ inches. (*Right*) The ornate "frame" with holes for a cord is made in one with this Staffordshire plaque shaped in low relief in the second half of the eighteenth century.

Plate 43a
Ceramic wall ornament. (*Left*) A fine example of the careful painting and elaborate "framing" given to early nineteenth-century specimens in bone china: a Derby view, its border perforated and gilded. (*Right*) Typical of many text plaques but made individual by the careful addition of the name Emma Jane Clements and the date. The border frame is in the familiar blobby lustre associated with Sunderland.

Plate 43b
(*Left*) Finely perforated and shaped in relief to suggest basketwork, touched with colours, and elaborately painted, this plate indicates the range of decoration that could be achieved in the 1760s in Staffordshire salt-glazed stoneware. The relief work is coloured green, turquoise, pink, light blue and yellow. (*Right*) Josiah Wedgwood (1730–95). This portrait medallion was modelled in 1777 by William Hackwood, chief modeller at Wedgwood's factory Etruria from 1769.

Plate 44
Vessels for flowers and bulbs. (*Top*) Wedgwood lidded flower bowl and bulb pot. The bowl, 4 inches across, is in drab-coloured earthenware, its applied pattern in white and lilac. 1810. The pot for two bulbs, 5 inches high, is in cane-ware shaped and painted to suggest bamboo. 1788. (*Centre*) Three covered pots with pierced lids for flowers or small bulbs. The vessels to the left and right are by Spode, the pot on the left in his rich japan colouring and the violet basket on the right brightly gilded over a red ground. About 1810. In the centre is a Worcester crocus pot of about 1765 with exotic birds and scale blue ground. (*Bottom*) Wedgwood bulb pots: (*left*) in jasper, 7 inches high, 1796; (*right*) in black basaltes, 5¾ inches high, 1820.

Plate 45

Figure comfit holders. (*Left*) Bone china work in the abundantly flowery manner of Coalport. The boy has a small girl companion similarly seated beside a large tub for comfits and a small tree-stump for toothpicks. (*Centre*) Derby shepherdess with lambs among the flowers at her feet. (*Right*) Superbly colourful "gold anchor" Chelsea, the dress pink as a background to the rich glory of colour and gold in the flower ornament.

Plate 46

Vinaigrettes at their most attractive in hall-marked English silver. Those at the top are open to show the inner hinged grids, typical of fine quality work. Below, the heart is by Lawrence and Co., Birmingham, 1823; the watch shape by S. Pemberton, 1818; the heavy cast design by John Bettridge, 1829; the bags by S. Pemberton, about 1810 and Lawrence and Co., 1823; the cast view of Windsor Castle by N. Mills, 1837; the engine-turned book by Taylor and Perry, 1830; the man and his dog and the shell by Matthew Linwood, 1811 and 1806.

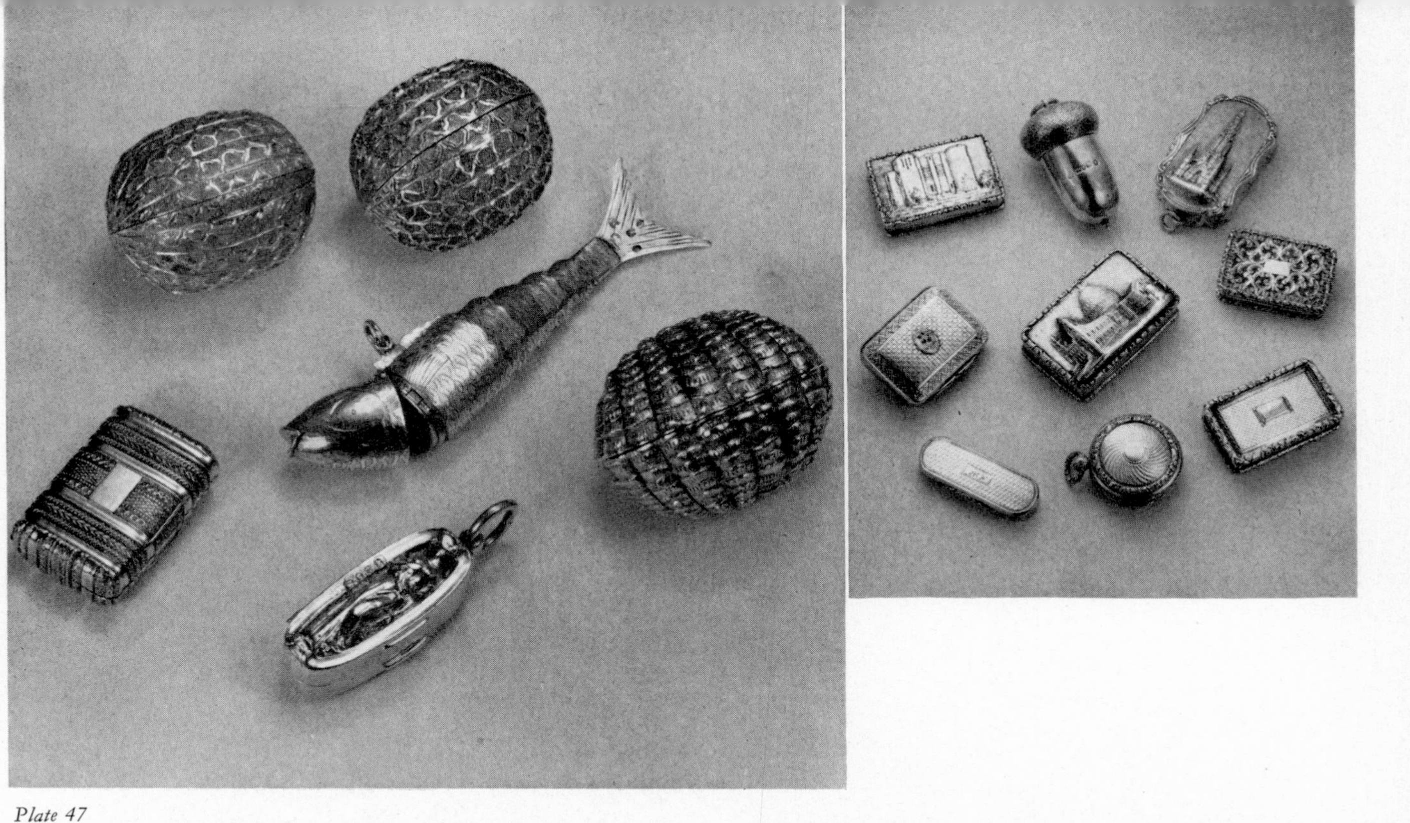

Plate 47

Vinaigrettes including interesting imitative designs and cast views of famous buildings. (*Left*) the two rare walnuts are by Taylor and Perry, Birmingham, 1836, one being fitted as a nutmeg grater. The articulated fish is by Joseph Wilmore, Birmingham, 1820. (*Above*) The acorn is by T. Phipps, 1816; the rare St. Paul's by Wilmore, 1842; the Scott Memorial a late specimen dated 1876; and the three engine turned at the bottom by N. Mills, 1835, Lawrence and Co., 1826, and W. Eley, 1828.

Such items suggest further collectors' hobbies. For the rest of us there is pleasure enough to be derived from the more homely likenesses of people whom history has forgotten.

The frames of silhouettes are important to the collector. Rich work of the eighteenth century was framed like a miniature in an oval mount of gilt metal enriched with borders of paste or pearls. Every collector hopes to find a silhouette still in the somewhat less rare early frame of thin brass stamped in raised gadroon patterns. By the early nineteenth century the typical frame was of black papier mâché with an inner oval rim of brass matching an acorn-and-ring hanger. Failing these, there are still bird's eye maple and pearwood frames with deeply mitred corners, unmistakably Victorian.

Frames were important sidelines even to the more expensive profilists. Miers himself was not above advertising his convex glasses and gilt borders. The labels that sealed the backs of these frames are, of course, invaluable sources of information, although their dates refer only to the year of printing, such as Mrs. Beetham's 1785.

Some profilists are known to have had several printed with different wording as they advanced: for instance, Miers may be traced through his early days in Leeds when he charged 2s. 6d., then 3s., then 5s. before he came to London. Some London labels indicate the introduction of his son; still later came the best known labels of this son of Miers and John Field. All too few profilists signed their work, but many pieces may be dated by details of costume or coiffure. Signatures such as Frith, Gibbs and Lincoln are noted occasionally.

Profiles, shadowgraphs, even such horrible pomposities as scissorgraphs and papyrotomic art . . . these treasures had many names but not until the late 1820s did England accept the name silhouette. Etienne de Silhouette (1709–67), France's finance minister in 1759, had a reputation for demanding economies which the ironic public quickly associated with his amateur enthusiasm for making "machine" profiles, and in France and Germany the word quickly took hold. But the earliest English reference to "the shadow of a shade . . . the silhouette of a bust" was in the *Monthly Review* for 1798, and it was only the Frenchman Edouart who succeeded in establishing it. Even then, so he records, people were indignant to find that his work consisted of the same old "black shades". For by then the family group, staring in bleak agony at the yet more modern contraption of that "apothecary picture-man" M. Daguerre, was beginning to take the place of the penetrating shadow.

Chapter Thirteen

DOLLS

AN ancient Roman rag doll has been excavated in Egypt, its features and hair stitched in the fabric, and Greek dolls of terra cotta have been found with jointed limbs. There is no beginning to the history of dolls and no limit to a collector's range, although those of us who have never entirely grown beyond our childhood companions usually want to talk about their characters and eccentricities rather than their age.

Maybe all that many of us are seeking is an excuse to relive rosy moments of nursery days, but in point of fact such pleasure may be less childish than our friends imagine. So completely has the custom vanished that we tend to forget today the important role once played by dolls in the strange, artificial but strictly adult world of high fashion. Not just for years but for centuries dolls were created with meticulous care and lavish expense, as gorgeously gowned and coiffeured as any small girl could dream, but intended solely for the lady of fashion, to keep her informed about each current detail of gown and hair-dressing and accessories.

Small wonder that the few "best dolls" included in enchanting child portraits of Stuart and early Georgian days are richly dressed, like the children themselves, as modish ladies in miniature, and that today's collector finds much of her pleasure in the clothes and accessories of her family. Indeed, the clothes often make the early doll, a cane frame holding out the skirts like a crinoline and supporting her body so that her small legs dangle or, like underclothes, simply are not.

Those early fashion dolls have tempted later imitators, but genuinely old dolls of many kinds are still to be found in the smaller antique shops. Many are of the prolific nineteenth century, but even the currently most popular genuine pedlar doll with her tray may be found as a triumph at ten guineas or less. A reminder of the late eighteenth century may cost as little as two guineas, and whisper of the days when even the merest "cap" could be reported in contemporary fashion gossip as "of tigre satin, embroidered with silver spangles and feathers of uncommon elegance, ornamented with a profusion of diamonds".

At first the fashion doll, or inanimate fashion model, was the size of its owner. As early as 1391 Isabella, wife of Richard II, received news in this manner from her mother regarding fashion at the French court she had left behind. Five years later Charles IV's embroiderer and *valet de chambre* Robert de Varennes was commanded to supply a complete wardrobe for a set of "lively effigies" of the queen sent from England at Richard's expense. In her turn Elizabeth of York, queen to the miserly Henry VII, rejoiced in a magnificently attired and jewelled effigy sent by Anne of Brittany in 1502.

Early models were of wood with faces of moulded and painted leather, but Tudor designers introduced the modelled wax associated with many of the most sensitive, vividly expressive doll faces—although associated also with many a childish tragedy, almost to the present day. By Elizabethan days Paris was firmly established as the hub of the world of fashion and a few of the leading designers soon found that they could inform clients of their style with smaller images, less than 24 inches high. The few large effigies recorded in the eighteenth century were for public display.

The first pair of these small mannequins were called La Grande Pandore and La Petite Pandore, and Pandoras they have remained. In some instances even the delicate handmade fabrics were specially woven for these dolls with their patterns correspondingly reduced in scale, and rouge, powder and patches were applied to their small faces. When Elizabeth I in 1600 sent to the King of France for news of

Paris fashions she received her answer by means of "model dolls".

Elaborate rules governed this important Parisian trade, and dressmaker and tailor had to submit their dolls for official inspection and stamping so that they would comply with the standardised measurements, a method that added enormously to the prestige of the industry. Exclusive rights to its fashions usually went with each doll, sometimes to a dressmaker, sometimes to an individual grand lady. Thus a dressmaker would announce in the press, "Last Saturday the French doll for the year 1712 arrived at my house in King Street, Covent Garden". And then, presumably, just sit back and wait. Towards the end of the seventeenth century London fashion houses began to compete with Paris in dressing and exporting fashion dolls but, inexcusably, English fashion dolls were never scaled accurately and dressmakers found it difficult to copy the styles displayed.

This seems a pity, for they were elegant little creations, their bodies composed of stuffed pads linked by ribbon, their faces of painted wood or more delicate painted wax, their long forkish hands usually cut from bamboo. There are many eighteenth-century references to the export of fashion dolls "to the Colonies and elsewhere", and it is easy to picture the thrill of receiving "a great lady and her blackamoor in scarlet livery" in the fashion of 1720. The *Gentleman's Magazine* gives records of "several dolls with different dresses made in St. James's Street" sent to the Czarina of Russia in 1731.

By the second half of the eighteenth century the doll's body, too, might be of wood but more often its body and characteristically short arms were of rolled fabric. A London hairdresser might display forty or fifty gorgeously dressed and coiffeured dolls and charge a fee for viewing them. Hair style and dress as well as the workmanship of the doll are important aids to the dating of fashion dolls, but it is important that the dress is of contemporary fabric and workmanship, for later dolls are sometimes dressed in mid-Georgian styles and sold as fashion dolls.

Before the end of the century, however, the fashion

magazine with hand-coloured fashion plates had arrived and the doll was abandoned to the nursery. Fortunately by then there was already a growing industry in the manufacture of children's dolls—children's babies they were called, although representing adults. Thus Daniel Defoe in 1722 reported from Paris in the *Daily Post* that "the Dutchess of Orleans made a Present to the Infant Queen of a Wax Baby Three Foot High, with Diamond Ear-rings, a Necklace of Pearls and Diamond Cross, with a Furniture of Plate for a Toilet, and Two India Chests, full of Linen, and several Sorts of Cloaths for the Baby, the whole for that Princess to play with".

Throughout the century these dolls tended to be somewhat stiff and long, some no more than wooden pegs with roughly carved heads. Great numbers of "Flanders babies" came from the Netherlands, recorded at the time in the lament:

> "The children of Holland take pleasure in making
> What children of England take pleasure in breaking."

In the late eighteenth-century English doll you look for a wooden head—occasionally wax—and short wooden arms and wooden slipper-tipped legs attached to a hand-sewn body of kid, linen or canvas stuffed with bran. The moulded papier mâché head arrived early in the nineteenth century, becoming a delightfully vivid creation by the late 1820s, and soon there were whole dolls of papier mâché. Wolverhampton, as centre of the paper ware trade, was an important source of these dolls which were first mass-produced by Evans and Cartwright. By 1830 prices were down and these dolls were being made in a dozen sizes. Noses and chins on these dolls are often badly battered. In 1858 Ludwig Greiner in Philadelphia took out a patent for heads with fabric to reinforce the joins and vulnerable projections and a head so labelled occasionally turns up.

Papier mâché heads continued to be made until the 1860s, when the ware was challenged by the cold gloss of china and by resilient gutta percha. From 1840 some lovely papier mâché dolls had wax-coated faces. At first eyebrows, lashes, lips and cheeks were painted on the wax: the final achievement from about 1855 was a clear, tough wax that allowed the features to be painted on the papier mâché under it.

Dolls' heads modelled in wax earned England a world reputation in the early nineteenth century, fitted to bodies of wood or bran-stuffed fabric. One London doll maker in 1850, Augusta Montanari, of Fitzroy Square, was inserting hair, eyebrows and lashes into the wax, and exhibited her skill at the 1851 Exhibition.

By then many English dolls were being made for real knockabout fun, and the factory processes that produced them led to price cuts and vast sales—hence our many opportunities of finding these treasures today. The factory doll was built up of ten pieces: a head-and-shoulders bust of china, papier mâché, wax or wood; a body of kid, linen or cotton stuffed with bran; teeth of straw or enamel; eyes of glass; hands of china, papier mâché, yellow kid or wood; hair curled or crimped and dressed; body-linen and stockings; complete outer clothing; hat; shoes.

As early as 1844 factory-made dolls were issued for the small home dressmaker to clothe in the unlikely garments that now puzzle and amuse us. Dresses and shoes on dressed dolls came from the cottage workrooms of countless out-workers, but the wig department was an important section of the doll factory itself, where changing hair styles were copied in astrakhan fur and, from about 1850, in the hair of Tibetan goats—much less frequently in "real hair". Small locks were rolled on wooden curling pins, wrapped in paper and boiled to achieve permanent waves. These were sewn to cloth skull caps to be fitted on to the dolls' heads, and could be dressed to suit the intended ages of their wearers. Child dolls became the rage only in Napoleon's time, during the childhood of the King of Rome.

In the same way wigs could be glued to heads of porcelain. We do not know whether any dolls were made with heads of the eighteenth century's fragile soft porcelain: certainly some cane heads tend to suggest that they were. But bone china heads are still very much in evidence, having proved more durable than wax in nursery battles. These are naturalistically coloured and attached to bodies of kid with pink kid arms.

Bone china dolls' heads have a well scrubbed look, less time-worn and ethereal than wax but better suited to jolly babies than to elegant *grandes dames*. Peach-bloom complexions came in about 1855, and for some fifteen years the loveliest dolls had faces of the delicately matt-surfaced porcelain known as parian ware and widely used for reproducing small models of marble statues. Hair, hair ornaments, even the string of pearls around the neck were shaped in the mould and afterwards appropriately coloured, and hands and feet were of the same material, complete with green or blue shoes, perhaps, touched with gold. But it must be admitted that such dolls were never meant to soil their pretty faces and hands with the rough and tumble of life in a plebeian nursery. However, an immensely strong biscuit porcelain, tinted but unglazed, was evolved in 1862 and soon ousted all competitors.

Many details we now tend to regard as modern were welcomed into the nursery surprisingly early in the nineteenth century. There were talking and walking dolls while Victoria was still a child—and what scores upon scores of dolls she had! Jointed dolls were no novelty, of course, for lay figures, ball jointed, had been used for centuries by artists and are mentioned by Vasari. In 1824 Johann Maelzel patented an arrangement of tiny bellows connected to the doll's arms that produced a squeaky "papa" or "mama" when the appropriate arm was raised. Two years later came walking dolls and dolls with movable heads. "Wire-eyed" dolls could be made to close their eyes by working projecting wires behind their backs, but in the mid-1820s these were outmoded by the introduction of the counterweight device. By then eyes were of enamelled glass or painted china, and were usually brown—occasionally violet or sapphire. Those familiar and somewhat disdainful light blue eyes date mainly from about 1840.

Even the bodies of dolls are a guide to the collector, the hand-sewn bran-stuffed kid or linen beginning to be replaced by machine-sewn textiles sometimes stuffed with sawdust by 1855. Papier mâché as an early nineteenth-century substitute for cheap wooden dolls was supplemented by gutta percha by about 1850. But many children still had to be content with a stump of wood, mounted, when not in use, on a turned wooden block.

Most picturesque of these block-based ornamental dolls —and the most collected, and reproduced, today—are the pedlars, which have now come out from under their glass domes. With their fascinating trays of tiny goods they are irresistible toys for children of any age. In their black frocks or poke bonnets and red cloaks, with white quill frilling, perhaps, around their weathered faces, women hawkers were familiar figures in the streets and the dolls followed them closely.

Early pedlar dolls of the late eighteenth century might wear petticoats of quilted chintz beneath their outer skirts; Victorian specimens might have fringed plaid shawls and skirts of patterned bombazine. Some are knitting stockings as they wait for customers. Pairs, man and woman, both with trays of tiny goods, are early Victorian. It is characteristic of the pedlar doll that she is primarily intended to stand and display her wares. Her body is of wood, her head of wood or well-modelled wax, and the firmness of her stance is ensured by replacing legs with a stem—sometimes two—of turned wood, on a base covered, perhaps, with marbled paper.

Conspicuous on the tray is usually her licence, a real hawker's necessity. This was printed in miniature, in several versions, of which the most frequent is "Polly Hawkins, Licensed Hawker, January 1st 1786". But the date bears no relation to that of the doll, and this licence is considered to belong to the 1820s. Similarly the broadsheets on pedlar trays may be ante-dated.

But what delightful trays of wares they are. A late eighteenth-century doll may proffer valuable tiny trifles in gold and silver inherited from the long vogue for these adult toys (see Chapter Four). All kinds of household objects in miniature were included, and for more than half a century from about 1790 the vogue for collecting such trifles continued, although precious metals were replaced by ceramics, textiles, glass, wood, paper and the like. A pedlar is a find indeed if her tray contains, for example, a tiny tea-set in hand-made flint-glass half the size of the usual miniature ware. But even in later dolls the original and subsequent owners have generally added to the assortments of miniature goods sold with them.

It is not always realised that the pedlar usually started with a specialised stock. She may concentrate on jewellery, such as tiny rings, lockets and imitation watches. Or laces, buttons, pins, ribbons, garters, purses and other minutely embroidered treasures for the needlewoman, the sewing machine being used for such work only late in the period. Even miniature song sheets were specially printed, which by their titles may suggest the date of a doll. "Home Sweet Home", for instance, was not performed in England till 1823. Reproduction pedlars mostly carry needlework items or "lucky bag" trinkets such as were not made at the time of their suggested origin. Hardware pieces in expensive, delicately finished cast iron were imported from Berlin, but were poorly reproduced by some Birmingham founders from about 1835 to appear on "late" pedlar trays.

The wooden pedlar doll, wax faced, with shells glued all over her stiffly sized foundation fabric dates from the late 1840s; the old pedlar women, with sponge covered china heads, to the 1850s. Then there is the market woman, factory made, dating to no earlier than the 1830s, with her basket of fowls and dairy goods. Sometimes she is paired with a man carrying fruit and vegetables. These are often labelled "C. & H. White, Milton, Portsmouth", or "Whites of Milton". Some pedlars are found in the individualistic manner of amateur work, with embroidered leather or cambric faces and minutely stitched clothes.

Dolls dressed in ecclesiastical robes are found occasionally. These may be of the eighteenth century, and some were intended perhaps as lay figures for artists, and some for use in religious instruction. But some at least were cherished just as dolls, as witnessed by a charming child engraving by the incomparable Chardin.

Another craze with early Victorians was the fortune-telling doll. This was emphatically a middle-class delight. Normally the doll of the period beguiled its small owner with layer upon layer of petticoats minutely featherstitched in cambric and flannel. The fortune-telling hussy has underskirts composed of paper slips, each printed with a prophecy, for the presumptuous to tear off in a haphazard snatch. It was even possible to buy books of replacements. There are birthday dolls, too, who offer printed advice that promises to be entertaining but in fact proves platitudinous, with emphasis on the dangers of gossip and greed. Even flannel petticoats might be preferable to such dull birthday admonitions as "One loses a little by too much frankness", or "Reflect before speaking. You will speak more to the point".

Chapter Fourteen

PEWTER TABLE WARE

TIN-AND-TEMPER, the old Georgian craftsmen called their finest quality pewter, an amenable tin-alloy with a mellow gleam that makes silver appear almost garish in comparison. Silver, mahogany, eggshell porcelain give a gracious urbanity to many a lovely house, but who does not recall a glowing welcome to some treasury of old oak, Staffordshire blue and unpretentious pewter?

For centuries, from Elizabethan to late Georgian days, the metal was a necessity rather than a luxury in the English home, and this basic requirement of everyday service has resulted in plain, shapely outlines and lastingly pleasing proportions that often make even Continental pewter seem overfussed with ornament. Today the collector must pay substantially for authentic specimens from the seventeenth century, but there are considerable opportunities among eighteenth-century work.

There is a particular attraction in a dresser set out with its garnish of antique pewter plates, arranged in time-old manner to display their unscratched backs, freshly scrubbed with oil and rottenstone or sand and rushes. Looking no further than such plates there are limitless possibilities among these products of the specialist pewterers known as sadware men, whose name, surely, went back to the days of apt colour-terms and whose metal soon acquired the gentle dun-colour known as sad. Theirs were the finest qualities of pewter, the tin slightly alloyed with bismuth and copper—later antimony—and never marred by the thundercloud tinge of lead.

Plates were usually shaped by casting in moulds, and then

scraped and rasped in a lathe powered by the woman or boy turn-wheel who was forbidden by guild law to advance beyond this endless task, throughout centuries when almost every craft and trade was astonishingly dependent upon "boy-power". But the mark of quality was the laborious hammering that strengthened the plate's bouge. After hammering it was lathe-turned again on the inside, but the hammer marks may be detected on the underside: the finest of all were entirely shaped by hammering. Finally, lathe burnishing with bloodstones or agates gave them their fleeting silvery lustre.

During the eighteenth century, pewterers became very conscious of their competitors in silver and in clay, and broke free of guild restrictions in their attempt to reach a wider public. The early eighteenth-century style of plate with a broad rim and wide edge strengthened with beading tended to be replaced around the mid-century by plain-rimmed designs. I have indicated some typical rim silhouettes. Their dates must not be taken as exact nor the outlines as invariable, but it is possible to be more specific here than in most details because the moulds that shaped them were heavy and costly and usually borrowed from Pewterers' Hall or shared by groups of manufacturers: their range was limited and changes slow.

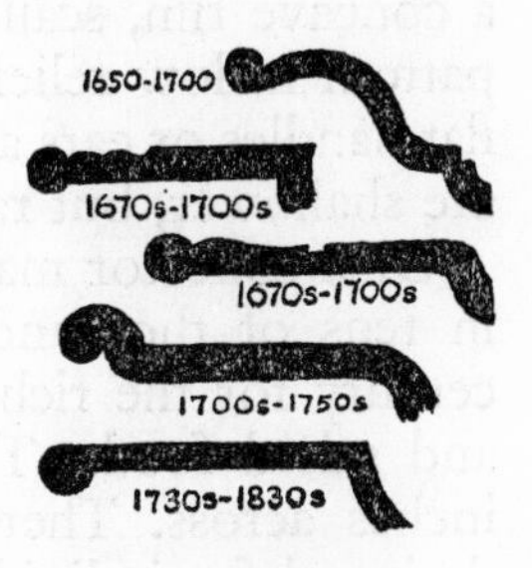

Fig. 15. Flatware rim outlines.

Plain ovals and circles gave place to more decorative outlines at this time, such as the octagonal plate, plain-rimmed at first but later with double or treble reeding, gadrooning, or reeding and beading. Some five-lobed plates have scroll and shell decoration. Touch marks are usually to be found on the plate rims.

There are further possibilities, too, for the sadware collector. There may be a chance to revive the old seventeenth- and eighteenth-century custom of marriage plates, for instance. Early pairs of these bride and bridegroom gifts are ornamental affairs appropriately engraved with mottoes and lively pictorial work, but the individual touch is, of course, the inclusion of initials and wedding date. The triangular arrangement of initials sometimes found on marriage pewter shows the husband's surname initial at the top and the christian name initials of himself and his wife to left and right below. This custom disappeared in early Georgian days. But there are other plates too.

Occasionally the chance comes to acquire small shallow banqueting dishes, as dessert plates were called until about 1820, sometimes with flat projecting handles. These were used for the fruits and sweetmeats of the fashionable drawing room repast that I describe more fully in Chapter Sixteen. A typical specimen is about 6 inches across, with a concave rim, scallop edged and decorated with a simple pattern in low relief. Thin ring handles were followed by flat handles or ears and specimens of the eighteenth century are shallower, but rare in pewter.

Or a collector may seek for saucers, such as were made in tens of thousands until as late as the mid-eighteenth century for the rich sauces that enlivened the many dried and salted foods. These are deep, rimless dishes about 6 inches across. There are mazarines for the finding, too, designed for individual servings of ragoûts and fricassées, to be arranged on a wide-brimmed charger around a central circular boss displaying an enamelled crest or coat of arms. There are even the heavy oval trays known as voiders for clearing empty glasses during a banquet.

Pewter trenchers are interesting, used by the wealthy when other folk cut their meat on hunks of four-day-old bread, and in lesser homes until late in the eighteenth century. They are essentially flat and plain, often square, and low rimmed, since their purpose was to save more valuable plate. Meat was served to the diner on a plate but transferred by him to the trencher for cutting. Even so, the trenchers had to be cleaned of knife marks after meals by the servant known as the trencher scraper, working away with tools and pewterwort rushes (*equisetum hyemale*) in the trencher house. In 1622 "Bingham's wife" was appointed by the Goldsmiths' Company to be "scraper and scourer of the Company's pewter".

Old inventories are full of intriguing lists of pewter, from the small pie dishes listed as "coffins" to the "counterfeits" which we know as porringers and some enthusiasts insist are all bleeding bowls. The porringer is descended from the older and rarer pottanger or soup bowl—the Scottish quaich. The ear is the bowl's most notable and decorative feature: two ears usually indicate Continental work. It is some help, too, in dating. An early bowl has this flat pierced or fretted handle or ear—I cannot find "lug" in old inventories—soldered to the bowl without any additional support. A later one may have a strengthening bar fixed along the join, or a projection, semi-circular or round, curving down from under the ear and fitting the curve of the bowl. A lidded porringer is a rarity indeed and usually commemorative.

Fig. 16. Porringer handles, 1650–1750.

The ideal accompaniment to a dresser of such wares would be a rack of old spoons and forks, but these are rare finds. Spoon makers were another group of specialists. Flat casting quickly formed the spoon's shape, but only endless hammering over a hardwood form rendered the soft metal hard textured and compact for the tough life expected of it. The knop or finial that is the spoon collector's special delight was cast separately and soldered on to the hammered stem, and the whole spoon might be gilded, not just for ornament but to make a world of difference to the user's pleasure in subtle flavours.

Spoons may be dated from hall-marked silver ones which they copied as best they could. Early knops include the pyramid, the acorn, the ball shapes with marks of ribbing or twisting known as melon and writhen knops, and the best-known Apostle designs popular as christening gifts to the saints' namesakes. There were wild men, too, as knops, and heraldic lions sejant among fifteenth- and sixteenth-century patterns, and seal tops pricked with initials or dates throughout Stuart and even early Georgian days, although knops generally were abandoned in the seventeenth century.

Subsequent styles are disappointingly orthodox. The plain early Stuart cut-off end, "slipped in the stalk", was followed by the mid-century square-ended Puritan, and then by the lobed, notched ends that heralded the change to spoons that were all curves in the manner of late Stuart furnishings, sometimes with low relief scrolling ornament. By the 1690s the wavy end was replacing the notched end on a spoon with a narrower bowl more pointed at the tip and a rat tail extending halfway down the bowl or more.

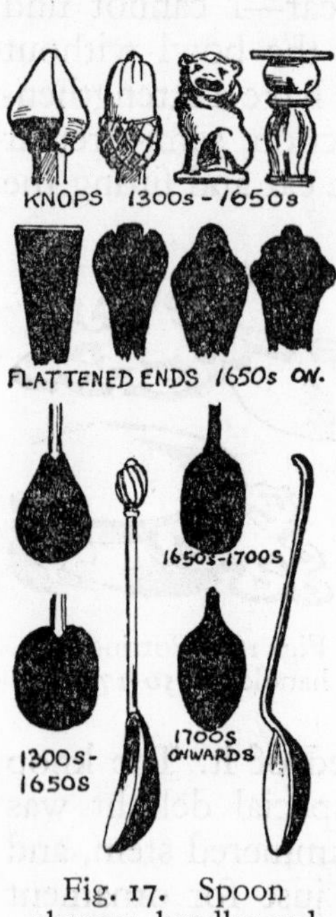

Fig. 17. Spoon changes, handles and bowls.

Within another twenty years there might be a tapering ridge up the front of the stem from the rounded tip, too, and by the mid-century the spoon had lost its last association with earlier epochs when the more or less elliptical bowl gave place to a tapering egg shape. This completely reversed the broad-ended fig-shaped bowl of most ancient design. Unfortunately the pewter spoon on sale today is most often of this "modern" type and considered scarcely worthy of a collector's interest. The metal is heavily leaded and merely cast in a gunmetal mould, lacking the strength of the old hand hammering. Such spoons were made until the mid-nineteenth century.

A more promising prospect is a group of pewter drinking vessels, lidded tankards with their sturdy thumbpiece ornament, and lidless mugs that at their best bear the names of their original owners. These were made of a quality of pewter known as trifle to the old guildsman. Until the early eighteenth century the tankard was formed out of sheet metal, usually shaped into a tapering cylinder and soldered in an invisible vertical seam. But the collector of Georgian pewter may find a charming tulip-shaped tankard with beaded rim, or one in the ogee outline that followed in the 1760s and 1770s. A revival dating from about 1810 may be noted in specimens with vertical rims.

Other late eighteenth-century tankards are barrel-shaped, strengthened with encircling ribs simulating the barrel hoops, at a time when barrel shapes may be traced in glassware, ceramics, even diminutive vinaigrettes. Volute thumbpieces were general until after the mid-century, when perforated styles were introduced and outmoded all the earlier rams' heads, fleurs de lys, pairs of billing love-birds and similar whims. A feature of the Georgian tankard is its massive handle, boldly S-curved or shaped in a recurved scroll. The plain handle with its tail soldered flat to the body came at the end of the century.

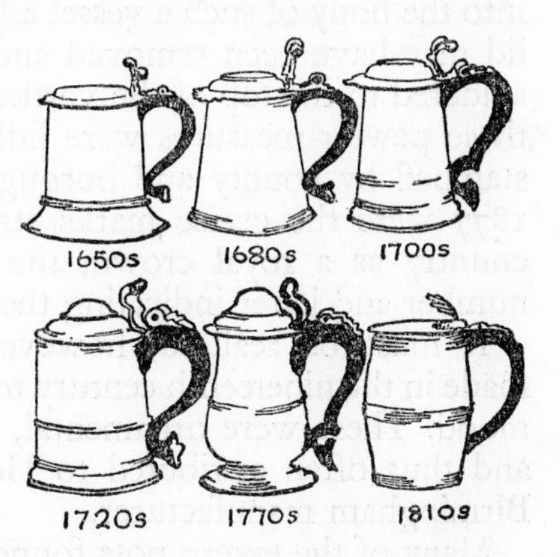

Fig. 18. Tankards, including skirted, tulip and barrel shapes.

The lead that in the nineteenth century spoilt pewter's impressive record of stalwart service had long been recognised as an allowable constituent in proportions as high as one-fifth for the lowest grade of pewter, the lay metal used for such collectable items as baluster wine measures. These are uniquely interesting little vessels because every detail in their design has a purpose: they represent the customer's indignant protest against the villainies of the wily potman.

Admittedly the protest might be ineffectual enough in the eighteenth century, when innkeepers often ordered their pots to be made short measure or "Birmingham measure", and remaining measures are remarkably varied in their capacity. Only in 1824 came the imperial system of weights and measures and this notable event, too, may be reflected in a collection of these vessels.

The wine measure or tavern pot introduced in the early

seventeenth century consists of an assembly of cast sections each specifically designed to defeat an innkeeper who sought to reduce the vessel's capacity without arousing suspicion. The curving body and the lines engraved around it and on the flat lid and the flat base all tend to make any dents or distortions conspicuous, while the "broad bottom" base is larger than the vertical rim so that no false base could be slipped inside.

When the imperial system was introduced short-measure tavern pots had to be enlarged. This means we may find that a section of plate has been soldered almost invisibly into the body of such a vessel a little above the base. Or the lid may have been removed and a narrow strip of pewter soldered to the top of the vertical rim. After 1824 most of these pewter measures were lidless. They were tested and stamped by county and borough authorities, and only in 1877 were the excise marks standardised throughout the country as a royal crown, the sovereign's initials and a number and letter indicating the county and date.

It must be realised, however, that pewter pots were made in the nineteenth century to meet the current romantic mood. These were ornamental, such as those marked HR and thus often attributed to Henry VIII instead of their Birmingham manufacturer.

Many of the tavern pots found today, of course, bear no seal of official testing, and many Georgian specimens lack even their makers' touch marks. Much provincial work was made many miles from any guild centre, and doubtless many other unmarked pots were intended for the huge export market to America.

For some reason hard to justify, any drinking vessel bearing the name of its original owner has a disproportionate appeal, and must be viewed with caution by those who value authenticity. Other surface ornament has always been a minor detail on English pewter. On the old soft pewter only light work was possible, called scratching by the superior silver engraver, but harder pewter could carry bold designs. Some is simple line engraving, a little is punched chasing, some is pricked, and some composed of the small curves known as wriggled or joggled work because the flat tool was held at an angle to the pewter surface and pushed forward with a rocking motion.

Specialists in this humble style of ornament travelled the country from pewterer to pewterer and their ornament may be considerably later than the vessels themselves. Much was personal, whether elaborate coat of arms or simple initials. But most frequently the only interruption of the mellow surface is the touch mark which may tell the initiate who made the piece and, from the guild records of his working years, its approximate date. Even in this detail, however, as the guild power waned the old standards were relaxed. Small punch marks were introduced on seventeenth- and eighteenth-century work, intended to be taken for silver marks. And the crowned X and rose and crown, symbols of high quality, lost their meaning on nineteenth-century pewter.

Fig. 19. Typical "crowned X".

These are particularly interesting marks, a connoisseur's puzzle for fifty years that my husband was the first, I think, to solve. Eighteenth-century English pewter plate is found marked in this way from time to time. More surprisingly, it may be struck with the words *Superfine French Metal.* This is a hard white metal containing more bismuth than ordinary pewter and recognised by its air of quality and its sonorous ring.

A turbulent Frenchman, James Taudin, first made and sold it, in the first half of the seventeenth century, long defying the Pewterers' Guild but eventually coming to terms with them and striking a special touch mark in 1657. This in itself caused trouble as a pewterer was then allowed only the one mark. Indeed Taudin was long dead and his son continuing this high quality work before a mark incorporating a rose and crown for export work and the letter X were permitted to any maker of this ware. The rose and crown was Taudin's mark and in 1657 he put E. SONNANT in a label above it, which has been elucidated as *écroui sonnant* or "hammered until sonorous".

It is easy to see how extraordinary ware thus came to

be known as the Frenchman's pewter and eventually as French pewter. Some pewter that is in fact Continental has initials worked into the crown or the centre of the rose. It is easy, too, to understand the Guild's eventual acceptance of this better metal: their members might still see disadvantages to themselves in a pewter that wore too well to need quick replacement, but at least it could put up a better fight against the Staffordshire potter's unwelcomely tough salt-glazed stoneware plates and drinking vessels.

The pewterers even improved on Taudin's formula by substituting antimony for bismuth, the result defined in 1755 as "a white, hard pewter with a clear sound". This, still better than the extraordinary ware, was marked with a crown over the X and any of the various phrases such as *Superfine French Metal*—but never pewter. By the 1770s plates, tankards and spoons were among the collectable pewter being made of this fine ware.

The list also and interestingly includes tea-pots. More than one collector I know possesses a prized "pewter" tea-pot and has been shocked to come across the current assumption that these are really of nineteenth-century Britannia metal. Often, of course, this is true, for the "hard pewter" known as Britannia metal in the early nineteenth century has left us many reminders of its brief popularity. All work marked DIXON, for instance, is of Britannia metal. But it is now established that pewter tea-pots were made in the 1770s, wooden handled, in five sizes, from a quart to a half-pint.

With so many possibilities open to the pewterer the list of collectable items covers a wide range. Candlesticks are among the most welcome in styles covering each phase of their long centuries of manufacture, if only because they provide the perfect change of emphasis when arranged with a garnish of flat ware. The pricket candlestick that sometimes turns up may be nineteenth-century "Elizabethan" rather than one of the squat designs really dating to the sixteenth century, but subsequent styles are to be found with memories of days when common candles were but poor, guttering and ill-odoured illuminants.

Some of the earliest of these remind us again that pewterers took their shapes from moulds that might be hired or shared—anything to cut down the heavy outlay, even to the using of trencher salt moulds to shape the heavy drip-tray saucer base of a late sixteenth- or early seventeenth-century candlestick. This design has a baluster stem—never long out of fashion on candlesticks and continued as an alternative to a pillar on the early Stuart design with a wide drip-tray and a bell-shaped base. The characteristic of the later seventeenth-century candlestick is the drip-tray or swelling knop in the middle of the straight stem on a trumpet base, and this was followed by a pillar stem and the same midway drip-tray on a round base. At the end of the century this style might be octagonal or scalloped on plan.

The candlestick that became established out of all these changes, however, looks altogether more prosaic and less experimental. With the awkward drip-tray abandoned the stem became a bulbous baluster and so it stayed for more than half a century until the 1770s reintroduced pillars and similar neo-classical outlines, familiar today because so widely made in silver.

A late pewter candlestick often has a slit in the side of the socket for poking out the candle stub, but the most efficient design for coping with this annoyance is the disc on a rod inside the stem attached to a brass button so that the last of the candle can be pushed up as required. It was 1830 or later before round pillared pewter candlesticks lost their place in the farmhouse kitchen.

Trencher salts have been mentioned already. Those early designs are rare enough now although they were made until the 1690s, the square, round or triangular block shaped with a central depression for the salt. The characteristic pewter salt of the 1660s is the waisted spool shape sometimes lightly engraved. From 1675 this was developed with an octagonal rim and base and between them a hollow baluster shape to hold the salt. The capstan salt of this period was popular until about 1720, plain or with beaded edges at first, then ridged with the light twinkling gadroons typical of silver in those sparkling years around 1700. There were more elaborate versions of the flat trencher salt between 1705 and 1730, too, but the last important salt design we find in pewter is the cup, made at first on a short stem and circular foot and then on four ball-and-claw feet until usurped by ubiquitous china and glass.

Pewter inkstands are mentioned in Chapter Five and pewter "toys" in Chapter Four. Other possibilities include pewter cruets, tea caddies, tobacco boxes, jugs. One curiosity that sometimes turns up is the pewter jelly mould. This is made in parts and opens to release the jelly or blancmange which can thus present an elaboration of surface ornament and "under-cutting" impossible in a confection that has to be turned out in the ordinary way. A diamond-shaped Victorian registration mark often makes it possible to date the design of such a mould. The Holborn firm of Watts and Harton displayed them at the Great Exhibition together with a collection of cups, meat dishes, hot water dishes and gravy boats, but by then the gentle grace of pewter was regarded as a poor substitute for the hard clean brightness of glass and china.

Chapter Fifteen

CHINA FRUITS AND VEGETABLES

EVEN the dessert fruits we buy nowadays tend to be beautiful and hard, decorative rather than luscious. In contrast, Stuart and Georgian housewives considered not only their fruits and vegetables but many of their garden flowers primarily for their value in kitchen and pantry and still-room, growing tansy for puddings and pickling marigold flowers for the porage. Their garden blackcurrants, raspberries and tiny wild-sized strawberries were brought in piled on their own greenery or on whatever strong leaves came to hand—cabbage, probably, or even bracken or mullein. So juicy ripe were they that the loaded leaves were placed undisturbed upon the big dishes of Stuart pewter or copper or early Georgian glass associated with the period's lavish display of food at dinner and dessert.

How lovely but how fleeting her garden produce must have appeared to the housewife striving to dress out a dessert. Small wonder that for more than a century the potter was called upon to fashion substitute garden freshness for the dessert table, and that his products still appeal to us today. Leaf plates are still easy and rewarding to collect, including the small pickle dishes. China fruits and vegetables are to be found, too, rare and costly in eighteenth-century porcelains but still selling for a few shillings in nineteenth-century bone china and earthenwares.

Even in Stuart days the very wealthy were offering desserts and pickles on the clean, untainting beauty of Oriental porcelain—the kind of "noble colation of dried Sweetemeates & Wine" recorded by Evelyn at Ipswich in 1677, or the "greate banquet of *Sweetemeates* and *Musique*" he attended "at the Duchess of Portsmouth's glorious Appartment" in 1682. So from China, inevitably, came the notion of clusters of little dishes in petal or lotus-leaf outline fitting together on padouk wood trays perhaps 2 feet across, forerunners of the eighteenth-century mahogany supper tray. Chinese bamboo tea-pots, pineapple jugs, pomegranates and the most satisfying melon shapes—all and many more were gladly accepted by westerners not for their original symbolism but for a charm naive enough to enchant the eighteenth-century sophisticate.

Not surprisingly it was the Chelsea porcelain manufactory that devised most of the English soft porcelain work in this mood, such as endearingly absurd cauliflowers, lemons and the like for offering the sugar plums and orange chips, jordan almonds and flower candy at wealthy banquets and desserts. Some copied Dresden work lent to Chelsea by the English Ambassador Sir Charles Hanbury, who was presented with a vast dessert service by the king of Saxony in 1748.

That enviable collector Lady Charlotte Schreiber in 1872 paid half a crown for a Chelsea apple 3 inches high, coloured red, yellow and pale green, sliced across from stalk to pit, with the slightly smaller half as a lid lifted by a stalk and leaf handle. Some specimens have fat looper caterpillar handles. Her purchase, now at the Victoria and Albert Museum, London, is the more interesting since Chelsea did much of its business through periodic sales, and Lot 100 in the catalogue for a sale in 1755 included "four fine APPLES for desart". In 1771 three apples, together with five lettuces, four sunflowers, four pears, two pomegranates, four lemons, six citrons, eight melons, two figs, two artichokes and a rose, sold for twenty-five shillings. Within recent years a pair of apples sold for one thousand pounds.

Lemons, about 4½ inches long, similarly took their place as small covered pots for the "dried sweetmeats" sold by fashionable confectioners under the sign of the pineapple. The knob for the lid might be a lemon flower bud or a stalk with a couple of leaves shaped in relief and coloured green. Staffordshire bone china lemons are somewhat less naturalistic. Some about 6 inches long follow the Dresden design with a flower spray and stalk as the handle on the cover. The fruit is attached to a circular stand about 9 inches across, modelled and pierced as basket work and painted with flower sprays. Bone china and fine earthenware oranges are mostly early Victorian.

"Groupes of figs" were listed by Chelsea in 1756. These may be little covered boxes less than 4 inches high shaped by trios of figs joined together. There were mid-eighteenth-century cauliflowers, too, trimmed for the pot, which might appear a strange choice now that we accept so casually the phenomenal mutation or freak change of nature that added the cauliflower to the cabbage family. Also to delight the epicure Chelsea made covered dishes shaped and coloured as tied bundles of asparagus—but then they even made asparagus-stick scent bottles. Coalport made and marked some asparagus bundles, too, in nineteenth-century bone china, and there are others unmarked.

Sunflowers lent themselves to gay little pots, perhaps to serve their seeds, as in China. The seedy flower centre forms the lid while the petals project as a flat rim to the sepal-covered vessel. There may be a stand, too, a 9-inch saucer casually flower-strewn, with a leaf partly overlapping the petals to form a vivid contrast, very much in the mood of today. Globe artichokes formed cups, as bought by Dr. Johnson in blue and white from the Chelsea-Derby sale of 1783. Chelsea took the Chinese melon shape, too, and the melon's satisfying colour scheme of green, yellow and purple tones, but this was a shape loved by all silversmiths and potters, that appears in pots and tureens in all sizes from 6 inches to 12 or more.

In Longton Hall porcelain of the mid-1750s melons were superbly modelled and coloured, placed on plates of lettuce leaves. They were classed by William Littler in his advertisements among "leaf basons and colliflowers" as "curious useful ornaments for desserts". Before the end of the century they were appearing in the cream-coloured earthenware of Wedgwood, Leeds and others. Some are naturalistic, some, like those of Leeds, conventionalised but with the melon bud and leaf handles and ornament. Others again are in the gay illogical Chinese mood, with the melon shape but the potter's favourite painted ornament of flower bouquets.

Even lettuces appear in porcelain, cos lettuces laid on their sides forming shallow oval-lidded dishes. Some Staffordshire bone china lettuces and cabbages and especially the emphatically crinkled savoys were, of course, among the most popular of the many "leaves" that found mention even on the covers of the Chelsea sales catalogues until 1770.

Pairs of large leaves 6 to 10 inches long might be piled with fruit; little 4-inch or 5-inch specimens might hold the pickles that had often to supplement fresh garden produce —green peaches that had failed to ripen, oysters, shallots, the gherkins that Pepys had found "rare things" in 1660 and the peppery nasturtium seeds of the following century. The old Christie sales catalogues of early English porcelain refer repeatedly to vessels for pickles—leaves, trays, stands, tureens. But the leaves had endless uses. Chelsea mounted some as chamber candlesticks, with stem handles and spur feet, and the notion continued a full century.

Four vine leaf dishes and four seven-leaf dishes were included in a dessert service listed in 1770. "Three fine vine leaves enamelled with natural flowers for a desert" were sold for a guinea and four small cabbage leaves for twenty-seven shillings.

Lettuce leaves were made at Worcester between 1755 and the 1780s in fine translucent soapstone porcelain, and "rose leav'd enamel desert plates" that cost forty-five shillings for two dozen in 1769. Worcester mulberry leaves were moulded in relief and painted with flower sprays in underglaze blue.

Bow as early as 1750 was making lettuce leaves, and here as at Worcester contemporaneous records and remaining specimens demonstrate the highly successful Chinese tendency to make light of the natural leaf forms with unassociated flower painting. At the Derby-Chelsea sale in 1773 fifty shillings was paid for four vine leaves "enamelled in flowers and fine mazarine blue and gold". In some Bow specimens of about 1750 the leaf rests on a spray of flowers in relief and Chinese tree-peony flowers ornament the upper side. Worcester painted many in underglaze blue: others from the same moulds were transfer-printed with pictures in black.

Many a currant, ivy and vine leaf around the mid-eighteenth century was mould-shaped from white salt-glazed stoneware, as thin and light and nearly translucent as possible, advertised at the time as flint ware. A foxglove leaf may be edged with green and have a stalk of its pink flowers laid upon it. Some indeterminate leaves bear flowers, fruits, insects, even exotic birds in low relief and on the underside vein mouldings and spur or flower feet. This is a style also found in Staffordshire earthenware where the reliefs are picked out in coloured glazes, green, yellow, grey. William Littler with his cousin Aaron Wedgwood made leaf dishes in brown earthenware covered with white clay-and-flint slip somewhat washily blue-painted under the glaze with leaves, berries, and insects and finally glazed with salt.

Josiah Wedgwood's famous green glaze evolved in 1759 was an obvious choice for leaf dessert services, so popular that they have been made ever since. From 1759, too, cream-coloured earthenware appeared in leaves, plain or painted with coloured enamels. Wedgwood's rivals did the same—Leeds with such designs as currants in low relief on a currant leaf 8 inches by 7. One Leeds design consists of three overlapping leaves with a looped stalk for a handle: this is painted nonsensically with green leaves and sprays of flowers.

Spode, Turner of Caughley and many others made these leaves, too. From about 1785 many bore underglaze transfer-printed ornament, some coloured over the glaze as well. These are found with rim bases instead of feet. Some unpainted fine white earthenware vine leaves may be discovered impressed "Hackwood". These were made by William Hackwood and Son of New Hall, Shelton, between 1842 and 1856.

There are other wares to watch for, too. Grainger, Lee and Company of Worcester from the 1850s used eggshell china, the leaves ground flat to rest directly on the table.

These are marked 1800, the year the firm was established but not the date the leaves were made. Miles Mason made not only his famous jugs but leaves in stone china, boasting that his ware was more beautiful and durable "and not so liable to snip at the edges" as the "Indian Nankin China". Spode made leaves in this fine-textured hard earthenware, but is associated more especially with bone china specimens, some in the intense reds, royal blues and golds of the Japanese Imari work.

Bone china fruits have been mentioned already. One other little nineteenth-century bone china detail for sweetmeats or custards in similar mood is the tulip cup, 2 or 3 inches high, coloured and gilded. Some of these flowers bear the mark of Spode, Bloor of Derby or Rockingham. These potters, and also Minton and Davenport, made vases too, in tulip shape, an inch or two larger, with rockwork bases. But many more, like so much of this lively dessert ware, are tantalisingly anonymous. The famous Aaron Wood himself is reputed to have spent much of his apprenticeship under Whieldon making models for pickle leaves, cabbage leaf tea-spouts and crabstock handles, for mid-Georgians not yet too sophisticated or remote from country ways to recognise those satisfyingly grippy handles as the gnarled and knotted twigs of the crabapple tree.

Chapter Sixteen

GLASSES TO DRESS THE DESSERT

THE deeper one explores into the origins of today's antiques the more one realises how little is really new. Even the modern cocktail party had its forerunner from as early as the fifteenth century in a gay, between-meals repast where wines and light refreshments were served informally and with the emphasis on their decorative presentation. This was known as a voyde, a word we have forgotten although the trays that served it may still be sold as voiders.

On formal occasions the array of fruits, cheese, the crisp cakes known as wafers, sweetmeats and the spiced wine hippocras were set off by an immensely elaborate centrepiece of figures, animals and the like, that went by the perfect name of a subtlety. By Tudor days the voyde might be an extremely impressive affair and at its most pretentious was known as a banquet, enjoyed in the small banqueting house that became an architectural feature of every gentleman's park; but it was still a dainty, ornamental meal of fruits and wines and fantastic confectionery.

Some Georgian banqueting houses still remain, like the summer houses of lesser gentry, raised high to command wide views, though that was mainly, I suspect, to impress the visitor rather than to delight his eye. Such fruit banquets served between dinner and supper continued as lively social occasions throughout the eighteenth century, the combined array of fruits and sweetmeats being known as a dessert. Even before the austere years of the Napoleonic wars, however, the dessert might be reduced in status to a simple course at the end of dinner, and in the nineteenth century its individuality and importance disappeared.

Fig. 20. Dessert glasses: The two upper rows, reading straight across both pages, show a chronological series of glasses for dry sweetmeats, easily identified by their various interesting rim treatments. An exceptionally large glass in one of these styles may be found, intended as a top or orange glass to form the centre-piece at the top of the pyramid, as shown bottom left. In normal size they might be placed on the pyramid or dotted about the dessert tables, filled with colourful fruits and sweets that could be taken and eaten with the fingers. The first three in the top row have the purled bowls of the late seventeenth century; the rest belong to Georgian days from about the 1720s to the 1820s, in the order shown. The fourth from the left has a knopped stem and domed and folded foot; the remainder in this first row have silesian stems, number six with an arch-and-point rim, eight and nine with open loops and ten with shallow-cutting.

In the second row the first three have silesian stems, and the central four

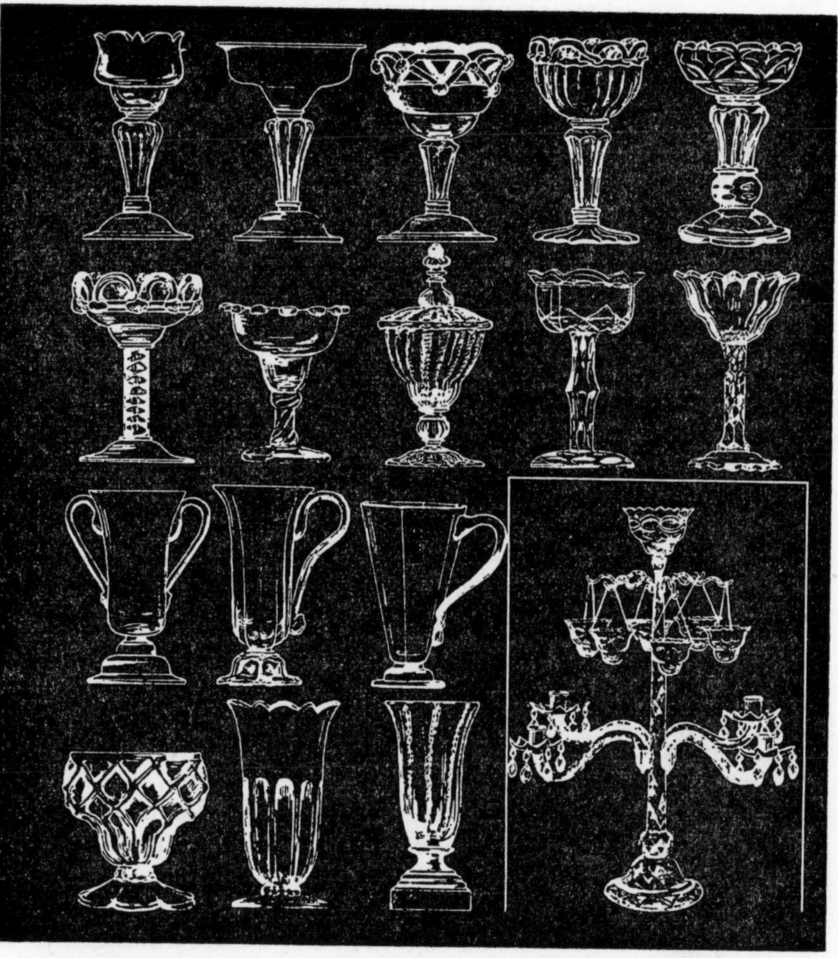

have ornamental twist stems. The rare covered sweetmeat has a blown-moulded body, and the two on the right have facet-cut stems and feet.

In the centre the third and fourth rows show jelly glasses and a low, open-topped comfit glass (see chapter on Comfit Holders). The jelly glasses in the third row are: George I specimen with ribbed bowl, stem and domed foot; ribbed bowl and pinched foot; ribbed bowl and double-loop handles; free-blown bowl with domed and folded foot; free-blown bowl with moulded foot; six-sided bowl with pinched foot. In the fourth row the five jelly glasses show bowls that are blown-moulded with trellis pattern, free-blown, shallow cut with scalloped rim, fluted, and notched.

The three-tier pyramid of salvers (left) would be presented for dessert fully loaded with glasses: those shown on it are the top glass and four syllabub glasses. The facet-cut chandelier centre-piece (right) has a top glass and hanging baskets for sweetmeats.

Here I am concerned with the Georgian dessert, served in the summer banqueting house or more frequently in the dessert room adjoining the dining room, to a chattering, moving throng. Often the guests were so numerous that the hostess hired the requisite dishes or entrusted the whole of the arrangements to a professional caterer, although the menus for those social gatherings that have come down to us tend to suggest present-day party fare for the very young, with their emphasis on individual glasses filled with jellies and custards, almond biscuits, candied fruits and whipped creams.

It would be interesting to stage such a dessert today. Many instructions are available from such authorities as Giles Rose, master cook to Charles II, Queen Anne's cooks who issued the *Royal Cookery Book* in 1710, and that mid-eighteenth-century treasure Mrs. Hannah Glasse. As for all the individual glasses that set off the vast array of colourful sweetmeats—even piled upon the chairs according to one account by Horace Walpole—these in all their distinctive shapes and styles are a fascinating study for anyone interested in England's world-famous glassware. Often they are much less costly than drinking glasses, and even more varied and individualistic since for once the glassman was free of the restrictions imposed by smooth rims and wide-spreading feet.

Such Georgian glasses for suckets and syllabubs, custards and jellies and orange chips can still be identified, dated and even given their rightful positions in the elaborate and wholly delightful "dressing out of the dessert". Even today specimens can be bought for five or ten shillings by those who know exactly what they seek.

It was the triumphant development of clear, sturdy and wholly English flint-glass in the late seventeenth century that transformed the dressing of the dessert into a lady's highly skilled accomplishment or caterer's show-piece. Special individual glasses then gave full value to the colours and variety of the repast, and by early Georgian times these were being built up into gorgeous pyramids by the use of footed glass salvers—forerunners of the modern pastry-cook's cake stands—placed one above the other in diminishing sizes.

As early as 1719 Lady Grisell Baillie described a table centre consisting of "a pirimide of sillibubs and orang cream in the paste, above it sweetmeats dry and wet". Within ten years she was reporting more elaborate arrangements, with glasses of French plums, apricots, almond biscuits and wafers on the lowest tier of each pyramid, fruit jellies, covered sweetmeats and unspecified tall glasses above, topped by a third tier of glasses filled with comfits surrounding a high and ornate centre glass. In her cookery book *The Compleat Confectioner* (1752) Mrs. Glasse recommended "bottles of flowers prettily intermix'd".

The collector distinguishes at once between wet sweetmeats and dry—between custards, ice creams, jellies, syllabubs which all required fairly deep, capacious glasses, and the dry suckets or candied fruits, dried bergamot chips and the like lifted with the fingers from open, tall-stemmed bowls. The typical dry sweetmeat or sucket glass of the early eighteenth century has a decorative bowl, hemispherical or in a waisted double-ogee outline, mounted on the shouldered, tapering stem known as the silesian, above a highly domed foot which is somewhat smaller than the bowl in diameter to allow of close-setting on the pyramids.

From about 1720 the bowl rim might be scalloped, and from about 1725 this was developed into the familiar arch-and-point outline: this is worth a critical look, for early glass-cutters ground their scallops on both surfaces to knife-edge sharpness, whereas in later work the rim indentations are chisel-edged, blunt and ground less deeply. Such ornament continued for some twenty-five years, but by 1730 the glassmaker was indulging in more elaborate escapes from the conventional style of rim required for drinking glasses and was introducing openwork loops of trailed glass in three or even four tiers above the rim.

Even in the conventionally smooth-rimmed sucket glass its purpose was never forgotten. Whereas for drinking a thin rim was desirable, in the sucket glass this could be strengthened and made more convenient by folding over the brim to thicken it and giving it an everted edge. These features, and the small foot, at once distinguish the sweetmeat glass from the thin-rimmed, wide-footed contemporaneous champagne glass.

In many sucket glasses the bowls themselves are decoratively shaped. Radial rib moulding, for instance, was popular for half a century. Some diamond-moulded sweetmeat glasses are fitted with matching high domed covers. More expensively, some of these glasses and covers are shallowly cut and sliced in geometrical designs, many of these reappearing later in the century.

Such bowls are often mounted on shouldered, tapering silesian stems cut with long flutes. But stems vary too. At first a beaded knop or more or less spherical swelling linked bowl and stem. Then came the use of triple rings above and below the stem; then from about 1750 a return to a knop, large and round. There are other shapes of stem dating to this period, too, but these are rarer. Variously swelling knopped and baluster stems are noted occasionally and also stems containing spirals of transparent or opaque white glass threads, dating between 1740 and 1775. Facet-cut stems appeared before the mid-century, too, early examples being cusped, that is, swelling sharply to the centre. Straight stems were facet-cut from about 1750, hollow diamond facets and fluted stems following in the late 1770s. The typical small high-domed foot to the eighteenth-century sweetmeat glass is appropriately decorated with radial ridging, moulded bosses, panels of slicing or the like.

Fruit baskets in glass for the dessert were being advertised early in the eighteenth century. They are not woven in the porcelain manner but built up of openwork loops, four to eight rows of this pinched or trailed work forming the flaring sides of the oval or round basket which may have D handles and a pierced foot rim. From the 1760s the baskets were matched by dishes with openwork rims and shallow cutting on the under surface. Dishes and plates and fruit baskets were formed into dessert services late in the eighteenth century, shallow cut in leaf designs until the deep diamond cutting took possession of our glassware around 1800. The plates often have a crude enough appearance because one part of a rim may be thick and another part thin, but every sort of ornament may be found, even gilding.

Such glasses for candied fruits and similar sweets took their place among others specifically designed for wet sweetmeats. Jelly poured in hot, and ices that had to remain, if possible, cold, appeared in thick little bowls, welcomed as a new fashion in the 1720s. Mrs. Glasse differentiated between coloured and clear jellies. The jelly bowl is a trumpet shape with everted rim above a narrower waist to offer a wide surface for the essential topping of whipped cream. At first these glasses were stemmed, but soon the stems were reduced to wide, flattish knops between bowls and deliberately heavy, domed or more or less conical feet.

Here again the bowls may be ornamented in the various styles of their day, shallowly cut, less expensively "sprigged" with the cutting wheel in slight, conventional motifs, or patterned in the course of forming the glass by the blown-moulded process. The thinner bowls of good quality jelly glasses, shaped by the glass-blower without the aid of moulds, testify to the improvement in glass annealing introduced in the late 1740s. The resultant double-annealing made the flint-glass far less liable to crack when the warm jelly was poured in. By then the glass usually held a quarter of a pint of jelly.

Scalloped rims were popular from about 1750 until well into the nineteenth century when they were associated with all the elaborate deep relief cutting. But a distinct find is a jelly glass with a bowl that appears wavy-outlined or hexagonal when viewed from above, on plan. The knop between bowl and foot offered obvious opportunities and collectors look for moulded ribbing upon it, or a cluster of silvery air beads within its smooth surface, but later in the century it grew less and less important and by 1800 had largely disappeared. High taxes prompted glassmen to save glass on such unnecessary features, especially on cheaper wares. The thick square foot was introduced in the 1780s and a circular moulded foot in about 1800.

Sometimes as a final touch a handle was introduced on a jelly glass. The swan-neck handle may be dated between about 1730 and 1750 but from 1740 until the end of the century the plainest of loops was in vogue and thereafter none at all.

Perhaps it is well to warn would-be collectors of jelly glasses not to be led astray by those poor quality stemless glasses with hybrid conical bowls and crudely shaped disc feet, bowl-rim and foot being of equal diameter. These were in wide use throughout the nineteenth century in confectioners' shops for serving ices and the like.

Syllabub is such a delightful name that its glasses simply ask to be collected. These were for the Hanoverian whipped syllabub of Georgian days, as distinct from the syllabub posset of the Tudors and Stuarts. Glass sellers of the period differentiated clearly between the glasses for jelly and those for syllabub, the latter having about twice the capacity with deep, notably wide-mouthed double-ogee bowls, narrow below to hold the sweetened sack or claret that was the basis of the syllabub, but essentially wide at the top to contain and support the all-important decoration of frothy whisked cream, the whole confection being lighter and less solidly easy to manage than the jelly-and-whipped-cream. By the 1770s the quality of syllabub glasses varied from "common ribbed" to "best diamond cut".

Early syllabub glasses designed to stand on the pyramid may be stemless, but others are found with the same characteristic double-ogee outline—an almost horizontal shoulder half way down the bowl—on a wide variety of stems and the small feet that distinguish them from other wine-glass stems. Baluster, shouldered silesian, spiralling air and opaque twist and cut stems may be found, the cut stems introduced in the early 1750s being misrepresented on many modern copies with vertical instead of the true horizontal facets.

Early Georgian stemless syllabub glasses have the same double-ogee bowls, plain or spirally ribbed to support the frothy whip, and thick, heavy, domed feet, plain or ribbed to match. But in examples dating later than about 1750 the glass may have a plain foot, sometimes no more than a flat disc, though still with a thick flange between bowl and foot, or a low moulded knop, omitted in nineteenth-century work.

Many stemless syllabub glasses are of mediocre glass, their decoration seldom amounting to more than notching of the rib crests. But in a glass of fine quality the whole bowl may be shallow-cut, or deep-cut in work of the 1790s and onwards. Solid square feet with high domes date from the early 1780s and hollowed gadrooned feet to the nineteenth century, ousted from about 1820 by disc feet pinched with radial decoration.

Custard cups are much more homely little pieces. The baked custard of the mid-eighteenth century, suitably flavoured with orange or almond, was poured into cups only about 1½ inches high and 2½ inches across the rim. This glass has a kick in the base, a hollow that helped in the old inadequate method of annealing the glass to strengthen it, and incidentally protected the table from the roughness where the glassblower broke the glass free of his punty rod. Glasses annealed by the improved process lack the kick and have the punty marks removed by "hollowing" or grinding smooth.

These glasses may have thick arching handles: the curly tail of the handle at the base is not to be found in the nineteenth-century version. Urn-shaped custard cups on short, expansive pedestal feet may date to the 1780s onwards. Both styles continued until the end of the eighteenth century but with the nineteenth century the cups became larger, some enriched with the deep relief cutting of their day in circuits of small diamonds. The urn-shape is still illustrated in a price list of 1831, with outspreading handles joining the bowl at rim and waist. But by then there were bucket bowls and convex shapes as well as the simplest style of cup without even a handle.

All these glasses, delightful in themselves, became a truly impressive collection when arranged on authentic pyramids. The glass salvers that were mounted above each other to form a pyramid may still be found. Three dozen or more might be required for a single eighteenth-century dessert party. The basic design is a flat glass plate with a low vertical rim or gallery mounted on a central glass stem with a spreading foot. In the second quarter of the eighteenth century the plate's small gallery might extend downwards, too, I cannot imagine why.

Eighteenth-century specimens show the various stems of their accompanying glasses, baluster, knopped and silesian on high-domed feet. (Moulded silesian stems, commonly used from the 1720s until the 1790s, reappeared in the nineteenth century on salver cake stands. Sometimes, too, a salver with a coarse rib-twist stem turns up, dating from the 1740s onwards, and this, too, may be regarded as a confectioner's display stand.) Air twist and opaque twist stems are rareties. Between about 1765 and 1790 there was a return to a seventeenth-century style of hollow pedestal stem but these, too, are seldom found today.

The upper tiers of a pyramid might differ from the ultra-sturdy base, introducing baluster and knopped outlines. There are also salvers with cut decoration dating to this period, sometimes with scalloped galleries and feet, and mounted on low, bell-shaped pedestals which soon acquired cut decoration, too. Even the under surface of the salver plate may be cut, understandably enough when it is realised how importantly they figured in these festivities, not only on the table but carried by liveried servants among the guests: when they were for this purpose they were given longer stems, and went by the name of waiters.

Some of the later pyramids are massive affairs, as they had to be to carry a load upwards of half a hundredweight. The base salver may have a broad, spool-shaped foot, or may even revolve on a metal pivot fitting into a bell-shaped pedestal. The early nineteenth-century taste for flamboyant cutting resulted in a salver with cut fluted stem and heavy square foot.

From about 1760 a more stable alternative to the pile of salvers consisted of a series of glass plates in diminishing sizes each with a hole in its centre so that they fitted on to a slender, tapering stem 2 to 4 feet high. These, too, may sometimes be found in out-of-the-way shops and attics.

The final touch in such a collection of dessert ware is the orange glass. This was the most important of dry sweetmeat glasses and topped the pyramid of glass salvers. Advertisements of the period distinguish clearly between orange and other sweetmeat glasses, some form of preserved orange or lemon or more costly pineapple being regarded as essential by such authorities as Mrs. Glasse for the "top glass". This vessel might be sold *en suite* with the pyramid salvers. It is tall-stemmed, 7 to 11 inches high, so that the bowl would rise above the jelly or sweetmeat glasses ranged all round it. It suggests a too-large wine-glass, sometimes in early work with a bowl in the double-ogee outline associated with dessert glass, on a shouldered tapering silesian stem moulded with long flutes and a highly domed foot. Rim scalloping developed into zig-zag cutting and the familiar arch-and-point. I have mentioned already that this arch-and-point outline deserves a second look.

As in other sweetmeat glasses, specimens of the 1740s onwards may be encircled with trailing loops of glass, sometimes in as many as four tiers, with rosette embossments or strawberry prunts to hide the ends of the trails. Stronger bowls followed these airy loops. They may be rib-moulded, or show the rough surface of "hammered" work or diamond trellis patterns, all formed in the course of making the bowl by blowing the blob of molten glass into a suitably patterned mould before expanding it to its final size and shape. The alternative is the thick-sectioned bowl free-blown without the aid of a mould and set a-twinkle with shallow cutting and slicing.

The stem is usually in the shouldered silesian outline, a suitably bold design, often further emphasised by nearly spherical knops above and below the stem, bright with air beads, or less costly triple rings. But there are other stems to be noted in the top glass, too, such as the early light baluster and knopped stems, the air twists of the 1740s and 1750s and the opaque twists that followed, along with the most sought-after facet-cut stems, cusped in early specimens. Hollow diamond facets and fluted stems date from the late 1770s onwards. The small foot is necessarily heavy.

The top glass was developed in its turn into that particularly scintillating alternative to the pyramid, the glass epergne for dry sweetmeats. From a knop immediately below the bowl of this ultra-massive 18-inch top glass project branches or hooks for carrying six or more of the little glass baskets that had long had a place on the dessert table. Towards the end of the eighteenth century the designs became very lavish and decorative, as cutting was combined with pendant lustres to make fascinating play with the period's dancing candlelight. For myself, however, much as I love the tinkle of glass lustres, I turn back to the lightly-cut graces of the mid-eighteenth century, when elaboration was left to the cooks who had to fill these glasses. Cooks like Mrs. Glasse, who suggested chocolate almonds and other sweets that she could call no better than "little things of sugar", and then advised her struggling emulators "in the middle of them have little pieces of paper, with some pretty smart sentences wrote on them; they will in company make much mirth".

Chapter Seventeen

COLLECTABLE CANDLESTICKS

TO those who love words for their shape and rhythm as well as their meaning there is magic in "candlelight". Here surely is a spell to exorcise all winter glooms. Lamps in endless variety have come and gone, but candlesticks that served, say, in an early Georgian home, are still sturdily serviceable today. Many craftsmen produced these satisfying forms. But here I am concerned more especially with the more decorative and collectable. Silver, as always, tended to set the fashion, but antique silver is for the confident and expert. The rest of us may prefer to set candlesticks of old brass on duty through the house, or transform a favourite corner with a flowery figure candlestick of porcelain or pottery. In brass especially, the choice is wide, their very variety making specimens from different periods associate the more happily together, provided only that the collector rejects that truly brazen hussy, the modern fake.

Candles and candlesticks are the oldest of lighting units, but today's collectors usually have to depend on museums for glimpses of the fourteenth century's three-footed brass stick or the fifteenth century's knopped stem design. English brass-ware was usually made from malleable Dutch or German ingots and plates until the 1700s, and the English metal, produced in limited quantities from 1588, was regarded by brass founders as "hard, flawy and scurvy". Then English manufacturing genius asserted itself. In the 1690s and again in the 1720s improvements in furnace heat and in copper refinery revolutionised this country's brass-making and even resulted in a wide export trade, while in the late 1730s new and improved rolling mills out-dated the old battery hammers for producing thin, even sheets of brass.

Occasionally a seventeenth-century specimen turns up, its long cylindrical socket often shaped like the beaded turning of mid-seventeenth-century woodwork. The broad encircling flange to catch the grease of the old guttering candles appeared lower and lower on such candlesticks as the century progressed, or was even omitted so that the grease trickled down the long straight side of the candlestick into the substantial saucer base.

There is, too, the seventeenth-century candle slide to be watched for, the gadget for pushing up the candle as required out of its long socket. Some have friction spring movements, others merely a series of catches along the side of the small vertical slit by which the slide is worked. But more generally the eighteenth and early nineteenth centuries provide most of the useful specimens. These are in a brass less pitted and blemished and more finely coloured then earlier work, and in designs that could not be made with the earlier metal.

While cast brass lacked malleability a candlestick could only be cast in a solid piece, and then turned and drilled. In the new metal of the eighteenth century it could be cast in two halves, brazed together with a faintly visible vertical seam, to leave the centre hollow, only the base being a separate, solid casting. Gradually further improvements brought more changes in the metal itself and in candlestick design, telling today's collector their place in the success story of English brass. Incidentally, they tell, too, of the success of English candle making, which allowed this country's candlestick designs to be well ahead of the Continental.

The brass of the early 1700s was less vascular, more pliable and yellower than before, a little lead being added to the old formula of 40% copper and 60% calamine. Then, and only then, could brass candlesticks follow the lead of silverwork. The plain and occasional pillar stems and rectangular feet of the late 1690s were followed by Queen Anne designs in which a baluster or inverted acorn stem was mounted on a highly-domed circular foot, high cushion moulding encircling the lower rim of the socket. One design with a hollow cylindrical stem resembles the seventeenth-century favourite, a slot in the stem being fitted with a slide for ejecting the candle end, but this shape was now cast in two vertical halves brazed together instead of being worked up laboriously by hand hammering.

English metal work down the ages has alternately scintillated and shone. The twinkling gadroon ornaments of the 1690s were followed by the smooth sheen of Queen Anne work, and this again was followed by the starry glitter of the early Georgian faceting and mid-century rococo gaiety, that preceded the stately simplicity of classic inspiration associated with the reign of George III. The faceting of early Georgian days was among the happiest of treatments for brass candle-holders. A slender stem, cast solid and faceted, might be mounted on an octagonal foot or on a square design with "hollow angles". Lobed feet date from about 1740 onwards, first four lobes then six, grooved and edge-shaped to emphasise the line. Scalloping to edge the foot followed in the 1760s and 1770s.

In all these eighteenth-century designs the most notable change is in the general proportions of the stick, the socket losing its old emphasis in deference to more graceful stem and tall foot. But the collector is reminded frequently by remaining specimens that simple kitchen candlesticks continued the well-proved design of a single-knopped cylindrical candle holder on a low domed foot that was notably shapely.

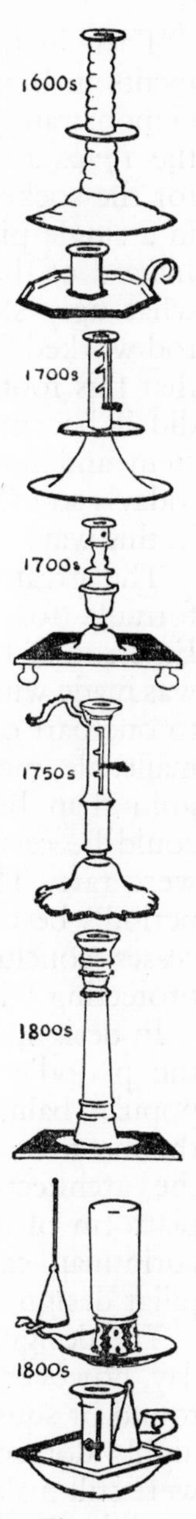

Fig. 21.

Then in the 1770s and 1780s came vast new developments in brass manufacture that a fortunate collector can demonstrate with particularly attractive candlesticks. In the 1770s a new process in brass casting made it possible for the socket and stem of a hollow candlestick to be cast in a single piece without the seaming previously required. Instead of the slide for moving the candle, with its somewhat ugly slot, there might then be a concealed central rod worked from under the foot. But it is important to note that this foot was still cast separately. Only in about 1860 did it become possible to make the whole stick—socket, stem and foot—as a single casting. Yet the majority of today's so-called antique brass candlesticks have been made in this way.

The great change of the period, however, was in the formula for the brass itself, first developed by James Emerson at Henham near Bristol in 1780. Emerson's brass was made with zinc instead of calamine: two parts of copper to one part of zinc made brass for fine candlesticks "more malleable, more beautiful, and of a colour more resembling gold than brass made with calamine". Mouldings, too, could be cast in more clear-cut relief and surface pittings were rare. The particularly pleasant golden sheen of this period's best candlesticks was achieved by a series of processes concluded by burnishing with a bloodstone and protecting with a clear lacquer varnish.

In design, specimens from the 1770s inevitably testify to the period's delight in classic elegance. Even the ever-popular baluster tended to become attenuated and one of the most usual alternatives was a plain or fluted column in the architectural manner, usually mounted on the flat platform of a stepped foot. Such a column has a proper corinthian capital instead of the moulded nozzle of the pillar design made in the 1700s.

The design of the 1780s and 1790s most often found today, however, has a stem wide at the shoulder and tapering, round or square in section and plain or fluted, on a round, highly domed foot. Some long-established brass founders were still making such stems in the mid-nineteenth century. In early specimens the foot is a pyramid encircled by an incised line or by cavetto moulding; the sparkle of gadrooning is noted occasionally on the base of what was now a vase-shaped socket with its expanded rim forming a nozzle. The whole emphasis tends to be on thin, tight-waisted shapes, the curves all concave, in contrast to the plump little balusters of the early eighteenth century. Even the sockets stress the same trend, with wide flaring rims or nozzles like the great hats of their day. Brass candlestick design in general followed silverwork, but glassmen, I think, gave the lead in the fashion for loose nozzles that became general in the late eighteenth century, for it was in glass that a low-burnt candle would break the fixed nozzle and render the whole stick useless.

Some stem designs at this time are excessively elaborate in their groupings of small knops or swellings around the main shouldered vase shaping. But at the close of the century many other brass candlesticks had to be produced as cheaply as possible to serve a cut-price market, in simple designs, depressingly poor of finish and made in the cheaper calamine brass. By the 1800s some baluster and knop-stemmed candlesticks were made with oval or rectangular feet and there was a long-sustained demand for the telescopic candlestick, the upper stem with its vertical-sided socket and rim nozzle made to slide into the trumpet-shaped lower stem or foot.

A delight all their own are chamber candlesticks. Most usual eighteenth-century type is the square or round tray made from sheet brass with a cast handle at the side. Some have little extinguishers accommodated in their handles; others even have snuffers tucked neatly through the socket base. There is also the type with a tumbler-shaped glass shelter around it, on a base like a perforated cup. Proper accompaniment is a very long extinguisher to reach down inside the shade.

One further practical point for collectors may be mentioned. Inscriptions and other incised ornament belong mainly to the seventeenth century, too early for today's collector to find inexpensive genuine examples, and from the mid-nineteenth century onwards, too late to rank as antiques. But as candlelight and firelight glow in contented harmony on a winter's night and the warm gleam of the candlesticks is mirrored in the horse brasses ranged by the hearth, it is pleasant to speculate how many of our loveliest antiques were fashioned by such gentle illumination in a world where the light of candles, like the power of horses, was still, as from time immemorial, the unquestioned basis of men's calculations.

Lovely, evocative candlelight, how happily, too, it illumined the pleasures of other centuries with its hesitant golden gleam. In magnificent candelabra and chandeliers the flames were tended by liveried flunkeys, to cast their enchantment over early Georgian revelry; and from elegant little silver candlesticks they twinkled on more intimate happiness. And when, instead, and very often, those flames flared and sulked and spluttered hot wax, a servant came running at my lady's querulous call to snuff and poke the wayward candlewick, for early Georgian candles and their ritual were masculine matters and my lady, tightly bodiced and splendidly hooped, was ideally attired for a role of helpless femininity.

Then, suddenly, to the delight of today's collectors, candlesticks became feminine, too. For over a century they proved a challenge to the English porcelain maker's delicate-fingered skill and the potter's sturdier handling of form and colour.

Technically, the change may be credited to the belated development of candlesnuffers that the most timid could use with equanimity. These spring-controlled snuffers snipped and extinguished and safely retained the glowing waxy snuff. Aesthetically, it reflected the mid-eighteenth-century delight in escaping from the urban sophistication of card-table and coffee-house into a dew-on-the-grass pastoral make-believe. English potters, experimenting with the soft paste porcelains evolved in the 1740s, eagerly caught at that evanescent May-morning radiance. And never was their achievement more endearing than when they first devised the nymphs and shepherds in their flowery rendezvous bearing fragrant wax candles.

The most prized English beeswax candles cost three or

four shillings each in the mid-eighteenth century: the porcelain maker worked for a rich clientele who had leisure and taste to revel in intricate modelling and exquisite gilded colour schemes. A few of the tentative early designs remain in their pristine whiteness, but by the early 1750s some of Chelsea's coloured figure groups were being created as candle holders, in pairs and sets of four, on matching scrolled rococo bases. Dining and toilet table candlesticks and letter-sealing tapersticks all are to be found in Chelsea work. The style, and even some of the designs, had a European beginning in Dresden, but Chelsea's original interpretation of the mood is unique. Soft porcelain specimens in perfect condition are museum treasures now, of course, but are all the more valuable to study, therefore, by those who seek to trace the fashionable beginnings of the china and pottery specimens, less ambitiously designed but produced in greater numbers and far more easily obtainable today.

Nowadays, perhaps, we have too little leisure to look for the stories these dainty creatures tell. Some are Aesop Fables brought to life; others show the cherubs or "boys" that romped through the eighteenth century; even the flirtatious couple embowered in hawthorn or jessamine are obviously acting out some scene, and never present the vacuous "ornamental" smiles of some later work. Some of these Chelsea creations are elaborate girandoles for the mantelpiece, each of a pair or a double pair carrying two or three branches. Christies sold a pair of "elegant Chelsea girandoles" among Thomas Turner's effects in 1767, each for two lights "with musical figures in arbours of jessamines" and the price even then was £3 14s. od.

In toilet table candlesticks, too, the figures may be grouped in these flower-encrusted bowers or *bocages*. Or Aesop's ox and ass, his goat-in-the-well, or his dog, fox and grapes, may raise porcelain candlesockets among their scrolls and flowers. For the table Chelsea and its rivals made figures to be viewed from all sides: little groups symbolic of the four seasons would adorn the dinner table until someone thought to raise the source of light above the diners' eye-level and the soaring curves of silver and Sheffield plate candelabra ousted such nonsense as

"Winter's" old man and chubby boy crouching over an illogically flower-girt fire. All work in this flowery mood required meticulous assembly, and hand-painting in enamel colours and gold to clothe the shepherd in magnificent brocades and his companion in sprigged calicoes that would have cost her life's earnings.

The candles themselves stand in bell-flower sockets with ornate calyx-shapes serving as expansive greasepans. Like the glassmen, the potters found it desirable to make the sockets detachable so that replacements could be fitted when low-burning candles resulted in cracks. But soon they devised an alternative safety measure, piercing the socket with four holes to release the wax into the pan.

The characteristic form of a Chelsea candlestick consists of C-shaped scrolls, supporting the socket and forming the footed base that is an important detail in the design. Bow candlesticks, too, rest on scroll footed bases, gilt-enriched, and strewn with flowers, but when looking at a collection you suddenly become aware of the problem involved in linking the socket with the figure design. Chelsea had the skill to make that appear easy.

One Bow solution is the single figure holding up the light, a flower-laden cherub, perhaps, supporting it on his garlanded head. Other sockets rest among the jessamine flowers on the tree stump behind the figures. But when, in the *Public Advertiser*, 1758, Bow announced that they were selling table chandeliers and girandoles, branches and candlesticks "for Chimney Pieces and finely decorated with Flowers and Figures", the branching lights were somewhat curiously devised. A hole was cut into the back near the base and this was fitted with branches of ormolu or green-enamelled metal. Some of these curving stalks were topped with porcelain candle sockets, some with porcelain flowers. Craftsmanship was meticulous—you can almost smell the rose, carnation or picotee—but the metal makes an uneasy accessory to otherwise attractive pieces, including some of Bow's individualistic birds, and plump small boys playing with this period's curiously popular goats and kids.

Worcester with its somewhat sturdier soapstone porcelain made wide-dished low-socketed chamber candlesticks, daintily finished with gilded scrolls and mask-trimmed handles. Derby's porcelain candlesticks are mainly pairs for the table and sometimes suggest that the freshness had gone out of the idea. Shepherd and dog, shepherdess and sheep are elegantly presented, but according to a guaranteed success-formula. A few candlesticks were made in the hard porcelain of Plymouth: a gardener and his wife may be found in plain white glazed porcelain and the same amiable pair in full colour and gold. But for a new approach there is more heart in the earthenware model catering for a far less monied public.

Salt-glazed stoneware was shaped into candlesticks while Chelsea and Bow were still establishing the vogue. These might be coloured by the late 1750s. There is recognisable character in a Ralph Wood shepherd or musician. His pairs of candlesticks follow the tree-stump plan with the socket nestling in the foliage and the base usually a flat-surfaced solid plinth. Some white-glazed earthenware, however, sought to reflect the style of Derby's unglazed biscuit porcelain.

Other work in white earthenware derives more directly from silver. Flowers and figures are forgotten in a classical, architectural mood, whether the columns are fluted corinthian with modelled capitals or square and moulded with festoons and rams' heads. Occasionally the candlestick nozzle is a balustraded capital. Leeds as well as the Potteries made impressive specimens. Wedgwood, using jasper ware, might rusticate the pillar and socket themselves into the shape of a tree-stump, ivy twined, with contrasting white figures. Victorian terra cotta may be found, too, in somewhat flamboyant designs classed at the time as "revived rococo".

There are simple *bocage* groups in earthenware, too. Of necessity these had to be inexpensive, shaped in two-piece moulds but carefully hand-finished and touched with colour. Walton's successful figure style appears in candlesticks made in his somewhat brittle earthenware. Figures and their tree backgrounds are notably consistent, the latter reduced to a handful of oak leaves carefully arranged and centred with what, I suspect, he intended originally for acorns and empty acorn cups, but were hand-painted into flowers of pink or blue. Other potters in the Walton tradition usually made their leaves and flowers dully nondescript.

By 1800 Ralph Salt was making a considerable contribution to this gathering of forthright figures for cottage table and mantelshelf candlestick. Demand continued until the 1860s. Like so many porcelain traditions, however, the eighteenth-century formula for effeminate candlesticks passed eventually to the bone china men of the 1820s and early Victorian days.

This was the magnificent period for "everlasting" flowers. Candlesticks from such inventive firms as Coalport contributed brilliantly to the craze. Flower encrustations and even children and cupids may transform conventionally shaped candlesticks mounted on all manner of flower-strewn scrolling bases. The Minton firm might dress their candlestick figures in the period's adored Louis XV fashion, either coloured or in the chaste statuary mood of parian ware. But there were many others. Chamber candlesticks of the 1840s are worth seeking. The dish may be a lotus leaf, its stem entwined to form a handle and its socket a lotus flower. Homely nasturtium flowers take to the design with equal grace and that bright-eyed favourite of the early nineteenth century, the gentian-blue convolvulus.

Chapter Eighteen

WALL PLAQUES AND PLATES

"He leap'd into the boat,
As it lay upon the strand,
But, oh! his heart was far away
With friends upon the land;
He thought of those he lov'd the best,
A wife and infant dear;
And feeling fill'd the sailor's breast,
The sailor's eye—a tear."

PRINTED on a slab of earthenware and "framed" with heavy copper lustre this "Sailor's Tear" was a best-seller in the early nineteenth century. Gay little flowers garlanded the lettering, a couple of rough holes were provided for a cord, and what better could be found to brighten the wall in any seafarer's home? Ceramic wall plates and plaques are collected enthusiastically today. Often they are bizarre, often entertaining. But mostly we cherish them for the same common touch that first made them sell. Here is sentiment unrestrained, a cheerful obviousness that could crowd a farmhouse kitchen with cow and milkmaid scenes, and a slapdash robust loyalty to the crown.

A representative collection can take us back through history with the vivid unreliability of the eyewitness, with great events no more than glimpsed among the urgent, unchanging business of daily living. Moreover, the result is as sweetly comforting as a mug of hot cocoa. Best-sellers in any medium must be optimistic: children could improve their minds with lugubrious sampler verses, but a melancholy wall decoration would be a poor greeting for the farm-hand after dawn-to-dusk at the plough, a poor companion for the sailor's wife at her solitary spinning.

However, if the sentiment becomes too sweet there is always the spice of sardonic wit:

> "This is a good world to live in,
> To lend or to spend or to give in,
> But to beg or to borrow,
> Or to get a man's own,
> It is such a world
> As never was known."

It is difficult today to realise what an important contribution plaques and rack plates made to the modest home. Yet most of us, probably, can still remember remote country cottage teas made fascinating by the last phase of uninhibited wall ornament, expressed in spectacular lithographs and monumental photographs; can even remember a childhood delight in flower-decked wall texts before obvious prettiness became taboo. Until nearly the mid-nineteenth century there was nothing, nothing at all, except ceramic plates and plaques for ordinary folk when they wanted gay colour to ornament their walls. Flimsy paper prints were little use, too small and detailed for dark little rooms, and made even more confusing when daubed with hand colouring. So the potters devised special plates and plaques for hanging, and the joiner knocked up hanging shelves known as delft racks to supplement the space on cupboard top and dresser for what came to be known as rack plates.

A representative collection of plates and plaques spans the years from Cromwell to Edward VII, expressed in almost all the ceramics known to those 250 years. Some of the earliest that remain are Lambeth plates of the seventeenth century made of tin-enamelled earthenware and known as delf or delft ware, although in fact potted also in Bristol and Liverpool, Staffordshire and elsewhere until early in the nineteenth century.

These round and oval plates are now most often collected—and reproduced—as "blue dash chargers": the oblique strokes in cobalt blue around their wide convex rims were intended to suggest stylised ropework, but their undersides indicate clearly enough that they were for display rather than for serving food. Turn one over and there is the flat ring on the back designed to take the hanging cord. This is more than the usual foot rim. Often it is grooved for the cord and in other cases is pierced. Here indeed is a point for the wary collector. The piercing was done with a couple of round wooden pegs pushed through the unfired clay and left there to hold the holes open and undistorted. Firing in the oven burnt them right away but left fragments of displaced clay at the edges of the holes, worth looking for.

The favourite cobalt blue glows richly on the greyish white ground of this tin-enamelled ware, occasionally enriched with a soft green, yellow, orange and purple. Often the design was sponge-painted and subjects range from figures and heraldic motifs to windmills, ships and lively groups of pinks and tulips and guelder roses. Trade guild coats of arms are immensely decorative, but I suppose first favourites now as at the time are the monarchs in their coronation robes, equestrian figures of military leaders and familiar Biblical scenes. Charles II in the Boscobel oak, a somewhat rakish, crown-burdened William III, plump Queen Anne or the Duke of Marlborough may be treated with the forthright simplicity of a popular memento.

Sometimes words replace the picture, probably to display in a place of public resort. They may remind you of "ye Pious Memory of Queen Caroline 1738" or aim to rally supporters at a Parliamentary election for "NUGENT ONLY/1754" or "CALVERT & MARTIN FOR TUKESBURY". The mid-eighteenth-century mood is reflected in lively little views surrounded by rims in more elaborate rococo patterns.

The other impressive form of decorative plate introduced in late Stuart days was the massive rack plate in slipware, as much as 3 feet in diameter, 3 inches deep and without a foot rim. Such a plate could be displayed ceiling-high on the top of a dresser or corner cupboard where the vigorous crudity of its ornament would be an advantage. Staffordshire potters such as Thomas Toft and Ralph Simpson are still remembered for such achievements, the ornament including a figure group such as Adam and Eve surrounded by a deep repetitive border composed of basket work, urns, or perhaps the heads of beady-eyed cavaliers associated with one of the several potters Toft, whose name and date, appropriately large, form a feature of the rim.

Here again we find the period's inevitable depictions of Charles II and Catherine, and of William III and Mary, as well as a range of subjects that suggest commissions from enterprising tavern-keepers, such as St. George and the dragon, the lion from the royal arms, a double-headed spread-eagle and a saucy mermaid. Such work continued into early Georgian years and was revived—collectors beware!—in the third quarter of the nineteenth century. The satisfyingly solid ornament on these plates was achieved by quick, primitive means that ruled out fine detail and expressive line but was therefore the more certain to be observed and remembered.

The basic dish is close-grained red or buff earthenware washed over with white pipe clay. This was dried leather hard, then ornamented on the flat and the deep bouge and the wide rim with designs laid on in creamy liquid red clay slip poured from a spouted can. Darker tinted slip emphasised outlines and important details, and the final touches of inspired peasant craftsmanship were contributed by lines of dots in white. Before it was fired the dish was sprinkled with powdered lead oxide known as smithum, and then clay, slip and smithum were fired in the one operation, the smithum melting into a smooth yellowish glaze.

The great mid-eighteenth-century ceramic adventure into translucent porcelains hardly concerned the maker of wall plates: porcelains were for those who hung their walls with miniatures, oil paintings or mezzotints. But you do occasionally find a circular anniversary plaque in Lowestoft soft paste porcelain dating between the mid-1760s and 1797. One side has an attractive, professionally painted flower design neatly bordered with a narrow convex frame, the other a contrastingly laborious, amateur flower-enflourished record that so-and-so was born or married on such a date. A single hole in the rim allowed for hanging on a nail.

In hard porcelain in the late 1770s, however, far more impressive plaques were produced at Bristol under Richard Champion. These are quite lovely and, among English ceramics, unique. They are of biscuit with the slight gloss of smear glazing, white or touched with colour, plain surfaced or, at their most fascinating, hand created in deep relief and lit with burnished gold. Some are oval—6 inches by 4 inches—and some circular—3½ inches in diameter. Ornament ranges from plain-surfaced blue or chocolate brown portrait profile busts to armorial work, monograms and flower groups.

The most elaborate profiles are surrounded by raised wreaths of leaves in thick matt gold with details burnished, and have outer borders of flowers modelled in biscuit, petal by petal, leaf by leaf, so that every detail has the sharp, almost metallic clarity that is the special appeal of true porcelain. Even at the time, and selling to the china dealers, such a plaque was priced at more than £5. Here again the nineteenth century discovered a renewed enthusiasm for mid-Georgian work, and plaques in this manner were made at Bristol in the late 1840s by Edward Raby. These, however, are in softer paste and the ground may be surface-stained blue before firing.

Less expensively, in the 1770s one could choose between glossy gaudy earthenware plaques and the austere stonewares evolved by Josiah Wedgwood. Wedgwood's black basaltes, fine grained and duskily opaque, were introduced in 1764, and his dense white jasper ware in 1771. At first he offered flat slabs of basaltes painted in colours with Etruscan designs, but late in the 1770s came plaques in the relief work, intricate and sharply defined, that is the ware's main distinction.

These plaques present compositions adapted from the frescoes of Herculaneum, sometimes against flat grounds painted or gilded. There are portrait medallions, too, and designs to meet the nineteenth century's craze for sporting scenes. The central motifs are framed either in smoothly convex moulding or with a ribbon-bound reeds design inside a broadly fluted surround. Collectors have to remember that many other potters issued black basaltes plaques, but few of such fine craftsmanship. A second series of these, too, appeared during the third quarter of the nineteenth century.

Panels of jasper were coloured with mineral oxides in the familiar restrained tones of blue, green or yellow, as backgrounds to bas reliefs in white jasper. Wedgwood advertised that for his bas relief work he employed "Some of the best artists in Europe", and Miss Meteyard has listed forty-eight modellers, but, of course, for Wedgwood they worked anonymously.

The more widely saleable alternative was the Staffordshire earthenware wall plaque with a design in relief to assert itself on a crowded cottage wall. Crude work of this kind has been dated to the seventeenth century, fired but unglazed, coloured sometimes, or even black-leaded. These developed into important wall ornaments in the 1770s, the designs cast in relief and brushed over with coloured glazes in separate washes in the Ralph Wood and Whieldon manner.

Plump geese and oxen, stalwart harvesters and finely frocked milkmaids were tricked out with coloured borders and cherub crestings in a day when there were no commercial calendars to rival their homely gaiety. A woman cutting wheat with a sickle is on view at the Victoria and Albert Museum, the plaque including a corded frame, a feature that was often elaborated and included a pair of loops for hanging. Richer effects in deeper relief came when high temperature colours were applied under colourless glazes—the so-called Pratt ware that invariably nowadays is dated to 1790 but in fact continued until the 1820s. These plaques might be oval, round or rectangular, and pairs were fashionable such as "Patricia and Her Lover" and "Ceres and Pomona". Patricia, then, could wear a vivid blue bodice and skirt, white apron, brownish yellow petticoat and blue and yellow spotted headdress, all set off by a frame with a bevelled rim moulded with a wavy line of shell pattern.

Pairs of plaques offer a challenge to the collector, and sets of the Seasons or the Elements may be assembled. Here again we find the ever-eager demand for portraits of royalty and other important personages. Princess Charlotte and her husband Prince Leopold in coronet-crested frames have been matched up, and to make the triumph complete, they were found to tally exactly as to frame and style with a pair of William IV and Queen Adelaide, obviously by the same potter but put on the market fifteen years later. A particularly appealing set in Queen Mary's collection consisted of the royal arms and, separately, the lion and unicorn supporters. But every possible subject was exploited. Queen Victoria's first visit to Scotland in 1842 was marked by the casting of a large equestrian portrait plaque at the important Portobello pottery, and, of course, every popular bloodthirsty sport of the period was offered for its champions.

Not all are painted. Cream-coloured earthenware was attractive enough in warm-shadowed high relief work, and appeared in some large plaques, such as a sailor and his girl of the 1780s measuring 11¼ inches by 8¾ inches. Irregular ovals may be as much as a foot wide, with moulded rims of dots and lines enclosing lions, elephants or other animals or more sporting scenes. Less frequently such plaques are found touched up with coloured enamels.

By the end of the Regency the cottager could buy pottery ornaments astonishingly cheaply. Lambeth and Derbyshire and Scotland were turning out huge numbers in rich "teapot-brown" salt glazed stoneware. Measuring about 6 inches by 5 inches in a plain convex border with two holes for hanging him, John Bull, Napoleon and many another celebrity in glossy relief was sold for a penny or two, along with hunting scenes, episodes from Punch and Judy, and ships in full sail.

Plaques depending wholly on relief effects were issued, too, in lovely, glowing terra cotta, the colour ranging from lobster brilliance to the matt warmth of brick dust. Nathaniel Smith's magnificent animal groups date to the 1760s, but the vogue came when terra cotta was rediscovered by the early Victorians. In the 1830s it was pressed into relief work as clear-cut as Wedgwood's jasper ware and suggested itself for similar classical scenes. Inevitably at that period some plaques were touched with gold, for the terra cotta maker was very much aware of a resemblance to Oriental carved lacquer work. A painted plaque may be found, but with the colours unfired. Minton made some striking plaques, such as Thorwaldsen's "Four Seasons", combining the terra cotta with bas relief ornament in the white, marble-like porcelain known as statuary parian ware.

All these relief plaques were simple enough, all emphatic so that they could hold their own among the aggressive furnishings of the strident early nineteenth century. Prints had their own plaque counterparts, too, however, in black transfer-printed plaques of white glazed earthenware—usually pearl ware—often over-painted in colours and with borders moulded in any of the fashionable silver patterns of their day such as gadrooning, reeding or feather pattern.

John Wesley, Washington or Nelson lost none of his fame for being printed in heavy black and often individually overpainted in the manner of the 1820s–50, and there were Biblical scenes, too, and landscapes, chinoiserie designs and sporting events for the choosing. "The Gretna Green Marriage" was among the best-sellers. Printing in blue dates later than about 1810 and was never greatly in demand anyway since so much "Staffordshire blue-and-white" was richly pictorial and transformed innumerable dressers and plate racks. There was a series of portrait plaques printed in a violet colour associated with the Reform Act.

All this cheaply printed work was intended for an uncritical happy-go-lucky market. Sunderland potters, especially, could count on a suitably jovial, sentimental and no longer illiterate market among seamen passing through the district. Heavy copper lustre was often combined with the blotchy purple or pink lustre now associated with the area, although made in fact elsewhere as well, to give substantial framing to every kind of current popular theme. The plaque is usually rectangular, less frequently square or round, and pierced for hanging. Some of the best are painted though their subjects keep within the usual bounds of popularity with sailing ships, farewell scenes, rhymes, songs and inscriptions to suit birthday, christening, wedding and funeral. Special presentation or souvenir plaques could be ordered from the local china seller.

Cheaper but more detailed were the transfer-printed specimens. Here you look for views of the once-marvellous Sunderland or Wearmouth Bridge, or religious themes including such forthright texts as "Prepare to Meet Thy God" enclosed in a wreath of flowers. Scott's Pottery and the High Southwick Pottery made a speciality of these. The evils of drink as portrayed in Cruickshank's drawings sold widely in the late 1830s. John Dawson's pottery at Low Ford issued decorated rectangular tiles pierced for hanging. Today none of this work is too banal for our delight—not even the ubiquitous sailing ship and the flowery cartouche pompously wishing:

> May Peace & Plenty
> On our Nation Smile
> And Trade with Commerce
> Bless the British Isle.

Wall plaques in bone china are in a different world, with an air of high fashion about their bright, carefully painted flower and bird groups, their Watteau scenes and souvenir landscapes surrounded by gilded frames. The Duchess of Sutherland set the fashion for using unframed slabs as wall dados. They date from the 1830s onwards, made by such firms as Copeland, Chamberlain of Worcester, and Coalport.

W. T. Copeland earned high praise from the Jury of the Great Exhibition, 1851, for the size and flatness and handsome painting of his examples. "Slabs and frames with paintings" catalogued by Copeland covered a wide range of subjects from paintings after Raphael and "Watteau vignettes with gold backgrounds chased and burnished" to landscapes and flowers and fruit. These are inscribed with titles and the "Copeland" mark in red. Madeley with its reputation for work as rich as Sèvres followed the popular Boucher and Watteau styles, the artist Randall being responsible for cupids and love scenes issued in the 1830s, and before 1845 Derby under the Bloor regime was offering painted views of cathedrals and churches in white glazed frames touched with gold.

The letters GFBBT on a plaque indicate G. F. Bowers of Brownhills, Tunstall, as the source, a copyist of famous English paintings. Gainsborough's "Cottage Door" gilt-framed was among his Great Exhibition entries. The letters WSK were impressed on plaques by William Saddler Kennedy of Burslem. A few of the finer bone china plaques were signed like canvas paintings, by Hurten, for example, who worked for Copeland, and Ballard of Madeley, and Hurstwood and Leyland of York. Other plaques have tiny initials hidden in the background of the painting, but disappointingly few have been identified. Occasionally, a pleasant little plaque turns up with a reminder of a minor early Victorian vogue for bone china painted with dogs' heads in vignette: celebrated dogs were commemorated and fine breeds.

Sometimes a plaque is found lacking the finish of a china frame. It may have had a frame of gilded wood or composition or of one of the fashionable polished woods such as walnut, rosewood or maple. And always there is the chance of finding a quaint, unclassifiable effort, for many "slabs" were sold plain for the genteel amateur decorator.

The Duchess of Sutherland was responsible, too, for another mid-nineteenth-century enthusiasm, not for plaques but for wall plates. Exquisitely enamelled plates had long been a feature of the glazed china cabinet, of course, but she had the notion of displaying them to greater advantage on wide mouldings around the room 2 or 3 feet below the ceiling. By 1850 the demand for brightly painted wall plates extended from palace to farmhouse. Even rooms without wall mouldings could be hung with the plates fitted into adjustable wire clips.

The result, of course, at such a period was that plates, too, came to be treated more and more pictorially: the range of decoration widened and ways were found to reduce the cost. The technique that gave picture pot-lids the right of entry into collectors' cabinets was developed into lavish full-colour under-glaze prints on plates of stone china and semi-porcelain. These picture plates have a finer velvety brilliance and body depth than the pot-lid though they came from the same firm of F. and R. Pratt & Company, Fenton, Staffordshire, where Jesse Austin devised the elaborate transfer-printing technique. Some are in gilded frames, some later examples in frames painted to resemble malachite.

Then came the turn of the art potter. English majolica was hailed as a new ceramic marvel in about 1850, devised by Leon Arnoux, art manager to Herbert Minton. Here the joy lies in the subtle rainbow iridescences that light the bold relief work on dishes and plates, from bluish purple to ruby red, and from golden yellow to green. The ware was made by a small group of potters until the end of the century but now is associated especially with the entirely dated but enduringly charming birds and fishes and flowers of William de Morgan, who made particularly effective use of a ruby red glaze lit by an underlying cream-coloured glaze.

It is easy to write and write about these later nineteenth-century art potters and artist decorators with their new art-school approach and their obvious delight in the creative possibilities of their job. The Doulton Pottery, Lambeth, for instance, welcomed these eager experiments. One result was the wall plate in a range of individualistic styles, such as salt-glazed low-relief impasto ware.

The Linthorpe Pottery near Middlesbrough was at work for ten years from 1879 and took great pride in the rich and varied tones of its coloured glazes. Many a big, heavy Linthorpe plaque dominated the back of a Victorian sideboard: some perhaps still do. Even the four Martin brothers of Southall Pottery, Southall Green, Middlesex, made wall and sideboard plates as well as their grotesque jugs and figures and these are now immensely valuable. Many of their colour effects were of their own devising and they took a special delight in designs of marine life so that today our quest for plate and plaque may be enlivened by a glimpse of crabs, sea anemones, even dragons among the earliest royalties, the classical motifs of Wedgwood's Etruria and the humblest but still fascinating doggerel made for the Sunderland sailor's lass.

Chapter Nineteen

POTS FOR FLOWERS AND BULBS

FLOWER arrangement is home-making at its most enjoyable, provided only that the flowers are allowed to go as they will, unburdened by rules of contemporary fashion. Every generation, it seems, has to develop its own cult, but just now a few flower lovers are turning away from the current enthusiasms and are finding wonderful possibilities among the vessels that served their Georgian predecessors —the myrtle pans and orange tubs, the bulb pots and mignonette boxes and jardinieres that brought the colour and sweetness of flowers growing and blowing through the house a hundred, or two hundred, years ago. Eventually perhaps we shall even rediscover our grandmothers' silver epergnes. Even when as a child I had to polish the awkward little tubes I delighted in their unabashed prettiness when filled with pink Zephyrine Drouhin roses and cascading gypsophila.

A Hogarth painting or a Torond silhouette may offer a glimpse of earlier flower arrangements. But most of all the vessels themselves declare their endless possibilities. As early as 1698 Sir John Verney described how he would have some new tuberose roots put "into the handsomest Potts & when they are blowne I may have 'em within doores". Some delft vessels may be associated with his day, but the most valuable period for today's collectors dates from about 1750 to 1850. In porcelain, earthenware and bone china, in basaltes and jasperware and Victorian terra cotta these vessels for plants and cut flowers and winter bulbs are a joy to the connoisseur's eye and a challenge to all green fingers.

So delightful are many in themselves that we hesitate to associate them with drippy leaves and thrusting roots. It becomes possible, even, to understand the eighteenth century's utterly un-English vogue for flowers fashioned in porcelain on slender stems of ormolu. Today these little scented beauties may still be found, rare and costly, as sweetly formal forerunners of the flower heads scattered over the surface of "flower encrusted" china. Indeed, porcelain flowers in a style created by Dresden were once the mainstay of the Sèvres porcelain works when Madame de Pompadour caught Louis XV's fancy with a veritable garden of scented porcelain and thus won his enthusiastic patronage for the new factory. Sèvres made the vessels for pot plants, too, of course, filled with perfume instead of water and mounted on additional elegant ormolu. Even today there is more than a hint of the gilt and brocade salon in the very word jardiniere.

Fig. 22. Quintal flower horn.

An enterprising collector, however, looks much further than the deep porcelain bowl, beautifully decorated. Some of the earliest and most challenging designs are associated with blue-painted Dutch delft ware. These may be as much as 12 inches tall and offer arrangements of small projecting sockets to be filled individually with cut flowers, a design used in Egypt four thousand years ago and later in flower-rich Persia and Mesopotamia. In a typical delft design sixteen sockets project from the domed cover over a large bowl; in another, twelve are mounted in three tiers on the corners of a hexagonal turret.

Less aggressively but with the same idea of wide-spreading display, English potters made five-socketed fan-shaped flower holders. Leeds advertised them in 1783 as quintal flower horns, in cream-coloured earthenware moulded in relief to suggest leaves; the Staffordshire potters of the 1830s called them flower or bulb tubes, and enriched them with colour or metallic lustre. The design to watch for consists of a long narrow vessel for a mantelshelf or window ledge on a rectangular foot, short stemmed and spreading above into five baluster-shaped sockets fanned out in a row.

All these vessels demand flowers in delicate trailing abundance to veil their somewhat ungainly usefulness. But there are many other pots and bowls only slightly less helpful for arrangements of floppy boughs and heavy-headed blossoms. These have flat, recessed covers dotted with holes, usually but not always regularly spaced. Sometimes crocuses or other small bulbs grew in sandy loam under the holes but the design is most suitable for cut flowers. An occasional specimen has a slanting lid with irregular piercings, copied, I suspect, from an open knife box. All Europe knew the design, it seems, and the late Chinese potters of Ch'ien Lung, as well as English potters who used it in a wide range of wares, so where indeed are all those vessels now?

For growing bulbs there is an obvious modification of this flower or bough pot design. This has only a few holes, with raised rims, each to hold a single bulb so that it will be only "a little immersed" in the soft water contained in the vessel below. A smaller hole in the lid may facilitate replenishment of the water. The pot can thus serve as a bulb glass, but the more decoratively since the bulbs' roots are hidden by the opaque ware, and this can become an opportunity for ornament that only the bulbs' own flowering can outshine.

Bulbs "to blow in the apartments of a house" were the delight of eighteenth- and nineteenth-century gardeners. John Abercrombie, for instance, in *The Gardener's Pocket Journal* in 1786—and still, for that matter, more than thirty years later in the nineteenth edition—listed hyacinths, dwarf tulips, jonquils, Persian irises and soleil narcissi. The old scented tulips must have been a joy, and hyacinths and jonquils invaluable in days when fresh perfumes through the house were the only refuge for a sensitive nose. The exquisitely fastidious might prefer the tantalising sweetness of mignonette, and here again Abercrombie advised autumn potting "for moving in said pots to adorn any apartment".

Occasionally a vessel turns up with a pierced lining suitable for the direct potting of such a plant, and in porous terra cotta there was a nineteenth-century demand for mignonette boxes. But mostly, it seems, the seedlings were potted up in the greenhouse and placed pot and all in an extravagantly handsome jardiniere.

So much for the range of vessels required by our predecessors. The joy in collecting them lies in the fascinating variety of wares, designs and ornament serving earlier generations of flower lovers. Most important are the vessels in porcelain and most famous the luscious creations of Sèvres, especially valuable when painted by known decorators.

These vessels are worth studying because to some extent they set the style for English potters. There are at least five typical shapes. First favourite perhaps was the *cuvette aux fleurs*, the oblong *bombé* commode design with a bow front, heavily gilded or leaf-shape handles and tiny feet or a shaped foot rim. Sometimes this has a partition from end to end. The *jardinière en éventail* was introduced by Sèvres, fanning out to the rim from a narrow base that rests in a separate stand, wide for stability but often pierced as well as painted so as to appear less dominant.

There are the more obvious tub shapes, too, in Sèvres porcelain, including the Chinese style of square orange tub footed and finialed at the corners, the cylindrical vessel with gilt scroll or shell handles, and the simple bucket form of the 1770s and onwards, showing its period's delight in projecting rams' masks and bands of rope pattern to set off the panels of flower painting. Inevitably such flower panels are associated with Sèvres elegance and the less hackneyed subjects occasionally encountered tend to be from other French potteries. Sèvres' handsome vessels continued importantly in production through the nineteenth century and can be dated by their marks.

Meanwhile among their rivals on the English market were flower pots from China. London china sellers liked the Oriental hard porcelain which stood up toughly to its journeyings. Many, always in pairs, were imported in the later eighteenth century, modelled in relief and deftly painted in the *famille rose* range of colours or in blue and white against backgrounds in the familiar cracked ice pattern. Some in blue and white are circular, but more of these vessels are in the fan (*éventail*) shape. Figures on cloudy scrolls and in garden pavilions, figures in landscapes and at their work are to be found on these vessels, but even here some are flower-painted in the European manner.

England, emphatically, had its own painters of flowers, too. A few at least of the richly-sepalled roses painted on flower vessels and ascribed to William Billingsley have the qualities of texture and liveliness that suggest his hand, jardinieres included, although collectors no longer shame his reputation by ascribing all massed roses to him alone. Swansea, for instance, made handsome flower vessels in the Sèvres manner, with pierced covers and small feet, painted with flower bouquets and with masks in relief.

Derby's porcelain flower and bulb pots are semi-circular, undecorated on the flat back, and often bear landscapes in the laboured style of their day in contrast to gayer subordinate flower bouquets. Duesbury, Derby's proprietor, paid Richard Askew nine shillings in 1765 for painting "a flower pot with a woman & cupet" and half-a-guinea in 1794 for two days' work painting a flower pot with a woman and child.

This semi-circular model was never Derby's exclusively, however, and I have met with it in the restrained silver inlay effects of resist lustre and in the gaudy brilliance of so-called Pratt ware. By the nineteenth century the vessel might be used for pot pourri, the recessed lid replaced by a lid with a knob handle.

In eighteenth-century Worcester porcelain my own favourites are the pairs of small scrolling wall vessels pierced for hanging on the wall, perfect for wisps of fern trailing over their delicious scale blue ground colour and reserves of exotic birds.

By the time bone china was established in the 1800s as a cheaper, stronger, more adaptable alternative to soft porcelain the vogue was beginning for old, pre-war Sèvres. Continental and Oriental porcelain could be imitated in fine bone china but by 1800 the genuine imports were almost unobtainable. We do not always realise today how intensely war conditions restricted—and stimulated—the craftsmen of the Regency. Thus the story of bone china flower pots is the story of how Worcester, Derby, Coalport and the rest strove to copy the lovely colours and comely flowers of the envied, hard-to-get rival.

Derby then made jardinieres with shell handles and flowers painted in garlands and festoons. Some are rectangular with handles of bird and rustic branch motifs. A set of three richly gilded Derby crocus pots may have figure scenes in landscape settings, each pot offering twenty or more holes for crocus bulbs or flower stalks. Rockingham made shallow, heavy-footed rectangular tubs with flowers in relief on the front framing popular views. To modern eyes the heavy feet often spoil these late Georgian designs. Spode included more graceful outlines, with upsweeping handles and square plinth base.

Worcester bone china appears in bucket-shaped pots, their handles in gilded lion mask and ring designs and their panels bright with flower sprays, but other potters made these, too. Coalport was still making them in the 1850s, larger then ever in the Victorian manner and painted, for instance, with Watteau-style shepherd and shepherdess, flower bouquets and jewelled borders.

Not every room can accommodate the vivid colours and richly detailed ornament of the Sèvres style. One of my own favourite flower vessels is my early Mason bowl, almost as thin and light as metal, its bright colours veiled with a wash of lustre and in pleasantly inarticulate patternings. Leeds and their rivals made cleanly-designed freshly golden earthenware pots and stands, with handles and swag ornaments in relief and pierced covers, and in the nineteenth century a range of near-china wares was developed in the Mason manner.

Even by the 1770s, however, the most obvious relief from the glossy prettiness of porcelain was to be found among such stonewares as basaltes and jasperwares, their surface matt, their texture heavily opaque, their colour and ornament deliberately subdued. Often you find a bulb pot in jasperware, square or rectangular, with the back undecorated for standing on window sill or side table. On the recessed cover are three rimmed openings for bulbs: some are intended for six bulbs in two rows, and a square, one-bulb vessel was made also, with a "tree stump" bulb cup, designed by William Hackwood for Wedgwood in 1796.

Ornament includes figure subjects in relief, such as the familiar Lady Templetown designs. There was a renewed demand for jasperware in the second half of the nineteenth century, especially for the Wedgwood blues patterned in white relief, and the firm met it with round tapering vessels as much as 16 inches high. These contain pierced linings so that they can be used for rooted plants. Bacchanals may frolic round them between borders of vines and flower garlands. The firm made an orange tub design, too, in white jasper dipped in one of the famous colours, with an oval reserve on each face for an applied plaque.

Black basaltes make satisfying bulb pots, heavily glazed inside and designed for a row of three bulbs in a long narrow vessel, 8 by 3½ inches, or for two rows, with the vessel's rim, ornamentally shaped, higher at the back than the front. Here, too, late eighteenth-century ideas on classical ornament are found, pressed in relief and decorated with dry-looking encaustic painting in red and white. There may be heavy-fisted cupids bearing wreaths, for instance, silhouetted in black against a tawny red background. By 1768, the records show, there was increasing demand for these somewhat pedestrian attempts to recapture the beauty of painted Greek vases. Myrtle pans were made, too, for evergreens, some grooved to suggest the laths of a wooden tub and with handles at the sides.

In cream stoneware Josiah Wedgwood's famous contemporary Thomas Turner made bulb pots in the familiar bombé outline of mid-Georgian commode and tea chest and jardiniere, with rimmed holes for half a dozen bulbs and a classic ornament in relief on the front. Both Wedgwood and Turner were among the makers of the fine-grained non-porous stoneware known as caneware. This is a charming nonsensical relic of its period, introduced in the 1780s and long exploited for its supposed likeness to cane and bamboo. Thus caneware bulb pots, glazed inside, may resemble lengths of bamboo arranged vertically as boxes bound at the top by thinner "canes" and showing the hollow tops of the bamboo around the bulb receptacles. Their joints are hand-painted in red with ornament added in blue and green even including a few small leaves, but not with the naturalistic effects of Chinese work in this style.

The ware continued until the mid-nineteenth century but by then the great garden ceramic was terra cotta. Baddeley of Longton, for instance, who started in 1862, distinguished between mignonette boxes, crocus pots, hyacinth pots and flower pots, all in the tawny red ware.

Victorian terra cotta was an ideal hard earthenware for the important Victorian conservatory. It was immensely decorative and shaped in bold relief patterns almost as sharp-cut as Oriental incised lacquer, or touched with colour over its own matt or glossy glowing red. But its virtue to the gardener was its porosity. Its hard, compact texture made glazing unnecessary, yet hollowware proved reasonably porous for growing plants, offering endless opportunities for hanging baskets and similar Victorian delights.

Ornament was still dominated by classical themes even when the well-known firm of F. and R. Pratt were painting their highly vitreous version of the ware with brilliant enamel colours. You may find a Minton plant vase with ambitious bas relief figures or a deep red mignonette box with a bas relief in parian ware, white and silky as the marble it was named after.

There is transfer ornament to look for, too, and matt and burnished gilding on flower holders by William Kirkham, and colourful birds and flowers and butterflies against backgrounds of gilded arabesques on jardinieres by Pinder, Bourne and Company. Charles Meigh and Sons of Hanley advertised "flower pot Flora shape; acanthus flower pots coloured and gilt". There is even some terra cotta to be sought in a sad buff tone, made by the Denby Pottery in Derbyshire. Its mignonette boxes are notably light and attractive enough as a completely negative background to the plant's delicate flowers and peculiarly vivid foliage, but it would be hard to imagine a vessel more remote from the Sèvres flowery radiance of a hundred years before.

Chapter Twenty

FIGURE COMFIT HOLDERS

MODERN homes offer few, perhaps too few, opportunities for sheer, unashamed ornament. We are still in reaction from the Victorian mania for purposeless accumulation. In this book my aim has been to confine myself to pieces that are of their essence decorative, but comparatively few among them were originated solely for their value as ornament. Often they please us today just because their rugged good looks or sparkling prettiness stem from the fact that basically they are well designed for a positive purpose. Garnitures of vases tend to be poor company, I find. Even a china cottage only comes alive when the warm sweetness of a burning pastille can rise from the gilded chimney or a window twinkle with a night-light mortar candle.

On the dessert table, especially, the items that have remained recognisable and individual today met this requirement. Among them none was more constantly in use, and none more essentially decorative, than the comfit holder.

The dessert and the banquet receive considerable mention in the course of this book. To those of us with a love of past skills they represent to perfection the grace and sparkle of their day, and we can only regret that both words lost much of their earlier significance during the nineteenth century while remaining in use to cause confusion today. Let me emphasise at once, therefore, that the dessert I have in mind, the dessert of the mid-eighteenth century, was a gay, informal party. Dressing out the dessert was still a genteel accomplishment, and hostesses who did not call in professional confectioners competed in their sweetmeats, their flower decorations and most especially their arrangements of small figures in porcelain to ornament their tables. These would be almost certain to include pairs of figures offering the contents of tiny baskets or bowls.

Collectors have given various improbable names to these dreamy gardeners, immaculate shepherds and shepherdesses, suave Turks and plump Orientals. Their open vessels—baskets, shells, trays—are only 2 or 3 inches wide across the rim, palpably too small for the usual "dry sweetmeats" offered in abundance on the tables around them, yet their gesture of hand or fan is unmistakable. In fact, their purpose was to offer the company tiny sugar comfits or cachous.

Their introduction was a sign of increasing sophistication. These comfits were richly flavoured and particularly strongly scented, designed to counteract refreshingly any lingering taste or smell of the dinner's lavishly sauced and pickled savouries. They were detailed in cookery books from the fifteenth century onwards and sold, for example, by the pound for 1s. 9d. in 1587, and 1s. 4d. in 1623. They were regarded as invaluable, too, after drinking and after smoking. Elizabeth I received "a box of pyne comfytts, musked" in 1562 as a New Year gift from her "poticary" John Hemmingway.

Kissing comfits Shakespeare called them, and likened them to hailstones, and more than two and a half centuries later Walter Scott drew attention to them in *The Fair Maid of Perth*: "Wine is drunk, comfits are eaten, and the gift is forgotten when the flavour is past away." Still later, in 1862, Charles Elmé Francatelli observed that certain towns were renowned for their manufacture, notably Bristol in England and Verdun in France.

The Howard household accounts in 1629 recorded the purchase of rosemary and violet conserves "to perfume my lady's breath"; and violets and many other fragrant blooms from the herb garden—even the small blue flowers of borage—were candied according to the recipes of Sir Hugh Plat in his *Delights for Ladies*, 1609, and of his successors such as Mrs. H. Glasse in *The Compleat Confectioner*, 1752.

For gentlemen, comfits were made with strongly aromatic

flavours. Often they were no more than single seeds jostled together in a syrupy-starchy paste over a charcoal fire until each became separately coated with the mixture. A pound of sugar would be needed to coat two ounces of the richly flavoured seeds to make sizeable comfits, but "fine small comfits" could be made with half the proportion of costly sugar. Caraway seeds from the herb garden made particularly pungent and diminutive ones, and suggested to Heywood in 1631 a typical play on words: "I will make bold to march in towards your banquet, and there comfit my selfe, and cast all carawayes downe my throat."

Home grown coriander seeds, too, distinctively sweet and round as bullets, aniseed and celery seeds were among the most popular, but cloves, too, and fennel and rosemary were used, and fragments of ginger and cinnamon, the coating coloured green with spinach juice, yellow with saffron or red with cochineal or mulberry syrup or the "red saunders" recommended by Mrs. Glasse. They were difficult to make. Plat recommended as many as twelve coatings for caraway seeds, and was emphatic that "the smaller that Anniseede Comfits be, the fairer, the harder, and so in all other". He estimated that "in every three hours you may make three pound comfits". Mid-Victorians favoured nonpareils made with orris root in gum arabic as the central flavour, and these might be coloured with carmine, "any other colour is considered in bad taste". All this is proof enough that, though small, they were important.

When the Chelsea porcelain factory began issuing brilliantly coloured figures in the 1750s, these made a decorative feature of a service previously furnished by simpler glass or silver vessels. (Comfit glasses have been noted among glass baskets and other furnishings for the dessert advertised in the *Liverpool Chronicle* during 1758.) The small Chelsea lady would offer her porcelain posy and her flower-scented sweets, the gentleman his more masculine comfits. For a large gathering several pairs of figures might be placed about the room, and sometimes a three-figure group on a single plinth is to be noted offering a wider range of comfits.

All these exquisites, some 7 or 8 inches high, were made in the soft porcelains of Chelsea, Derby and Bow, and in the hard porcelain of Dresden and other Continental centres. From about 1800 they were made, too, in the English bone china of such celebrated potters as John Rose of Coalport, Herbert Minton of Stoke-upon-Trent and the Bramelds of Rockingham. The one feature shared by all is the open vessel, whether basketwork hamper or tray, bowl or escallop shell, distinguishing them at once to the would-be collector from the normal run of ornamental idlers in the china cabinet. An unambitious but pleasant little comfit figure may still be bought for half a guinea or less, but always, of course, the hope is to find an eighteenth-century specimen.

Each detail in such a purchase is worth studying. A porcelain figure tends to look so self-assured that it is difficult to remember all the hazards it has passed, the moulding of various body sections and their assembly, with the detailed tooling this involved, and the firing of the figure within a framework of supports that the assembler—the repairer to give him his contemporary name—hoped would ensure graceful limbs and the perfect tilt to the head. Always there was the inevitable shrinkage, by as much as one-third, that the first firing involved. A second firing in the oven set the glaze, and hand painting in enamels provided the colour.

The baskets on these comfit figures were made with particular care. Oval, round or square, deep or shallow, they suggest the woven wicker-work perfectly. Some are white, some touched with gold. They are smooth within, but the lids simulate wicker on both sides. Instead of baskets some figures are in Levantine costume and sit by the shells instead of holding such awkward vessels. Many pairs were sold at the Chelsea auction sale of 1756, catalogued as "Two Figures in Turkish dresses, sitting with shells".

Even the minor details are noteworthy, and may help to indicate a date or origin. Often the setting consists of a flower-encrusted tree stump, the flowers made individually, some even petal by petal, and meticulously coloured. Sometimes there is a dog in the foreground, and it is tempting to think his master bore aniseed comfits. How those eighteenth-century sophisticates loved shepherds and their silly sheep. Even at the time they paid 36s. to 48s. for a Chelsea pair.

Chelsea probably made the first English comfit holders, and the finest. Some of the Turkish couples are in the lovely porcelain evolved in 1753. More belong to the "gold anchor" period of 1758–69, however, when the paste was denser, more translucent and chalky white under a limpid glaze. Sometimes the gold anchor mark itself is inconspicuous, but the figures jauntily proclaim their identity. Coalport, indeed, made similar figures, and with their marks, almost a century later, but in bone china.

Bow was presenting its own vigorous interpretations of Dresden basket figures by 1756, the early ones distinguished by their flat rectangular bases until in 1758 Bow set the fashion for pierced scroll-work bases, giving the lead to Chelsea and Derby. But Bow never achieved quite the perfection of finish that distinguishes very similar Chelsea work, for only at Chelsea, it seems, did the assembler go over the surface of the figure with a wet brush before firing.

Derby had its own technique for these figures, achieving a thin-glazed brittle delicacy in keeping with their dessert table setting. The folds of their garments may be almost knife-edged and the glaze never accumulated in the slight blobs associated with Chelsea work. Their flowery dress, often lined with a rich crushed-strawberry pink, required little gilding beyond buttons and garment edges. It may be noticed, too, among the flowers clustering around such a Derby figure, that the petals and light green-yellow leaves are appreciably thicker than those in soft porcelain made elsewhere. Chelsea-Derby specimens of the period may be no more than slightly tinted with pale washes of greens and pinks and a clear bluish-turquoise.

When bone china revolutionised men's ideas of the possible strength and versatility of translucent ceramics there was still a demand for these figure comfit holders. From about 1800 they were made in this wholly English ware, and indeed are more English than ever in appearance and expression although less adventurous in design. They lost nothing of their delicacy in the course of firing, sharply defined forms and delicate modelling being preserved in the kiln in a manner impossible with soft porcelains, and their wealth of colour and gold is set off by flower encrustations that are a study in themselves, each petal and leaf painstakingly modelled.

Among the more notable nineteenth-century makers, Coalport issued girls and youths standing before flowering tree-stumps, holding baskets and smothered in colour and gold, with more scrolls and flowers in high relief enriching their circular bases. Some are children, their dress a romantic recollection of earlier porcelains and their baskets or staved tubs too large to carry, so that they sit instead, flower-surrounded, between the flower-entwined tubs and smaller vessels intended for toothpicks. Marked Coalport or C Dale (Colebrook-Dale), these may be dated between 1828 and the 1850s.

Derby at this time was colouring its basket figures in a notable range of delicate shades, especially between the early 1830s and about 1845. Rockingham, too, under the Brameld brothers, made charming and original bone china examples from the 1820s. John Davenport marked his work with his name, but other specimens of the period are unmarked and as yet their makers have not been identified. Indeed by the mid-nineteenth century it had become possible to obtain a less costly figure cast hollow with its basket in a single piece. For this the tiny flowers were pressed or stamped from a mould in low relief and applied in masses. They were cheap and are therefore the more numerous and less expensive today. They are attractive, nevertheless, and highly symptomatic of an age that was rapidly abandoning the simple homely pungencies of the herb garden comfit in favour of grandiose liqueur bon-bons and gaudy little pastilles, harshly perfumed and flavoured, and so quickly made that a single workman could turn out three or four hundredweight a day.

Chapter Twenty-one

VINAIGRETTES

VINAIGRETTES were the toys of fashion for little more than sixty or seventy years. Since then they have had a century of despised neglect. Yet today no book on small decorative antiques would be complete without them. They made a notably successful contribution to their period's vaunted "art-manufactures", and one of the few that was unique to those extravagantly experimental years, launched, developed, perfected and routed in defeat. At the longest estimate the whole story of the vinaigrette is contained in the years between 1770 and 1860.

The name vinaigrette was introduced in about 1800, and even then the real vogue had but newly begun. Previously a vinaigrette had been a pungent vinegar condiment: Evelyn in *Acetaria*, 1699, referred to "vinaigrets to sharpen the appetite"; but even this use of the term had become unimportant when George I's cooks introduced German notions about sauces. As late as 1801 Hannah More received from the Duchess of York "an elegant gold aromatic box" at a time when the usual name was the still clumsier "aromatic vinegar box".

It is not difficult, indeed, to trace the box's lineage back to the early Tudor pouncet box and the aromatic orange, associated with the many-spiced pomander. The principle was the same. Sponge was soaked in aromatic vinegar, compact, springy, absorbent Turkish sponge, in a vinegar concocted with rosemary, sage, mint, bitter wormwood and pungent rue. When the sponge was enclosed in an orange skin the user carried it in his hand, but when Henry VIII introduced the jewelled pouncet box this might fit the head of an ebony staff, or hang from the waist on a long cord. By the 1660s it was known as a sponge box, and already the eventual vinaigrette design was foreshadowed by a box that was circular, like an exceedingly deep snuff box, and neither small nor dainty, but had the vinaigrette's arrangement of double lids hinging on the same pin, so that the sharp fragrance could be enjoyed through the inner perforated grille or preserved under the outer, tight-fitting lid.

We can find pictures of pouncet boxes on Holbein portraits, and of sponge boxes on mid-eighteenth-century trade cards, but we can find vinaigrettes themselves among family bygones and in the secondhand shop, awaiting the arbitrary change in date that will transform them into antiques. At present this date is 1830, when vinaigrettes in vast numbers were coming on to the market.

It is easy to be over specific regarding the dates of these various attempts to cope with the ill-odours endured even by the well-to-do throughout all centuries until our own. In fact, the early Tudor aromatic oranges continued in some demand until the end of the seventeenth century, and sponge boxes were used in the nineteenth century, and, to add to the confusion, were called pouncet boxes during the early years of that century when girls' heads were dizzy with Scott's historical romances.

The sponge box had a rival, too, in the essence box. This design has only a single, lift-off lid, without a hinge, and whatever favoured perfume emerged through its decorative grille was contained in a rectangular pastille of scented rice starch, magnesium carbonate and powdered orris root. But the real advance towards the vinaigrette was the evolution of a more powerful vinegar with a basis of strong acetic acid, that could be sweetened with concentrated perfume oils.

This advance may be dated to the 1770s, with a further improvement in the 1820s. The delicate scent of some of these early nineteenth-century toilet vinegars still lingers in many Nailsea toilet table flasks. Mint, rosemary, juniper, sage, mace, cinnamon, lavender, lemon and cloves in various combinations might supply essential oils for scenting the acetic acid and alcohol base, as well as more strident camphor and rue. The result was that the sponge and its receptacle could be more effective and at the same time much smaller—and that sighing and fainting and similar manifestations of sensibility could be cultivated without fear of losing their effect through undignified resuscitation with cold water or burnt feathers.

It is to be expected, then, that the earliest vinaigrettes we find suggest too-small sponge boxes, round or oval, their lids flat-chased or bright cut. But much-used hinges are better suited by straight-edged boxes, and in this case there was acid involved, to corrode any metal less resistant than gold, so that the majority of specimens in an average collection are likely to be in the more or less rectangular box designs that gradually replaced these small experiments of the late eighteenth century.

Always the box is small and slim, and essentially perfectly-lidded to guard the volatile contents. Inside the lid is a perforated grid, to retain the vinegar-soaked sponge when the box is opened, both lid and grid swinging on the same seven-lug hinge. This is the basic design, small and simply treated around 1800, becoming more adventurous and more ornate as goldsmiths and silversmiths explored its possibilities, but lighter in weight as factories took over from master craftsmen in Regency years, often acquiring a fob or chain in the 1830s, and finally becoming more massive and pompous in appearance in the late 1830s and the 1840s, staid and solid as the matronly women who might still be seen, as Charlotte Brontë mentions in *Jane Eyre*, "offering vinaigrettes and wielding fans". By the 1850s double bottles of coloured glass were available, stoppered at both ends to provide new artificial perfume and new solid smelling salts, and vinaigrettes were faced with extinction.

So much for a general outline. As in so many small toys of Regency and early Victorian days the favoured materials and manufacturing methods largely fashioned their own pattern of changing design and ornament. This may be traced in any considerable collection despite the individual characteristics that show up to interrupt this pattern, and despite the contrasts between hand craftsmanship in traditional techniques and the new bustling factory output, a contrast never displayed more strikingly and never felt more intensely than during the years under review.

The vinaigrette may be regarded as a piece of jewellery, and indeed many vinaigrettes are lockets, too. But it comes in a category all its own, because its whole purpose was to contain, with lasting safety, extremely potent acid. Silver and all base metals were quickly corroded by it: only gold, glass and various gemstones suffer it unharmed. Very occasionally we may find a gold specimen. One I have seen with particular pleasure is a small heart—not a later pompous, flower-engraved silver heart design but one that could be worn like a locket, hanging from the loops of an encircling snake and thus dating itself to the early nineteenth century "snake period". A late gold specimen was shaped as a skull, exhibited in 1851 by Phillips Brothers of Cockspur Street.

Sometimes the gold is enamelled and may even be mounted with small diamonds, for this is the vinaigrette at its most exclusive and expensive. For the same reason the design tends to avoid the conventional box, and we find a thimble, perhaps, or a basket, or even a ring for the smallest of vinaigrettes, twinkling with jewels. One in the Christie collection has a hinged circular lid only ⅜ inch across, with a flat amethyst centre encircled by pearls and more amethysts. Other vinaigrettes are hidden in seals. There was a costly late Georgian vogue for a vinaigrette mounted on a tiny musical box.

An effective alternative is the use of gold for the sides of the box and for the grille—the most exquisite of grilles, these, pierced and engraved with birds, flowers, foliage —combined with top and base in well-striated agate, or cornelian, topaz, or glowing bloodstones. Pearl shell combines brilliantly with gold in interesting imitative "toy" shapes. Sometimes part of the box is porcelain, or the opaque white glass easily mistaken for it, or clear cut-glass: the vinaigrette designed as a locket may have a small glass window at the back to disclose a curl of hair. Any of these would probably be sold in a leather case to preserve the soft gold from the rub of wear.

Occasionally, too, a specimen may be found in the gold-coloured alloy known as pinchbeck, but even this had to be covered thickly in gold and was more usefully replaced by silver that would show some warning when the gold wore thin. In silver, too, after the mid-1820s the metal might be combined with more colourful materials such as a step-cut panel of agate, cornelian, amethyst, onyx or bloodstone. Somewhat later the whole box might be made from such stones with silver mounts and grid. One of my own favourites is in that sparkling amber-coloured glass known as aventurine, but the pale blue opalescent gemstone known as Uttoxeter paste was an equally popular alternative. Or a cairngorm may be found, set in the lid of a vinaigrette shaped as a tiny silver-mounted horn, a miniature of the Scottish snuff-mull.

Any collection of vinaigrettes today is likely to be composed mainly of silver specimens, some gilded all over, but all invariable double or treble gilded inside the box and on both sides of the grille. Birmingham became the great centre for silver vinaigrettes, the city's watch-case makers turning out great numbers between 1810 and the 1850s.

Hall-marks are often helpful in dating these. Sometimes the marks are found inside the lid, but when this is polished mirror-bright they are often on the front edge of the case or on the base. Then only the standard mark and maker's mark are inside the lid, and only one or other of these on the inner grille. These marks indicate that even by the mid-1770s Birmingham had still no part in their manufacture, for the Assay Office, established in 1773, makes no record of them in its 1777 list.

Any good silver book will help in the interpretation of these marks. Birmingham's city mark is the anchor, sometimes struck horizontally, and for a full set of marks this should be accompanied by the lion passant gardant, the date letter, which was changed each year on July 1, the maker's mark and, from 1784 to 1890, the duty mark. For the date letter the full alphabet was used, a different letter for each year until the alphabet was all used, then beginning again in another style of type. The only exception was the letter J, easily confused with I: this was used only for the cycles dated 1798–9 to 1823–4, and 1849–50 to 1874–5. The shapes of the punch marks as well as the styles of type help to distinguish between the later cycles, but some are easily confused nonetheless.

The duty mark is an outline of the monarch's head, so that here, too, changes may be noted, usually somewhat belated—William IV's head appeared in 1834 and Victoria's in 1839. Sometimes assay marks of the years 1797–8 include the head stamped twice because duty was doubled that year. Usually the head was in an oval shield but more often followed the shape of the head between 1797 and 1812.

Fig. 23. Birmingham hall-mark used during the twelvemonth July 1, 1834 to June 30, 1835: king's head duty mark; anchor, Birmingham's town mark; lion passant of sterling silver; date letter (L in black-letter caps); maker's mark. These may appear in any order. The duty head appeared 1784–1890 sometimes struck twice in 1797–98 when duty was doubled. From 1797 to 1812 the punch outline most usually followed the head outline. There was delay in changing: William IV appeared on Birmingham work only in 1834, and Victoria in 1839. Until 1821 the lion was passant gardant, head turned outwards: since 1821 it has looked ahead. The date letter was changed on July 1 each year, working through the alphabet from A to Z, then beginning again in another style of lettering. Full alphabets were used for the years 1798–99 to 1823–24 and 1849–50 to 1874–75, but for the other year-cycles a twenty-five letter alphabet was used, omitting J.

Among makers' marks may be mentioned the initials of Matthew Linwood, Joseph Taylor, and also Taylor and Perry, John Shaw, John Lawrence, Samuel Pemberton, Joseph Wilmore, Gervase Wheeler, Nathaniel Mills and Cocks and Bettridge. London makers associated with the London assay marks of lion passant gardant or lion passant and the leopard's head include Peter and Ann Bateman, William Fountain, Thomas Holland, Thomas Robins.

Many silver vinaigrettes, of course, are not hall-marked. The reason is involved and interesting. In about 1830 the silversmiths Wardell and Simpson introduced a fashion for hanging the vinaigrette on a chain or fob. A tiny collared eye was soldered to one of the shorter ends of the rectangular vinaigrette (the top or right side according to the way of the ornament on the box) and fitted with a loose ring. Less frequently a fine chain was attached to both sides of the box. This was a period when high necked dress made it difficult to display a jewellery locket, and the dangling vinaigrette served this purpose, too. The prolific Samuel Pemberton had a liking for them, ornamented with the word SOUVENIR or the inevitable and not very decorative spray of forget-me-nots. But from our point of view the trouble is that these vinaigrettes were classed as lockets by the assay offices, and as such did not have to be hall-marked or subjected to duty payment. Many of these unmarked vinaigrettes prove to be of poor quality silver that would never have passed the test of assay.

Sheffield plate is found, too, in silver shapes. It is of little account to the collector, however, once it reveals itself by the warm glow of its copper core.

Silver vinaigrettes make a fascinating study in themselves. Early specimens until, say, the end of the Regency years, are the most interesting as small expressions of their period's toys. Some are the extremely plain small ovals of late eighteenth-century fashion, associated with such excessively famous factory silversmiths as the Bateman family. But it is among specimens of this period that we find, for example, the door knobs and verge watch outlines, some early reticules and purses (more were made in the 1820s), the early book shapes by Matthew Linwood, the smooth spun egg and acorn shapes opened by unscrewing like tiny nutmeg graters, the curling snail and cowrie shells, perhaps engraved on the back with merman or other sea creature, and some of the more attractive fish. Even among fish of this inventive period there is a world of difference, to modern eyes at least, between the heavily-built big-headed creature like a whale and the lithe, curved dolphin, even though both are in the segmented flexible design and both date to late Regency years.

In silver vinaigrettes of the 1820s and 1830s we find an increasing use of substantial flower and foliage ornament, engraved at first against matted grounds, then embossed and chased. Sometimes this is enriched with applied cast ornament or, in work of the 1830s onwards, given a very similar appearance by machine-pressed embossing. Such ornament could achieve an impression of costliness and yet in reality be thin, light and correspondingly inexpensive. This more aggressive decoration is frequently contrasted with that most impersonal, restrained and peculiarly satisfying form of ornament known as engine-turning. A vinaigrette shaped as a book, or two books, by Gervase Wheeler, for instance, may have chased rosettes on a matted ground as spine ornament and engine-turning on the covers.

This insistence on all-over ornament is in tune with the period's opinions, but to the factory silversmith its purpose was to make the best of the thinly rolled silver, giving it slight additional strength and masking the dents and scratches of wear. A moulded thumb piece may take some of the rub of use. The more imaginative among these vinaigrettes have pictorial ornament on their lids—curlew in a landscape, a tramp and his dog—and by the late 1830s castings of historical buildings were in production.

The early Victorian work is attractive in a heavier, more florid manner. Nathaniel Mills made many of the cathedral, castle and mansion boxes, and must have made them well for so many to remain. He ornamented snuff-boxes, too, in this way and even silver cases for visiting cards. But these magnificent buildings cast in high relief—especially Windsor Castle—appear on vinaigrettes by Thomas Spice, too, and John Shaw, Taylor and Perry and N. Morrison. The design usually fills the whole of the rectangular lid, with engine turning on the sides and base.

It is typical of this late work that the box seldom deviates far from the rectangular outline. The ovals and globes of the 1800s were long forgotten, and the snails and barrels and travelling chests and foxes' masks generally left to the few craftsmen working in the old traditions of the master silversmiths. This is easily explained by the factory processes involved, of course, but at the same time reflects closely the trends in texture and outline found throughout domestic design of the period.

Many late Georgian vinaigrettes are comparatively uninteresting at first glance. But they become brilliantly individual when the outer lid is opened. Gold vinaigrettes set the style of inner grille or grid that long remained the most exquisite detail in the less expensive designs. Some of the most delicate are in the silver filigree of the early 1800s found, for instance, in work by John Shaw of Birmingham. Other grids are pictorial: I have even seen one showing H.M.S. *Victory* and rejoicing over Trafalgar, and there are endless groups of swans in reeds and other birds, baskets of flowers, leaping fish, bowls of fruit, cornucopias, and handsome heraldic motifs. Piercing and engraving are often enhanced by the sparkle of bright cutting and, occasionally, by embossing.

Even from the mid-1820s, however, there was a tendency to shape the holes by tool piercing instead of the earlier hand-saw frets, and all too soon the Victorian factory silversmiths were using up all their enthusiasm on the vinaigrette's cover and, for reasons of cost, were leaving the grid comparatively plain. The holes are round, drilled in a concentric rectangle, perhaps, or from corner to corner in a St. Andrew's cross. Sometimes, too, such a grid is found as a shockingly disappointing replacement in an earlier vinaigrette, and then we suddenly realise how far we have come from the vinaigrette's brief spell of perfection and how easily the sturdy mid-Victorian could dispense with its small service.

Index

(*Plates are indicated by italic figures.*)

MORE SMALL DECORATIVE ANTIQUES

A. Fruit stand, dishes and plates in green-glaze ware. The dish (*upper left*) shows a favourite design suggesting basket-ware covered with leaves.

Frontispiece

THERLE HUGHES

MORE SMALL DECORATIVE ANTIQUES

BOOKPLAN

First published 1962

CONTENTS

ACKNOWLEDGMENTS

I am particularly grateful to the owners of the pieces illustrated in colour for permitting me to borrow these for photography: to Mrs. C. A. L. French, Dr. Nigel Loring, Miss Mabel Aldridge and Miss Moira F. Doolan. The group on the jacket is from the Bethnal Green Museum, assembled with the generous assistance of the Curator, Mr. C. M. Weekley.

The black and white plates include many pieces in private collections, and I here acknowledge appreciatively their owners' kindness in allowing me to use them as illustrations.

LIST OF ILLUSTRATIONS

COLOUR PLATES

BLACK AND WHITE PLATES *between pages 128 and 129*

6. Green-glaze Wedgwood leaf dishes and jug; Wedgwood cauliflower soup plate; pineapple coffee pot.

7. Silver caddy ladles, including tea leaves, shell and jockey cap; *and* caddy ladles including a hand shape and a heavy vine casting (*all Messrs. Delieb Antiques Ltd.*).

8. Silver caddy ladles, including Onslow and fiddle handle designs (*Messrs. Delieb Antiques Ltd.*); Georgian mote skimmer (*Victoria and Albert Museum*).

9. Cottages in bone china made as pastille burners and night-light shelters (*Messrs. Delomosne and Son*).

10. Cottages for an inexpensive market, including a "crime piece", villa and church (*all Brighton Museum*).

11. Tunbridge ware: late 17th century backgammon board (*Victoria and Albert Museum*); view of the Pantiles in Tunbridge ware mosaic.

12. Tunbridge ware souvenirs *and* boxes showing cube mosaic and marble veneer (*all Tunbridge Wells Museum*).

13. Birds in porcelain: white partridges and parrot by Chelsea (*Cecil Higgins Museum, Bedford*); Chelsea mandarin duck and hen harrier (*in the collection of Her Majesty the Queen*).

14. Bow porcelain pheasants *and* three Bow parrots (*all Messrs. Christie, Manson and Woods*).

15. Derby model of a peacock *and* birds on a Longton Hall perfume vase (*both Victoria and Albert Museum*); Plymouth hard paste porcelain phoenixes (*Wernher Collection, Luton Hoo*).

16. Birds in earthenware: cock and hen *and* hawk (*Victoria and Albert Museum*); exceptionally well-modelled cock.

17. Birds modelled by Chelsea as covered tureens: crested duck (*Cecil Higgins Museum*); hen with chicks (*Victoria and Albert Museum*).

18. Door knockers: wrought iron, late 16th century; cast iron, late 18th century, *and* brass of the late 18th and early 19th centuries (*The General Trading Company*).

27. Lustre jugs: with silver lustre subsidiary to a gay coaching scene (*Brighton Museum*); with the purplish mottling of Sunderland ware; patterned in silver resist lustre; with silver resist as background to chinoiserie scene in blue (*all Messrs. Delomosne and Son*).

28. Copper lustre mugs, jugs, goblet and shaving dish (*all Sunderland Museum*).

29. Sweetmeat vessel and teapot *and* lidded basket with encrusted ornament, all in Belleek mother of pearl lustre (*all in the collection of Mrs. Kenneth Symes*).

30. Coventry woven picture ribbons made by Thomas Stevens, "The Good Old Days" and "The Present Time" (*in the collection of B. W. Blades, Esq.*).

31. Coventry woven picture ribbons: "The Start", a horse racing scene, and "Are You Ready ?", showing the Oxford and Cambridge boat race (*in the collection of Mrs. C. A. L. French*).

32. Perfume sprinkler shaped as a watering can in a Spode japan pattern; flat dishes in piecrust ware for stewed fruit (*all Hanley Museum*).

33. Wedgwood game pie dishes in cane-coloured stoneware known as piecrust ware (*Hanley Museum*).

34. Victorian lockets shaped as hearts, padlocks, purse, etc. (*in the collection of Richard Ogden, Esq.*).

35. Tortoiseshell set with gold in 18th century piqué work: étuis and snuffboxes.

36. English piqué work in silver on ivory and in gold on tortoiseshell.

37. Money boxes in earthenware: two hens with their chicks *and* two moneypots in red earthenware (*Victoria and Albert Museum*); cottage design with figures of boy and girl (*Brighton Museum*); cottage and figures in "Pratt ware" (*Victoria and Albert Museum*).

46. Wedding fan richly painted on finely pierced sticks (*in the collection of Mr. and Mrs. Marshall R. Anspach*); cabriolet fan with double mount (*in the collection of Her Majesty the Queen*).

47. Fans with pictorial ornament: with a stipple engraving after Adam Buck (*in the collection of Mrs. George Neilson*); with country house scene and carved pearl sticks (*Victoria and Albert Museum*); marriage fan for the Princess Anne, 1733; medallion bridal fan of the mid-1770s.

48. All-white fan with lace mount and ivory sticks, 19th century; brisé fan painted with Mrs. Fitzherbert and the Prince of Wales.

Line Diagram

Chapter One

STAFFORDSHIRE BLUE

COOL and gracious as the old oak furniture on which it looks its loveliest, yet with the homely welcome of chintz at a lattice window, Staffordshire blue china claims an unshakable but remarkable position in the collector's affections. Much of it, post-dating 1830, is not yet even acknowledged as antique, yet the "picturesque views" decorating plate and jug and soup tureen record an utterly vanished world. The familiar blue ornament ranges from Don Quixote illustrations to romantic Italian scenes, from Grecian, Persian and Oriental patterns to American landscapes, yet the results remain as essentially English as the rich borders of roses and acorns and shells that collectors today try to recognise as the various makers' "signatures". Most of this ware was manufactured for a comparatively low-price market and for tough everyday service, yet now its value has soared. Indeed, few collectors' pieces cover such a gigantic price range: quite lovely specimens are still to be found for ten shillings—some for as little as half a crown. Yet an American view may sell for several hundred pounds.

Fundamentally the term Staffordshire blue covers all manner of more or less translucent bone china and opaque earthenwares and stonewares decorated in innumerable tones and shades of blue. But collectors discover that practically all their finds come under the heading of useful wares, the decoration applied not by the old style of costly hand painting but by the quick inexpensive mass-production method of transfer printing. Even the choice of colour began as a manufacturer's necessity, for the heat required to fix the glaze ruined many shades. In the 1830s the method was used with black and various tones of green, red and yellow but these never ousted the more satisfying blue.

Perhaps the most important reason for the tremendous development of the ware in the early 19th century is to be found in the quality of the ceramic itself which became identified with the giant production of Staffordshire blue. Wedgwood had delighted the world with his strong white pearlware, developed in the 1770s from the earlier cream-coloured earthenwares. But when felspar replaced china clay in the formula the result was a hard white stoneware, compact-textured, light in the hands, with a rich ringing tone when tapped. As the potters succeeded in achieving greater heat in their kilns they found they could quickly give this stoneware a hard but manageable surface: this showed the transferred print clearly in every detail yet would receive and hold a fine glaze.

The glaze that was evolved specifically for this work was known as printing body, and is another notable feature contributing to the deserved and hard-won success of this ware. This is a lead glaze, intensely hard and glossy, resistant to acids and the cracks and crazings that tend to reduce old earthenwares to the awful condition called "quaint".

Thomas Turner of Caughley as early as the 1770s developed the revolutionary idea of printing under the glaze on inexpensive wares in the way introduced for ornamenting such small *galanteries* as enamel snuff boxes and applied at Worcester on 18th-century porcelain by the renowned Robert Hancock. In this way a design engraved on a copper plate could be printed, in a single colour, on to a huge number of transfer papers and thus conveyed to pieces of earthenware with a speed and cheapness previously unimagined. William Adams of Cobridge introduced the method to Staffordshire in 1775 and in about 1780 Josiah Spode developed its underglaze application so that many generations of scullery maids should not obliterate those dainty shepherdesses under April skies or the endless pursuit of Oriental lovers over the bridge of willow pattern fantasy.

The copper-plate engraver's skill is easily taken for

granted in this work. It is interesting to observe the early technique in heavy line engraving practised by Hancock, taught to Thomas Turner at Caughley and thence spreading to the innumerable master engravers of Staffordshire and their anonymous employees who include such important firms as Sherwin, Hordley and Sherwin.

A less obvious skill in the development of this craft was the blending of suitable ink. The tricky, costly cobalt-derived zaffre and smalt of the 18th century were soon abandoned after the invention in 1802 of an artificial ultramarine by the French chemist Thénard, a substitute that cost a penny an ounce in 1817 as compared with genuine ultramarine at more than thirty pounds. Perhaps equally important, however, and least likely to be realised today by the collector, was the development of suitable paper, made by the new Fourdrinier machine, for conveying the ink from the engraved copper plate to the surface of the stoneware. The firm of R. & J. Clews who worked a pottery at Cobridge from 1817 declared in 1820: "Had not an improvement taken place in the manufacture of the tissue paper, the new style of engraving would have been useless, as the paper previously was too coarse to draw from the engraved plate anything like a clear or perfect impression".

As the ceramic surface and the paper both improved a more elaborate line engraving technique developed with the lines cut to different depths, and by about 1810 fine mass effects were being achieved by the inclusion of stipple on the same engraved copper plate. So perfect was the method by Regency days that remarkably delicate effects of light and shade, of three-dimensional solidity and distance could be produced within the limits of the single colour. Not until the 1840s did the quality decline, at a time when the pencil-drawing effects of lithography in six-colour printing were ousting the sharply articulate copper-plate engraving.

From a purely technical point of view it is interesting to note how cleverly the engravings were designed so that the transfer prints should cover plate or hollow-ware without leaving any large white spaces to reveal imperfections in the stoneware itself. Puffy clouds fill the skies, and in the foreground figures and water appear while the borders are loaded with detail, mainly consisting of flowers and leaves and other naturalistic motifs in the exact, full manner of the early 19th century. A piece of hollow-ware such as a jug or sugar bowl may be ornamented with three or four different pictures on inner and outer surfaces. On a table service there are at least a dozen different but related subjects as the main pictorial decoration, all richly framed in matching borders. On the backs, temptingly inaccessible during the meal, titles are frequently supplied, giving details both of the series and of the individual pictures, but not, unfortunately, by any means always naming the maker.

At the time when the finest of this work was appearing on the market—say between 1815 and 1840—the main decoration was not so much a pattern or design as an honest attempt at a picture. Many of these favourite blue and white subjects are cathedrals, famous London buildings, English watering places, and above all the "picturesque views" that, with the fact-loving, topographical-minded early 19th century, rivalled the alternative romantic escapist "Italian" landscapes, Oriental imaginings and the tamely pretty rural domestic scenes then threatened by the march of industrialism. At least one artist was sent to America to make drawings for such decoration to help the export trade at a period when these English views would be likely to prove unwelcome. Well might the potters be startled at the prices such pieces command today.

This is a fascinating subject. In the United States, too, the old rural communities and pleasant small townships were being threatened by industrial expansion, and the desire to retain some record of the vanishing beauty was rivalled only by an upsurging pride in state achievements. Some of the most interesting and highly valued plates and serving platters bear the arms of various states and yet link them with their period by landscape backgrounds and closely patterned naturalistic flower borders. Others show valued old buildings such as New York's Columbia College or the original St. Patrick's Cathedral or typically pleasant views of Columbus, say, or Chillicothe, Ohio, from early 18th-century prints, or Albany, New York, in colonial days.

It was not difficult to obtain engravings: apart from other

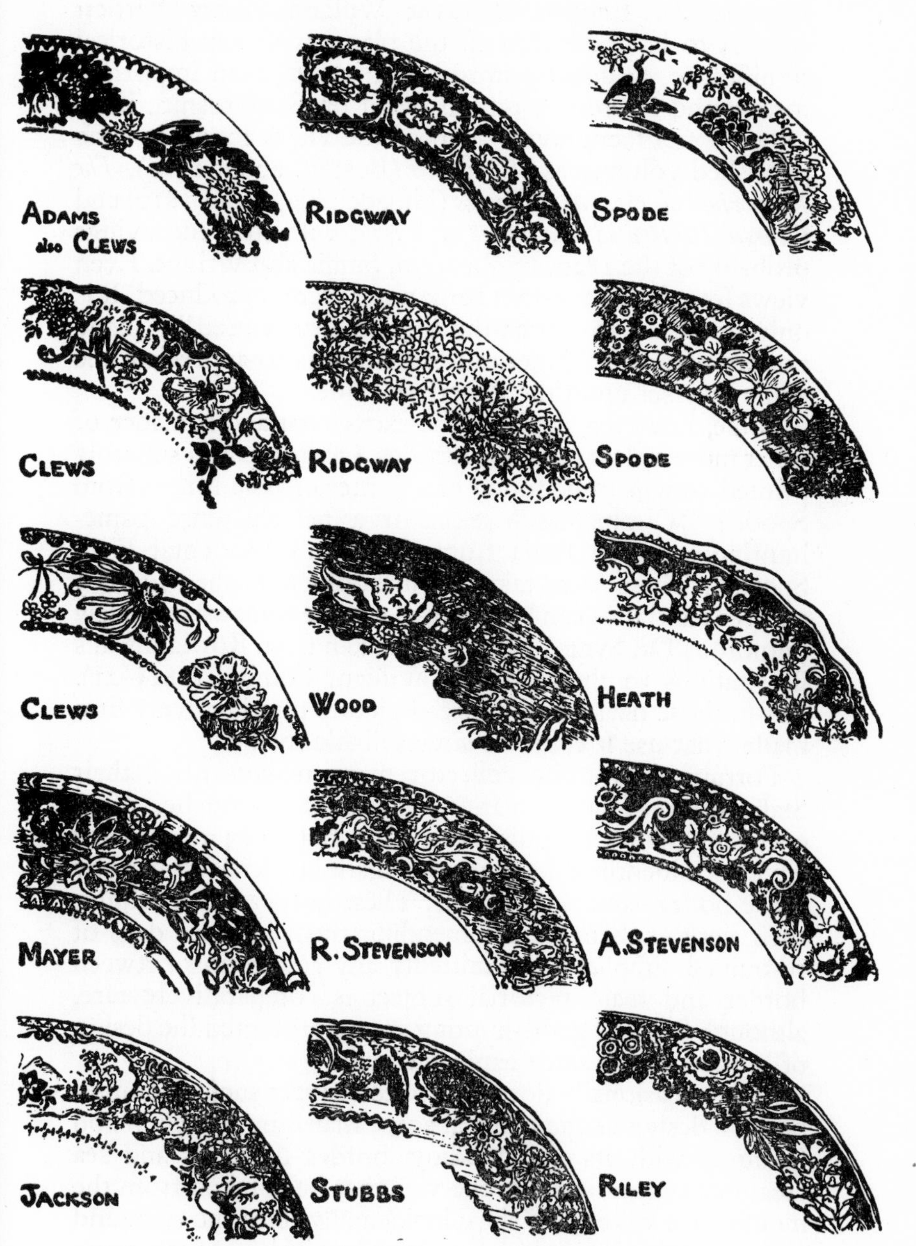

Fig. 1. Transfer-printed blue and white plate borders.

sources, the English engraver William Henry Bartlett appears to have covered all the places with any historical significance, frequently introducing water as an important foreground interest, a typical detail on Staffordshire blue. Other potters' engravers adapted the views found in such published volumes as *Polyanthus* (Boston, about 1810), *The Emporium of Arts and Sciences* (Philadelphia, about 1810) and *Georgia Illustrated in a Series of Views*, with steel engravings probably of the 1820s by Rawdon, Smilie and Wright. Even views found on American bank notes were reproduced. It is only necessary to notice the printed marks used by many potters with their American eagle motifs to appreciate the value they set upon the American trade.

Some, however, depicted the excitement and romance of other more or less remote countries. Occasionally a superbly printed view is to be found of a corner of Asia Minor from Spode's "Caramanian" series or a naïvely tense game-hunting scene in India from this firm's "Oriental Field Sports". These were taken from books published in 1803 and 1805 and thus can be dated, as can the somewhat crudely humorous Dr. Syntax adventures taken from Rowlandson's illustrations to the verses of William Combes (1815–21). But in those days of widespread picture pirating every firm made what use it chose of any available theme.

Fortunately for the collector many makers titled their Staffordshire blue in various styles of cartouche, often enclosing minute or indistinct initials. But many more pieces have been identified by the extravagant borders favoured by those potters and their clients. These borders are a delight, their very exuberance commending them in these days of restrained simplicity. Admittedly any association between border and main pictorial subject is comparatively rare, although Spode's game-hunting scenes prompted the design of borders in the same explosive vein.

Only occasionally does the collector meet such a comprehensive design as the nautical scene issued by Enoch Wood (plate 2) with its surrounding border of shells and sea creatures suggesting that the view has been taken from the mouth of a cave. The ship, incidentally, flies the stars and stripes, indicating a bid for American sales. Much more often the border designer could give his imagination full play, whether with massed effects of rose or oak leaves or with such simple symbolism as a combination of corn and olive and vine, all in the rich profusion of the period.

Fig. 2. Top row: Four Caughley marks (S for Salopian); Minton and Boyle (1836–41); Minton and Hollins (1844–76). Second row: E. Wood and Sons (1818–*c.*1846); J. Clews (1818–29); Stubbs and Kent (1798–1829); two arrow marks of J. Shorthose (to 1823). Third row: Four of the Meigh pottery, Hanley (1790–1902): Job Meigh and Son (1812–35); Charles Meigh and Son (1851–60); Old Hall Earthenware Co. Ltd. (1862–87); Hicks and Meigh, Shelton (1810–35).

It must not be imagined, however, that it is possible to attribute most Staffordshire blue to individual makers or even dates. Although little more than a hundred years old it is often tantalisingly untraceable. Just because a few well-known potters are particularly associated with all that is best-loved in this ware it is sometimes forgotten that it was produced in thousands of tons by innumerable manufacturers. Here it is only possible to mention a few notable contributors.

Beginning as early as the 1780s, Josiah Spode, father and son, made some of what is now considered technically the most perfect, in the most lovely luminous blue. Designs include the "Tiber", "Lucano" and similar views in the romantic Italian mood, the "Indian Field Sports" and "Caramanian" series already mentioned and such widely different individual designs as the "Milkmaid" introduced in 1814, the "Warwick vase" (1821), "Waterloo" (1818) and the "Gothic Castle"—in a Chinese setting. The elder Spode was an early maker of willow pattern and it is a find indeed when a specimen of his first design comes to light with only one figure on the bridge. (See Spode marks, p.56.)

Fig. 3. Top row: C. Harvey and Sons (1799–1853); J. and R. Riley (*c*.1802–26); W. Hackwood and Son (1818–56); W. and J. Harding (1864–69). Second row: Two marks of the Ridgway firm, Shelton: J. and W. Ridgway (1814–30); John Ridgway (1834–40); W. Ratcliff (1837–*c*.1840). Third row: T. and R. Boote (1842–); Middlesbrough Pottery (1834–52); Don Pottery, Swinton (1790–1893); Barkers and Kent Ltd. (1889–).

The name *WOOD* or *E. WOOD & SONS BURSLEM WARRANTED* or merely *EW & S* may be found impressed on a piece of high quality Staffordshire blue, the first indicating a date prior to 1818. Continuing until 1846 this Enoch Wood and his sons produced a remarkable range of more than five hundred views, English, French, American, of London, of fashionable spas, of cathedrals, castles and country estates. Rivalling Spode and Wood for delightful colouring was Andrew Stevenson of Cobridge. Between 1810 and 1817 he issued more than thirty English scenes as well as much work for the American market where he had his own young artist W. G. Wall sketching views for him on the spot. As well as borders of large flowers, roses and leaves and later a wide vine leaf design he sometimes included medallion portraits in the border detail.

Confusingly, another Stevenson, Ralph, worked at Cobridge between 1815 and 1840, enclosing his English views in particularly handsome acorn and oak leaf borders and his American views in vine leaf designs. A few of his early pieces are impressed with the one word *STEVENSON* but mostly lack even that aid to identification. In the late 1820s, however, he was joined by W. Williams and they used the marks *RSW* and *R. STEVENSON & WILLIAMS*.

Fig. 4. Marks of A. Stevenson (1810–18); Dimmock and Co. (*c.* 1840–80); William Adderley Ltd. (1870s–).

Yet another firm known to have issued nearly two hundred "English", "Picturesque", "Select" and similarly popular views was that of James and Ralph Clews, successors to Andrew Stevenson from early in 1817. But today they are more especially associated with three other series, each enormously popular at the time and still to be found and treasured. The "Three Tours of Doctor Syntax" already mentioned cover some eighty Rowlandson designs easily identified. The "Don Quixote" series runs to about twenty subjects in appropriate borders while their other favourite, "The Pictures of Sir David Wilkie", a series of twelve, includes such familiar scenes as "Playing at Draughts" and "The Valentine". The Clews firm issued more than seventy-two American views including a series of twelve with scalloped borders carrying the names of fifteen states with stars between. Another twelve "Picturesque Views" on the Hudson river are from Wall's engravings made in 1823.

Some attractive milkmaid scenes came from Joseph

Stubbs of Longport. Here again a named piece is a rarity, but possibly his English series may be recognised by borders of leaves and pointed scrolls. His successor from 1834, Thomas Mayer, edged some of his views with fine lace decoration set in borders of vine leaves and trumpet flowers. His table ware is rimmed with narrow edge decoration of classic husk and spoked circles. Significantly, Mayer's printed mark, one of the largest found on English ceramics, is one of the many adaptations of the American eagle motif with a scroll from its beak bearing the familiar phrase *E PLURIBUS UNUM*. Another user of lace effects was Ralph Hall of Tunstall while a distinctive flower

Fig. 5. Marks used by the firm of William Adams of Greenfield (early 1820s–1865).

and leaf border with wide reserves containing children and goats was much used by John and William Ridgway, associated with views of Oxford and Cambridge colleges.

Such firms were but a few of those engaged on this spectacularly successful work. It would be possible to mention many others, such as E. J. Phillips & Company of Longport who produced the Eton College series, the Adams family who issued innumerable series of English churches, castles and manor houses and ambitious multi-coloured American designs marked with lively American eagles. Job Ridgway, established at Hanley by 1794, was producing Staffordshire blue from 1817, clear and unblurred but lighter in tone than that of his rivals. The great Minton firm made Staffordshire blue from 1798. Minute initials incorporated in the title cartouches help in dating: *M*, 1822–36; *M & B* (Minton and Boyle), 1836–41; *M & Co.*, 1841–44; *M & H*, Minton and Hollins, 1845–61. There was a change from *Minton* to *Mintons* in 1883. *England* included in a mark post-dates 1891.

Other well-known makers include Charles Meigh of Hanley, J. & J. Jackson of Burslem, Thomas Green of Fenton and many others. Indeed, some "old" Staffordshire blue is still being manufactured: after leaving the factory this may be given signs of wear that deceive the unwary. In general, however, modern reproductions tend to lack the surprising lightness of late 18th century work. More important, they usually fail to delight the eye with the subtleties of glowing colour that will make old Staffordshire blue live on when the modern work has long fallen out of fashion.

Chapter Two

POSY HOLDERS

WHEN the Guild of Blacksmiths in Cromwellian days entertained their wives and families to dinner "nosegays and twinings" were listed on the bill; a century later the Pewterers' Company paid fifteen shillings for nosegays on their election day. From earliest times the fastidious have sought to escape the ill-odours of their environment and the jubilant to proclaim their happiness by surrounding themselves with flower fragrance. When plague was at its most terrible in London, pungent rosemary went up in price from a shilling an armful to six shillings a posy handful, although some preferred "a nosegay made of the tasselled end of a ship's rope".

In other chapters I have written of our ancestors' delight in perfume, Elizabethan pomander and Georgian smelling bottle being succeeded by the astonishing wealth of sweetness enjoyed by the well-to-do Victorian. But none of these fragrant toys proved as lastingly appreciated as the heady sweetness of a flower nosegay. Now old-fashioned pinks and sweet williams are in vogue again, flowers that perfectly recall the vanished art of creating a Victorian posy.

Late Victorians with their unwieldy shop-made bouquets killed this charming forerunner of modern flower-arrangement studies, but it is fully time for a revival, and for an excuse to bring back into use one of the Victorians' most beguiling small inventions, the flower holder of the jewellers' catalogue, now cherished by collectors as the posy holder. This attractive little vessel, some three to five inches long, now ranks as a collector's piece, but how it cries out to be primed with shapely, fragrant flowers—violets, lilies of the valley, the Victorians' adored moss rose. Such essays in floral art were immensely important to the Victorian young lady, as artistic accomplishments and as expressions of a hundred moods and emotions too exquisite for clumsy words. William Powell Frith perfectly caught the spirit of the task in his painting of the 1850s, "Making a Posy", now in the Birmingham City Art Gallery.

There might be a perfectly round camellia in the centre, perhaps, surrounded by concentric rings or patterns of colour, with maidenhair fern or dodder grass and sweetly scented geranium leaves to lighten and edge the little dome or cone of flower heads. All would be tightly bound so as to remain fresh and sweet through the jostle and heat of a ball.

A collection of posy holders reveals many fascinating glimpses of the last century's fine craftsmanship. They are becoming rarer every year, however, in gold, silver, porcelain, tortoiseshell, mother of pearl, even in the cheapest gilt metal pressed and milled and fretted to suggest gold filigree.

Not even the artificial nosegays created at great expense by both men and women in the mid 18th century could rival the radiant fragrance of fresh flowers, and the *porte-fleur* and *porte-bouquet* have taken many forms since Nosegay Nan became arbiter of mid-Georgian fashion and the macaroni sported a buttonhole that reached his ear. Even as early as the late 1730s little gold and silver tubes were devised, merely rim-engraved, to be filled with damp sponge to keep their flowers fresh, and were important enough to be featured on trade cards of jewellers and toy-makers. At first the corsage might be made with a special pocket for such a holder, but by the 1740s a design had been evolved which included a spring dress clip.

The next obvious step was a cheaper imitation, and soon glass holders were on the market, trumpet-shaped at first, and then flattish flasks in clear flint-glass, and trumpet-shaped in common glass for the florists to sell with their nosegays. At the same time ornamental brooches were adapted to hold flowers with jewels or paste to add a dew-drop sparkle, and the fashion continued in some degree throughout most of the 19th century, as witnessed by specimens at the Great Exhibition and among the designs registered at the Patent Office to prevent copying by rival firms.

Queen Adelaide tucked fresh flowers into her sash, but it was the hand posy that most especially expressed the 19th-century's delight in flowers as refreshing "toys". Small bouquets sheathed in gold were carried by ladies of high fashion in the 1820s, as delightfully recorded by Croker in 1827: "Ladies now wear bouquets not merely in their bosoms but they carry them about in their hands as large as brooms, and when they sit down to dinner they stick their nosegays into the water glasses and the table looks like a bed of flowers". (Water glasses as distinct from tumblers are mentioned in Chapter 22.)

The posy holder was no more than the obvious development of the foil or filigree paper of the florist's bouquet, ensuring that dress and gloves should remain immaculate. Collectors recognise four main styles: the diminishing tube or trumpet-shape for long-stalked flowers, the cup with a stick or crook handle for a close pattern of flower heads, the curving cornucopia or horn of plenty, and the trumpet or cup modified into a folding tripod design that would stand when required like a vase.

Each is to be found in a variety of shape and material and ornament, from the gold of the earliest cup-and-stem patterns, supplied expensively by goldsmith and jeweller, to the cheapest of gilt-metal from the toymen of Birmingham, packed off to the spas and resorts of fashion by the dozen gross and even given away free by fashionable florists. It says much for the quality of their craftsmanship that even with the hasty manufacture and flimsy materials of their heyday these posy holders retain today a charm and individuality that make them extremely collectable. Even the occasional imitation is still to be found, proof in itself of their popularity: a delightful example in the Harris Art Gallery, Preston, has brilliant feather flowers and leaves in a holder of plaited straw.

In gold they are rarities now, sometimes set with diamonds or paste. Fabergé himself created them in gold and enamel to the commission of the Czarina, one with a cluster of flower-patterned "leaves" made to compress with a sliding ring around the posy stems, another with a cup of delicate gold "feathers". Bright & Sons of Scarborough displayed a gold and enamel specimen at the International Exhibition of 1872. Cast in gilded silver they may be set with tiny emeralds, turquoises or other touches of colour, and are finely hand-chased or engraved. Some late specimens are lined with white enamel. But when the exclusive fashion became the popular vogue the materials had to be reduced to less expensive imitations of such grandeur and in the main these are what we find today. Silver is represented by silver plate, gold occasionally by the attractive gilded alloy known as pinchbeck or priuces metal, but more often by thin gilded brass alloys generally classed asgilt-metal. Some of the most charming are wholly or partly of painted porcelain or delicate tortoiseshell, amber or mother-of-pearl.

Some early posy holders retain the tapering tube or trumpet shape of the *porte-fleur:* silversmiths tended to keep to this shape as a background, perhaps to turquoise forget-me-nots or to grapes in purple enamel. But more often the funnel is modified to take a short-stalked posy in a small cup mounted on a pencil-thin stem. A popular cup and handle design follows a tulip outline with petals to hold the posy stalks and leaves and stalk as the handle. When cast in expensive gilded pinchbeck each petal may be mounted with pavé seed pearls, and occasionally a lovely specimen turns up decorated with marcasite and enamel, with cameos, silhouettes, or even a tiny locket: these may be represented less expensively with mounts of Scotch pebbles, translucent and opaque, medallions of carved mother-of-pearl, or a reducing mirror.

Many designs suggest clusters of flowers and fruit in full relief, linked perhaps by the period's popular coiling snake. A pinchbeck holder shown at the Great Exhibition by Mr. Balleny of Birmingham had fruiting vines in deep relief on the cup and the twisted stem forming a loop handle. But a more frequent find is the less costly cup in thin steam-rolled brass alloy, each petal with its rim and collar shaped and ornamentally fret-cut in deep relief by a hand fly-press, and four or six soldered together in alternating patterns. Even in such inexpensive work the surface ornament is intricate and dainty, usually composed of flowers and leaves and birds closely interlaced.

After assembly the whole cup would be electro-gilded and perhaps polished but the fastidious woman might suspect that some taint from the underlying base metal would stain her white-gloved fingers, and the most charming of these cups have tapering pencil handles of enamel, queerly shaped coral—a delight of the sixties—turned ivory, hardstone, glass. Amber is light and warm to the fingers: mother-of-pearl refreshingly cool but so liable to slip from the grasp that the tip is usually a tiny scroll or a cluster of flowers and leaves, casually engraved. Cool handles of porcelain are painted with tiny posies: here the dominant colour note may be given by a gilt-touched ground of blue, red, yellow or green. Even among glass handles there is a range of styles to be found—coloured, engraved, colour-striped, or patterned with gilded diapers and painted flowers.

The popular mid-century alternative shape was the cornucopia, fashionable until the 1870s. This horn of plenty is a diminishing tube, curving from rim to tip. This again is a shape often made in porcelain, entirely Victorian-English but painted with cupids and flowers and touches of gilding to imitate 18th century Chelsea, or given a mark of crossed swords to suggest Dresden. Among metal cornucopias, too, one finds many with solid bodies, their ornament engraved and their note of colour introduced in semi-precious stones. Others in delicate openwork show the factory manufacturing methods already described, the segments of pattern pressed in high relief in close-set flower designs, assembled and soldered and finally gilded or silver-plated.

A welcome find is a cornucopia in the twists and curls and intertwinings of wire filigree. The wire may be gold or silver, but is more often pliant tin from the Combe Martin tin mines in North Devon, stiffened with an alloy and assembled with virtually invisible solder. In a flower-shaped cornucopia every petal and sepal is outlined with a twisted cord of the wire and filled with extremely delicate filigree flowers and leaves, soldered detail by detail, and coils of wire form a pleasant grip. F. Allen of Birmingham showed many at the Great Exhibition. By 1865, however, even filigree effects were being achieved by the gilt-metal toymen, the very twist of the filigree wires being suggested by clever use of punch and press.

Very occasionally a cornucopia is to be found with folding legs that spring out at a touch so that the posy holder may be put down without damage to the flowers. This is a development often found in funnel and cup-and-stem designs. In about 1840 the firm of Hilliard & Thomason of Birmingham offered a stem design with concealed springs that opens out into a tripod stand when the cap finial is unscrewed, the cap being secured on a guard chain. Soon the spring-operated tripod feet—often in out-curving leaf shape—could be controlled by moving a ring along what appeared when closed to be a normal slender stem.

Even then, however, the holder is seldom complete without one, often two, other small and extremely dainty, sometimes elaborate, chains. One is for the finger ring that let the posy dangle prettily during a dance, usually plain but occasionally chased, and sometimes split so as to fit any finger. A cornucopia or crook stem design may end in a loop for a ribbon. The other chain is attached to the head of a large pin passing across the cup of the holder and securing the knot of flowers, though even for this essential requirement of the posy holder there is a small range of alternatives, none, I suspect, entirely satisfactory. Sometimes the pin is split from the thick end to fit the more tightly in holes drilled for the purpose on opposite sides near the top of the cup; sometimes the pin shank is flat although still ending in a point. Sometimes in a late holder the pin is more effectively fixed, being threaded to screw into the perforation in the side of the cup.

Before this idea had been developed, however, the firm of Heeley & Sons, Birmingham, devised two more reliable alternatives. One was a series of four downward-projecting spikes inside the cup so that the flower bunch could be pushed in easily but less easily fall out. The other was a cup design consisting of separate petals or leaves that could be drawn tightly together around the flowers by moving a compressing ring. This is an attractive design found in gilded silver and occasionally in springy tortoiseshell bearing exquisite piqué ornament. Adam Dixon and Josiah Pumphrey of Birmingham patented the most convincingly effective device, however, in 1863, fitting the cup with a pair of slightly toothed spring grips that hold the flowers between them but can be pressed to open.

This improvement is also to be found on the dress *porte-fleur* which might be made to harmonise. Indeed in some examples the posy holder could be worn instead of carried, but is not improved by the long hook on one side. Such a toy all too easily loses its essential daintiness, and there is little beyond novelty to recommend, for example, the gold cornucopia claimed by its maker, Andrew Campbell of Tottenham Court Road, London, to "combine the three several uses of a dress brooch, a flower holder and a watch protector". Perhaps one should blame the mood of a period that could wear a posy of flowers high on the hips where the monstrous ball dress was caught up to accentuate the bustle.

There is a period interest even in the solid-looking little posy holder that hinges at the centre to contain a vinaigrette below the flowers and has a glass bottle for scent or salts as a handle. But all too soon, then, it could degenerate into something mundanely serviceable, instead of flaunting or whispering its nonsense among girls and their squires so well versed in the language of flowers that even a pink, according to its variety, could declare every emotion from aversion to ardent love.

Chapter Three

GREEN-GLAZE WARES

MRS. DELANY in 1752 was completely charmed by a grand ball where the ballroom was transformed into an arcadian forest of trees and rocks and rococo cascades, the musicians and singers were tricked out as idyllic shepherds and even the waiters were in "whimsical dress". Pretended rusticity was a pleasant vogue among ladies and gentlemen of fashion that lasted into the 1760s, and fortunately for us the notion returned time after time: one result has been an enduring fashion for green-glazed wares.

Elsewhere I have written of the wares in the more obvious naturalistic shapes of fruit and vegetable, inspired by Meissen and charmingly interpreted by Chelsea, including the best known yellow and green style developed by Wedgwood called pineapple or cauliflower ware, but such work met demands that were comparatively short-lived. The ceramics known briefly as green-glaze have proved lastingly satisfying, and constitute a clearly defined group of considerable merit, produced over more than a century, yet seldom studied and as seldom understood.

Less obvious than blue-and-white, less precious than genuine antique lustre-ware, these ceramics suggest wonderful possibilities for home colour scheming. Typically the whole surface of the dish or bowl or vase or teapot is a rich deep green, but every part of the vessel is given interest by surface patterning, and the green colour itself comes alive in the subtle undertones of light and shade thus introduced by the relief detail. Often the pattern is charmingly obvious, representing overlapping leaves and fern or bracken fronds: the outline of plate or bowl may follow the asymmetrical form of a vine leaf with curving stalk handle, or a conventional shape may contain leaves, fruits, tendrils and small creatures as intricate surface relief work.

To the 18th-century housewife fresh green leaves were so much a part of summer pleasure, and so sadly lacking throughout the winter, that the enterprising even learnt how to "green" leaves from the garden and introduce them as the perfect foil for their dishes of fruit at dessert. Mrs. Hannah Glasse in *The Complete Confectioner*, 1753, suggests as a dessert centrepiece "a large dish of fruit of all sorts piled up, and set out with green leaves" and she describes in detail how to green the leaves of the pear tree and cut them to shape to go around a dish of apricots because their own leaves are "too tender for greening". From such hard-won effects of table decoration it must indeed have been a relief to turn to the cool green beauty of dessert sets—plates, fancy-shaped dishes, bowls, centrepieces—in richly glazed green earthenware.

Today's collector can hope to find specimens of green-glaze dating from the 1760s to the 1870s: indeed some pieces are too handsome and useful ever to have gone out of production. The expert traces improvements in the quality of the glaze and the texture of the earthenware. The rest of us deliberate contentedly among the different tones and surface brilliances, the shadowy pools of heaviest colour in deep-cut veins and the sunny highlights on tendril and berry, or find particular delight in the cauliflower vessels where the green leaf-work is crowned with flower heads in creamy yellow.

To us the very irregularities of colour are pleasing, the small flaws and cracks in the earthenware recall those more leisurely days when men or boys used strong, practised fingers to force the heavy clay into moulds whose all-over patternings were intended to mask and minimise these faults. Every detail in the pattern had to be filled, more clay being added as required and formed into a homogeneous mass without the smallest bubble of trapped air. It is hard to realise, therefore, that to its originators green-glaze ware was hailed as a triumph for the comparatively smooth, even intensity of its colour, and only gradually was improved to the less exciting, mechanically near-perfect quality of the last Victorian revival.

The genius basically responsible for green-glaze, as so often we find when exploring the history of English earthenwares, was Josiah Wedgwood. The letters and more especially the Experiment Books of this extraordinarily determined, hardworking, ill-health-defying potter offer brief glimpses of the endless struggle for success.

There had been green-glazed earthenware in England for centuries before Wedgwood took up the quest, of course. The somewhat haphazard unreliable glaze on everyday pots and crocks was achieved with finely ground natural sulphide of lead—smithum or galena—mixed with about one-twelfth oxide of copper. When this powder mixture was sprinkled on the clay vessels a single firing in the potter's oven baked the clay and covered it with a thick green glaze. A puzzle jug thus glazed in the Victoria and Albert Museum is dated 1571.

Wedgwood, however, as soon as he established himself as a master potter at Ivy House, Burslem, in 1759, determined to perfect his evolution of more reliable green ware. The charming blotchy, streaky glazes then in production, that we treasure as tortoiseshell and agate wares, came easily from his glost or glaze-fixing ovens. His long search, as he explained later, was for a liquid glaze in "an even self colour" which could be produced as economically, and his method was to add copper oxide to a clear glaze: the concentration of the copper oxide determined the intensity of the colour. The result was "a new species of coloured ware to be fired along with the tortoiseshell and agate ware in our common gloss ovens".

At the time all that his Experiment Book noted—for March 23, 1759—was, "Experiment No. 7, the invention of Green Glaze Ware. A Green glaze to be laid on Common white biscuit ware. Very Good". The yellow glaze came later: experiment 93, dated March 10, 1760, marked an early "Tryal for Yellow glaze" and a month later experiment 100 recorded the achievement of a "*full yellow Glaze*".

By then his green glaze was already on the market, including dishes shaped as leaves and bunches of grapes (still in production) for pickles, sweetmeats and fruit, rectangular and cylindrical tea canisters and sets of tea ware, chocolate cups, jugs, candlesticks, piggins, basins, sauce-boats, tureens. The combination of green and yellow suggested more naturalistic forms, such as apples, pears,

REGISTRY OF DESIGNS

Index to the letters for each year and month from 1842 to 1883

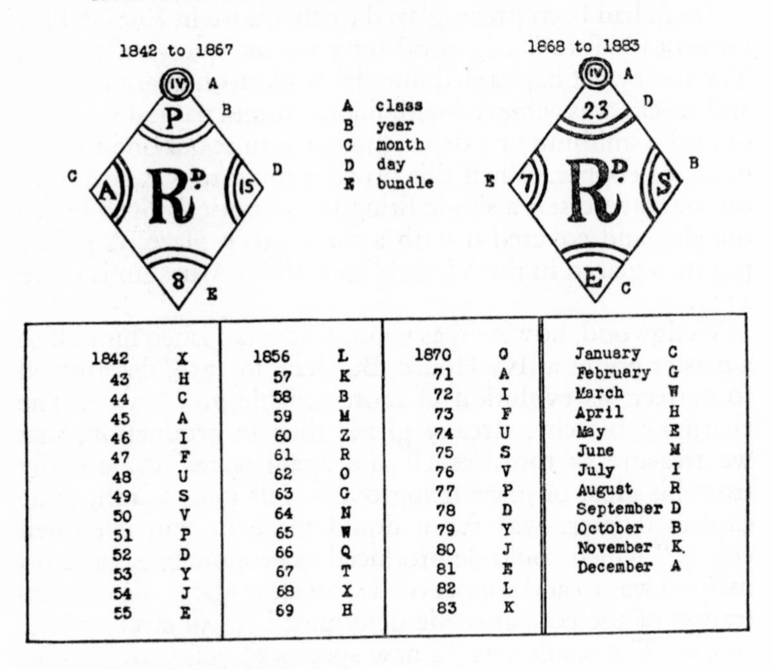

1842	X	1856	L	1870	C	January	C
43	H	57	K	71	A	February	G
44	C	58	B	72	I	March	W
45	A	59	M	73	F	April	H
46	I	60	Z	74	U	May	E
47	F	61	R	75	S	June	M
48	U	62	O	76	V	July	I
49	S	63	G	77	P	August	R
50	V	64	N	78	D	September	D
51	P	65	W	79	Y	October	B
52	D	66	Q	80	J	November	K
53	Y	67	T	81	E	December	A
54	J	68	X	82	L		
55	E	69	H	83	K		

For September 1857 ?R used from September 1st to September 19th.

For December 1860 ?K used.

For March 1st to March 6th 1878 the following mark was issued:

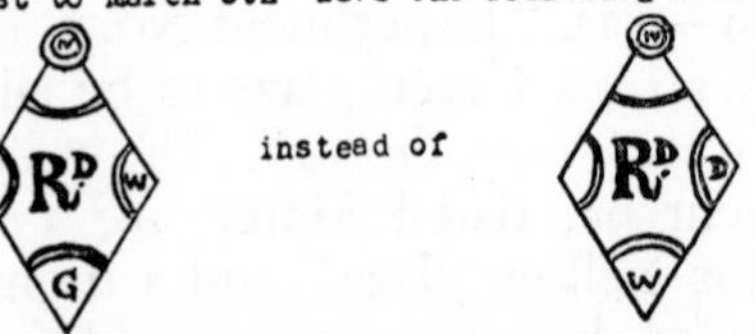

Fig. 6. Much ware between 1842 and 1883 bore a registration mark, and the corner letters and figures are here explained. The date was that of the design's introduction. Class IV covered all ceramic wares.

lemons, quinces, cucumbers, used for complete tea services and still to be found occasionally in particularly attractive teapots and jugs.

Staffordshire potters had been losing ground to the porcelain makers of London, Derby and Worcester, and thankfully seized upon Wedgwood's notions in green-glaze ware and the "cauliflower" or "pineapple" ware as abundantly obvious successes. But they scamped the detailed care of the Wedgwood work, the tool modelling and sharp undercutting that gave his ware a fresh cool crispness. It is interesting to note the success of the green dessert ware in the hot brilliance of the West Indies, mentioned by Wedgwood in 1766 with the comment, "I have a few crates in hand, some gilt, some plain". When Wedgwood received his first order for the royal household, early in 1765, it included six fruit baskets and stands in green glaze rimmed with gilding.

Inevitably Wedgwood's zest for improvement and invention did not long accept the "common white biscuit ware" of rough, flawy, uneven consistency that may be found under the green glazes of his early imitators. First he made it lighter by hand-washing the unpurified clays shipped to him from Devon and Cornwall. But his major triumph came in 1775, when he won a lawsuit against the porcelain maker Richard Champion and thus broke the monopoly that had denied potters the purified ingredients required for fine earthenware. Thereafter Wedgwood's creamware became renowned, and the fine texture and clear light tone of the earthenware gave a new brilliance to his rich green glaze. From about 1790 his stronger but heavier pearlware was used too. No Wedgwood marks have been found on the early green-glaze and only occasional symbols on the ware of the 1770s, such as an O with a symbol consisting of two outward-pointing semi-circles joined by a straight line. But from 1780 he impressed the name *Wedgwood*, changed in the 19th century to *WEDGWOOD* and augmented, after 1860, by date symbols composed of two letters and a numeral.

Among collectors the improved green-glaze ware made after 1775 is classed as belonging to the second period: the third came towards the end of the 18th century when the colour might be supplied by chromium oxide, giving a splendid range from yellow-green to emerald, more solidly opaque and less shading to blue than the copper greens. Josiah Wedgwood had died in 1795 and the ware never wholly recaptured the quality he infused into it by his relentless intolerance of imperfection. But more is known of other green-glaze potters in the 19th century.

Fig. 7. Wedgwood marks always display the name. All the above are dated between 1769 and 1780.

Dessert services were in demand again, a typical set consisting of four shells, two hearts, two circular tureens, dishes and stands, twenty-four plates and a decorative centrepiece. Among interesting specimens at the Victoria and Albert Museum, London, are two plates marked *BRAMELD + 8*, indicating production by the famous Rockingham firm at Swinton in about 1810, before the Brameld brothers began making their sparkling bone china in about 1820. The plates are modelled in relief with wicker-work rims and leaf and stem patterns under the green glaze.

Two flower vases, twelve and a half inches tall, in a bright green glaze, are attributed to the same firm, probably made a few years later. These are in a design of vertical overlapping leaves of a water plant, flaring out at the top where moths rest on some of the tips. An elaborate five-lobed stand consists of a water lily leaf with applied stems, flower-buds and seed-pods.

In early Victorian times green-glaze ware had an improved body and a thicker, crystalline glaze. The body consistency might be bulked out with twenty to thirty per cent of chalk which helped to minimise the different reactions to atmospheric changes shown by body and glaze, the cause of the glaze's tiny cracks or "crazing". For the glaze the formula might require sulphate of copper dissolved and precipitated by a solution of borax and then mixed with transparent glaze, in the proportions of six pounds of copper sulphate to ten quarts of the glaze.

The shades of green were many and lovely, from sea green and water green to bronze green and apple greens, from meadow green to Chinese sage. Calcium fluoride was used to make a tone called Victoria green. Pieces from a grass green dessert service may be found, for example, or bread trays, or cheese trays, in the relief water lily pattern made by Adams & Bromley of Shelton who changed their mark in 1873 from *Adams & Co.* to *Adams & Bromley* or *A & B*. Instead of the laborious hand moulding of Wedgwood's day these patterns in relief of vein and rib and berry were shaped with hand presses: careful scrutiny will reveal traces of thin lines where the pressure has forced a little earthenware into the cracks or joints of the press tools.

Earthenware treated in the majolica manner dates from the 1860s. The basis for this work was a coarse cane-coloured earthenware shaped with patterns in relief. This was covered with a white opaque glaze and fired in the kiln. Only after this preliminary preparation was the green glaze applied and fired, acquiring a lustrous glow from the glistening white beneath. Much of this went to the United States, but Harvey Adams & Co. of Longton issued tea and breakfast ware. This might be decorated with shamrock but more interesting patterns were derived from various arrangements of ferns and tree leaves—fifty or more groupings—modelled from specimens grown in the Duke of Sutherland's garden at nearby Trentham Hall. Strangely, these bear the diamond-shaped registration mark that protected the designs from copyists, but lack the firm's trademark.

Green-glaze ware marked *S & S* was made by Daniel Sutherland & Sons, Longton: candlesticks may be found, and stands for stilton cheese, bread and fruit dishes, many styles and patterns of jug—all the "extras" to the lunch or tea table that green-glaze presented so attractively—were marked by this firm between 1863 and 1875, when, for some reason, marking of their wares was discontinued. *GJ* impressed in a monogram is the mark of George Jones, Stoke-upon-Trent, established 1861, the monogram being enclosed in a circle after 1875. Jones won medals for his green-glaze in Paris, London and Vienna, and produced a wide range of vases, honey skips, trinket caskets, dessert ware and ambitious imitations of Palissy figures. A bee with wings expanded and the inscription *MW & Co* marks dessert ware by Morgan Wood & Co., Burslem, established 1860; and there are other known makers such as Banks and Thorley of New Street Pottery, Hanley, established 1873, whose products show faultless craftsmanship, the natural groupings of ivy, ferns, anemones, being embossed in low relief on plates and dishes with twisted rope handles.

The final phase came in the late 1860s when Poole, Stanway & Wood of Stoke-upon-Trent applied green glaze to the marble-like porcelain known as parian ware. Edward Steele of Hanley, too, developed this ware, impressing his monogram *ES* in a circle on notably well-modelled dessert services, vases and jugs. The parian ware gave the green glaze a clarity and restrained brilliance that time has not spoilt with any blemish of crazing. Even the first Josiah Wedgwood, surely, would have approved. He, more than anyone, shrewdly envisaged the lasting appeal of the ware he had launched upon the world. As early as 1774 he wrote to his partner Bentley: "The Agate, the Green and other coloured Glazes have had their day and done us pretty well, but they are certain of a resurrection soon for there ever will be a numerous Class of People to purchase *shewy* and *cheap* things."

Chapter Four

SILVER CADDY LADLES

TODAY, when so many of us collect old silver caddy ladles, it is surprising to realise how imperfectly we know their history. Tea became a luxurious necessity early in the 18th century. "Honest smugglers" abounded, and ash woods were stripped and ruined for substitute leaves that would make the precious tea leaves appear more plentiful. Under such circumstances, with tea so costly and so widely appreciated, the lady of the house took care to have it in her own safe keeping, and to perform herself the small ritual of tea-making.

Tea with cordials and thin bread and butter kept the ladies entertained while the men lingered around the dining-table, but in many households it constituted a repast in itself. That wonderful late-18th-century recorder of meal-times and menus whom I mention elsewhere in this book, Parson Woodforde, refers frequently in his diaries to this pleasant way of entertaining neighbours and chance callers around six o'clock, most often as a preliminary to "getting down to cards"—"sixpenny whist", perhaps, or "a pool of commerce".

It is rare today, however, to find a silver ladle dating earlier than the 1780s. What, then, did the tea-maker use before? A teaspoon, perhaps, or the flattish perforated bowl of the mote skimmer described later in this chapter, or a scoop in home-carved box wood? Perhaps she used a shell, for early Georgians were fascinated by shells, and many early ladles have bowls in the attractive scallop shell design. There are several possibilities. But the fact remains that ladles were never exempted from assay or duty payment or the associated hall-marking. Even when, in 1790, other very small and light silver weighing less than five pennyweights was excused the disfigurement and rough handling involved, the caddy ladle was specifically retained within the jurisdiction of the assay office. Yet that office's price list as late as 1777 makes no mention of them: the caddy spoon as an individualistic, identifiable piece of silver had still to arrive.

This is the more remarkable since the Chinese supplied not only the tea and the inspiration for its lovely equipage but sometimes, it appears, included spoons as well in the tutenag-metal vessels that brought the leaves to Europe. These are recorded as small and flattish with open bowls and short curving handles and were of ivory or of the same tutenag alloy described by Lovell in 1687 as "more lovely and fine" than tin.

One obvious answer is to be found in the tea canister of late-Stuart and early-Georgian days. Most hostesses, I imagine, followed the ritual perfectly caught by Hogarth in his conversation piece "The Walpole Family", probably dating to the 1730s. Here Lady Walpole is seen in the act of making tea, surrounded by all her dainty paraphernalia. She has lifted a silver tea canister from its place in the shagreen-covered tea chest and is measuring the leaves into the canister's domed lid. Necked canisters continued until the 1760s, permitting such careful pouring and measuring of the leaves, even though the small opening made such a vessel so awkward to fill with the big rolled leaves of the period that it soon became usual to make it open also by sliding off either the top and shoulders or the substantial moulded base.

The real need for a caddy ladle came as other, more interesting, box designs were developed in canisters that acknowledged the popularity of the beverage by being more than twice as large of those of Queen Anne's day. Very occasionally we find a plain, flattish little spoon like a too-short teaspoon, just right to fit a lid recess in the handsome wooden tea chest that guarded the pair of silver canisters. In a typical design the plain mitred and apparently fixed end of the mahogany chest slides upward when the lid is open and from behind it at the bottom a tiny handle is revealed for pulling out the shallow drawer. In this way the lock of the chest secures also the silver ladle.

In most of the early ladles found today, however, the bowl is a deep scallop shell set almost at right angles to a stem that ends in one of the teaspoon designs of its day. A wide finial such as the scrolling Onslow pattern permitted the ladle to be hooked into the arching handle of the mid-Georgian vase-shaped canister, but an occasional ladle is found with a small hook soldered to the back of the stem for hanging on a loop inside the chest.

Occasionally at this period the ladle handle was of turned ivory, ebony or black-stained boxwood, affixed to a bowl raised by hammering the silver plate, or more rarely shaped by casting. In general, however, the ladle was developed as a very short-stemmed little tool made from a single piece of silver or invisibly joined bowl to stem. This was suitable for being placed unceremoniously inside the silver tea canister among the leaves, at a period when a new market was being found for the less exclusively expensive silver canister sold as a single entity: the name caddy, like its ladle, came late in the 18th century, one of the earliest references to "caddy ladles" occurring in the Assay Act of 1790. The term "cadee shell" has been noted in use in 1839 and caddy spoon in the 1860s.

These early caddy shells remain among the most attractive ever designed and may be found with hall-marks as early as the 1780s. Joseph Taylor of Birmingham made charming specimens in the 1790s embossed with sprigs of flowers in the flutes of the shell. Usually the handle is no more than a broad, flat thumb-piece made with the bowl or invisibly hard-soldered to it. It may be ornamented with a line-engraved crest or cypher surrounded by the sharp-edged sparkling engraving known as bright-cutting. Not all are the obvious fan-shaped scallop shell or deeper cockle shell: interesting asymmetrical outlines are to be noted, suggesting mussel shells rather than leaves, the handle attached either to what would be the hinge side or to the wider end of the shell.

Sometimes in the tradition of the miniature silver "toy" the ladle is a tiny shovel or scoop with rounded corners to the square-cut bowl and a businesslike T handle, but, like the toy, it is garnished with delicate chasing. Ladles in the shouldered spoon design known as fiddle-shape date from 1805 onwards. An early ladle usually measures about three inches long and one-and-a-half inches across and weighs ten pennyweights.

Today the early caddy ladles have to be sought with patience and a watchful eye for reproductions. All that most late Georgians wanted was an inexpensive little piece, pleasant to handle, free of the taint of base metal, and sufficiently original in its design. Today such a specimen may be bought for a few pounds even when the hallmark is clear and the maker known. These are the factory silversmiths' ladles, made from the lightest of thin-rolled silver plate, most often in Birmingham (marked with an anchor) but sometimes in Sheffield (a crown) or London (so-called leopard's head) or Dublin (crowned harp or figure of Hibernia). Hand-worked ball presses gradually shaped the thin silver, using tools of the hard steel that only came into general use in the 1790s.

All are welcome today, but the collector soon looks for the more interesting, individualistic designs. Some of the most attractive are shaped and veined as tea leaves, their handles being gracefully curled stalks. Some leaf ladles are delicately engraved, others left plain in the leaf's natural curves. E. Morley was making them in London in the 1800s, and other imitative shapes as well, such as an acorn in its cup with a leaf-engraved handle. Samuel Pemberton, a notable Birmingham maker of collectable small silver, might enliven the leaf with an inset of silver wire filigree. At the other extreme, some leaf shapes are cast and finished with chasing and occasional engraving, producing heavy, handsome ladles in the ornate manner of the 1820s that could be condemned as florid in larger work. William Smiley of Camomile Street, London, was still making them in the mid 19th century with the bowl as a tea leaf and the handle as a sprig of leaves.

Some leaf ladles are gilded, and vine leaves and grapes, with wire tendril handles, appear among ladles as well as among decanter labels, both facts reminding the collector that this was a period that still regarded tea drinking as an after-dinner ritual which included also cordials. These were sipped from extremely elegant little glasses similarly ornamented with a wealth of delicate flower work around the rims, so that every detail of the equipage should be in keeping with the sparkling, gilded, hand-painted porcelain tea servcie.

Other designs are singularly hard to associate with the tea equipage but are all the more perfectly of their period. There is the fish, for example, that would remind Georgians merely of the mother-of-pearl fish counters lost and won at the card table. There is the rare eagle design of the "American eagle period" at the end of the 18th century, delicately chased to suggest plumage, the head and neck serving as a handle with a gleaming burnished eye. This was another of Joseph Taylor's designs, introduced in the 1790s, repeated less perfectly in the 1830s, and reproduced in the present century without the duty mark obligatory on silver ladles made between 1784 and 1890.

Another prize is the ladle as an open hand, with a neat little cuff as a handle, the whole design quickly shaped and finished and less attractive perhaps than the equally well-known and much-sought jockey cap. This too has been reproduced. Some of the most elegant caps are in silver filigree of the 1830s and—less exquisite—of the 1850s. Stirrup designs were made too during this period, when every silversmith sought the custom of sportsmen, and some of the many small tea scoops are edged with horseshoe markings. Scoop designs are particularly attractive to modern eyes among the simpler shapes that yet avoid the conventional spoon outline, such as hearts, octagons and the like. Some bowls in plainest elliptical outline are quite elaborately and improbably ornamented, such as the victory celebration souvenirs embossed with war trophies that were made in Birmingham between 1804 and 1815. Sometimes one is found with a name of a battle and its date engraved on the stem, such as Trafalgar.

One obvious reason for unconventional designs was the unwelcome competition of Sheffield plate. This could not be stamped into complicated shapes, but shells and smooth-bowled spoons were in production by 1790 and at less than half the price of silver. For the same reason silversmiths quickly abandoned the narrow bead mouldings and thread edgings that Sheffield platers found convenient for hiding the core of copper. Hence the delicate sheared edges in silver, often in interesting outlines. Specimens are found so delicate that they have broken in use, generally at the junction of thumb rest and bowl, and have been mended not quite perfectly. Sheffield plate catalogues of 1800–25 invariably illustrate caddy spoons among their domestic wares. By 1839 David Cope of Birmingham listed caddy shells also in British plate, a variant of Sheffield plate with a core of silver-toned nickel or of the alloy known as German silver instead of the self-revealing copper.

British plate caddy spoons were made widely in the 1830s and 1840s, but they form only one group among several that may confuse today's collector. Very many more were electro-plated on German silver by the process patented by Elkington and Mason in 1842. These were priced from one shilling and tenpence to four shillings and twopence each with a range of handles matching contemporaneous silver tea-spoons—threaded, beaded, kings pattern, fiddle, lily, French, Victoria and Albert. By then the old method of shaping the spoons by stamping was being superseded by machinery processes and the same patterns are to be found in silver.

There was another alternative, too, for inexpensive kitchen caddy spoons. This was Britannia metal, a hard, strong type of pewter. Such spoons may date to as early as about 1815, but only a few discoloured specimens remain. They were restricted to smooth, simple shapes as they could not be stamped in complex patterns, but when new they shone almost as brightly as silver itself.

All this made the Victorian master silversmith determine to produce massive, deeply-shaped caddy spoons. Even among these minor furnishings of the tea table we find the heavy castings of the period. The tendency was to produce an extremely solid little tool, its shape and ornament prosaic and naturalistic, and with a longer handle than on earlier ladles. Francis Higgins of Hatton Garden, London, for example, made a limpet shell bowl of gilded silver and mounted it on a handle of pond flowers, and regarded it highly enough to show it at the Great Exhibition of 1851.

The collector pottering through a tray of small silver may find another small item of the tea table equipage that is perhaps puzzling. This is a spoon with a long, pointed handle and a nearly flat bowl pierced in attractive patterns that would obviously be hopelessly inadequate, nevertheless, as a modern tea strainer. This is known as a mote skimmer, but had two purposes for the hostess or her maidservant pouring tea. As a skimmer it could be passed over the surface of a cup of freshly poured tea to remove any dust or other motes associated with the tea leaves of its period; the other purpose was only revealed if the harassed hostess found the strainer on the inner end of the teapot spout entirely blocked by the big tea leaves that uncurled in the boiling water to fill the bottom of the pot. It is interesting to find a tool so obviously evolved from sheer necessity from the ordinary teaspoons. That they were evolved quickly is shown by an entry in the *London Gazette* referring to "long or strainer tea spoons with narrow pointed handles" as early as 1697.

Occasionally a skimmer is to be found clipped into the lid of a tea chest instead of a ladle, as it would serve this purpose too, but could not be kept in the canister.

The earliest skimmers have the rat-tail design of their period's teaspoons, and their bowls are plainly pierced with round holes. These piercings were followed by rows of saw-cut crosses in the early 18th century, and more decorative piercing soon appeared, so that by the mid-18th century the designs began to suggest the saw-cut charm of the sugar caster. Elaborate foliated scrolls, crescents, diamonds and the like were in use throughout George III's reign. The barb finial also changed, being short at first but increasing to about half an inch in the early Georgian skimmer, and often, but not invariably, being twice as long by the 1760s. By the last quarter of the century it had proved necessary to introduce a giant version of this small "period piece", to deal with the same problems when tea was served from the gloriously fashionable but remotely haughty silver urn.

Chapter Five

CHINA COTTAGES

THE first antique I ever bought was a china cottage, an elegant little villa, the very essence of trim white urbanity, with doors and windows, roof tiles and chimney pots picked out in richest gold . . . But enough of that. Only fellow enthusiasts will understand the urge for personal reminiscence on this absorbing theme, and they will have their own favourites—a summerhouse, perhaps, smothered in fantastic great ivy leaves or convolvulus flowers, like something out of Jack and the Beanstalk, or a cottage all white save for a vividly coloured goldfinch, or a pottery model with a completely different air about it, such as the naïvely gruesome Potash Farm, sold by the thousand as a memento to a famous mid-19th-century murder.

Be it romantic castellated tower or frankly cosy flower-laden cottage, our early-19th-century ancestors liked their architecture to be picturesque. They embroidered impossibly elegant mansions in endless cross-stitch, they decked themselves in flowery cottage bonnets, and they filled their drawing-rooms and boudoirs with tiny china and pottery models of ivied church and pagoda summer house, sham-gothic arbour and high-roofed toll lodge.

Today we may smile at their enthusiasms, yet we gladly pay pounds for china ware that cost them shillings or even pence, and that for the mere decorative charm of what they bought for positive use. The very self-assurance and prettiness of these absurd little creations appeal quite monstrously to our mid-20th-century tastes.

First, however, for some basic facts. Today's collectors distinguish between cottages of porcelain and bone china and those of pottery, between those made solely for ornament and the various "useful" pieces, between the few bearing manufacturers' marks and the multitude unmarked which were made by a considerable number of famous potteries, between the genuine antiques and the very many more recent imitations, created in response to a demand for these delectable scraps of nonsense that grows year by year.

A whole village of brilliant Meissen porcelain was presented to the English ambassador, Sir Charles Hanbury, at Dresden by the king of Saxony in 1748—as many as a hundred and sixty-six cottages, barns and the like, to be set out as table ornaments among the dessert dishes. The ambassador lent the gift to Chelsea, but record of Chelsea cottages is restricted to a couple of items in the 1756 sale catalogue, each "a most beautiful perfume pot in the form of an old castle or pigeon house decorated with pigeons".

Derby produced some soft porcelain cottages in the mid-1760s, embowered in hawthorn flowers, and others in hard porcelain, with a hard, lustrous but somewhat flawed glaze, were made at Bristol. These were pastille burners, for it had been found that a tiny porcelain or pottery cottage, like a hollow box inverted over a separate flat plinth, made a perfect cassolette or vessel for burning sweetly-scented pastilles.

In those days such pastille burners were regarded as essential in a well-ordered household. The small, richly perfumed cone of charcoal, benzoin and gum arabic was lit upon the plinth and the cottage placed over it so that the perfume rose from the tiny gilded chimney. Less than a hundred years ago cottage pastille burners were still contributing to the heavy sweetness of the Victorian drawing-room. In a reference as late as 1856 Theodore Hook "put three or four pastilles into the burner on the mantelpiece".

Other cottages are found with cut-out windows, Gothic arched shapes being popularly romantic. These were designed to reveal the tiny glimmer of the nightlight that was important at a period when it was difficult to produce a light in a hurry. The most exciting of these are the lithophanes, some of which were made by the Worcester firm of Grainger, Lee & Company from 1828. Unlit, such a piece looks dull, lacking the detail of the conventional design:

often only the back is fashioned as a cottage or arbour, with a central aperture for inserting the light.

Instead of a cut-out window the front consists of a piece of glassy porcelain, smooth on the outer side but very skilfully mould-shaped into steep humps and sudden hollows within. The light shining through such a window shows brightly or more faintly according to the depth of the porcelain it has to penetrate, so that the deeply uneven surface produces a remarkably detailed monochrome picture.

Non-guttering, slow burning candles that did not require endless snuffing appeared only a few years after the development of self-consuming candle wick in 1825, but some of these cottages were intended for little mortar lights with wicks floating in open vessels of whale or other oil: occasionally a late cottage has a hollowed base for the oil. In the majority the whole cottage lifts off its base for the light to be inserted, but sometimes a cottage is found with the roof lifting off the walls like the lid of a box: Derby and Spode produced a number. Sometimes one wall lifts out, as in the model of All Saints Church, Derby.

Cottage money boxes are mentioned in Chapter 18, and there are also cottage tobacco jars for the seeking: some large cottages open to reveal themselves as inkstands, but many others are merely mantelpiece ornaments, elegant, romantic, topographical or unashamedly pretty. Perhaps the most usual is the old-world cottage in a wealth of flowers, but castles, gateways, watermills, clock towers, thatched farms, summer arbours are to be found, and even summer-house adaptations of Chinese pagodas.

Even apart from their general air of fragile daintiness, porcelain and bone china cottages are at once distinguishable from those of pottery, being more or less translucent when held against the light in contrast to the solid opacity of the pottery. Bone china, translucent yet essentially sturdy, the discovery of Josiah Spode, was the basis of the 19th century's spectacular development of lovely table wares. Rockingham, Coalport, Spode, Derby and Worcester were among the famous firms making lovely bone china cottages in the most notable period between, say, 1820 and 1840.

B.1. Lustre jugs. *Upper row:* leaf pattern in silver resist; canary yellow with transfer portrait of Sir Francis Burdett, Bart, M.P.; silver banded with transfer print of country scene. *Lower row:* hand painted; resist patterned in a bronze tone; copper with white relief ornament.

B.2. Lustre jugs. The lustre rims and borders enrich ornament mainly applied by transfer printing. The church (*upper left*) is hand painted, the lively scene (*below*) hand coloured over a transfer print.

facing page 48

Rockingham, only just launched into china manufacture as distinct from earthenwares, has become the accepted name for many of the most exquisite, but very few are marked. In particular Rockingham is associated with the notably charming style of cottage edged on roof and chimney with minute flowers, and with gold-bordered steps running up to the door between the gay flower beds that encrust the apple green base. The very white Rockingham china has a hard, glassy glaze, sometimes bearing exquisitely lacy gilding in the firm's distinctively dark, slightly coppery gold. John Wager Brameld continued to make delicate flower pieces, working in Bayswater, London, until the late 1850s, after the Rockingham works at Swinton, Yorkshire, closed in

Fig. 8. Rockingham marks. Top, 1826-30 printed in red, brown or purple. Below, before 1826, as an applied medallion, impressed, or printed in red or purple.

1842. When a mark is found on a genuine Rockingham piece it is the name of the proprietor, Brameld, and, on work made after 1826, a griffin from the crest of the Fitzwilliams on whose estate the pottery was established. After 1830 a royal crown was added to the mark, and the words "Manufacturers to the King" changed to "Manufacturers to the Queen" in 1837.

Coalport and the Chamberlain factory at Worcester must also be credited with many splendidly flower-laden fantasies, each flower coloured and placed in position by hand among the shavings of china paste introduced as grass.

The everlasting flower was a newcomer to the English garden in Regency days. In the drawing rooms of the rich, however, everlasting flowers had long been the precious darlings of flower-loving English women, clustering around figure groups and massive painted vases. In the 18th century's fragile porcelains these were costly, and the texture of paste and glaze were never entirely suited to petal delicacies. But flowers of china reached an infinitely wider public of late-Georgian and early-Victorian England.

In 1820 the Brameld brothers began creating, petal by petal, leaf by leaf, the blooms now associated with their Rockingham china works. For the next forty years countless factory girls spent their days shaping the petals that still show the touch of their fingers, assembling them into individualistic and never wholly identical flowers, and grouping them on cottages and inkstands, bowls and candlesticks, ready for firing in the oven, glazing into sparkling brilliance and final colouring. As Robert Dossie pointed out as early as 1764, "where latitude may be given to the fancy" the worker's fingers with a small, flat, pointed stick, a pair of pliers and a wet sponge, shaped the flowers better than any plaster moulds.

The early 19th century liked its flowers realistic and of recognisable species, such as pinks and auriculas, bright blue convolvulus or morning glory, and tawny zinnia. But the size of such flowers in relation to the cottage they adorn is often as incongruous as the fittings to a doll's house of that period. Rockingham is thought to have kept the flowers mainly to scale, including delicate gilded posies, although some of the big pink convolvulus flowers on cottage roofs have been credited to this firm.

Many of the sweet peas, ranunculus and carnation flowers may be attributed to Coalport, where flower-decked ornaments were made for almost thirty years. Much of this work is in white felspar china, the most translucent china of its day and stronger even than Oriental hard porcelain; bone china was used from the early 1830s. Coalport colouring is vivid and clear, in fresh light tones, and the low-temperature leadless (and thus non-poisonous) glaze has a bright, attractive clarity. From 1828 to 1850 the name was Colebrook Dale, tribute to the one-time fame of the nearby iron works: hence the occasional mark *C.D.* on a Coalport cottage or a turreted castle on a craggy base.

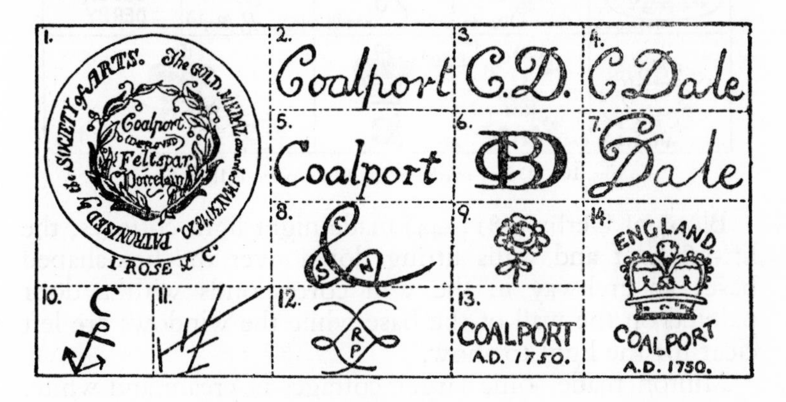

Fig. 9. Marks used by the Coalport firm:

1. From 1820 onwards, printed in red.
2. 1815-28.
3-7. "Coalport" and various shortenings of "Coalbrookdale" used 1828 to *c.* 1850; No. 6 possibly to 1861.
8. 1861-75, the letters standing for factories which they claimed to have incorporated—Caughley, Swansea, Nantgarw.
9. Rare—for John or W. Rose.
10-12. Adaptations of other firms' marks—Chelsea, Meissen, Sèvres.
13. 1875-81. This mark shows the introduction of the date 1750 which the firm claimed as its date of foundation.
14. A later specimen, used from 1895, when the word "England" was required by law.

On many cottages the flowers are less ambitious creations, mould-pressed or stamped in little more than low relief. Cottages may be loaded with such suggestions of flowers, flooding over the roofs and walls and gardens of some quite elaborate buildings, such as a house and water mill, or a gabled mansion.

The most emphatically rustic flower-smothered cottages were made by Spode, quite small, with porches around the doors, climbing roses and masses of small pink flowers. The walls may be bright lilac colour and the base emerald green. A Spode summer house may have a round, domed roof resting on a circle of pillars, and Spode made circular cottages, too, with lifting lids. Occasionally one is found marked either *Spode* or *Spode Felspar Porcelain*.

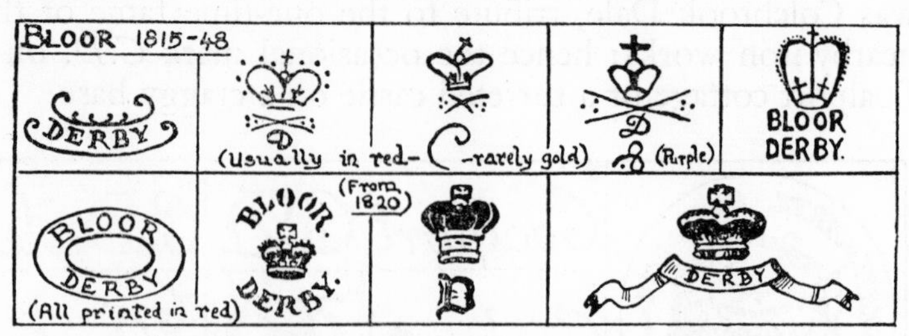

Fig. 10. Derby marks in the Bloor period, 1815-48.

Bloor of Derby (1811–44) made night light cottages, the lift-off roof and walls fitting down over the box-shaped base: an archway in the wall corresponds with a door painted on the wall of the base while the windows are left clear for the light to show.

Minton made some larger cottages in cream and white, their only touch of colour being a goldfinch on the roof. In some other white cottages the effect is of snow upon roof and flower encrustations. Worcester cottages include some marked *Flight, Barr & Barr*, indicating manufacture between 1812 and 1840: here the flowers may be painted on the walls where gold lines mark the brickwork. Late Worcester specimens are sometimes mounted on little feet.

Gilt-outlined salmon-scale roof tiles are associated with porcelain pastille burners from Swansea, probably made between 1818 and 1822, although many anonymous cottages show delicate gilt and colour detail of tiling and brickwork, and emphasise, say, a bird's nest under the eaves, a figure at a window, even a bright brassy knocker or a horseshoe hung over the door. Davenport, too, may be mentioned for finely-finished cottages.

In contrast to all this brilliance it is almost startling to find a cottage in colourless, matt-surfaced biscuit porcelain: an ivy-clad Derby church pastille burner of the 1830s, perhaps, or a rare Wedgwood cottage, a primly dainty pencil drawing among the glowing paintings.

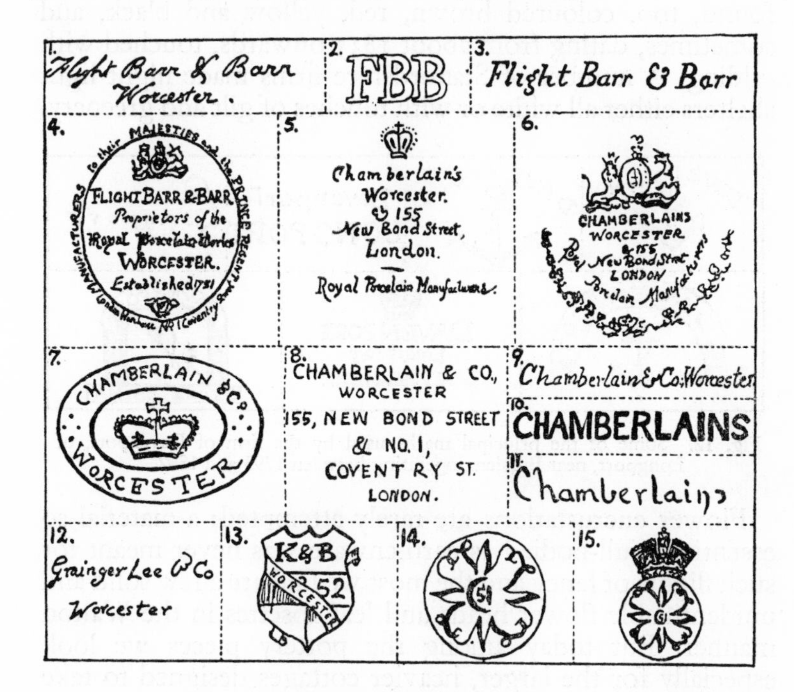

Fig. 11.

1-4. Marks of Flight, Barr and Barr, 1813-40; (1) in red or black; (2) impressed; (3 and 4) printed in red or black.
5-6. Chamberlain's marks, printed in red: (5) 1816-20; (6) 1820-40.
7-11. Some of the marks used after the amalgamation of Chamberlain and Barr: (7) 1850-51; (8) 1840-45; printed in red, until the Coventry Street address was given up; (9) printed; (10) printed or impressed; (11) incised.
12. One of the marks of Grainger, Lee and Company after Lee joined Grainger in 1812.
13-14. Marks of Kerr and Binns, 1852-62; (13) on best-quality work, printed; (14) printed or impressed.
15. Mark of the Worcester Royal Porcelain Company Ltd., founded in 1862.

In pottery as in china the 19th century was the great period for cottages, but a few in slipware of the 18th century are known, and others hand-modelled as half-timbered cottages in the mingled colour effects associated with Thomas Whieldon (at work 1740 to 1780) and his period. Early-19th-century potters made cottages glazed with red lead and sometimes stained nearly black with powdered manganese. Lines scratched in the surface roughly indicate details of brick and tile. Half-timbered cottages are found, too, coloured brown, red, yellow and black, and sometimes, dating from about 1835 onwards, touched with gilding. A number of Staffordshire firms made night light shelters either all white or with touches of gilt and greenery.

Fig. 12. Some of the principal marks used by the firm of Davenport, of Longport, near Burslem, operating between 1793 and 1882.

Flower encrustations are rarely attempted: a material so essentially full-bodied as earthenware was never meant for such flights of fancy and the most we find are a few solid and unidentifiable flower heads and leaf rosettes in the Walton manner. But today among the pottery pieces we look especially for the larger, heavier cottages designed to take prominent place among the comforter dogs and lustre jugs on the farmhouse mantelpiece. These were immensely popular between 1825 and 1850 and are found in all shapes, sizes and colours. Some of the finest were made by Sampson Smith of Longton and William Kent of Burslem. Architecturally they range from splendidly coloured castle keeps on rocky bases to labourers' cottages picturesquely thatched. An interesting pair in Brighton Museum show how variously the same basic thatched cottage pastille burner could be handled. One is a trim little dwelling neatly finished in every detail from the chimneys to the pointing of the bricks and has a row of large simple flowers and leaves as a border each side. The other has an added penthouse for the cows around its door and every quickly-daubed feature suggests the struggling, rough and ready life of the cottage-smallholder.

Some of these cottages have attractive decoration on the base leading to the door in scroll patterns suggesting the figure ornaments of Ralph Salt and John Walton and their followers. But individual attribution is impossible. Some were made as watch holders, a circular hole for the watch being worked into the design of cottage or castle keep, sometimes as much as a foot tall, so that the watch would serve as mantel or bedside clock. Some in stoneware, large and heavy, were intended as door porters.

Many pottery cottages purported to be representations of real buildings, such as the Copeland firm's white stoneware models of Shakespeare's house at Stratford-on-Avon, in vogue from 1840. Other famous buildings, sometimes slightly startling in their bright enamel colours, include Westminster Abbey and Temple Bar, Wesley's house in Bunhill Fields, Cheshire's familiar Moreton Hall, and Boscobel House in Shropshire that sheltered Charles II, all made with an eye to the souvenir hunter, and certainly with no thought for the eventual collector of antiques.

Among such models the real lowbrows of the period chose the so-called crime pieces. There was the Red Barn at Polstead, for instance, commemorated in 1827, complete with figures of Maria Martin and her murderer William Corder. Most popular of all were Potash Farm, home of the murderer James Rush, and Stanfield Hall, home of his victim Mr. Jeremy, Recorder of Norwich, and scene of the once-familiar crime. These of course were shaped by the speedy method of pouring wet clay into plaster of paris moulds, so that the same hollow shape was produced many times, and inscribed by hand with whatever name the public might demand.

The most usual Potash Farm/Stanfield Hall model was produced by at least three potters, and may show a brilliant underglaze prussian blue roof set off by the dullish, flaky overglaze enamels, red, black and green, that fill in the details below. These date to 1848 and appear in various versions, some even with tentative attempts at the flower encrustations of happier dwellings.

It goes without saying that cottages of every kind have been reproduced, often given signs of age and wear, and

Printed in Blue
(1784-1789)

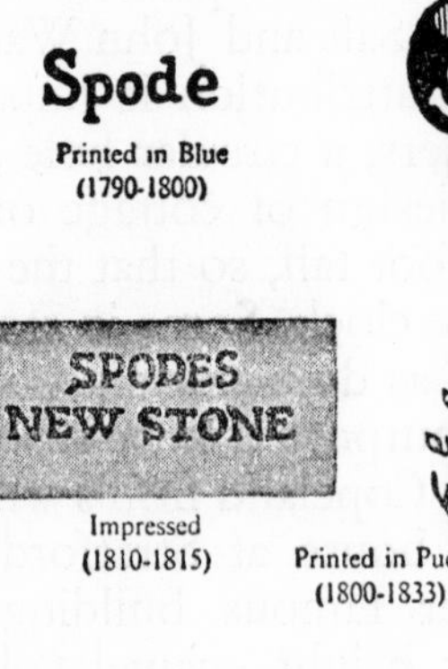

Printed in Blue
(1790-1800)

SPODE

Printed, Blue Ground
(1795-1805)

Stone-China
Printed in Blue
(c. 1805)

SPODE
Stone China
Printed in Blue
(c. 1805)

SPODES
NEW STONE
Impressed
(1810-1815)

Printed in Puce
(1800-1833)

SPODE
Felspar Porcelai
Printed in Blue
(1800-1833)

Printed in Blue
(From 1810)

SPODE & COPELAND,
Printed in Blue
(First used in 1815)

Printed in Blue
(1833-1846)

Printed in Blue
(1833-1846)

COPELAND
& GARRETT
Impressed
(1833-1846)

Printed in Blue
(1833-1846)

Copeland
Late Spode.
Printed in Blue
(1847-1867)

Copeland late Spode
Impressed
(1847-1867)

Printed in Green
or Blue

Impressed

Copeland
Stone China
Printed in Blue

COPELAND
Printed in Green
Late 19th Century

COPELAND
Printed in Green
Late 19th Century

SPODE
COPELANDS CHINA
ENGLAND
Modern Mark
Printed in Green

COPELAND
SPODE
ENGLAND
New Stone

Modern Marks, Printed in Various Colours

Fig. 13. Spode and Copeland trade marks, with their dates.

sometimes even the marks of famous potteries, so that specimens with marks and especially with such familiar marks as the ubiquitous Chelsea gold anchor and the Rockingham griffin are always to be viewed with particular caution. Sometimes detection is easy, when the fresh delicacy, the spontaneity of early-19th-century work is obviously lacking. But subtler differences of texture, glaze and colouring can only be learnt by handling the known work of the various firms: to generalise is as misleading as to give all lavender, mauve and purple cottages the label of Rockingham. Indeed there is much to be said for allowing these happy little absurdities their anonymity, and enjoying each for its own personality.

Chapter Six

TUNBRIDGE WARE

CENTURY after century men and women have turned to wood for their warmth, comfort, elegance. Much of social history can be told in tinder boxes and snuff rasps, games boards and nutmeg graters—a homely, fundamental story for the beauty of smooth unpainted wood in its endless variety of grain and tint transcends all the petty ins and outs of fashion. Men and women today are as universally attached to those sweet-smelling products of saw and plane and lathe as when, over two hundred and sixty years ago, that intrepid horsewoman Celia Fiennes made her way "through much woods and lanes and some pleasant shades of lofty trees" and found on sale at Tunbridge "all sorts of curious wooden ware, which this place is noted for (the delicate neate and thin ware of wood, both white and Lignum vitae wood)".

Already, in the 1690s, Tunbridge Wells was noted for its waters, taking its name from the older neighbouring Kentish town that is now spelt Tonbridge but with similar pronunciation. Lord North had discovered the chalybeate springs as early as 1606 but the first patrons, such as Henrietta Maria, had to set up their own encampments in the neighbourhood and it was the sojourn there of the Court during the plague of 1665 that developed the fashionable spa. Every holiday town has its souvenirs and the best of these are usually entertaining little samples of the most decorative local crafts. Tunbridge happened to be exceptionally fortunate for some two hundred years in possessing both the craftsmen and the local materials to produce a succession of lastingly attractive wares, culminating in the famous mosaic.

The Tunbridge ware most highly valued and widely collected today was made mainly after about 1800 and more especially in the 1830s–50s, but the skill behind its production resulted from centuries of such craftsmanship. Mid-Victorian games tables and pen trays continued the tradition of the popular 17th-century table skittles and the innumerable boxes—for lace, jewels and all manner of treasures—that figure in the letters of 18th-century patrons such as Fanny Burney in 1789 and Samuel Derrick in 1762 who exclaimed ruefully: "Were this ware smuggled abroad and then imported as a foreign commodity I am persuaded people would run after it; but alas! everyone knows it is English and the encouragement is therefore poor".

The collector may look for every sort and size of article, from reading desk to egg cup, and priced in pounds or shillings accordingly. Boxes are probably the most common, but every detail of desk equipment may be found, from book rest to sealing set, even to the rare pens and propelling pencils. (A "Cleopatra's Needle" thermometer and other similar monoliths date of course no earlier than 1878). There is much for the smoker and much, too, for the needlewoman, from silk winder and needle case to miniature table and teapot serving as pincushion and tape measure. Work tables themselves are less common, and another fairly unusual find is a tea caddy. When not sewing or writing letters souvenir-seeking visitors might be expected to pass their time with games, and here again the local trade sought to meet their interests with a wonderful range of equipment from substantial games tables to cribbage boards.

Basically the wood in a specimen of Tunbridge ware will probably consist of pine, sometimes beech, occasionally rosewood for fine work and for the solid turned legs and spindles that are an important feature of the work. But usually what will catch the eye will be the covering veneer which is the distinction of these wares. During the period now attracting collectors there were two quite different styles of treatment, often both appearing on the same article. Both were veneers, but whereas one consisted entirely of formalistic designs built up of geometric shapes based mainly on square, diamond and triangle, the other reproduced the whole range of floral patterns, birds, butterflies, and even pictorial scenes associated with early Victorian needlework, and here expressed in a range of lovely varied colours all directly produced by English and foreign woods without stain or paint and, in the finest early work, without the cheap varnish that has discoloured late examples.

From the earliest days of Tunbridge ware the staple material was wood in its natural colours. When colour and range of grain were required beyond the limits of local products the craftsmen had the good sense to seek foreign woods rather than to add artificial dyes. Only a steely greyish tone was deliberately achieved, by steeping the wood in the local chalybeate spa water. Even the deep greyish green sometimes noted was caused naturally by a fungus, *chlorosplenium aeruginosum*, which is often to be found on the sapwood of fallen branches of such wood as oak and birch.

At first, materials and tools limited Tunbridge ware to simple turnery. Already in 1699 John Jackson "at the Unicorn, [a turner's trade sign] the corner of Wood Street, Cheapside, London", was advertising his "Tunbridge ware" but it must be acknowledged that it is impossible now to differentiate these early products from those of other well-wooded regions until these men applied their long skill at traditional small-wood work to create the entirely different and distinctive Tunbridge ware mosaics. Visitors' comments confirm that the early work consisted mainly of treen, a term that has direct association with the verb to turn. This, when in common use, appears to have implied the platters, candlesticks, drinking vessels and the like wholly or partly made on one of our oldest machines, the lathe, as distinct from the wooden wares of joiner and cabinet maker, a probability put forward by Mr. Edward Pinto, who has assembled the extraordinarily interesting and comprehensive "Pinto Collection of Wooden Bygones".

The white wood wares noted by Celia Fiennes would include kitchen bowls in sycamore, strong, clean and suitably grained for long service, or lime, easily carved for butter and gingerbread moulds, sweet chestnut and fruit-woods, all immediately available. Box and pear were highly prized; beech reserved for coarser work. The lignum vitae that she also noted, one of the hardest woods and new to England in the 17th century, was the one foreign wood considered essential for enduring turnery. For goblets, ladles, pestles and mortars it was calculated to sell well at the spa to people concerned about their health for it was long credited with imparting health and vigour to liquors and foods that came in contact with it. "Lignum vitae and Tunbridge wares" were associated in the advertisement of Alexander Wetherstone, Portugal Street, near Lincoln's Inn Gate, in the early 1760s.

The contrasts in colour between heart and sap wood associated with lignum vitae were exploited too in glowing yew wood and in small work of immensely decorative laburnum with its "oyster shell" patterns when cut across the grain. By the 19th century the turnery of the Tunbridge region was still sufficiently renowned for a London turner, Thomas Jacques of Leather Lane, Holborn, to be described in the 1811 London Post Office Directory as an "Ivory Turner and Tunbridge-ware Manufacturer". Jacques's trade card, of about 1790, distinguishes between Tunbridge ware and work in hard woods. In the 1840s and 1850s leading makers of Tunbridge ware were still advertising turned "stickwork" under its more grandiose name of "inlaid turnery".

Such references indicate that through the 18th century such treen continued in demand. By the third quarter of the century there was a notable pleasure in small furniture with galleried rim and ornament. A broad oval tea tray may be found, for example: Mrs. Pendarves mentioned "Tunbridge voiders" (trays) as early as 1727. In an example of the 1770s or 1780s the tray may bear a central marquetry motif such as a shell or ten-petalled flower and be rimmed with a gallery supported by wholly delightful little spindles, and a similar delight in ornamental spindle shaping on the lathe is noted in countless tiny 18th-century souvenirs, such as nutmeg graters, pipe stoppers, goblet stems, the finials of tobacco jars and long-handled stemmed and galleried cruet stands—the "elegant turnery ware" for which Tunbridge was described as famous in 1788 by Aitkin in *England Delineated*.

In 18th-century journals and letters small souvenirs may be described as having handles or spindles of lathe-turned "stick-work". This is interesting as it confirms that marquetry as well as turnery was in production: left-over scraps and fillets of many differently coloured woods glued together revealed an attractive variety of pattern and colour by the shaping of the lathe.

Obviously, by the early 18th century these craftsmen of the Kent and Sussex border were appreciating the decorative value of texture as well as colour in their work. The cutting of wood for joinery work was limited by structural necessities but the smooth surfaces of small boxes and trays and games boards could be decorated effectively with thin glued-on slices of wood and of these no strength was required, so that they could be cut at all angles to catch the finest patterns of grain and colour.

Inlay in such light woods as holly had been used on furniture since the end of the 16th century, shallow hollows being cut in the surface of the solid oak or walnut to fit scraps of holly or boxwood similarly shaped to form chequer patterns and simple flower arabesques. Trade card illustrations of about 1700 have been noticed showing tables with their tops and frames inlaid in geometrical patterns of various woods, bone and ebony, including the black and white eight-pointed stars noted occasionally on long-case clocks, contemporaneous references already using the term "musaique". But the more ambitious Continental marquetry work established in England late in the 17th century prompted the development of more elaborate patterns achieved with thin veneers and it appears more than probable that Tunbridge participated in the vogue.

At its most ambitious the marquetry was an elaborate craft. The whole surface of an article might be covered with a thin veneer composed not of a single sheet of wood but of delicately fret-cut patterns in several different woods perfectly shaped to fit into each other, jig-saw puzzle fashion, and together form a smooth, unbroken surface. Late in the 18th century a more restrained style of marquetry gave furniture makers an opportunity to join in the fashion for neo-classical ornament: although many resorted to short-lived surface painting the marquetry has proved its superiority in use. Cabinets, desks, tea trays, every kind of box, might incorporate panels of marquetry including long-popular fan and shell motifs. These were constructed from small pieces of thin veneer in a few light tones of holly—shaded as required by heat—and the bronze-green sycamore known as harewood to ornament lovely veneers of satinwood. By then furniture makers obtained these motifs from marquetry specialists such as they might find around Tunbridge, along with the end-of-century bands of dark and light chequered patterns thought to resemble twisted rope. These were known as stringing and are found applied in outline panel effects on good quality provincial work in mahogany.

Even in the 19th century Tunbridge ware craftsmen included one Robert Russell who, it appears, continued this traditional method. Occasional specimens of his work are still to be found, beautiful arabesques in furze wood from the famous nearby Common and all manner of other local and foreign woods. Russell showed a lady's workbox of this "Tunbridge ware marquetry" at the Great Exhibition of 1851, styling himself the inventor, though by this he may have meant to imply no more than originality of design.

Tunbridge ware is thought to have included various other styles of elaborately ornamented wood during the 18th century, but these were merely passing phases, interesting when recognised in a display of minor curios. There was the popular imitation of tortoiseshell, for instance, made from veneers of white holly wood scorched with hot sand. There were pictures printed directly on to the wood by a method patented by Stephen Bradford of Birmingham in 1759, a practice that prompted the production of cheap little souvenirs pasted with printed paper engravings. But these were minor trifles. The finer craftsmen kept alive the traditions of ornamental inlays, marquetry and veneers.

The Regency's delightful vandyke patterns and cube complexities associated with the term parquetry work are considered the earliest expression of the new phase in

Tunbridge ware and at the same time must be regarded as the direct descendants of the combined chess and backgammon boards—the 17th century's "pairs of tables"—which required similar patterns and diverted the earliest visitors to the watering place. This was a skill never lost by the Tunbridge ware men. Many a delightful little games table was devised, becoming more elaborate late in the 18th century with drawers for storing the pieces and a reversible top giving access to recesses for the more complicated form of backgammon known as tric-trac. Early 19th-century specimens often follow the pleasant sofa table design with rounded ends and lyre-shaped legs linked by an ornamental stretcher.

Boards, too, were made with lavish care to serve the sets of draughts, solitaire pegs and even chessmen produced not only by the Tunbridge turners but by amateurs, such as the Duchess of Portland and her daughters, using their own small lathes to work in ivory, amber, jet, pursuing a hobby fashionable in the third quarter of the 18th century. From these games boards it is easy to trace the development of the individualistic mosaics of Victoria's reign. In stickwork, from the early days of Tunbridge wares, variously coloured woods had been glued together so that cutting them revealed a haphazard pattern and an occasional box is noted covered with a veneer of such colour mixtures, suggesting marble. In the 19th-century Tunbridge ware mosaic veneer, the patterns were achieved by glueing and cutting the variously coloured woods with an exactitude that permitted the creation of pictorial scenes.

The transition was gradual, and many of the pieces of Tunbridge ware most prized today show a particularly pleasing combination of the traditional marquetry and the newer phase of mosaic. A good example is the games table in Kensington Palace made for the Prince Consort in about 1845, the top opening to show the plain squared surface required for chess and the points for backgammon surrounded by bands of flower mosaic and flanked by more elaborate pictorial medallions, all edged with various sizes of stringing and with the legs carrying mosaic arabesques.

Before the development of the tessellated mosaics, long

triangular vandykes in alternate light and dark woods might border designs consisting of various diamond shapes so arranged as to produce an effect of solid cubes depicted in perspective, their seeming solidity emphasised by the clever contrast and alignment of grains and colours. This large-scale, simple cube mosaic is associated with the Regency years but continued much later. The borders may help in dating it, simple at first, then in smaller-scale geometric patterns of increasing intricacy and finally, less happily, with flower mosaic bandings.

These perspective cube designs were never bettered, but an age that admired Florentine marble mosaic inevitably prompted experiment with combinations of very much smaller squares of coloured woods, measuring as little as one-sixteenth of an inch across. Borders and small insertions are noted on early work of this type: the designs consisting of varicoloured stars and innumerable geometric patterns, composed of small squares, triangles, diamonds and the like fitting perfectly together. From this it was a natural step to reduce the shapes of the pieces to a uniform square comparable with the period's cross-stitch embroideries on square canvas known as Berlin wool work, and make the patterns more appealing to their period—around 1830—in uneasy naturalistic flowers and butterflies.

With as many as a hundred and sixty variously coloured woods available it proved possible by about 1850 to present pictorial motifs such as local views, perfect for the souvenir hunter. These could be just as detailed as those in Berlin wool and indeed border detail was often worked direct from the squared patterns of the embroiderer and were claimed when "viewed at a distance" to be "perfect imitations of nature". The views most frequently found include the Tunbridge Wells Pantiles, part of BayhamAbbey (shown at the Great Exhibition by Edmund Nye on a work-box, the picture composed of thirteen thousand pieces of wood), Hever and Tonbridge Castles, Gibraltar House (Tunbridge Wells) and Eridge Castle both before and after removal of the pinnacles from the towers in about 1870.

On the face of it such work would have been prohibitively expensive. The triumph of the mosaic veneer was the fact that it could in a sense be mass produced. An elaborate pattern could be created in these tiny squares and yet be commercially feasible because once a block of pattern was built up it could be sliced into a large number of thin veneers each carrying the same pattern for glueing to various plain wooden articles. Specimen tables and boxes shown at the Great Exhibition by Nye contained as many as 129,540 and 110,800 tiny squares of variously coloured woods, all in their natural colours. Mr. Pinto has noticed a stamp box, an 1840 introduction, with a mosaic representation of a stamp, of normal size, composed of about one thousand tesserae.

At first the small-scale mosaic was used only for narrow borders, little more than the familiar stringing, but by the late 1840s the whole lid of a work box or cover of a folio might be filled with a mosaic view enclosed in flower borders as elaborate as anything in cross stitch and showing a range of softly blended colours in welcome contrast to the strident tones associated with Berlin woods and even perhaps the inspiration for the cross-stitch pictures sometimes noted which are restricted almost entirely to shades of brown and fawn and dull green.

For those interested in how things are made the processes in this mosaic are fascinating. The underlying article was simply constructed of pine and the pattern composed of tiny squares of different woods was mounted upon each of its flat or gently rounded surfaces as a single sheet of veneer less than a tenth of an inch thick. This sheet of pattern may be understood by visualising the contents of a box of matches glued into the neatest possible solid block and then cut across into thin slices so that each slice is composed of fragmentary squares, one from each matchstick. But in the mosaic the sticks were selected and arranged in order according to the colours required for the pattern. This was slow, careful work. The bandmaker, as he was called, worked from a squared chart: remaining specimens show every square lettered to indicate the required wood.

Each column was dealt with separately, the bandmaker beginning with slips of wood some six inches long and one inch wide although only about one-sixteenth of an inch thick. These were convenient to handle and he glued them together by their inch-wide faces. All he required for the pattern on the chart was a thin vertical slice off the resultant block, which would contain in its row of tiny end squares the equivalent of the chart's first column. He could saw about eight to ten veneer slices to the inch so that one assembly of the column served about eight to ten final groupings of the pattern. When he had treated each column in the same way the bandmaker glued together a slice representing each column—each measuring six inches by one-sixteenth of an inch by the depth required of the final mosaic—so that he had a solid cube, still six inches deep, carrying on its end face the whole pattern shown on the chart.

From the same original assembly of each column he could make up another seven to nine exactly similar cubes. He could then cut slices off these cubes, obtaining about fifty to sixty from each, and every one with an identical design. Work prohibitively expensive for decorating a single article became economic when used for six hundred. By the second half of the 19th century however haste was sometimes spoiling results. Such details as the corner where borders meet often lacks the meticulous matching of earlier work. Even more damaging perhaps was the gradual change shortly before the mid-century from a simple polish to a finish of ugly varnish that now tends to have a yellowish tinge and to craze whitely when scratched. Collectors must also beware of the 20th-century reproductions made in large quantities between-wars in traditional shapes and patterns.

Collectors delight especially in specimens carrying the labels of their makes. Small manufacturers engaged in the craft are now forgortten but the larger on usually attached paper labels to their work. Such firms include Fenner and Nye who dissolved a century-old partnership in the 1830s and continued independently, Fenner in 1837 announcing a Regent Street, London, address for his "mosaic and inlaid fancy-wood furniture"; John Barton whose family was employing about twenty men on stick-work turnery by 1728 and who in 1811 invented a circular saw for cutting the veneers; I. J. & A. Sharp; James Friend; George Bennett; Henry Hollamby who showed at the Great Exhibition, and the long-established Tonbridge firm of Wise which continued into the 1870s. A coloured print published in 1822 of "H.R.H. Princess Victoria Returning from a Morning Ride" shows background details of signs announcing the "Tonbridge Ware Repository" and the "The Original Manufactory of Tonbridge Ware" with the name Jordan Place above. This had been acquired from Jordan in the 1740s by a predecessor of the two Burrows firms producing Tunbridge ware in the 19th century. Several of these firms, tracing direct descent from the earliest days of Tunbridge ware manufacture, have led to some confusion among collectors who do not realise that the fascinating cube patterns and pictorial mosaics were but notable phases in the long history of a local souvenir craft unique in Britain.

Chapter Seven

BIRDS IN PORCELAIN

FORTUNATE indeed is the collector who can boast of a mid-18th-century "Chinese Chippendale" wall bracket, and doubly fortunate when spell-bound among its fantastic carving is poised a brilliant porcelain bird. The cascading scrolls of the mahogany offer the perfect setting for beady-eyed parrot or cherry-thieving bullfinch, their form and pose as homely and natural as the potters who created them. Occasionally bird and carving may be contemporaneous, for the Chelsea potters had but recently embarked on the exciting and, to England, entirely new venture of making translucent porcelain when they began to include birds among their figures, for cabinet and bracket ornament, and more especially to set on tables dressed for dessert. Thereafter Chelsea, Bow, Derby, all the famous makers of 18th-century porcelains, furnished a limitless aviary, and potters in stoneware, earthenware and bone china added their own contributions to the lively throng.

Some of these birds are so perfect that they suggest instant flight, some are dullards, earthbound, but the collector of ceramic birds assuredly has the most companionable of specimens and the most decorative. Not all are costly. Chelsea porcelain bird tureens may sell for many hundreds of pounds, but unmarked birds in the 19th century's bone china or in less finely finished earthenware are sometimes to be found for a pound or less. Not all, of course, are antiques. Nor is age any assurance either of fine quality or of a likeable crudity.

Instinctively the china bird fancier looks for specimens with plumage shaped in the modelling rather than dependent upon colouring to suggest the subtleties of feather movement—in the turn of a neck or the droop of a tail. For what can only be called character, an owl-like Chelsea hen harrier bearing the red anchor mark of the factory's early years, 1754–56, may be far more real than many a laboured "portrait" of the 19th century. The perfect modelling and mellow glaze of a Chelsea swan may suggest closely overlapping plumage without any painting at all, but then glossy water birds, like some of the sleeker preening finches, glow superbly under the rich wash of the potter's glaze, whereas it would be hard to imagine a successful recreation in 18th- or 19th-century porcelain of such a naturally matt-plumaged bird as a house sparrow.

Not that the 18th-century potter was likely to think of sparrows: remaining specimens testify to a strong country sale, and the birds are game, such as stout-legged partridges, the parrots of the gentleman's private aviary, canaries as the customary companions of his home, and the cocks and hens of his barnyard. China had made them, and Meissen had copied China: the English potters of the 1750s had no lack of models. If they never caught the elusive charm of a K'ang-hsi goose, at least Chelsea made some of the most spectacular soft porcelain birds, including the famous covered tureens.

The account book kept by William Duesbury and his staff when he was still in London decorating porcelain sent to him from Chelsea and other factories refers to many birds, to "houls" and "hostorredg" (though the birds were long-beaked, clumsy-legged cranes), to drooping birds and flap-wing birds, pheasants, parrots and goldfinches. The main source of Chelsea detail was a book published in 1743, *The Natural History of Uncommon Birds*, by George Edwards. But the interpretations were their own. Usually these birds rest solidly on simply-suggested tree stumps bearing a few scattered flowers and mosses. Sometimes breast or tail receives extra support from a minor branch, but one test of success is the subordination of the stump so that only the bird catches the eye.

Some are miniatures, such as the pigeons for the "magnificent perfume pot in the form of a Pigeon House with Pidgeons, a fox, etc." catalogued in the Chelsea sale of

1755. Other small scent bottles were formed as peacocks and parrots at Chelsea for those who would accept the convention of the metal collar around the bird's neck to receive the head stopper. But in Chelsea's more ornate gold anchor days after 1758 even birds became more elaborately set out, and a candlestick, for instance, might be adorned with a bird and her nestlings in a cherry tree on an encrusted rococo base, in gay defiance of the neo-classic orderliness then descending on well-to-do Englishmen's furnishings.

Bow, like Chelsea, made bird tureens in the mid-1750s, carefully modelled and laboriously painted, and also bird ornaments somewhat more angular and lively with interesting suggestions of movement in head and wing—strutting cocks and hens, for instance, with querky heads and strong, grippy claws, and coloured in bold contradiction of nature. Even Bow peacocks are an unnatural blue and without eye markings on the tail. A hen pheasant may lack the subtle detail of an almost identical Chelsea model, and may display colours ranging from mauve-marked blue for the head, through pink, red and yellow to the browns and yellow of wings and tail, yet retain the anxious, hesitant pose characteristic of this bird.

Many more of the birds now collected came from the long-continuing Derby works. These are often charming: even the blue tit's quintessence of life was attempted. But the first rich vigour has gone. Peacocks, especially, trail their lovely tails over exquisite flower encrustations, and canaries released into flowery bushes perch in anxious conspicuousness, but it is never possible to forget they are painted toys. When Chelsea made a bird teapot with forward-thrust head and open beak as its spout the bird was the hideously raucous guinea fowl: Derby, I feel, would never have made such a choice.

There are birds to be noticed, too, from Longton Hall, nestling among that pottery's particularly lovely flower encrustations. Occasionally, also, a hard porcelain bird turns up, a finch perhaps or a somewhat ungainly pheasant, or a pair of phoenix, wings spread in the classic pose, on broad, flaming plinths. These are Plymouth birds of about 1770. Some were issued in the white, some brightly coloured

—red, yellow, blue, crimson, purple, brown, black. But hard porcelain, cold and slightly greyish, was a poor medium for the pheasant's warm radiance. Indeed, by the 1770s, porcelain potters were tending to turn from the gentleman's aviary, but the earthenware craftsmen were very much aware of the wicker cage over the cottage door.

A collection of earthenware birds may lack the accomplished grace of porcelain but today it has the immense appeal of traditional craftsmanship, touched with the humour never far away from the tough Staffordshire potters.

A few early ceramic birds were made in the clear-cut white salt-glazed stoneware of early Georgian days. By the mid 18th century some were given beaks or feathers emphasised in brown or blue, and later more were made gorgeous with enamel colours, such as the swans and their cygnets in the Schrieber collection at the Victoria and Albert Museum, London, one swan with purple neck and body, the other, smaller, turquoise blue, their feet black, their wings blue, green, red, orange, yellow.

Nottingham in the 1750s made rich brown birds, including owl jugs, with fragments of rough clay to suggest their plumage. But earthenware, lead glazed, as a medium for this work came into its own when Thomas Whieldon blotched and dappled his bird figures. Pigeons, owls, game birds, appeared to perfection in the purplish browns and slaty blues, the yellows and greens achieved by this impressionistic method of allowing the glaze to mingle the dabs of colour derived from copper (green), manganese (purple and, with iron, a deep brown), cobalt (blue and grey), and ochre (yellow and orange).

Unmarked birds cannot be ascribed to a known potter, merely admired for the hauteur of a hawk or the plump self-effacement of a finch, their plumage sketched in with a few incised lines. Other birds of around 1780 and 1790 may be noted in much the same range of colours, but in orderly rather than spontaneous effects, as the colours have been brush-applied in the Ralph Wood manner. Thus tits—birds that have appealed to every generation of potters—have been noted with brown bodies, blue and yellow on their wings, dark head patches and blue eye rings.

Before the end of the century, however, potters were using vividly coloured enamels painted on over the lead glaze and, more durably, a limited range of hard bright colours under the glaze to achieve the somewhat heavy effects of the so-called Pratt ware, found for instance in a cock crudely modelled as a wooden toy but majestically coloured with a blue body, an orange comb, and a tail daubed with blue, yellow, orange and brown. These bright colour effects soon had countless unnamed potters working on cocks and pheasants and canaries "painted after nature" as gorgeous as any in porcelain. An occasional bird may be found with a whistle, either projecting from the typical green mound of the base or from the bird's out-jutting tail.

Hawkers carrying long trays of little earthenware figures on their heads were familiar in the streets of the early 19th century, recorded for instance in Henry Alken pictures. And very welcome their wares must have proved while women dressed so much in dingy white, and while so many towns were thronged with homesick country folk. Some of these early-19th-century earthenware birds are cheaply ambitious, clumsily attempting with a few disproportionate leaves and flowers to represent the flowering bush effects of the porcelain maker's fragile *bocages*. But who could deny the attraction of a treeful of birds, tiny nestlings above, plump parents on the lower branches?

By the earliest years of the 19th century, bone china was proving a successful alternative to more fragile porcelains, and infinitely more susceptible than earthenwares to the delicacy of detail in crest and beak and feather. Occasionally a tiny Spode thrush comes to light, or a brilliant green and red and yellow parrot from the Chamberlain Worcester pottery. Rockingham's Brameld brothers, who began making bone china in 1820, are associated with such birds as miniature parrots two and a half inches high. Many Derby birds, too, date to the 19th century, lacking subtlety but meticulously painted with that century's delight in exact representation and set among delicate flower encrustations. Peacocks especially are Derby's bird, every eye on the tail, every feather in the breast scrupulously detailed.

For the everyday collector most of the bird vessels found

today belong to the 19th century too, although the masterpieces, Meissen-inspired, date right back to Chelsea's red anchor days of the mid-1750s when such bird tureens contained sweetmeats at the informal after-dinner buffet party known as a dessert (a delightful affair that I describe in more detail in *Small Decorative Antiques*). *The Daily Advertiser* in 1764 notes their use for this purpose.

The Chelsea sale catalogues of 1755 and 1756 list such items as, "A most beautiful TUREEN in the shape of a HEN & CHICKENS as large as life in a fine sunflower leaf dish". A specimen of this in the Victoria and Albert Museum is extraordinarily attractive (plate 17): the hen's head is a delightful study, and she sits with wings slightly fluffed out to shelter her chicks peeping from among feathers suggested by light brush-work in purple shades, browns and red. A horizontal division from the breast to the upper side of the tail separates the bowl from the cover, a chick on the hen's back serving as a lifting handle. A dish of sunflowers completes the model, twenty-one inches by fifteen, shaped in relief with flowers and laurel leaves vividly coloured.

The most imposing Chelsea tureen, a swan fourteen inches tall and twenty inches long, with arching neck and long slender head and beak was a major triumph for the soft porcelain of its period—a whiter, more translucent paste than that of Chelsea's earliest work, and with a smoother glaze. Yet the bird and its flat oval dish sold in 1768 for as little as thirty-five shillings.

Other covered dishes were modelled as crested ducks, gruesome fighting cocks and the smaller partridges that proved particularly popular for the dessert table. Chelsea frequently advertised them, such as "two fine partridges in a beautiful dish with corn etc.", remaining dishes showing basket work around embossed designs of yellow wheat-ears and coloured flowers. Partridges proved popular models with Bow and Derby too. Bow made attractive oval tureens from about 1756, with the birds sitting in nests wreathed with flowers and wheat, their dishes measuring eight inches by six, sometimes less. Pigeon tureens are found, too, in Bow's hard, dense, heavy porcelain and in the firm's harshly white phosphatic porcelain dating from about 1760 to 1765. Derby pigeons and partridge tureens date from about 1756 onwards too, in a glassy paste with a creamy translucency but all too seldom are marked. This is the greater pity since these small homely tureens had a wide sale, although specimens of the 1770s lack the earlier fine finish.

Even the Chelsea tureens have their early-19th-century imitations as well as 20th-century fakes. They were exactly copied by Madeley, but in bone china instead of soft porcelain. Although they were issued unmarked some in the course of time have acquired the desirable red anchor. The early tureens are museum pieces, but hens and their chicks of the 19th century are to be found still in many qualities: a collector who put a small advertisement in his local newspaper was astonished at the number he could acquire. Those of the 1820s may be a little less than life-size and vividly enamelled: a few bear the Bloor mark of Derby (1815–48). Some served like the cradles I described in Chapter 10 to convey congratulatory small gifts and good wishes to mothers and their new babies, and by the 1830s, smaller still, sometimes carried valentines.

Stolid-looking Victorian hens, often fully life-size, may be found in styles freely shared among the bone china and stone china potters, rarely marked and impossible to distinguish. The whole hen usually forms the lid to a yellow wicker-basket nest. Warmed, she could be used on the table to cover the family's breakfast boiled eggs. Outstanding models of the 1850s may still be found, however, finely modelled in ivory-tinted parian ware with the smooth, matt surface produced by a process known as smear glazing. Charles Meigh & Sons of Hanley made some of the best; others are marked by T. J. & J. Mayer of Hanley. Today, however, we even collect the small hens in coarse pottery of the 1840s to 1860s regarded at the time as little more than throw-away containers for sweets and prizes at country fairs.

Conspicuously different from the general run of very humble 19th-century earthenware bird ornaments were the grotesques and caricatures of the Martin brothers' stoneware, in dull greens, blues and browns. These are now highly prized and are either hated or loved on sight. The four brothers' production period extended from 1873 to 1915 and many of their fantasies are dated. Bernard Moore was another creator of birds who sometimes signed them, working around the beginning of the present century, fashioning red-glazed ducks and turquoise owls and all manner of specimens of Oriental and Continental inspiration. Among tomorrow's antiques in this line the Royal Worcester and Crown Staffordshire marks may be found on a range of birds designed for a new generation of garden bird-lovers who might be hard-pressed to identify the superb Chelsea hen harrier but delight to differentiate between, say, a coal tit and a great tit, or a shrike and a nuthatch. Only among these comparative newcomers, it appears, is to be found the essential specimen of a robin.

The Royal Worcester birds designed by Dorothy Doughty have no place yet in a consideration of antique birds in porcelain, but already, of course, are avidly sought for what have already become priceless collections. Here each bird and its setting is treated as an individualistic creation, and it is indeed fascinating to watch as skilled fingers fashion even each tiniest stamen of each smallest background flower and, after it has received its first drying, others build such tiny details into the required composition, others again add colour, process by process, and the wonderful surface texture that gives the warm glow of life to these bird figures, the most delicately exquisite, surely, ever produced in the long tradition of the potter's craft.

Chapter Eight

JUGS FOR MILK AND CREAM

FOR two and a half centuries our English ritual of tea-time has been enriched by the charm of what was long known as the tea equipage. First in finely-proportioned silver, then in a wealth of coloured ceramics, English craftsmen have produced some of their most brilliant, imaginative creations in the service of this delicate repast.

Only very fortunate collectors can assemble typical examples of all the vessels contributing to the early Georgian's splendid tea table array, but there are fascinating possibilities for collectors who concentrate on a single detail of this equipage. They can thus build up a little group of specimens, each an individual treasure, together displaying, decade by decade, the changing styles and shapes and decorative details of form and ornament dominating the whole tea-service design.

The jugs for milk and cream are a perfect choice for such a collection, small yet important, functional in the tradition of all good design yet addicted to every kind of minor decorative diversion. And what a wealth of varieties are available. In silver they may be traced right from Queen Anne's day. But innumerable other specimens are to be found in Sheffield plate, in earthenwares and the lovely soft porcelains of Chelsea, Worcester, Bow and the fine bone chinas that succeeded them, in pewter and painted enamels and Nailsea glass. Many of these are still available for a pound or two—many for less. Some collectors even concentrate entirely on those oddly likeable cow designs, although modern reproductions are now making these a somewhat hazardous choice.

There is still some doubt as to how the earliest English

tea drinkers took their costly "tay", and considerable argument in favour of the theory that for tea as for coffee a tall hot-milk pot accompanied the teapot. However that may be, by about 1705 tiny "milk ewers" were being created by the silversmiths to hold a mere eighth of a pint. The design of these little jugs was so simple that it continued in silver and ceramics while other fashions came and went, the body smoothly pear-shaped, on a narrow cast foot ring, the rim straight with the open beak-shaped spout added as a separate, cast unit and balanced by a plain cast scroll handle topped by a minute thumb-piece. There was a gradual tendency for the foot rim to be made larger and more spreading, noticeable even by 1727 and very marked by 1760.

Probably the earliest wide-lipped vessels for slow-pouring cream were designed for the dessert table. Delightful small cream-boats of the 1720s are known, such as a rounded nautilus shell with a dolphin handle or the more usual sauce-boat shape, oval with outward curving rim, its sheared edge in scalloped or cyma outline, and with a high arching, double scroll handle or a free-standing handle topped by a motif shaped in the round. Sometimes there is a mask under the lip and frequently three shapely feet, the mask strengthening the curve of the lip and the feet ensuring a steady balance despite the small size and light weight of the vessel and the bumps of careless cleaning.

A hand-raised cream-boat may show applied ornament in relief but deep relief work is associated more particularly with cast designs made from the late 1730s onwards, their tiny cows and goats, flowers or other motifs prominent and shining with the rub of wear. Sometimes such a vessel has a round moulded foot ring instead of the dolphins, shells or other shapely feet.

With the creation of colourful dessert services in English porcelains, cream-bowls tended to oust the silver boats from the dessert table, but by then small jugs for cold creamy tea-time milk were appearing in a more graceful curving design that had been introduced in the 1730s. This is a miniature version of the long prized "inverted helmet" ewer, the rounded body topped by a curving rim with wide flaring spout and mounted on three small feet. Within a few years even the more prosaic pear-shaped, plain spouted jugs were often given similar tiny legs and scroll feet and even in porcelain and painted enamels the same fashion had to be observed, although for painted enamels especially it was entirely unsuitable.

Some of the most delightful little silver jugs ever made date to the 1730s and 1740s, the baluster or pear-shaped body often narrowing to the neck then flaring out in scalloped or cyma shaped rim which rises to a fine, wide curving lip for pouring. To balance this the rim rises high, too, to support the arching handle which is often a series of small opposing scrolls and returns to the body at its widest part with a final flourish. By the late 1730s it might be given a cast and chased leaf for a thumb rest and sometimes ornamented with beading or gadrooning. The very small feet or stem and foot ring contribute to the poised, jaunty air: sometimes in the charming manner of its period the whole vessel from lip to foot rim is octagonal or hexagonal on plan to catch the light with added brilliance.

Even by the 1740s however the gleam of smooth silver is often interrupted by elaborate ornament. On jugs as on cream-boats this is often chased on the hand-raised vessel but becomes most conspicuous in the heavy embossed motifs easily achieved by casting. Feet may be in scroll-and-leaf design or lion's mask-and-paw or shell patterns. On the jug's body instead of the early crest there may be hunting scenes, farm animals and even tiny figure groups from classical legend, but many show merely flowers or fruiting vines or irregular scrolling cartouches. Many small silver jugs, however, in inverted pear-shapes on hollow pedestal stemmed feet, produced from the 1760s onwards, are pleasingly simple, being inexpensively lathe-spun instead of hammered from the plate. They were assembled with a minimum of ornament, such as pressed beading to strengthen the edges of rim and foot. From the 1770s the jug might be shaped by stamping out two halves in machine-rolled silver to be joined vertically—and invisibly—and mounted on a separately shaped foot.

English silversmiths never elaborated the rococo notions

of swirling scrolls to the extent found on the Continent but it is easy to understand nevertheless the new-found delight in neo-classic styles that came as an obvious reaction to these extravagances and dominated the tea tables of the 1770s. Today these plinth-mounted jugs, their plain looping handles emphasising the smooth upward and outward sweep of body and spout, may seem too chaste—and too easily knocked over—for homely tea-times. Often the body is eight-sided on plan, tapering from rim to base where a slender stem links it to the eight-sided round or elliptical pedestal foot sometimes resting on a four-sided plinth. Bright-cut engraving dates from the 1780s—tiny sharp-edged fragments cut from the metal like delicate chip carving.

By then some of these jugs were in narrow-necked classical vase or ewer shape with upswept everted spouts. They were soon replaced, however, by the comparatively squat little pitcher, still with high out-curving lip and arching or square-shouldered handle but with the body, round, oval, barrel-shaped, even seven-sided, resting flatly on the tea-tray. The silver is thin and the rim often protected with moulding. For steadiness there may be four ball feet, associated with Regency days when tea-pots were thus raised from the table surface. Gadrooning and fluting on urn-shaped jugs is an early-19th-century development and an abundance of embossed scenic ornament and heavy applied mouldings are associated with the 1820s when some attractive jugs matched tea-pots in the early silversmith's melon shape. The 1830s brought mainly a more flamboyant rendering of the rococo styles outmoded nearly a century before.

It may be mentioned in passing that these jugs and even the dessert table's silver boats were intended for milk or fresh cream, both sadly perishable. The serving of hot boiled milk with tea and coffee was one obvious solution: with desserts an alternative was scalded or clotted cream and this too has its silver vessels, exceptionally attractive. In the 1740s small milkmaid pails were devised, often marked to resemble the wooden vessels and lifted by tall bail handles. Their accompanying ladles, often with shell-shaped

C. Card cases in papier mâché painted on both sides: that on the left is rendered more brilliant with inlays of pearl shell.

facing page 80

bowls, are seldom found with them today. Mrs. Delany was charmed to receive a pail and spoon in 1752. By the 1770s these vessels had lost their bucket details but appeared very splendid in pierced silver or in silver wire lined with Bristol blue glass. By then the alternative was the cream basket, pierced and glass-lined too, but in a bowl or vase shape on stem and foot. A comparative rarity is the helmet cream jug in pierced silver, never wholly satisfactory in the line of the blue glass spout.

There is still some doubt as to when tea was first served with cream. The Hon. John Byng, well up in the London fashions of his day, mentions in *The Torrington Diaries*, as late as 1785, tea with cream as "a great curiosity". Yet in the 1770s Chelsea was including cream ewers among the porcelain tea equipage. Inevitably the story of milk and cream jugs from the mid 18th century is dominated by the launching of porcelain manufacture in England—in 1743 at Chelsea and between 1744 and 1748 at Heylin's Glass House, Bow, and between 1748 and 1750 at Bristol. Previously porcelain had been no more than a costly rarity. Now such details as cream jugs at once appeared, but for a century to come the potter tended to follow the silversmith's designs.

At first even the decoration consisted only of embossed ornament on the colourless glazed body of the pear-shaped jug and the narrow pointed spout and three or four small feet were all separately applied units. Even the most famous Chelsea goat-and-bee jug—the vessel supported by two goats lying head to tail—was taken from a silver model. But the rim-curving, wide-spouted ewers more appropriate to the new materials quickly followed, including some double handled and double spouted. Some were oval in section and spirally fluted, or reeded and scallop rimmed, some octagonal. Bristol made one design in fan-shaped panels rising from a six-sided base.

Now lovely decoration in enamel colours contributed to the rich effect. Even the base of a jug interior sometimes displays a flower spray, perhaps to hide a minor flaw. A jug of the 1750s may be found with low relief moulding as its main decoration—in chinoiserie designs for instance—and yet with blue flowers inside. Catalogues of the Chelsea sales listing tea and coffee services mention these vessels, a typical entry reading: "A compleat tea and coffee equipage containing 8 tea cups and saucers, 8 handled cups; a tea pot and stand, slop bason, sugar bason, cream ewer, and plate", the last item being for the tea spoons. One set of saucers served for both tea and coffee cups, a custom continued even in the early 19th century in much bone china ware. Five types of enamelled decoration were noted in one Chelsea list: flowers, insects, birds, cupids and green landscapes.

Worcester too made delightful little pear-shaped cream jugs, narrow-necked, wide-mouthed and three-footed in the silver manner, moulded with relief ornament and with smooth surfaces decorated in enamel colours. Worcester is associated with the earliest porcelain to be decorated with the time-saving transfer prints we now expect to find on almost all china tea ware. The earliest were in black; later they were over-painted in colour, but transfer-printing is associated most especially with lovely tones of underglaze blue. This possible quest for a would-be collector was considered in Chapter 1.

Other porcelain factories produced their own individual little jugs. Derby set the fashion for the design with an ovoid body and long, slightly tapering neck. Derby may be credited, too, perhaps with the earliest porcelain examples of the mask jugs which delight many collectors, a silversmith's strengthening feature on jugs with sheared rims. Such a jug in porcelain has a mask moulded in relief on the outer surface of the lip, a fashion which included not only the commonest bearded head but also the heads of satyrs, cupids and the like, developing in the 1770s and 1780s into the vogue for celebrities' heads, such as the Derby Lord Rodney in a cocked hat, General Wolfe, Kitty Clive and the Young Pretender. Bristol cream jugs in hard porcelain have coloured masks of spring, summer, autumn and winter taken from the moulds used for the heads of the familiar sets of the seasons.

Elaborate relief moulding may be found also on the bird handle of the lid that often accompanies such a cream jug, low or high domed, plain or richly decorated, but leaving the spout uncovered.

Other imaginative moulded design of the 1760s and onwards is to be found among jugs composed of leaf panels. These were made by Longton Hall and indeed most of the porcelain factories: sometimes the leaf stalks serve as tiny feet. Handles shaped as twigs or crab-stocks, canes, knotted stalks and the like had been popular at Chelsea and Longton Hall from 1750 although on the jugs from other factories it is more usual to find plain loops, straps and scrolls, and by the last quarter of the century the innumerable urns and vases dominating current neo-classic ornament had established their familiar patterns.

Classic emphasis on smooth, upsweeping curves never really suited the English tea table, however, and by 1800 in ceramics as in silver there was a return to low, broad-based tea services such as may still be found in every kind of ware. Here the cream jug may be almost too solidly squat, but in a good design it is a particularly attractive little pitcher, its spout curving up somewhat above the rim.

The 19th century has its own special opportunities for the collector: the lovely mellow but fragile porcelains of the previous half-century were almost abandoned and bone china ruled the day, thin, translucent, dainty ware, but far stronger as well as whiter, so that many a delightful specimen remains. Its correct dating is a skill that comes of long familiarity with this exuberant century, but it may be mentioned in passing that any jug with "England" included in the maker's mark is likely to post-date 1891.

If porcelain and china followed the fashion set by silver they in turn were mimicked by earthenwares, fresh, homely, unsophisticated. Their range includes among others the early white salt-glazed jugs, usually lidded and with relief ornament in the silversmith's manner, jugs of the mingled colour glazes known as tortoiseshell ware, with tiny claw feet and sometimes masks on their lips, and lustre wares less elaborate in form and treatment than their bone china counterparts. Lustre ware jugs are, of course, a collector's joy despite the modern imitations, and are mentioned in Chapter 12.

The collector looks beyond ceramics, however. There are specimens for the seeking in South Staffordshire enamels, for instance. This interesting product, associated with all that is most dainty in snuff box, étui, thimble case and chatelaine, makes another specialist hobby. The white enamel is delicately painted and set in fine metal mounts so that no trace is seen of the underlying core of copper that supplies its remarkable strength. My favourites here are the little pear-shaped, wavy-rimmed variety on scroll feet, flower-painted like porcelain but with a character all their own.

Pewter cream jugs may date to the 18th century: those in Sheffield plate often to Regency days. Even in glass there are many antique cream jugs for the finding and to the enthusiast no other craftsman's material can compare with glass, possessing the miracle quality of water, now limpid smooth, now rippled into a thousand flashing fires.

The jugs worth collecting are nearly all made of flint-glass, the wholly English invention of George Ravenscroft in the 1670s, lustrous silky glass that never wholly lost its dusky tone until the 19th century. A Ravenscroft jug in the Victoria and Albert Museum tells its own tale of early difficulties in strengthening this glass. The bowl and foot are ribbed, the handle twisted and the most vulnerable edges of lip and foot are folded back on themselves, for it was so susceptible to atmospheric changes that it might fall to pieces even when standing in the cupboard.

By early-Georgian days flint-glass jugs were welcomed on to the tea table for serving hot milk. These are delightful, sharing the miniature quality of all tea equipage of the 1730s, perhaps two-and-a-half or three-and-a-half inches tall in the rounded baluster outlines of contemporaneous milk pots of silver and pewter and with similar sharply beaked spouts. A feature to look for on such a jug is the considerable hollow under the base, the centre still rough to the fingers where it was broken from the glass maker's punty rod. This shape was still made early in the 19th century, but improvements in annealing reduced the need for the hollow base kick.

Some glass milk jugs from the mid 18th century onwards show another silversmithing notion, the small plump body raised on three stumpy feet. As the milk for tea was then served cold the lip could be shaped more suitably for a richer, creamier liquid, rising upward and forward in a wide, graceful curve. This lip may be noted folded outwards to strengthen the edge, with the fold concealed under narrow glass frilling or trailing. The design called for a longer neck and the body below became more rounded.

By the 1770s the whole outline reflected the current fashion for neo-classic design, with shouldered body and round foot. The result is the perfect small cream jug but it was still advertised as a milk ewer. However, glass cream jugs were being advertised by 1787, and more homely little shapes became popular in the 1790s, wide-bodied and resting flatly upon the tea-tray. Early-19th-century specimens are sometimes found, often oblong on plan, but by then high fashion had banished glass cream jugs from the tea table and they are to be found mainly among the cheaper styles of glassware.

Not only their general design but more especially the ornamental treatments of these jugs help the collector to date them. Engraving is particularly fascinating and associated with the late 18th century and early-Regency years when the lustrous glass gave a rich beauty to the delicate linear work. But far more jugs bear the cut ornament unique to glass and here the most important guide to dating perhaps is the change from shallow cutting, which retained the lovely translucency of the glass, to the deep cutting composed of deep V-shaped grooves crossing each other so that the small pyramids between them appear to project from the surface with a diamond fire and glitter. The deep cutting became technically possible in the 1780s but mainly took effect from about 1805.

At its finest a glass jug is shaped and ornamented individually—free-blown, hand-cut, hand-engraved. But by the 1760s glassmen had begun to devise less expensive ways of achieving what they hoped would pass for the same effects. They never quite do, of course, but today this blown-moulded and press-shaped glass is greatly valued and collected. I describe something of this work in Chapter 22.

Nailsea jugs are a subject in themselves, flamboyantly patterned with splashes and zig-zags, stripes and threads of contrasting colour, whether they were in fact made around Bristol or as far away as Newcastle, Alloa, Warrington and Sunderland. Those in brownish-green bottle-glass may be dated 1790–1820; light green bottle-glass with notched ornament, 1800–20; mottled ornament on opaque coloured glass from 1815 onwards and on translucent coloured flint-glass from 1845; lattice patterning in white and pink on pale green glass, 1815–45, and thereafter on clear flint-glass—all these dates being, of course, only approximate. Most Nailsea jugs are of cheap, low-taxed bottle-glass but coloured flint-glass jugs are delightful finds, blue, amethyst, purple, amber, perhaps given the superb enrichment of gilding in a scrolling cartouche around a cautionary "Be canny with the cream". Most surprising find perhaps is an opaque, milk-white glass jug dating from about 1820 onwards, utterly dull until held against the light when it may reveal a fiery opalescence to which even the prosaic glassmen were moved to give the lovely name of sunset glow.

Chapter Nine

DOOR KNOCKERS AND PORTERS

THE traveller knocking at the moonlit door can still stir a romance-loving heart: in these coloured-plastic days there is a peculiar attraction about the massive iron knocker that could send its thunder to the remotest slumbering servant.

Collectors can still find splendid specimens and demand is increasing. So too is the renewed interest in that other, still weightier, piece of door "furniture", the door porter or door stop. Both at their best are decorative, whether our choice is a gilded shield-of-arms knocker that once roused an earl's household, or Doyle's Mr. Punch, bright with brass polish or black-lead, chuckling a welcome as he holds wide the door. There are changes in style and technique that make it possible to determine a specimen's period, and a range of metals from japanned iron to bronzed work and brass.

Even the more ornate may still be bought for a few pounds, but they have to be sought. You do not find them in showy window displays and their discovery, I have found, can supply the authentic thrill as an unenthusiastic dealer drags out the dusty iron from some dark, cluttered corner.

Knockers developed in the 16th and 17th centuries. Early Elizabethans rapped on the door with their staves or perhaps with a wooden mallet hung beside it for the purpose, or clattered the wrought iron ring that pulled the door shut. But later 16th century writers refer to early knockers: Picciatio Florio, a visitor to London in 1598, for example, mentions "a hammer or striker to knock a door with". In 1611 Cotgrove referred to "the ring, knocker or hammer of a door". As local blacksmiths began to fashion their own designs in wrought iron the rapper might follow the traditional shape of either handle or hammer, but now the ring or iron hammer shaft pivoted on a shaped escutcheon of plate iron and was provided with an iron stud to strike on.

Design has always been simple enough, but has changed more importantly in the course of centuries than may at first be realised, considering that it consists merely in the three units, the leaf escutcheon bolted to the door, the bolts passing right through the wood to nuts and washers on the inner side, the handle or rapper, weighted towards the bottom to ensure a forceful knock, and the striking stud, also bolted to the door, to receive and magnify the rapper's blows.

The spur-shaped rapper that was developed later in the 17th century was one of the first designs made from standardised units produced in quantity. The spur swings from loops wrought to the flat plate or escutcheon of metal, which may be leaf-shaped or pierced in geometrical designs or take the form of a time-weathered face.

The way the rapper hangs is an important point. Simple knockers in wrought iron never really went out of production until the end of the 19th century but this rapper attachment was abandoned late in the 18th century. It is surprising it lasted so long for every dare-devil young man about town, it seems, had to test his strength at knocker-wrenching. As early as 1709 Steele in *The Tatler* noted that "one can hardly find a Knocker at a Door in a whole Street after a Midnight Expedition of these Beaux Esprits". And as late as 1844 J. T. Hewlett could look back on his youth and remember "knocker wrenching and sign removing were in vogue in my day". The pivot was the weak point, of course, and the rapper could be torn from its plate by any ill-mannered roisterer, though most people today credit them with the strength to wrench the whole knocker unit from the door, backplate, bolts and all.

By the 18th century the typical knocker was of iron, but cast instead of wrought, and weighty to escape cracking in vigorous use. Some of these date from the 1730s and 1740s, usually with simple wrought iron ring rappers swinging from elaborate escutcheons cast in high relief. A lion's head, for instance, may be nine inches long, seven inches wide and four inches deep, with the rapper swinging from its mouth, a wrought iron ring, round or oval with a heavy knop or other simple motif to give the rap. Eyes drilled in the rapper allowed it to swing loosely on a riveted bar passing through the lion's mouth. Smaller sizes were made too, but the full range of size and ornament came when the rapper itself could also be in cast instead of wrought iron, fashioned from the malleable cast iron that was invented in 1804 by Samuel Lucas of Sheffield and was in use by the 1820s, with little danger of fracture when comparatively small.

Every maker then developed more ambitious patterns. The rapper may be found as a twist of cable, or a fruiting vine, or a handsome coat of arms. The expansive spread-eagle escutcheon and palmette rapper are found with a frequency that points to long popularity, and the hand grasping a bar and swinging a laurel wreath. A lyre rapper of about 1800 may be found hanging from the head of a sphinx. Vase shapes date from the neo-classic vogue of the 1760s onwards through the 19th century, the intricate surface ornament made possible by the casting method appearing attractively on some elliptical rappers with back plates in urn outlines. Such a backplate, shaped as an urn or vase or more ambitiously as a caryatid figure, served not only to attach the rapper but also to receive the knock. But in a design such as the lion and ring there had to be an additional stud attached to the door where the ring would strike. This important detail should harmonise with the rest of the knocker: it may be as decorative as a Tudor rose or as plain as the concentric-ringed neo-classic patera.

For many years black japanning was often used to protect the iron from the weather but the best of these early-19th-century castings are highlighted with bronze powder. Hubball of Clerkenwell invented the process in 1812. Metallic bronze powders ground in turpentine varnish were applied to projecting details, tinted by an undercoat of blue or yellow paint.

By then the rapper-wrencher had been thwarted by a

change in design, the rapper head being sunk into the escutcheon and swinging loosely from a fixed rivet that passed through it. This meant that the knocker could become the small, neat little ornament that is most in demand today. The London firm of Baily & Sons began with a well-modelled head attached to the door by a single bolt: this had a slender acanthus leaf rapper and expansive ornamental striking plate.

A special method of making extremely well finished castings which could be hand-chased and highly burnished was introduced by the Coalbrookdale Company, Shropshire, in 1839. They were among the firms that often registered their designs at the Patent Office to prevent piracy by competitors and it is always worth looking for the diamond-shaped mark on a knocker: this shows its design was registered between 1842 and 1883 and the symbols can be interpreted to supply the date (see page 34).

Coalbrookdale applied the brief brilliance of electro-gilding to some mid-19th-century knockers and many late Georgian firms offered their knocker patterns in three qualities: in iron bronzed all over; with a bronzed escutcheon and a brass rapper; and all brass. Trade catalogues show the difference in cost. For a crested palmette escutcheon and a loop rapper, for example, the prices might be three shillings, six shillings and sixpence, and ten shillings and sixpence. For current values the shillings might be changed to pounds.

A gleaming brass knocker is delightfully welcoming. It is difficult to realise today how comparatively recent was their heyday. The soft brass alloys were altogether too tempting to the 18th-century knocker-wrencher and not until the early 19th century were these loveliest of knockers in high demand. By the 1820s, however, they were as floridly rococo as even that decade could desire. There are lions, goats and other animal heads shaped by casting in high relief with ring rappers, and female heads from classic legend such as the best-known Medusa with foliage festoons. There are Egyptian motifs, sphinx heads and lyre-shaped rappers and a range of less inventive designs such as the hand with a wreath, the vase with a festoon and the spread acanthus leaf or fleur-de-lys with a long loop rapper. In some, even when the escutcheon is round or horizontally elliptical, it is deep enough to do duty also as a striking stud, the whole design suggesting a handle on a chest of drawers. By the late 1830s there was already a "hatch knocker", a design with a letter flap as well as the scroll-shaped rapper. Brass knockers were sometimes protected from the weather by an elaborate lacquering process that was known, confusingly, as bronzing.

The perfect accompaniment to an old door knocker is a door porter. The same firms made both, and gave them the same range of treatment in cast iron, bronzed cast iron and brass. Some have only the handle in brass on a base of cast iron and would be bought and assembled by merchants. Some from about 1850 are vividly but somewhat fleetingly painted and some again are to be found in quite other materials.

The majority of door porters are in iron or brass, however, and date no earlier than about 1775 when John Izon and Thomas Whitehurst patented a "secret" cast brass "rising hinge with steel roller" that caused a door to rise slightly as it opened so that it would close again slowly unless actively prevented. Early porters are cast in the round, such as the basket of flowers in gilded brass with every petal burnished: from the centre of the weight rises a tall, thin handle ending in a plain loop or a solid finial in the form of a pineapple, symbol of hospitality.

Flat-backed stops date from the 1790s onwards, such as the winged lion illustrated, with pineapple handle, assembled from three castings, or the long-handled half-bell design which might be over-elaborated in the early 19th century with ball or lion paw feet. A lion's paw in iron or brass was itself a popular design in Regency years, topped by a collar and a stylised acanthus leaf merging into a "loop of rope" handle. In brass this cost twelve shillings in 1822. Samuel Kenrick of Summit Foundry, West Bromwich, made some of these, impressing them with his mark *KENRICK*.

By 1810 many door porters were made without handles,

some fifteen inches high—lively inventive designs, however inconvenient it might prove to shift three or four pounds of crouching sphinx or winged leopard, horse or greyhound or seated lion. An eagle clawing a ball might measure more than fourteen inches from wing-tip to wing-tip. Sometimes a brass door stop turns up declaring itself made to order by its original owner's coat of arms. More frequent is the outspilling cornucopia, a design of the 1820s, and this was soon followed by full-length celebrity figures with attractive bronzed finish in the period's new-found malleable cast iron.

These are particular treasures, splendidly sturdy little flat-backed figures, often shaped to lift easily—Wellington by his cocked hat, Punch by the curve of his cap. William III may be found as well as George IV and Nelson and the Duke of York and Sir Robert Peel. The early soldiers in uniform well suit the rigid upright pose required of the guardian of the door and may be vivid with colour. William IV carrying the Reform Bill sold well in the early 1830s and Queen Victoria in her robes formed a coronation souvenir.

The Coalbrookdale Company made door porters as finely finished as their knockers, including an armoured knight with spear and shield under a gothic canopy. This figure, originally bronzed, may carry an inscription cast into the back of the plinth: "The Coalbrookdale Company. Registered—October 28th 1841". (A specimen has been noted with the date reading "February 28th 1842, N° 89".) Modern copies of this knight are about an inch shorter than the original's height of seventeen inches.

This firm virtually monopolised the trade in door porters of good quality and at the Great Exhibition, 1851, they displayed pairs of whippets, deer and eagles, outstandingly modelled and brilliantly burnished. Less expensive bronzed porters were shown at the Exhibition by Andrew Handyside of Derby.

The door stop figures that delighted the rest of the 19th century are fascinatingly varied—from Jenny Lind to kilted Scotsmen. Mr. Punch in iron and in brass appeared with other grotesques in the third quarter of the century: he was taken from Richard Doyle's celebrated drawing which first appeared on the cover of the magazine *Punch* in 1849. Punch and Judy as a pair are to be found too, and that other popular pair of grotesques, Mr. and Mrs. Caudle, while nearly a quarter of a century later came the small, ill-clad Ally Sloper, the celebrated figure that appeared in the magazine *Judy* early in the 1870s and later in the comic journal *Ally Sloper's Half Holiday*, founded in 1884 by Gilbert Dalziel.

Jumbo, illustrated on plate 19, in iron with bright-painted harness, was a mid-Victorian celebrity of the London Zoo and is of particular interest because she bears the Patent Office's diamond registration mark. This may be elucidated and indicates a registration of the design on May 18th, 1882 (see page 34).

With luck an old iron door porter may be found in its original finish of japanning, paint or bronze powders. But more likely such short-lived brilliance will have gone long ago, replaced by the nearly-forgotten glow of strong-armed blackleading.

Door porters in other materials are not always recognised. These range from obelisks in Minton terra-cotta and Derbyshire marble to a tipped-over basket of flowers brilliantly coloured in wood-mounted plaster.

Some of the loveliest are in glass. An early type of these is the West Country "dump", a high-crowned egg-shaped dome given character by long bubbles of air trapped within the clear greenish glass. On a roughly finished dump the flattened base was left concave towards the centre, where a rough scar shows how the lump of glass has been broken free of the punty iron on which it was held while hot for holes to be pierced and more hot glass added smoothly over the resultant air pockets or bubbles, and while the whole mass of hot glass was swung to elongate these crude decorations. A flat-ground base indicates higher quality, and many of these glass door porters are in considerably more elaborate designs only a little coarser and larger than some paperweights. Bristol and Nailsea were making them from about 1828 and Birmingham and Castleford a few years later in harsher tones of green bottle glass.

Clear flint-glass in porters, smoky-hued from its weight

of lead oxide, dates from the 1840s onwards, the dome often decorated with fountains of small air bubbles seeming to rise from the centre of the base and cascade down the sides. In more elaborate designs solid motifs such as flowers in a pot might be introduced. The pot was composed of glass dipped in wet white clay and the flower petals merely drops of water introduced when the hot glass was pierced with a clay-dipped stick. The result has a dewy freshness, however, more appealing perhaps than the coloured glass flowers found in other flint-glass porters, green, blue, purple, red, yellow, although here again tiny bubbles of air were caught on the petals as the motifs were enclosed within their dome of glass and give an unreal beauty to the whole.

Here as in the millefiori style the flowers and their round base of many-coloured glass fill only half the dome yet appear so magnified that the whole glass is full of colour and sparkle. Even the cushions of "flower heads" familiar as millefiori work and associated with mid-19th-century paperweights are found among door porters of the 1850s. Some of these pass today as outsize paperweights, their real attractiveness lost until their clustered florets are seen at floor level.

Chapter Ten

POTTERY CRADLES

AS recently as a hundred years ago the bearing and rearing of children was fraught with perils and alarms unthought-of today. Even the boldest, least imaginative mother sought encouragement and advice of friends and neighbours and mother and child alike thrived on a wealth of elaborate ceremonial and equipment stemming from shared apprehension, well-wishing and ultimate rejoicing. Throughout centuries when bed furnishings were paramount status-symbols, and in farmhouse and cottage were the only evidence of comfort, let alone luxury, the finest bed was magnificently draped in preparation for the weeks when mother and baby would be on show to visitors. Rich fur coverlets and silk-embroidered pillow-covers were represented in less lavish homes by exquisite quilting.

Even the mother's convalescent drink of wine-spiced caudle was shared with all comers: just before and after the birth of the Prince of Wales in 1762 Queen Charlotte's well-wishers accounted for eight gallons of caudle and one hundred pounds' worth of cakes daily. In return, visitors would seldom call empty-handed. There is something peculiarly charming—poignant even—about the small gifts that remain to us from those noisy, jolly scenes when the callers crowded among the resplendent draperies around the bed, laughing with the nurse, rejoicing with the mother, and only the baby wailed.

Silver spoons were rare gifts from godparents, and the presents most mothers might expect would be humble enough; but how charmingly they were presented. One may still find an occasional pincushion bearing highly prized pins stuck to spell out good wishes too dear to the recipient to be destroyed by use. But most highly valued today, perhaps, is all that remains of a gift of equally unmistakable intention, a tiny cradle, often complete with the figure of a baby, leaving little space for the silver-mounted coral or other simpler, more perishable gift: an anodyne necklace for teething was a notion much favoured in the mid 18th century.

Very occasionally the cradle was of gold set with jewels, and in Stuart days the baby might be carved in alabaster. But very many more, both cradles and babies, were made in the various kinds and qualities of simple earthenwares and stonewares that bear record to so many of the customs and pleasures of ordinary folk throughout the 18th and 19th centuries.

At first the child was hand-modelled, the clay rolled and pinched and tooled into crude semblance of a figure and placed in a plain cradle made from coarse reddish-burning clay covered over with a smoother, more fluid clay known as slip. Slip-ware cradles were made throughout the 18th and early 19th centuries: as late as 1811 Richard Waters of Lambeth patented an improvement in decoration technique. The earthenware itself improved progressively and details of glazing help the collector towards approximate dating, although many regions using different clays are known to have met the widespread demand, including London, Kent, Sussex, North Staffordshire, Derbyshire, Yorkshire. In the third quarter of the 19th century these gifts were still being made by Edward Bingham, Castle Hedingham, Essex, and by Bridgend and Ewenny in Glamorganshire.

Early slipware cradles may be some four inches long or as much as twelve inches. Vertical sides and ends are usually flat bats of clay, the base resting on simple rockers and the low rounded hood perhaps flanked by tall finials for rocking, matched by another pair at the foot. This shape is as plain as the wood and wicker furniture it represented but here verisimilitude ends for its ornament is true to the potter's idiom of the day, showing skilled, specialist work in lines and dots, figures, medallions, flowers, geometrical formalities shaped in the watery clay slip by trickling it on to the surface through a goose quill.

Occasionally there is a date, or the first few letters of the alphabet as in a child's sampler: one in the Hanley Museum, about eleven inches long, is inscribed on the end "M.T. 1740" and on the sides "Made by Ralph Shaw October the 31 Cobridg: gate". A delightful specimen has been noted with a bird peeping into the cradle, wings a-flutter, eyes big blobs of dark slip. The clay slip may be white, buff, black, reddish-brown but the distinctive colour of these cradles is the golden tone of the transparent lead glaze, often intensified into a richer brown with manganese oxide. Finely powdered natural sulphide of lead was sprinkled over the cradle: firing at a moderate temperature baked the clay and melted the lead so that it spread over the ware. The early alternative was a glossier colourless glaze attained by using calcined lead oxide similarly ground to a fine powder but this was costlier. From the 1750s a liquid lead glaze might be used but the older method was continued on slip wares until the 19th century. Study of museum pieces makes it easy to distinguish the three styles of glaze.

An early slip cradle is a find indeed. A Staffordshire specimen in the Victoria and Albert Museum attributed to about 1700 is of red earthenware covered with white slip ornamented with trailing in blue slip: there are letters of the alphabet one and a quarter inches high along the sides and leaf and dot patterns on the panels of hood and end. The slip cradle illustrated in plate 23 is early Georgian, twelve inches long by four inches wide. The edges are scalloped, the trailed ornament and dots in white on the dark brown slip that covers the basic red earthenware. But the interesting feature here is the additional ornament, the fiddler straddling the hood and the six heads hand-modelled in the round in a white earthenware containing ground calcined flint instead of sand, with beady black slip eyes.

The designs of earthenware cradles became more interesting when the potters learnt how to shape their wares by casting in moulds as was done with white salt-glazed stoneware from the 1730s. These were made far into the 19th century. Curved outlines are to be noted and ornament in relief, the shape often being built up of three units separately pressed in moulds to make the two halves of the hood.

Mould-shaping made it easier to include a baby in the design —or at least its head and shoulders—with the coverlets tossed aside to show a gaily patterned "robe" finished, like face and hair, according to the whim of the individual decorator. Such a cradle is a decorative ornament for the mantel shelf, handsome enough to require no additional gift, and often lacking the space to contain it. Pleasing wicker effects were easily and variously achieved, often merely touched with colour but edged with wide rope-work bands of a deeper tone. Occasionally the effect suggests vermicular quilting, as if the cradle were encased in this draught-excluding fabric.

The white salt-glazed stoneware that was all the rage towards the middle of the 18th century is found in valuable but cold-looking cradles: an "orange skin" surface to the ware suggests a date earlier than about 1760 when this defect was overcome by covering the surface with red lead before firing in the kiln. Cradles in this "poor man's porcelain" are remarkably thin and delicate. Early examples of the 1740s are the most intriguing, where the potter has "sprigged on" numbers of small motifs hand-stamped separately out of pads of clay. In the 1750s the relief ornament became repetitive, being cut into the brass or copper moulds that shaped the cradle sides. Collectors must be on their guard, however, for many white salt-glazed cradles date no earlier than the third quarter of the 19th century, the Victorian maker's mark now discreetly obliterated. By then the cradle had become a cabinet show piece, sold as "Elizabethan ware" and relief-decorated with pseudo-medieval designs.

An exceptionally interesting little cradle of about 1785 in the collection of Viscount Mackintosh of Halifax shows sprigged-on ornament applied in a curiously haphazard manner, both inside and outside. As well as tiny flowers, swags, urns and the like this includes medallions of Admiral Rodney, and it is thought that this is a unique little piece commemorating the death of his infant daughter (plate 23).

Mould-shaped cradles in earthenware, less sharply defined than those in stoneware and attractively mellowed by the limpid, rich-coloured glaze, are to be found in the lovely green-glaze ware developed by Josiah Wedgwood in partnership with Thomas Whieldon which I have described in Chapter 3. Many are patterned to suggest wicker, but others are merely edged with rope-work and are adorned with the groups of classical figures associated with Wedgwood and his designer Flaxman and popular from the 1770s. The small baby sometimes found in such a cradle is in the same rich green ware. As with other specimens of this ware the collector may experience the triumph of finding variants similarly ornamented but with a golden yellow glaze. These were slightly cheaper imitations of the green-glaze and tortoiseshell-ware cradles, showing similar use of moulds to produce relief patterns. An early type in this rich golden glaze, eight to twelve inches long, continued into the 19th century, being made in Leeds, Staffordshire and Newcastle. One in Brighton Museum, twelve inches long, in yellow glazed earthenware, is patterned in low relief by the use of moulds and shows delightful babies at play among other classical figures, only the edges being shaped to suggest twisted wicker. I have seen identical relief patterning on a green-glaze cradle.

Green-glaze cradles too, however, may be no older than mid-Victorian days. Few bear potters' trademarks, but the type of earthenware under the glaze makes it possible to attribute a date within wide limits. Early specimens were in dark cream-coloured earthenware; from the late 1770s a light-weight, light-hued creamware was general; from the 1790s and in the 19th century the material was hard, heavy, white pearlware.

Every cradle collector looks for an example in the mottled colour effects known as tortoiseshell ware, or Whieldon ware after the celebrated potter Thomas Whieldon (at work 1740–80). This ware was in constant production in Staffordshire until the end of the 18th century. Soft shades of green, yellow, slate blue, dark brown, blotchy grey may blend delightfully under a glaze now finely crackled or crazed. The colours—metallic oxides—were applied to the unglazed earthenware, the liquid transparent glaze causing them to flow and fuse in a peculiarly satisfying manner. From this developed the most fascinating effects in so-called coloured glazes brush-applied, the method associated with Ralph Wood, still in a limited range of soft metallic oxide colours kept separate by the brush-painting technique.

From these it is an effort, perhaps, to turn to what must have appeared far more exciting to the late 18th century—the brightly painted cradles dating from the 1780s onwards, made at first in a thin, light-weight cream-coloured earthenware, their glaze as smooth as if floated on to the surface and even today seldom crazed. Yellow, green, red, blue and black compose the usual colour schemes, all fixed by a single firing in the kiln. The painting is lively with vigorous brush-work: a Yorkshire specimen is often dominated by a bold round rose on the hood, and initials and date on the footboard.

Colours that could be applied more permanently under the glaze were introduced in the 1790s, passing unscathed through the high temperature kiln firing. Characteristic are a hot tawny yellow and a pale yellow, a deep rich blue, rusty browns, dull greens and touches of black.

That other great vogue of the early 19th century, decoration transfer-printed under the glaze in lovely tones of blue, may be discovered among cradles, too, and becomes wholly delightful when a cartouche on the hood contains a name or initials and perhaps a birth-date, painted in black over the glaze by an obliging china seller.

Occasionally a Victorian cradle is found which is more than merely an appealing little ornament, being fitted to meet the Victorian's insatiable demand for pincushions. Here there may be a survival of that charming custom of spelling out good wishes in pinheads, the inscription usually being the simplest "God Bless the Babe".

Even in parian ware cradles are to be found and their babies—that austere ivory-tinted porcelain invented in 1842 which took its name from parian marble. This lent itself to delicate cast and pressed effects of woven basketry and suited its period, the matter-of-fact 1850s, but it lacks the imaginative freedom of less imitative earthenwares; there is a macabre marble-tombstone touch about some of these parian babes, who soon passed with a fashion too naïve and uninhibited to survive save as a collector's foible.

At no time were these endearing small items regarded as important by the potters concerned: few marks are to be found. Even Wedgwood's marks are rare here, occasionally found impressed on a cradle of green-glazed ware. The initials *EB&S* impressed mark some cradles made by Ephraim Booth & Sons of Stoke-upon-Trent. But for the rest the potter usually remains as anonymous as the child whose arrival occasioned the gift—an expression of good wishes so deeply treasured that the fragile pottery was preserved through a lifetime of charming uselessness and can still form the perfect "gift wrapping" for a similar occasion today.

Chapter Eleven

DOUBLE SCENT BOTTLES

THE whole 19th century was enchanted by perfumes. By the beginning of the century perfumiers were skilled in extracting the attars of fragrant plants and prolonging their volatile beauty in sweet resins and oils. There were sweet bags and sachets of flower powders for the pocket, and perforated boxes or cassolettes of resinous pastes to warm over a candle flame or carry in the reticule. Richly scented pastilles of resin and charcoal smouldered in bedroom and boudoir in the tiny china cottages (see Chapter 5) that today prove as endearing to collectors as that other small 19th century delight, the vinaigrette.

By the middle of the century, however, the vinaigrette was beginning to be considered old-fashioned. The basis was the too-long-familiar concentrated acetic acid aromatised with camphor and such intensely fragrant attars as roses and English lavender, absorbed in snippets of fine Turkey sponge within the perforated inner lid of the small silver box. The new craze of the 1870s and 1880s was the invigorating ammonia of the smelling bottle, and the new shape was the double bottle. Collectors are only beginning to look for these articles, as completely Victorian as, say, the skirt lifter or the feather posy, but as varied and charming as glassmaker, silversmith and gilt metal manufacturer could devise.

In the private collection from which this chapter is illustrated the earliest hallmark is for 1851 (Birmingham) on a bottle three and a half inches long and one and a quarter ounces in weight, but many specimens are nearly twice the length and four times the weight. Although basically the shape varies little they offer considerable scope for material and surface ornament. Almost without exception they are beautifully made, pleasant to the eye and a joy to handle. Some may be found still in their original leather cases.

Smelling salts, eau-de-luce, sal volatile, under various names the revivifying scents required by the over-dressed Victorian in her over-furnished rooms were based upon pungent liquid ammonia or alcoholic ammonia. A drachm each of English lavender and rosemary attars, half a drachm each of bergamot and cloves, would together enrich a pint of liquid ammonia. A favourite name was inexhaustible salts, but they lasted at most only two or three months: a warm hand quickly dissipated the ammonia, which accounts for the thickness and the deep cutting of many of the finest bottles. The immense popularity of these bottles may be attributed to the fact that the design incorporated two bottles, joined base to base, so that one half could be filled with the fashionable salts while the other contained a perfume—one of the sweet flowery "handkerchief scents" then equally appreciated, tubereuse, violet or the most powerful patchouli long associated with genuine Indian shawls until both shawl and scent were imitated in Europe.

In most of these bottles the centre part is of glass. Two bottles were made separately and welded together, base to base. In clear glass it is possible to see the junction, a slightly convex surface fitting, not always quite perfectly, on to a concave surface. But to the fingers the whole double bottle offers an entirely smooth piece of glass save for its cut or moulded ornament. Some bottles are of china with enamelled decoration, some of glass-lined silver, flatly decorated with hand-engraved scrollwork or engine-turned in basket work or other geometrical pattern, and others again are of imitative engine-turned nickel alloy.

At each end is a metal lid, silver too, perhaps—sometimes as a very thin casing over brass—but more often merely of a gilded brass alloy. This may be delicately tooled or stamp-embossed in an all-over foliate design or mechanically patterned with severe engine-turning. Sometimes there is a plain cartouche for a crest or cypher on one end, a Christian name on the other, and occasionally the ends are mounted with tiny turquoises or other inexpensive gems. A fashion of the 1870s put a facet-cut "gem" of coloured glass in the centre of each mount, matching the glass bottle, ruby, sapphire or emerald.

It was important to the user to differentiate at a touch between the ends of her bottle. Usually one end springs open on a three-lug hinge by pressure on a small stud: this is the end for the smelling salts. Inside the lid is a glass-covered metal disc controlled by a hidden spring so that the small vessel is entirely sealed when closed. This was important. The vinaigrette makers had avoided leakage problems with their aromatic vinegars by ensuring that the liquid was absorbed by fine scraps of sponge. The ammonia compound of the smelling salts was often treated in the same way. But in a glass bottle the sponge trimmings looked unattractive. The perfumier's reaction was to replace the sponge with "insoluble crystal salts" (sulphate of potash), more attractive looking but no safeguard against spilling, so that the neck of the bottle might be filled with white cotton. Fleeting but safer was sesqui-carbonate of ammonia —known at the time as white smelling salts or Preston salts.

The handkerchief scent that filled the other half of the vessel was less instantly available. This end of the bottle usually has a cap that screws down on to a metal thread cemented to the glass. Occasionally a specimen is found that screws directly on to the glass itself which has been thread-cut to receive it. Inside the cap is a minute glass stopper, three-eighths or even a quarter of an inch across, ground to fit really tightly in the ground neck of the bottle.

The spirit basis made these scents fleeting but an occasional trace lingers as a reminder of that lush period when the manufacturing perfumier was taking over from the home stillroom. He still extracted his odours from the long-familiar sources but delighted in concocting imitations: for example he would combine half a dozen ingredients from vanilla extract to oil of almonds in order to suggest the simple charm of heliotrope; only jasmine proved inimitable, and in consequence its distillation sold at nine pounds for a fluid ounce in 1862.

The perfumier always had to contend with the oxidising influence of the air and the fit of the stopper was immensely important: many pure extracts had to be mixed with other ingredients to avoid a sickly odour, lemon attar suffering from particulary rapid oxidisation. Benzoin, storax and tolu extracts in spirit solutions helped to make volatile scents more permanent, but the traces found today in these bottles declare little of their original perfumes. The manufacturers blended with a view to lasting fragrance: in a mingling of jasmine, rose and patchouli each would predominate in turn. Musk proved particularly enduring. Even the mid-Victorians had their "economical scents", however, and recipes of the period recommend dilutions such as a pint of spirit of wine to an ounce or less of santal or bergamot attar brightened with a little magnesium "to fill little fancy bottles such as are sold at the bazaars, toyshops, arcades, wheels of fortune etc.".

As an alternative method of securing the cover it may be fitted with a cork instead of a stopper, ensuring a leak-proof fastening when the lid is screwed down. There are several variants. One of the most attractive harks back to the vinaigrette and the hinged cover springs open to reveal a fretted grille over sponge once saturated with aromatic vinegar. Some of the smaller bottles made in the fifties and sixties, two and a half to three and a half inches long, disclose such dainty fittings. A more elaborate style is hinged in the middle where the two bottles meet, one bottle being plain-based, the other based with a dainty perforated vinaigrette.

This central cache was sometimes treated as a locket, and one may feel slightly intrusive on discovering a tiny photograph, more private than the frequent engraved monograms, dates and names that give personal interest to many shield-shaped cartouches on the mounts. Variants in the design of the bottle itself include the rarer waisted outline and the swelling barrel shape. One, with a chain attached to each end, was designed to hang horizontally from the chatelaine.

Mainly, however, the collector finds variety in the rich metallic oxide colours and fine cutting of the glass. Translucent deep blues, sea-greens and ruby reds tone splendidly with the gilded mounts but other tints range from vaseline, amber, pale blue, dark yellow and manganese amethyst to a uranium opaline green. Even the plainly-panelled, opaque, dull-looking bottle in whitish opal glass proves to possess a wonderful sunset glow when held against the light. Occasionally, as an aid to differentiation, the two halves are different colours, such as blue and green.

A rare late series are in flashed glass. This was a simple process dear to this colour-conscious century. The clear glass of the bottle was thinly covered with colour. Ornament cut into the surface then appeared in clear glass greatly enhanced and intensified by the background of colour. The knowing collector distinguishes such work from the specimens ornamented not by cutting but by blowing into a patterned mould and coloured by brush-staining. In Chapter 22 some details are given of the various blown-moulding and pressing techniques available by then to the enterprising glassmen seeking to cut their prices and widen their markets. The moulding made these surface-coloured bottles slightly cheaper, but the colour still required a kiln firing to fix it and finishing touches on the cutting wheel.

Many of the most impressive double bottles, six or seven inches long, six ounces in weight, are in clear flint-glass deeply cut on the wheel and showing the slight irregularities of hand work. But these too have clever imitations only slightly less sharp-edged, created by blowing the molten glass into patterned moulds. All the familiar designs of the glass-cutter are to be found. Long smooth diamonds and triangles are perhaps the most usual. One may note sharp starry points of light where projecting diamond shapes have been cut across and across in strawberry or hobnail cutting so that handling the bottle requires minimum contact with the glass. Bold convex Roman pillars add weight and strength and were easy to shape by moulding but even more effective are the spiralling ribbons of square-edged panel cutting. Many are merely divided into six, eight or, more usually, ten panels by V-shaped channels cut vertically between them, their surfaces rendered silky smooth by a series of processes on the polishing wheel. A rarity is a bottle with flowers engraved on the flat glass panels. A rarity too, now, is a bottle still retaining its original gilded scrollwork or stars upon the smooth glass.

Sometimes makers of these handsome trinkets may be elucidated, and some indication of date. The bottle may be found in its original case bearing an inscription such as, "Howell, James & Co. Goldsmiths and Jewellers to the Queen and Prince and Princess of Wales, 5, 7, & 9, Regent Street". Or the bottle itself may bear the maker's name in a circle inside the cap—of the hinged mount, of course, since this would be the more often displayed in company. The name is usually in a circle with *LONDON* across the middle—*MAW & SON*, or *MAW, SON & THOMPSON*, for example, or *HOWELL & CO.* The firm of S. Mordan & Co. who made some centrally hinged bottles, showed the name around a crown.

Often a silver mount bears clear hallmarks and a book on silversmiths' marks will then indicate a date. Some bear the London Assay Office mark of the leopard's (lion's) head, others the Birmingham anchor, and initials may determine the actual manufacturer. Sometimes when the silver is richly embossed in high relief with bold scrolls, often lightly engraved, it has escaped hall marking, and in any case many of the late examples capped in silver have such light-weight metal that they were exempt from excise duty and assay and therefore bear no marks. They may be highly domed to cover large stoppers, even occasionally with both ends screw-mounted and identical save for details of ornament.

Many more mounts are of common metal alloy cast in high relief and brazed into the hinge or screw mount and splendidly though thinly gilded by the electro-deposit method patented by Elkington and Mason, Birmingham, in 1842. Others were shaped in the press and engraved before double-gilding. When these have lain unused in some boudoir drawer they still appear brilliant as gold, but they lack the appeal of the worn stopper, the bottle glass faintly blurred with acetic acid, the opening powder-whitened with sesqui-carbonate of ammonia, the minute stopper releasing a trace of frangipani or lemon verbena. This may well appear more pungent today by contrast to our ascetic surroundings than ever it was in the days of its introduction when sandalwood-scented notepaper vied with heliotrope sachets in the linen, scented wadding in jewel case lining, scent-steeped shells in the work box, scented book marks to banish mould, "scented gems" in boxes lined with resin-impregnated card, scented paper spills for warming or smouldering, when musk and ambergris defied the laundry maid and civet clung to the posted valentine. Small wonder is it indeed that the spring cap of the smelling bottle was snapped open to clear the air with the clean, fresh tang of ammonia.

Chapter Twelve

LUSTRE WARES

IT is not necessary to be even a minor connoisseur of antiques to fall in love with lustre pottery. Today those mugs and jugs, tea sets and mantel-shelf ornaments are among the most popular of collectors' treasures. They possess an inconsequential "rightness", an unself-conscious association of colour and shape and pattern that makes them the natural successors to earlier folk potteries. There is a direct, obvious appeal in their range of colours—the gold lustre in tones from richest guinea-yellow to soft coppery bronzes, the cold clear silver tones of platinum, the pinks and mauves and purple-browns—all enriched with the metallic, lustrous sheen that supplies their distinctive beauty.

It is easy to imagine the popularity of these lustres in shadowy farmhouse kitchen and best parlour: although they are at home today in sophisticated surroundings they are essentially soft-contoured, homely pieces, with the breath of the country about them. Their decoration is frequently naïve in both subject and treatment, but entirely distinct from the lazy crudeness of the heavy, gritty modern lustre jugs now flooding the market.

Old English lustre is a joy to handle, its colour and sheen an undemanding delight to the least observant eye, even while to many the special charm of this ware lies in the range of decorative detail to which the lustre serves merely as an additional garnish. Today's prices for exclusive specimens may be fifty or even a hundred pounds, but for those who will overlook occasional cracks and chips there are genuine old specimens to be sought out from among their plebeian modern rivals and bought for a few pounds. A range of lustre jugs showing the different styles of treatment offer fascinating possibilities to the collector who is prepared to buy slowly and wisely.

Any survey of lustre ware must cover an immensely wide range of lustre effects and decorative techniques. In order to clear up frequent misunderstanding, however, it may be stated at once that the basic principle consisted in covering various qualities and colours of biscuit—that is, unglazed—and smooth-glazed ceramics with a translucent substance that gave them an iridescent soap-bubble sheen. In this survey I include also the less familiar but equally fascinating type of lustre known by the few who love it and seek it as mother-of-pearl ware.

The craft, famous in medieval Spain and Italy, was only rediscovered in England near the end of the 18th century and brought to perfection in the 19th, the earliest experimenters including John Hancock at Spode's factory, Robert Wilson of Hanley, and Josiah Wedgwood. Their primary intention was to achieve effects comparable with the Hispano-Moresque, while replacing the Spanish tin-enamelled earthenware with the creamware then proving immensely successful throughout the Staffordshire potteries. Such wares must have been produced by most of the major English potters and by many makers of bone china, and are often so elaborately handsome that most surely they must have delighted their makers. It is curious, therefore, to find so few marks, so little contemporaneous acknowledgment of any kind that these lovely lustres were on the market.

As late as 1807, L. W. Dillwyn of the Cambrian Pottery, Swansea, advertised a ware "ornamented with an entirely new Golden Lustre" and this appears to be the earliest commercial success for a lustre produced with gold oxide. Collectors look also for the "silver" and pink lustres developed at this time by potters who found gold scarce and costly. For grey metallic effects they used not tarnishable silver but platinum oxide, adding manganese oxide for the deep tone of polished steel, and for the pink lustres used "purple of cassius", a less expensive precipitate obtained from a mixture of gold chloride and tin chloride.

Always the film of lustre is extremely thin. The metal oxide or chloride was held in suspension in an oily mixture while brush-painted on to the ware so that firing in the kiln—a muffle kiln where it was shielded from the direct heat of the furnace—destroyed all but the metal deposit which was thus firmly fixed and rendered remarkably durable.

Gold lustres are found in a range of tones on wares that tend to be pleasantly light in the hands. Some of the early work has the distinctive yellow tones of the gold guineas that potters used as a source of the metal, while copper in the gold alloy is indicated by proportionately deeper, bronze tones. Iron and ochre mixed with the gold show as a reddish-brown surface with a greenish lustre. Always the tone and quality of the underlying earthenware or china affect the tone and brilliance of the lustre. When this was realised a special reddish-brown clay was used to give a splendid rich glow to heavily alloyed gold lustre, a development thought to date from 1823 onwards, invented by John Hancock. Dark brown earthenware in the unglazed biscuit state may produce wonderful purplish tones of lustre: Wilson of Hanley contributed a splendid crushed-blackberry tone. Painted ornament among such lustres was applied over reserves prepared with thick white glaze.

Meanwhile, silver lustre, an English invention, was being produced by the Wedgwood firm by 1805, and in 1806 John Davenport devised a way of using stencils so that gold and silver lustres could be applied in delicate patterns over the clear creamy white of the glazed earthenware. The most familiar and, to many, most desirable resist lustre developed from this in about 1810 with the patterns of birds and flower, fruiting vine and geometrical forms appearing in the glossy white or cream-toned earthenware against backgrounds of metallic lustres. This was known as resist ware because the pattern was painted on the white or tinted glaze not in lustre but in a substance that would resist the metallic solution—either glycerine or brown shellac in spirits of wine, later removed by washing. The ware could then be covered with the lustre solution which would adhere permanently only where there was no resist. In 1810, too, Peter Warburton of the New Hall China Manufactory patented a method of decorating bone china and earthenware with gold and silver lustres by a form of transfer printing.

Patterns in blue, yellow, buff or the rarest rose colour against the lustre backgrounds of resist wares date from the late 1820s onwards, being a result of Henry Daniell's new ground-laying process which I mention in Chapter 14. By then another use had been devised for the silver lustre, to achieve to a remarkable extent the effect of costly silver plate. The ware was silvered inside and out with two applications of the platinum lustre and left smoothly plain save for the flutings characteristic of the period's silver and the silversmiths' beaded rims that masked the thickness of the earthenware body. Jugs and other domestic wares may be found and sets of the goblets used for funerals and even church "plate".

Edward Deakin of Longton showed teapots, egg-frames, candlesticks, mustard pots and many other pieces at the Great Exhibition, 1851, but already by then the attempted illusion was beginning to be forgotten. More of the vessels found today are lined with white glaze and painted with flowers or rings of colour. In 1852 John Ridgway & Company developed a cheaper way of applying the lustre so thinly that the pieces found today are usually distressingly worn and shabby looking to the discredit of the earlier, finer work.

Lustre today appeals for its own rich glow, and in our eyes may lose more than it gains, perhaps, when other ornament forces it into a minor background rôle. Ornament in relief on lustred wares dating from the 1820s may be found which is far more elaborate than the silver effects, being sprigged on in the 18th-century manner. A jug may be boldly patterned all round with plump huntsmen and hounds, coloured with enamels and lustre and framed with bands of lustre above and below. Enoch Wood and Elijah Mayer moulded the ornament directly upon the ware.

All the other easy contemporaneous methods of decorating ceramics are to be noted too. Sometimes the ornament, such as crude flowers, is painted directly upon the lustred surface but more often on bands or reserves of white or colour: for example, lustred jugs impressed with a *B* may show flower patterns on bands of brilliant yellow, the work of Thomas Barlow of Longton.

Instead of enamel-bright flowers there may be austere little views painted in sepia, or any of the period's popular pictorial scenes, portraits, famous buildings reproduced by the process of transfer-printing in blue or black, sometimes hand-coloured and sometimes to be found completely washed over with a light coating of lustre. In more delicate china, New Hall, Swansea and Minton issued delightful tea services lightly touched with lustre. The strawberry design was popular, used by both New Hall and Swansea, the berries red, with green and pink for leaves and stems and tendrils.

Much background lustre is in the pink-to-purple colour range. This was originated by the Wedgwood firm at Etruria, but is now associated especially with the cheap happy-go-lucky work of Sunderland. Marbled effects achieved by mingling the various tints were introduced by Etruria too, and the splashed or mottled variants developed by Staffordshire, Liverpool and Bristol as well as by the Sunderland potters now credited with a monopoly of this style. The lustred vessels were spattered with oil blown through fine muslin on the end of a tube: the heat of the kiln expanded the oil, forming small bubbles. I have written elsewhere of the sentimental wall plaques and similar sailor mementoes in this gay Sunderland lustre which cries out for the crowded, uncritical surroundings of cabin or cottage.

The cheap lustre made from copper oxide was intended for cottage and fairground too, impressively rich looking, lustred inside and out and often quickly dabbed with colour as well, but basically a heavy, poor ware spoilt by innumerable small specks and bubbles.

Perhaps the greatest range of quality in lustre pottery, however, is found among the purely decorative figures. At their most ambitious these consist of finely modelled classical figures copied from the porcelain of early Bow, Chelsea and Derby. Their most eminent makers included Robert Wilson of Hanley, Enoch Wood and the Wedgwood firm. The celebrated figure of a mounted Hussar in the British Museum, attributed to Wilson, is the most ambitious piece of lustre statuary in existence. Among later makers working in the mid 19th century was Ralph Salt of Hanley. Salt's delicately modelled figures are very different from those made by his contemporaries in Staffordshire which tended to be irregular in form and carelessly lustred. In Victorian days much lustre ware was made to be peddled by hawkers for a few pence, yet today even this finds itself honoured and admired.

If lustre is essentially an early-19th-century expression of man's delight in soap-bubble iridescence, so too is the enthusiasm for the nacreous sheen of mother-of-pearl. The 18th century enjoyed especially the fantastic shapes of shells, but the 19th century appreciated the pearl-shell's urbane colour effects and glossy texture on chair and cabinet, on card case and scatter pin. It is strange to find here, too, how unfamiliar to most collectors now is one aspect of this lost enthusiasm—the effort to reproduce the shapes and textures of shells in more tractable ceramics.

Some of the most interesting and collectable results are in the form of a lustre known as mother-of-pearl ware. Many charming little pieces still sell for shillings rather than pounds, and the collector can assemble literally hundreds of different specimens, from conch shell comport to dragon teapot, from figures and mirror frames to exquisite fragments of costume jewellery.

As early as 1778 Josiah Wedgwood sought to follow the silversmiths' lead and create nautilus cream jugs and sauce tureens and spread the dessert table with gay little cockle shells. His creamware offered a clear, fine background to overglaze enamels which suggested the delicate cream and pink tones of sea shells but lacked their soap-bubble iridescence. The triumph of creating this nacreous lustre effect in ceramics was due to a Frenchman's invention in the 19th century, and was developed brilliantly in Ireland and was so obviously a triumph that English potters quickly acquired both the technical know-how and the licence to use the patented process. Consequently it is possible to find a number of familiar English potters contributing their different skills to the design and ornament of this most delicate, enchanting ware.

The Frenchman was Jules Joseph Henri Brianchon, partner in the firm of Gillet et Brianchon, Paris, who marked their wares *G B BREVETE PARIS* in a circle. Brianchon took out his English patent, 8th July 1857, for "unalterable coatings" of ceramic substances, imparting "the colour of gold, white and coloured mother-of-pearl" and the "variegated and changing reflections of shells". But the British success of this glaze was due to a series of fortunate chances.

The discovery of fine felspar in County Fermanagh, Ireland, prompted a London architect, Robert William Armstrong, to establish the Belleek Pottery there in 1857, making a felspar porcelain beloved of the Victorians and known as parian ware. At its most perfect, unglazed parian does suggest the colour and surface texture of marble, and it was immensely popular around the mid 19th century for small statuary. But when made to a simpler formula—67 parts felspar to 55 parts Cornish stone—its fine granular surface was easily soiled and difficult to clean. Ordinary lead glazes were unsatisfactory, but the Brianchon formula, based on resin, proved perfect. Other ceramics, containing phosphate and lime, stained this glaze but on parian it has retained its wonderful glossy sheen, not even acquiring the tiny cracks or crazing associated with ageing pottery. The resin could be mixed with bismuth nitrate for a clear lustre: chloride of gold produced the rich brilliancies of shells. It is perhaps necessary here to emphasise that this was entirely unlike the metallic lustres described earlier in this chapter: hence Brianchon's triumph and the distinctive individuality of mother-of-pearl ware.

In Belleek ware the result of this triumph is seen in a wide range of vessels ornamented with shells, coral, sea urchins and other real and imagined marine life, in wonderfully thin, shell-shaped teacups and teapots, and in comports where seahorses prance or dolphins play. But the suggestion of Oriental splendour was developed too and one may occasionally discover a magnificent Victorian dragon partly enamelled in vivid colours.

The delicate strength of the parian ware made it possible to produce some of the finest flower encrustations ever created—roses and daisies shaped in full relief tossed on the swelling skirts of tall jugs, or rose, thistle and shamrock rimming the parian baskets composed of thin threads of porcelain that are a particular feature of Belleek. But there are simple pearl-washed jugs and beakers and plates for the finding, too, and a wealth of lively designs from flower holder to piggybank moneybox. Some of the figures are unusually attractive, including Irish peasants with their creels, children, animals, even insects. The Belleek mark is easily recognised: *BELLEEK POTTERY* impressed on parian made before 1863; and the more familiar transfer-printed design of an Irish round tower, wolf hound and harp over a shamrock-trimmed ribbon inscribed *BELLEEK*. A crowned Irish harp was sometimes printed or impressed, too, apparently an early mark. Armstrong and his partner died in 1884 but the firm continued, their wares less exquisite but still full of charm. Those with *IRELAND* in the mark post-date 1891.

Fig. 14. The two Belleek marks, both printed.

Meanwhile, almost as early as Belleek, Worcester acquired a licence to use a slight modification of the Brianchon formula. Parian figures may be found in the bold, experienced Worcester manner, sometimes enriched with touches of brilliant enamel colours but leaving the flesh and much other detail to display the lovely pearly iridescence. Pieces from dessert, tea and cabaret sets sometimes turn up. The earliest bear the Worcester mark of four script Ws encircling the figure 51: this lacks the crown that was added in 1862.

Much more, however, of the exquisite small ware that gleams with the mother-of-pearl radiance came from the firm of W. H. Goss. The Goss parian factory was launched in 1858, its particular aim being the lady's dressing table and boudoir and most especially her costume needs for brooch, scarf pin, shawl pin, hair pin, bracelet, necklace, pendant. Many of these trinkets are ornamented with delicate floral work. In 1872 Goss patented a method for modelling his jewellery with even greater delicacy, its glistening iridescence sometimes faintly tinted primrose yellow and the flowers enamelled in their natural colours. Goss made many of the wares associated with Belleek, but one searches especially for swan vases, scent bottles, tazzas, rice powder jars, scent diffusers. All may be found impressed *W H GOSS* or *W H G.*

Samuel Moore of Longton was another maker of mother-of-pearl ware in the 1860s, and in 1870 he was followed by his sons, who became renowned for delicate modelling and brilliant lustre on elaborate tea ware. Among their specialities were large mirror frames. A small frame for a miniature, silhouette or photograph is an attractive piece. A red-letter find is a teapot, impressed *MOORE*, shaped as a camel, its handle formed of the Arab driver fastening its load.

The great Herbert Minton was renowned for his parian and made particularly attractive use of the mother-of-pearl lustre. One of his most attractive notions expressed the period's delight in contrasts of texture by ornamenting elaborate mother-of-pearl ware pieces with figures in unglazed parian. A tall dish for fruit in the lustred porcelain

Fig. 15. Minton: the Roman M, and the crossed L's of Sèvres somewhat modified, with the addition of an M, are early marks. The ermine mark with three dots above is post-1851.

may have statuary parian figures grouped round the stem. Flower-encrusted flower pots may be found and a wide range of tea ware: this might suggest Belleek work but for the impressed mark *MINTON* until 1862 and thereafter *MINTONS*.

Yet another maker of note was W. T. Copeland. He issued considerable quantities of the table ware, flower holders, vases, trinket sets and shells expected of those who developed this ware. But the firm is associated also with many pearl-lustred figures. It had a splendid reputation for parian figures reproducing the marble statuary of its day, but its mother-of-pearl ware includes gay little cupids, animals and the like. Here again the mark may help in dating a piece: *COPELAND LATE SPODE* was used until 1867 and afterwards *COPELAND*.

Disappointingly, however, great quantities of this ware lack all marks. Much, it is thought, came from the Cauldon Place Pottery, Hanley, made by T. C. Brown-Westhead, Moore & Co., who were appointed potters to the queen in 1862. One of their specialities was a be-ribboned basket-work sandwich box with a fern frond laid across the lid and upon this an azure butterfly serving as a handle. Other baskets suggest bound cane, and there are mugs and pieces of tea ware for the finding with flower and foliage ornament in relief; but some work on record as being made by this firm for a cheaper market may be found less brilliantly iridescent.

Exceptionally fine mother-of-pearl ware was recorded too as being made by another firm of the 1860s. This was the pottery of Robinson & Leadbeater, Stoke-upon-Trent. It is known that comports, flower holders, centrepieces and many other pieces were made but, tantalisingly, none has yet been found bearing this firm's mark.

Chapter Thirteen

WOVEN PICTURE RIBBONS

TANTALISING, too, are some of the records of exhibits that triumphed in 1851 yet now are vanished without trace. A particularly successful venture at the 1851 Exhibition, selling to the crowds as fast as they were made before their eyes, consisted of gay snippets of ribbon woven with pictorial notions and including the names of designer and manufacturer, intended to demonstrate the skill of the Coventry ribbon weavers. From decade to decade since then fashion has welcomed or spurned decorative ribbons. Those particular novelty souvenirs are rare, perhaps non-existent, now, but their more elaborate successors developed later into a considerable and enduring Victorian enthusiasm.

These small loom-woven pictures once selling for sixpence and a shilling—eighteenpence when framed and glazed—now appear quite astonishingly vivid and appealing, not only in their colours but in their unabashed defiance of good sense if not good taste, cramming the whole crowded scene of the Lady Godiva procession, say, or a hunt in full cry, on to a few inches of silk ribbon so that the picture is formed in the actual weaving and, at that, entirely produced by machine.

The Illustrated London News in 1855 described an early specimen shown at the Paris Universal Exhibition where visitors could watch the process of manufacture in a machine worked by steam power. This was the "Alliance Ribbon" issued by James Hart of Coventry. It shows Victoria placed under the tricolor with Louis Napoleon under the Union Jack and both surrounded by the arms of both nations and wreaths of flowers. Underneath, in English and French, are the words, "May God Bless the Alliance". All this was welcomed as "proof of the advancement made by this country in her appliance of steam-power to arts and manufactures", and all sounds today as gaudy and lovable as a similar group in Staffordshire pottery. It is small wonder indeed that the enthusiasm now for picture ribbons is to be found among collectors, but as yet they are inexpensive, selling for a few shillings in their labelled cardboard mounts.

Coventry ribbons first became famous nearly three hundred years ago when Huguenot refugees brought the craft to this ancient weaving centre. In the mid-19th century one ribbon merchant alone could boast of over two thousand outworkers, and in 1839 no fewer than eighty-nine ribbon firms were listed in the town's directory. By the mid-1830s the Jacquard loom improvement was beginning to make it possible to weave multi-coloured patterned designs automatically: hence the woven "landscapes, figures, portraits" on show in 1851, condemned for their "gaudiness and over-decoration" by the Great Exhibition judges and seized upon joyfully by the happy-go-lucky public.

The success of these early souvenirs was remembered, and at the exhibition of 1862 a machine was on view producing woven ribbon pictures showing the front and interior of the Crystal Palace, selling as quickly as they could be produced. Their maker was Thomas Stevens, established as a ribbon maker in 1854. Stevens began with comparatively unambitious little mementoes, such as birthday greetings and children's nursery rhymes. By the 1870s, however, he was issuing fans, scent sachets, Christmas cards, even silk-centred valentines with similar ornament, and in 1875 could list no fewer than five hundred subjects of "Illuminated Pure Silk Woven Book-Markers", some with bead trimming and tassels, some woven with words and music of popular songs, some mounted in ivory for pulpit Bibles.

Stevens made a notable success of his business during a period of decline in the ribbon trade. He sold tens of thousands of book-markers ornamentally loom-woven with hymns and texts or with verses by Shakespeare or Byron, George Eliot or Eliza Cook, and today pictorial ribbons are most usually known by the awkward name he invented for them—Stevengraphs. From these he advanced to the better-known pictorial pieces measuring about six inches by two inches, mounted on card for hanging on the wall. These are the collector's major trophies today—minutely detailed scenes of sports, coaching ("The Good Old Days") and other mid-Victorian delights expressed in lively line and intensely vivid colour. The drawing is simple but good, suggesting the jostle of horses at the start of a race—the riders absurdly low in the saddle by present-day standards—or oarsmen tense for their gun.

The effect is brighter than any water colour, the glossy silks, introduced with mechanical accuracy, gleaming with every change of light, and the detail so minute that it is difficult to realise the threads must all follow the warp and weft lines of the weaver's loom. The many sporting scenes such as the utterly Victorian tennis game or "The Last Lap" of a penny-farthing bicycle race, or the railway series from "The First Train" to "The Present Time—60 Miles an Hour" are set in outdoor backgrounds and a considerable effect of three-dimensional perspective is achieved by using extremely fine, close weaving to subdue the colour and transform the clear black-and-white and sepia-and-white of the glossy silk threads into a remarkably wide range of grey and tawny tones with a silky matt surface.

This is a feature of the work that no photograph can illustrate: under a magnifying glass even the faces of the crowds on their coach roofs or lining the rails to watch a race are seen in some detail, with here the features emphasised and there the shadow of a hat brim. In the boat race scenes the background of ships at anchor, the boats crowded with spectators and the distant trees are represented with perfect clarity yet in such subdued greys and browns that they never obtrude on the lively foreground scene. It is only when a label is torn or missing and the back of the ribbon revealed that it is possible to appreciate the large proportion of vividly glossy black or brown silk that has been kept to the back of the ribbon so as to reveal only the extremely fine stitches that create this subdued effect: the sky a hazy golden, the foreground usually grey in a steel engraving effect created by an elaboration of stitch that details shadows and reflections, uneven grassland and the sparkle of rippled water.

In contrast, the foreground details are emphatic with bright dyes—Coventry-made by the firm of Rotherham—and the heavy broché weaving stitch that shows the colour in solid shimmering patches of parallel threads on the surface of the work—in an engine driver's shirt, perhaps, or a horse's glossy coat, or the wreath of rose, shamrock and thistle in red, crimson, green and purple set against the monochrome greys of a head-and-shoulders portrait. In some equestrian subjects the colour range is restricted to browns, fawns, soft golds and other tawny shades with the occasional emphasis of solid black.

The raised effects created by the introduction of long broché stitches in close masses is restricted to the weft or cross threads—horizontal in portraits but vertical in the most usual landscape pictures where the ribbon runs from side to side. The maximum amount of contrast is achieved by restricting the longest stitches to the immediate foreground, suggesting the embroiderer's satin stitch: even a horse's tail may be represented by a number of lines, each composed of a tiny row of these bright glossy stitches. For slightly less prominent detail this hard-edged satin stitch effect may merely outline a basket-work stitch, still achieved merely by a series of closely parallel weft stitches on the surface of the fabric but with each stitch comparatively short and placed in an overlapping stepped arrangement.

Further distant detail may be in similar stitchery on an ever-decreasing scale. Throughout, it is the size of the stitch that determines the gloss and colour and thus the emphasis on a feature. Yet small detail is carefully filled in: only the clothing of the cyclists is in vivid colour but every man has clearly defined features on a face measuring one-tenth of an inch (and middle-distance faces may be a quarter this size) and in this particular subject, "The Last Lap", the artist craftsman who set up the machine has achieved an astonishingly clear complexity of spokes where the wheels of the penny-farthings overlap.

Portraits form a group on their own. One of the earliest by Stevens is of Victoria and the Prince Consort issued for the 1862 exhibition. Another Victorian portrait, taken from the Winterhalter 1846 group and garlanded with full-colour rose, shamrock and thistle, sold in enormous numbers, affixed to cardboard ready for framing. Another portrait was issued for the 1887 jubilee. Many portraits are of foreign royalty; Russian, German, Austrian. Mostly they are head-and-shoulders studies: W. E. Gladstone (four inches by two and a half) his features as clear and sympathetically reproduced as in a photograph, his flower wreath as bright as jewels, may be joined by Joseph Chamberlain, John Bright, Charles Stuart Parnell and the Marquess of Salisbury.

Sportsman portraits include full-lengths of John L. Sullivan, Fred Archer and Tom Cannon. Portraits of jockeys were popular, sometimes wearing an owner's colours, and lively sporting scenes were among the most extensive issued. Collectors look for "The Start" or "The Struggle" and, very similar, "The Finish", or "The Water Jump" in the steeplechasing series, for instance, or "Are You Ready?", "The Final Spurt" and "The Finish" of the Oxford-Cambridge boat race, or "The Home Stretch" (trotting) or cricket or football scenes. These measure approximately six by two inches, each ribbon having been woven with repeats of the same design for cutting off and mounting. One delightful series glories in the speed of progress with a steam locomotive and an express train, a lifeboat ("Called to the Rescue") and a fire engine drawn by dashing horses.

Inevitably there are scenes of Coventry's famous Lady Godiva procession: three that probably date to 1880 are of Lady Godiva on her horse, peeping Tom and the procession itself, perhaps taken from an engraving signed D. Jee in volume two of Withington's *English Pageantry*.

For many years the pictures were mounted to sell for a shilling each on cardboard in a soft tone of green, now faded to pale brownish-grey; sometimes a biscuit-colour was used. The card measurements are eight by five-and-a-quarter inches and the opening is bevelled and gilded: in small letters under the picture is the explanation: "Woven in silk by Thomas Stevens, inventor and manufacturer,

Coventry and London (registered)". Below this in large decorative letters is the title of the scene. A black wood frame with a gold inner line and black corner bosses took the price up to one shilling and sixpence. The mount is important as a guarantee of genuineness as it bears the firm's trade label, and this cannot be copied today as the firm is still in business.

It is difficult to date many Stevengraphs exactly, but on the label of some of the fox hunting and steeplechasing scenes may be found the diamond-shaped mark with a large central "Rd" indicating that the design was registered at the Patent Office to protect it for three years from use by rival firms. The marginal letters and figures on these marks indicate registration at various dates during 1879 (see page 34).

A typical label announces "Stevengraph Pure Silk Woven Pictures" and gives a list of the subjects that "can be had beautifully Illuminated in 10 or 12 colours". This list indicates clearly enough that such pictures were more highly regarded than the general run of Stevengraphs: valentines, book-marks and the like receive no mention here. The length of the list varies. There may be six or seven on a label bearing the registration diamond indicating a date between 1879 and when the design was registered and 1883 when this type of mark was discontinued. Already by then, according to the label, Thomas Stevens had been awarded "ten highest prize medals and diplomas" and the eight medals are illustrated, obverse and reverse, over the engraving of the Stevengraph Works that heads the label. Stevens' catalogue for 1876–77 shows only six medals and claims seven awards ("Seven highest prize medals and diploma"). On another label eleven subjects are listed and its later date is confirmed by the diamond-shaped registration mark with the code letter J for the year 1880. This mark, when omitted from the label, may be found impressed in the soft card framing the picture but is inconspicuous and may be overlooked.

This new Stevengraph Works was built as convincing proof of Stevens' success in the mid-1870s: it is more than possible that the ribbons gave the name to the factory for the catalogue of Stevengraphs adapted for American sale as late as 1876–77 is illustrated merely with a diploma heading. It has been argued by some that the factory was named first, however, from the fact that writers in the early 1870s tried to call the ribbon pictures by other equally tiresome names such as textilegraphs. An early-20th-century mount has been noted with a printed inscription: "Woven on Silk by Thomas Stevens (Coventry) Ltd."

Perhaps the greatest disappointment to the collector is to find one of the later series of silk pictures, measuring five-and-a-quarter by two-and-a-quarter inches, lacking the earlier charm and fine workmanship. Their poor colour and less perfect technique point to a declining, price-cutting industry. The stitches are loose, the colour predominantly grey, and the scenes tend to be overcrowded and poorly copied from engravings. Historical subjects include Wellington and Blücher at Waterloo, William III crossing the Boyne, the death of Nelson and the signing of the Declaration of Independence, a picture made in 1893. Once their popularity vanished many silk pictures remained stored away in warehouses before being sold. Never having been exposed to the light these are still as fresh as when new and their colours unfaded, but their mounts lack the original Stevens labels.

Other Coventry firms known to have woven pictorial ribbons include W. H. Grant, who showed at the International Exhibition, 1885, and J. Hart. Even grandiose cigarette "cards" were produced as recently as the 1920s. Stevens himself had a keen eye for the American market and the retail price list in dollars and cents which he issued for 1876–77 is impressively comprehensive. This is amusing today for its page of "Eulogiums passed upon these goods by various Journals". It is curious indeed to read *The Bookseller*, August 1870, regarding "these works of art". "... In future ages collectors will glory and pride themselves upon the number and beauty of their specimens."

Chapter Fourteen

CHINA WATERING CANS

NOW that we are all on such intimate terms with our cactus, coleus, ficus and house-trained ivy, a delightful notion has been revived, and lovers of old china are being presented with exquisite little "watering cans" of the 18th and 19th centuries. When men take the shape and style of a homely tool and produce instead a fragile toy, all gilt and painted flowers, they have a gift worthy of Marie Antoinette herself, and when its tiny purpose is the diffusion of fragrant perfume the gift is surely irresistible.

From at least as early as the 14th century, watering pots in different designs and materials have been in demand, and until less than a century ago the most lovely have served the women of the household for imparting sophisticated fragrance to their surroundings. It is small wonder, therefore, that these little pots are still in demand today, including the most charmingly nonsensical miniatures of such vessels, toy versions of articles that themselves are scarcely more than playthings.

As early as the 15th century, Valentina, Duchess of Orleans, chose as her badge a perfuming pot, long-necked, bulbous, suggesting the shape of a Georgian decanter. This style of pot was made in 14th- and 15th-century England in coarse crimson or brownish earthenware for scenting and freshening the absorbent rushes strewn on dusty floors. The design is interesting as it was lost in the later spouted cans and depends on the principle of the pipette. The servant immersed the pot in sweetened water so that it filled through some thirty holes in its slightly convex base. He then lifted it by the neck between two fingers with his thumb over its small hole some three-eighths of an inch in diameter. So long as he held it thus no water could escape, but by uncovering the hole he released a slow sprinkle through the base holes on to the floor below.

The early pot was some nine inches tall and six inches across the base. For decoration there might be bands of white clay slip around the body or it might be covered wholly or partly in a green or brownish-yellow glaze. Fifteenth century improvements resulted in a somewhat larger vessel with a thicker, shorter neck and a larger mouth opening. The lip of the mouth was then joined to the high curved shoulder by a substantial handle with a trefoil terminal. Late in the century the vessel—usually green—might be urn-shaped and the perforated base rounded so that it could not be set down and forgotten while the contents seeped away.

In Elizabethan days, however, this old design disappeared and a style of watering pot developed that continued in use until late in the 18th century. Now that dust is such a minor annoyance in English homes it is difficult to imagine the endless trouble and sickness it caused down the centuries, and the importance of the sprinkler moving slowly from room to room. Hone's *Year Book* as late as 1838 illustrates such a watering pot and the writer records: "I remember to have seen at some old almshouses, when I was a boy, an aged feeble widow tottering with one of those earthen vessels slowly dribbling the water; since then I have seen only the usual painted tin watering pots".

One may still find such a vessel, though rarely in good condition apart from museum specimens. It is usually about twelve inches high, the bulbous body now mounted on a slight footrim, but instead of the perforated base it has a flat-fronted perforated rose jutting out and slightly up from the shoulder on a short, wide spout. A handle from lip to shoulder became essential with this design as the vessel had to be tilted, and a hood to cover half the opening at the top of a neck some three inches wide.

In a fine specimen in the Hastings Museum the union of spout and body is made a decorative flower petal feature matched by the half-hood over the neck. This 16th-century vessel is in red earthenware covered with a light brownish-yellow glaze. Such a pot would serve in the garden too for watering the knots of flowers and sweet herbs that were ever in demand for kitchen and stillroom. A slight modification of the design was developed early in the 18th century in vessels made of strong but heavy brown salt-glazed stoneware. In these the only openings were perforations in the rose and larger perforations in a top entirely covered to minimise evaporation. A century ago they were already rare.

By then carpets on the floors were replacing moisture-loving rushes but halls, passage-ways and far-reaching kitchen premises still suffered from the dust of rough-paved street and yard. Watering pots with spouted sprinkler roses were beautifully made in copper and brass and these in their turn were copied by the potter in warm red earthenware. These are modifications of the Elizabethan vessel with the small mouth about equal in diameter to the spout and half the diameter of the conspicuous rose which may be made a more decorative feature with lozenge-shaped piercings instead of haphazard roundish holes. Glaze may be limited to the points of greatest wear, the finely powdered natural sulphate of lead, known as smithum to its users and as galena to collectors, applied before firing to the rose and the front of the body. Three examples of these pots are in the British Museum.

To the collector today, however, the most fascinating watering pots are the small vessels some six inches high that were developed fairly late in the 18th century not for water but once again for distributing fragrance. From the late 18th century through the 19th century flower scents were quite extraordinarily important to the houseproud. Marie Antoinette swayed fashion away from strong, heavy scents towards delicate flower perfumes, but throughout the century Englishwomen had bought and made their own flower-perfumed waters. English lavender was considered far better than the French, and a few ounces of its essential oil could be distilled with several quarts of rectified spirit to produce delightful lavender water.

Recipe books offered many suggestions for the women who concocted their own distillations and infusions. Mrs. Hannah Glasse in *The Compleat Confectioner*, for instance,

1. Staffordshire blue and white ware showing transfer-printing at its most impressive. The "Triumphal Arch" (*above*) from Spode's Caramania series shows the vivid three-dimensional effects that could be achieved with a single colour printing and the elaborate harmonising border is typical of the best work. The romantic view (*below*) with a wide rose border is a Wedgwood piece of about 1830.

2. Staffordshire blue and white. *Upper left:* imaginative design with the shell border suggesting the mouth of a cave. The ship flies the stars and stripes, for sale in America. Impressed *Wood & Sons Burslem Warranted.* About 1835. *Upper right:* Spode's earliest version of the willow pattern, lacking the fine detail of later transfer work. *Below:* a delightful teapot, 4 ins. high, in Spode's Milkmaid design introduced 1814.

3. Two examples of Staffordshire blue transfer-printing intended for the American market and now eagerly collected. *Above:* "Boston State House and Common" with Job Hancock's house on the left: the border includes eagles among the flowers and scrolls. A 16-in. dish by Joseph Stubbs. *Below:* "Park Theatre, New York" in a border of oak leaves and acorns, impressed with the mark RSW for the firm of R. Stevenson and Wilson.

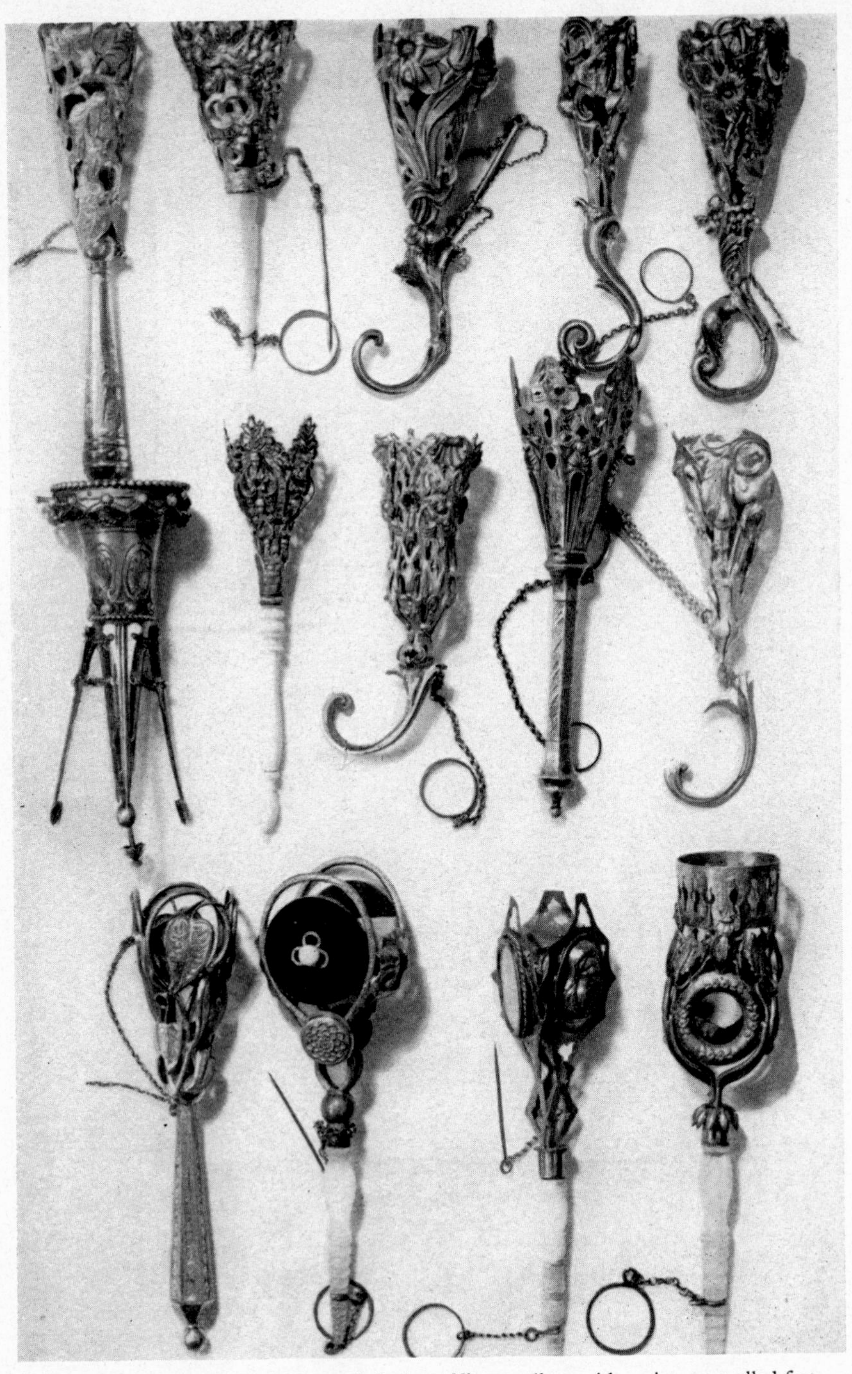

4. Posy holders, mainly of gilt metal. *Left, middle row:* silver with spring-controlled feet.

5a. Translucent olive green glaze covering an early stirrup cup in the Ralph Wood manner, modelled as a hound's head.

5b. Cabbage cream jug and cauliflower teapot, moulded in detail to suggest the leaves and flower and glazed in lovely tones of green and cream. These date to 1860 following designs taken from Wedgwood's early pattern book of 1759.

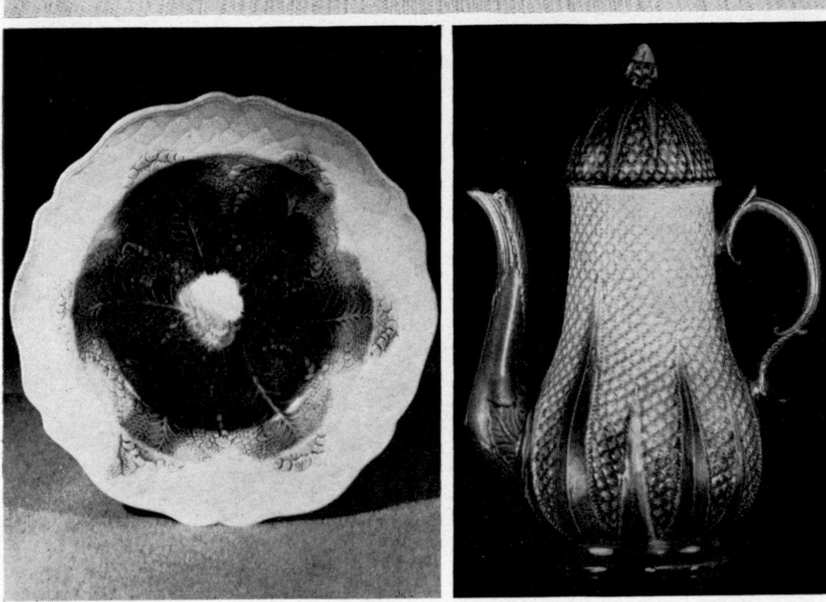

6. Green glaze wares. *Above:* typical Wedgwood leaf dish and plates and a shapely jug in a pattern of fruiting vine. *Lower left:* Wedgwood soup plate in green and cream glazes intended to suggest a cauliflower. About 1770. *Lower right:* "Pineapple" coffee pot in cream and green, delicately moulded to suggest the surface of the fruit. 1760s.

7a. Silver caddy ladles including tealeaves, shell and jockey cap. The plain spoon shape is thought to have preceded the more decorative styles.

7b. The tealeaf inset with filigree is by Samuel Pemberton, 1806. The hand is a rare design. The heavy vine casting is finely made by Rawlins and Sumner, 1828.

8a. Silver caddy ladles. The shell with the Onslow handle is hallmarked for 1794; the eight-sided bowl with fiddle handle, bright-cut, is by J. Taylor, 1806; tealeaf and acorn are by E. Morley, 1810, and the shovel by J. Wilmore, 1820.

8b. Georgian mote skimmer or skimming spoon with finely perforated bowl for taking dust from the surface of the poured tea and barb finial for clearing the teapot spout. Made by Thomas Northcote, 1777.

9. Popular designs in delicate bone china pastille burners and night-light shelters of the early 19th century. Castle and toll house are frequent subjects but the period delighted especially in the *cottage ornée* with its contrived rusticity, here represented by innumerable gothic windows and spectacular flower encrustations.

10. Cottages for an inexpensive market. *Upper left:* "A View of the Red Barn at Polestead", a chimney ornament "crime piece" complete with Maria Martin and William Corder at the door. Staffordshire enamelled earthenware, 1828. *Upper right:* thatched cottage, 4 ins. high, with cows and byre; a pastille burner of the 1820s in unpretentious earthenware with an attractive simplicity of design and colouring. *Lower left:* Villa $7\frac{1}{2}$ ins. high, ventilated for burning scented pastilles or a night-light that would glimmer through the translucent bone china: by the Worcester firm of Grainger, Lee and Co. who developed the more elaborate cottage lithophane. *Lower right:* earthenware church in the homely style of the village potter, perfect wedding souvenir for the sentimental countryman of the 1790s.

11. Tunbridge ware. *Above:* walnut board finely inlaid for the game of backgammon, such as was made in Tunbridge Wells in the late 17th century. *Below:* high quality pictorial work representing the final phase of Tunbridge ware mosaic. The design, wholly composed of fragments of variously coloured woods applied as a veneer, shows a view of the Tunbridge Wells Pantiles.

12. Wooden articles suitable for souvenir sale finely made in Tunbridge ware. *Above:* miniatures for workbox and desk. The table has a rim of pins, the teapot a pincushion lid and the barrel a tape measure. The thermometer shows both cube mosaic and the small-scale flower mosaic. *Below:* cabinet and box are veneered with the fine cube mosaic or parquetry and vandyke pattern. The box behind has a veneer of marble pattern sliced from suitably glued-together shavings.

13a. Porcelain birds at their most splendid, designed as dessert table ornaments in the mid-1750s. These substantial white partridges and brilliant parrot are from Chelsea, marked with the raised anchor.

13b. Chelsea's outstanding capacity for catching bird-like pose and expression are perfectly illustrated in this mandarin duck and owl-like hen harrier.

14a. A lovely pair of Bow pheasants, their colour ranging from the mauve-marked blue of their heads through pink, red and yellow to the browns and yellow of wings and tails.

14b. Parrots have always attracted the bird potter. These Bow specimens are in tones of green on flowery treestump supports. Those left and right are in a pose frequently adopted for models but the central bird is outstanding.

15. Bird modelling at its most exquisite. *Upper left:* the Derby peacock dates to the mid-1830s, meticulously hand painted and set among flowers created petal by petal and naturalistically coloured. *Upper right:* a masterpiece of Longton Hall porcelain dating to about 1755, the covered perfume vase smothered in flowers animated by the birds above. *Below:* Plymouth hard porcelain fashioned into an impressive pair of phoenix rising from the flames that envelop their scroll supports.

16. The broader, less detailed treatment required for bird modelling in earthenware, here combined with interesting colour brilliance. The cock and hen (*top*) are gorgeously painted with the "Pratt ware" colours associated with the 1790s—orange combs, blue bodies, blue, yellow, orange and brown tails. The cock is $8\frac{1}{4}$ ins. tall. The Staffordshire hawk of about 1750 (*lower left*) combines mingled-colour glaze—mottled green and brownish grey—with formal incised detail. The cock (*lower right*) is notably well modelled and sympathetically painted with an attempt at a flower-encrusted base.

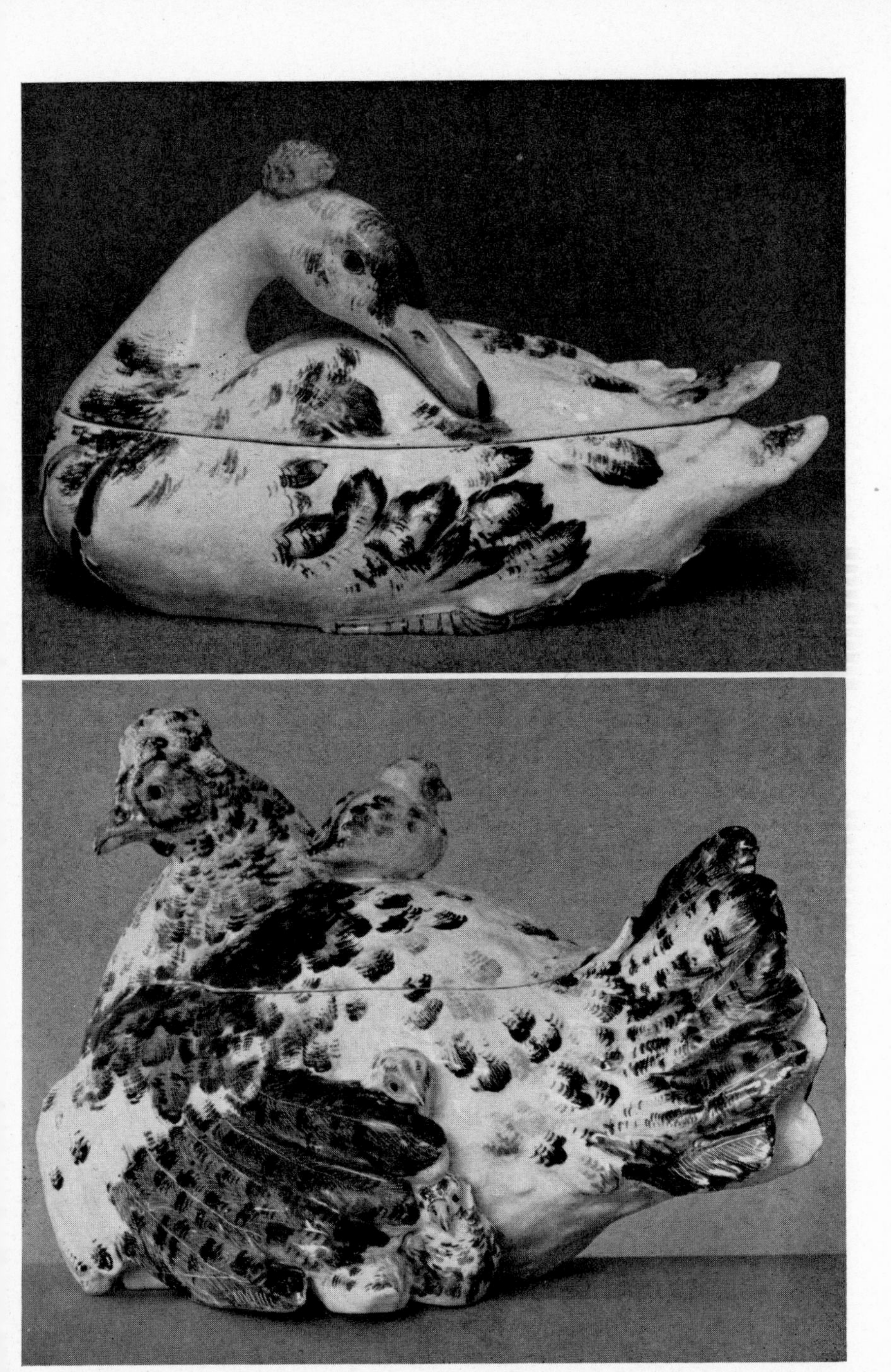

17. Birds modelled by Chelsea as covered tureens. The crested duck (*above*) is marked with the red anchor of 1753–56. The hen (*below*) is forerunner of innumerable sitting hens, with chicks nestling under her wing.

18. Door knockers. *Upper left:* wrought iron of the late 16th century with the ring rapper swinging from the mouth against a striking stud. *Upper right:* cast iron of the late 18th century, the mask escutcheon attached by two bolts. *Lower left:* brass, late 18th century, the rapper swinging on steel rivets screwed into the escutcheon. *Lower centre:* brass, early 19th century, with rapper and upper eye bolt cast in a single piece. *Lower right:* iron, the spur rapper easily wrenched away.

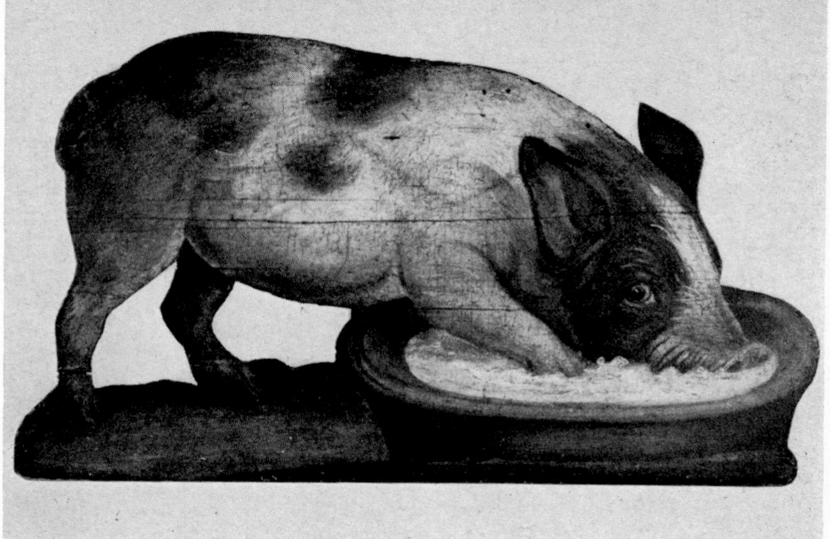

19. Door porters indicating the very wide range of materials and treatments. Jumbo in cast iron commemorates the celebrated mid-Victorian elephant at the London Zoo. The harness is painted in brilliant colours. The glass dome (*upper right*) is in a style sometimes mistaken for a massive paper weight. Coloured enamels combined with air bubbles inside the heavily leaded glass create an ocean-bed effect. The greedy pig of the late 18th century is painted on heavy wood.

20. Jugs for milk and cream. *Top left:* lively design with chased ornament and dainty feet, 1736. *Top right:* the earliest style, with beak spout and moulded foot ring, 1725. *Centre left:* cream boat by Edward Feline, about 1740. *Centre right:* stemmed design by David Willaume, patterned in relief, 1743. *Bottom left:* cream boat with cow embossment and lion's mask legs, 1750. *Bottom right:* typical helmet design. This was made in Cork, 1760s.

21. Silver vessels for milk and cream. *Upper left:* cream pail, 2½ ins. high, with a Bristol blue lining, made by Charles Aldridge and Henry Green, London, 1779. *Upper right:* quickly ornamented milk jug in the somewhat graceless style of pear-shaped body on hollow pedestal foot. This, London made, dates to 1781. *Lower left:* substantial little pitcher, oval on plan and with characteristic handle, 1799. *Lower right:* finely proportioned Dublin example of the 18th century's neo-classic style. Height 6¾ ins. 1799.

22. Glass jugs for the tea table. *Upper left:* rare engraved jug commemorating William III's triumph at the Battle of the Boyne, 1690, the glass probably mid-18th century and the engraving somewhat later. *Upper right:* "A Trip to the Fort"—Yarmouth souvenir pictorial engraving on a jug with the substantial square plinth fashionable around the end of the 18th century. *Lower left:* richly ornamented jug showing a range of cut patterns including radial cutting on the foot: second quarter of the 19th century. *Lower right:* very early example of a jug in flint glass: this is marked with the raven's head of George Ravenscroft and may be dated 1675–80.

23. Antique earthenware cradles such as still make delightful christening gifts. *Upper left:* dainty 5-in. specimen containing a brightly dressed child. *Upper centre:* probably unique, this is decorated haphazardly with applied medallions including several of Admiral Rodney and is thought to commemorate the death of his baby daughter, about 1785. *Upper right:* magnificent early Georgian cradle in slip ware, 12 ins. long, dark brown with white ornament: the fiddler and the six heads are in white earthenware with black eyes. *Lower left:* glazed earthenware, hand coloured, the low relief pattern suggesting a quilted cradle cover. *Lower centre:* bonneted baby in a cradle of about 1800 moulded and coloured to suggest coarse wickerwork. *Lower right:* yellow glazed earthenware of about 1800 moulded with lively classical figures: this is found also in green-glaze ware.

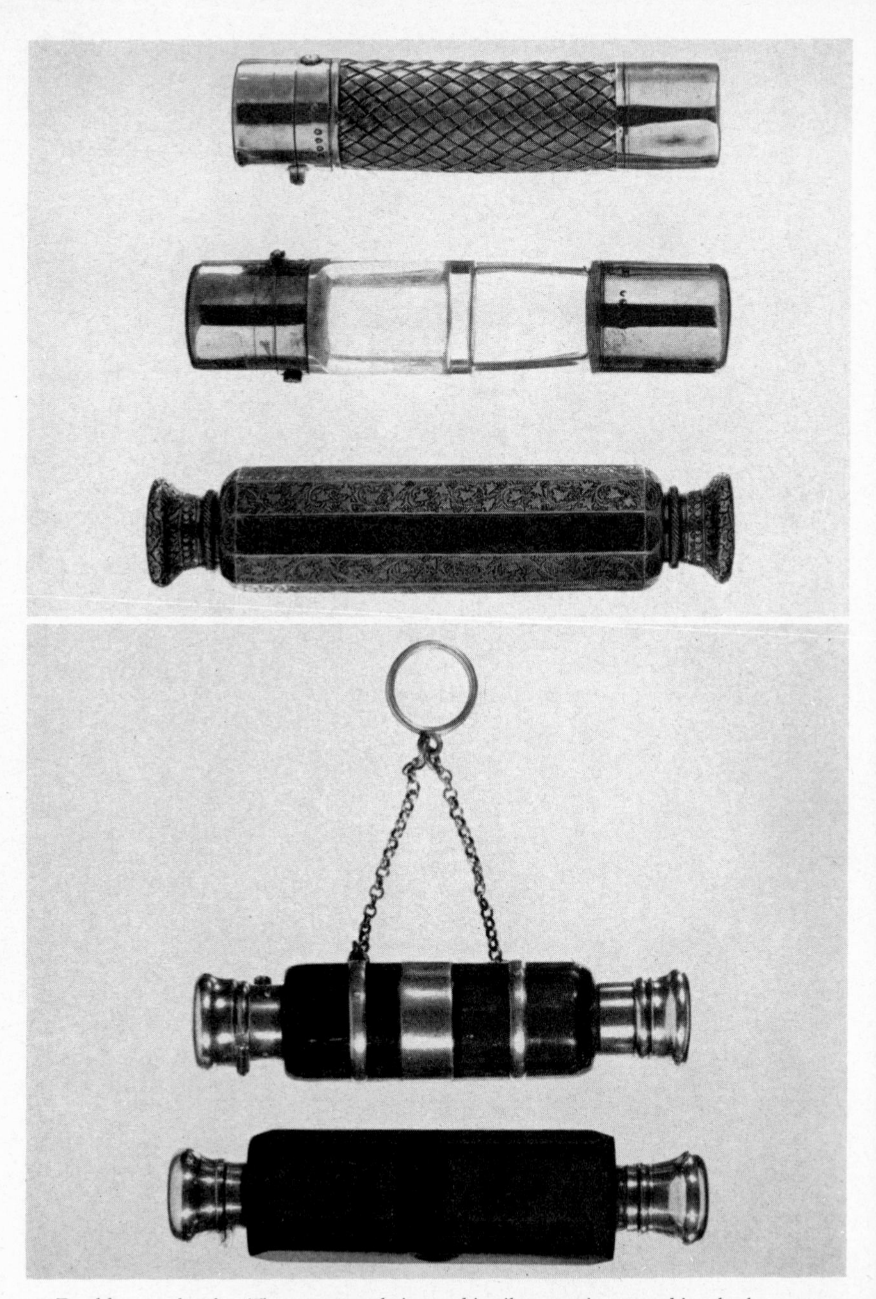

24. Double scent bottles. The top example is cased in silver, engine turned in a basket pattern. London, 1881. The plain glass example, $3\frac{1}{2}$ ins. long, has silver lids hallmarked for Birmingham, 1851. The scroll-engraved bottle is in a nickel alloy, its caps, both screw-attached, differentiated by their relief patterns. This still retains its leather case. The bottle fitted with chain and ring for carrying is in blue glass, the spring-fitted lid bearing the supplier's name, S. Mordan & Co., London. The amber glass bottle below with silver plated mounts clearly shows the join of the two bottle bases.

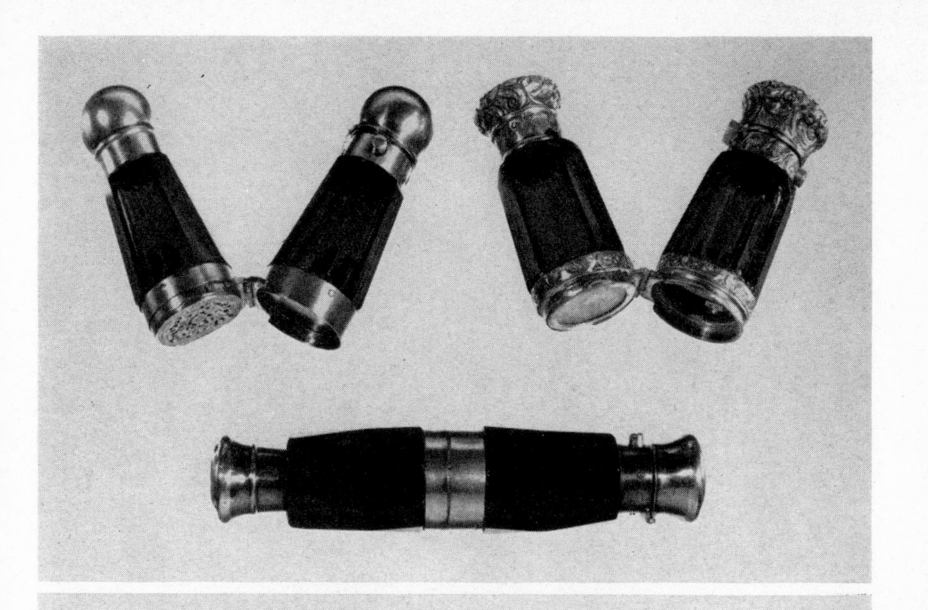

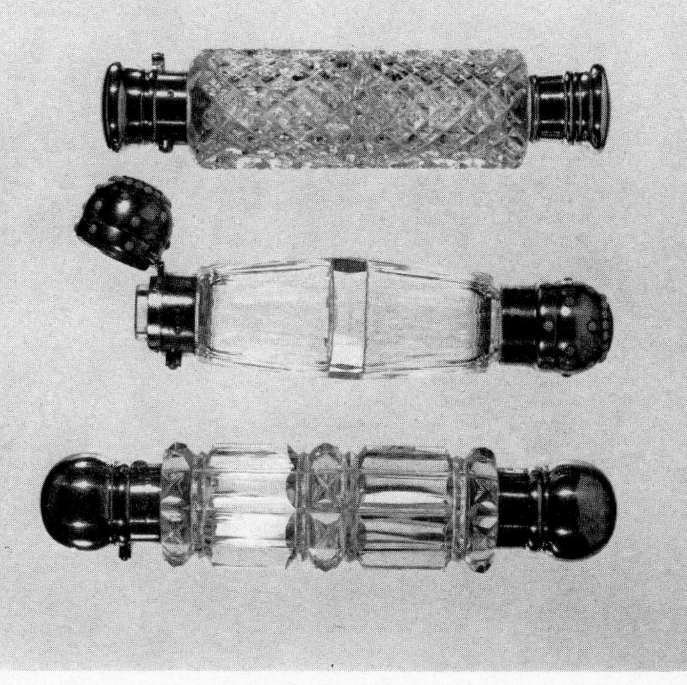

25. Double scent bottles. The hinged style above is unusual. The top left example is in ruby glass and has a vinaigrette at the bottle base with perforated grid; that on the right conceals a photograph. The three in clear glass below show the range of cut ornament. The top example has a strawberry-cut diamond pattern; this is $5\frac{1}{2}$ ins. long. The central facet-cut barrel is unusual, its engraved caps marked Birkenhead Iron Works. The heavy 6-inch specimen below has ball shaped silver mounts. London, 1888.

26. Lustre wares, the ceramic entirely covered by metallic lustre glaze to suggest solid metal. The Wedgwood incense burner is in red earthenware covered with gold copper lustre, 1805. The early-19th-century teapot is moulded in relief with the silversmith's beading and fluting and covered with silver lustre.

27. Jugs showing a wide range of lustre work. *Upper left:* subsidiary decoration in silver lustre above a gay coaching scene. This has been inscribed with the name Jacob Goodwin and the date 1810. *Upper right:* purplish mottling in the style known as Sunderland ware. *Lower left:* typical silver resist lustre, the patterns appearing in the glazed creamy surface of the earthenware against the dark silver background. *Lower right:* silver resist as a background to a chinoiserie scene in blue.

28. Copper lustre ware such as was made in Sunderland and elsewhere. The upper mug is an early shape, surprisingly light in the hands. On this and the goblet the painted ornament is restricted to white reserves. The tallest jug is a fine example of imitation metal. The centrepiece is a shaving dish with flowers and foliage painted in colours over the glowing lustre.

29a. Lustred porcelain with an iridescent gleam—Ireland's mother of pearl ware made at Belleek, Co. Fermanagh, in the second half of the 19th century. Typically, the sweetmeat vessel is a shell and the teapot a sea urchin set in coral.

29b. Lidded basket composed of strands of parian porcelain and ornamented with rose and shamrock and thistle. For colour this depends on the lustrous mother of pearl glaze.

30. Mid-Victorian Coventry picture ribbons measuring 6 by 2 ins. framed in their original cards, as issued by Thomas Stevens, their inventor and manufacturer. Colour contrasts and extremely intricate detail are achieved entirely in the mechanical weaving process. The "Lord Howe" travelling at 60 m.p.h. has a charming companion piece "The First Train".

The Start.

Are you Ready?

31. "The Start" is one of several equine subjects found in Coventry ribbons, the variously woven silks in fawn, yellow, cream and black providing effective contrast for the horses' glossy coats and riders' shirts. Extremely fine weaving even shows the features of the spectators' faces. The boat race is full of background detail in tones of grey and sepia contrasting with the blues, pink and yellow of the oarsmen and the scarlet and green of officials. This has a registration mark impressed on the card mount.

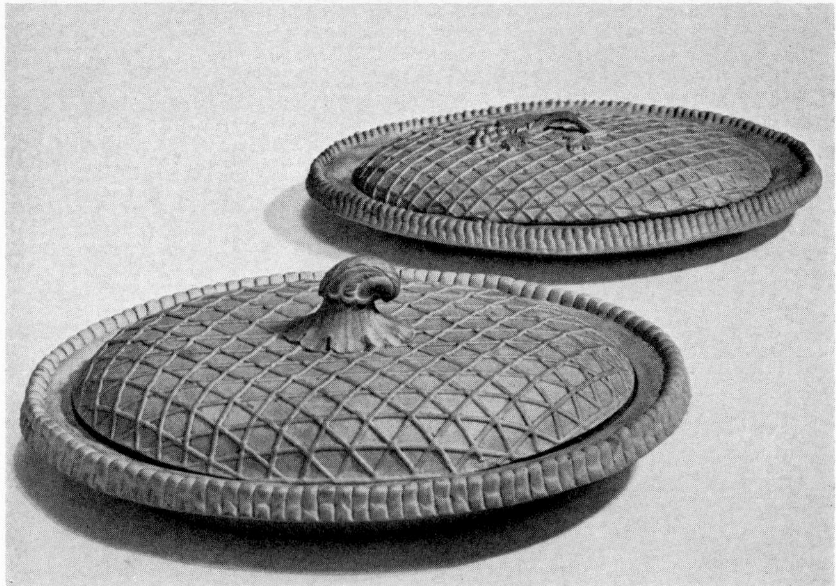

32. *Above:* perfume sprinkler shaped as a watering can. This would be fitted with a deeply recessed lid and a wide saucer. Spode bone china of the early 19th century vividly ornamented in colours and gold in a japan pattern. *Below:* flat dishes in unglazed buff caneware shaped and coloured to resemble pastry. These would be filled with stewed fruit.

33. Game pie dishes such as were made by the Wedgwood firm from the 1790s, continuing in production for some eighty years. The scarcity of flour during the Napoleonic wars created a great demand for these lidded dishes in cane ware reproducing in shape and colour the appearance of massive raised pies. The upper specimen is particularly fine, the ornament shaped separately as it would be by the pastrycook. The lower, later specimen has an elaborate moulded design of dead game.

34. Victorian lockets. *Top row:* heart shapes: set with ruby and diamond star; set with initials in turquoises; closely set with black onyx. *Second row:* padlock shapes: moonstone set in chased moulding; set with an amethyst; glass-fronted to show a plait of hair. *Third row:* set with convex amethyst and rock crystal; pressed with diagonal ribbings; snake setting to cameo memorial portrait. *Bottom row:* set front and back with heart-shaped cairngorms; set with trefoil of garnets; shaped as heavily strapped purse, with press stud for opening.

35. Tortoiseshell set with gold in the delicate designs associated with 18th-century English piqué work. The four corner articles are étuis, oval on plan, with hinged covers and compartmented for scissors, memo tablet and the like. The shuttle-shaped boxes might be for snuff, tortoiseshell perfectly preserving the delicate aroma.

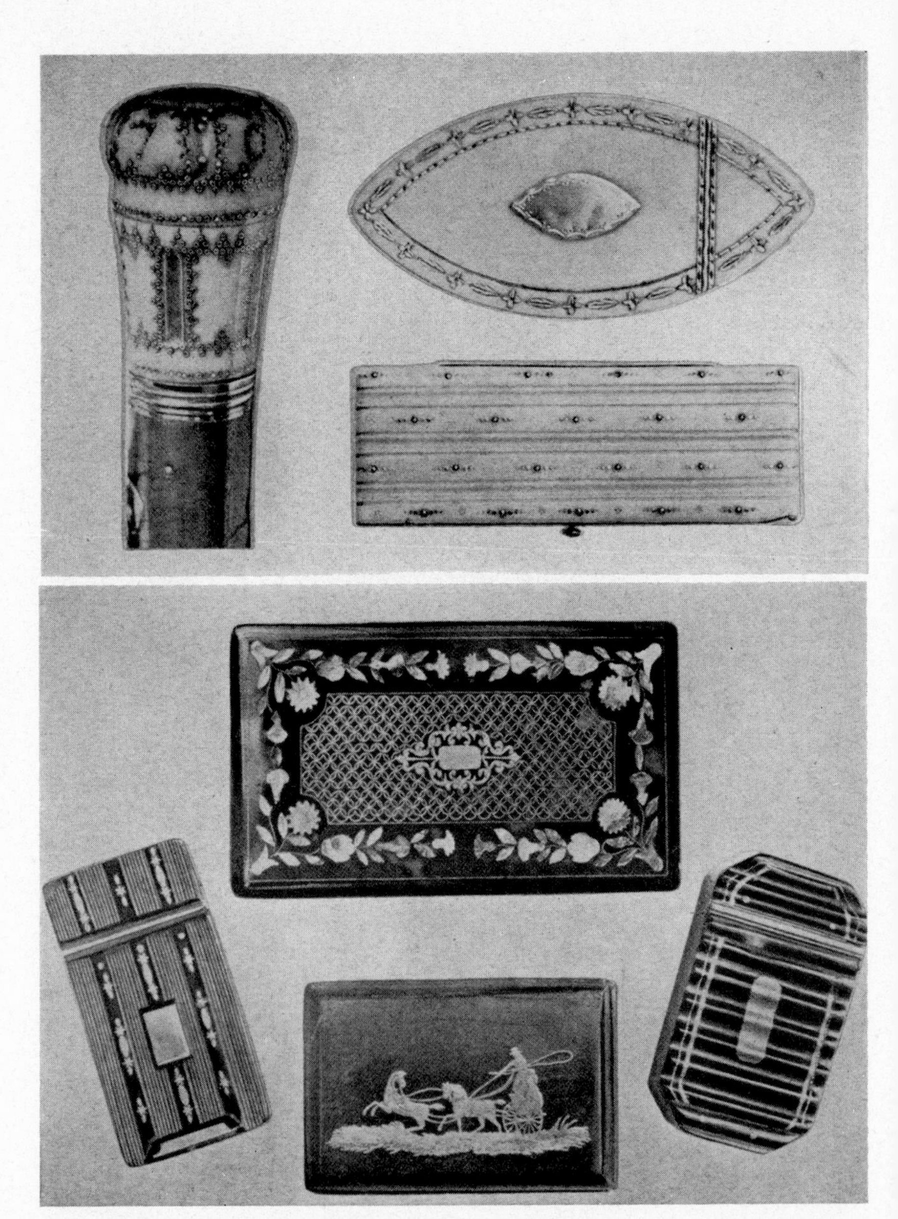

36. English piqué work. *Above:* the nail head or clouté style of ornament applied with effective restraint in silver upon ivory. The cane head pattern is composed entirely in this manner. *Below:* an interesting range of early-19th-century patterns in gold on tortoiseshell, pictorial work contrasting with meticulous formal detail.

37. Moneyboxes in earthenware. *Top:* two 18th-century hens surrounded by chickens: (*left*) 5 ins. high, the feathers suggested in white clay slip on a chocolate brown ground; (*right*) from Gorsty Hill, Worcestershire, splashed with manganese brown under the yellow glaze. *Centre:* two 18th-century money pots from Brede, Sussex, in glowing red earthenware under a yellowish glaze. *Bottom:* early-19th-century cottages showing different treatments of the same basic design. These are slotted behind the chimney.

38. Pressed papier mâché at its most ornate, made into substantial furniture. The tip-up pillar table (*left*) shows an oil painting of Queen Victoria's children with Windsor Castle behind. The border has green and pink shell among the gold ornament. By Jennens and Bettridge, early 1850s. The chair (*centre*) is black japanned and painted with flowers in colours with bronzed enrichments. The flower and gold enriched teapoy is fitted with mâché canisters and cut glass vessels for sugar and for blending the teas.

39. Papier mâché. *Upper left:* paper rack painted in the Wolverhampton style of bronze work, the stained glass window in full colour. Marked *Jennens & Bettridge*. Mid-19th century. *Upper right:* tea caddy with Chinese landscape in gold on black. *Below:* decorative tray made by Shoolbred and Loveridge of Wolverhampton in about 1825.

40. Salt-glazed stoneware partly stained brown, with lively ornament in relief. *Above:* Fulham tankards dated 1729 and 1761. *Below:* detail from a John Wesley centenary bowl by Doulton, about 1839.

41. Vivid figure-moulding in tough, inexpensive brown stoneware finished with salt glazing. These were issued by Doulton and Watts from about 1820. *Upper row:* Queen Caroline, consort of George IV, who in fact was never crowned; the Duke of York who died 1827; Queen Victoria; the Prince Consort. *Below left:* Daniel O'Connell the Irish patriot: this figure-flask sometimes holds a scroll impressed *Irish Reform Cordial. Below right:* "Seahorse", over 24 ins. high, modelled by Mark Villars Marshall, about 1890.

42. Crystal cameos. Superb examples of Apsley Pellatt's work. The cup (*above*) carries two portraits in the delicate silvery relief work within the thickness of the glass—George III and the Prince Regent in the guise of Roman emperors. The scent bottle below shows a portrait of Princess Charlotte in a setting of richly cut diamonds. The paperweight in cushion shape is cut to form a frame enclosing a portrait of George IV in coronation robes against a ground of cross-cut diamonds. 1821.

43. Effective use of crystal cameos among the glitter of lustres and heavy cutting designed to intensify the brilliance of candlelight. *Left:* a pair of magnificent lustre-hung girandole candlesticks, the superb glass set with cameos of Princess Charlotte and George III. *Right:* candelabrum set with a classical figure, with in addition a coloured rose medallion in the centre of the cut star ornament.

44. Silver tumblers and beakers. *Upper left:* from a William III travelling set engraved with a hunting scene. Made by Charles Overing, 1701. *Upper right:* simple beaker hallmarked for 1672. The triangle of initials suggests that this was a wedding gift, the husband's surname initial at the top and the Christian name initials of himself and his wife to left and right below. *Lower left:* straight-sided, heavy-based beaker with simple, flat-chased ornament. Made in Norwich, 1691. *Lower right:* more sophisticated lidded bell shape of the same period. By John Bodington, London, 1697.

45. Richly ornamented tumblers and beakers. *Top left:* enamelled glass in the waisted design known as a tun. *Top right:* enamelled in full colours with the royal arms of George III and the Prince of Wales, about 1762. *Centre left:* engraved glass wishing "Success to the Integrity In^{o} Gibson Com^{R}". *Centre right:* heavy cut-based tumbler richly patterned with cut diamonds and fluting. *Bottom left:* gilt-marked Chamberlains Worcester beaker with yellow ground and gilt border. About 1810. *Bottom right:* beaker bat printed with subjects from Pyne's *Microcosm.* Impressed BFB for Barr, Flight and Barr, Worcester. About 1812.

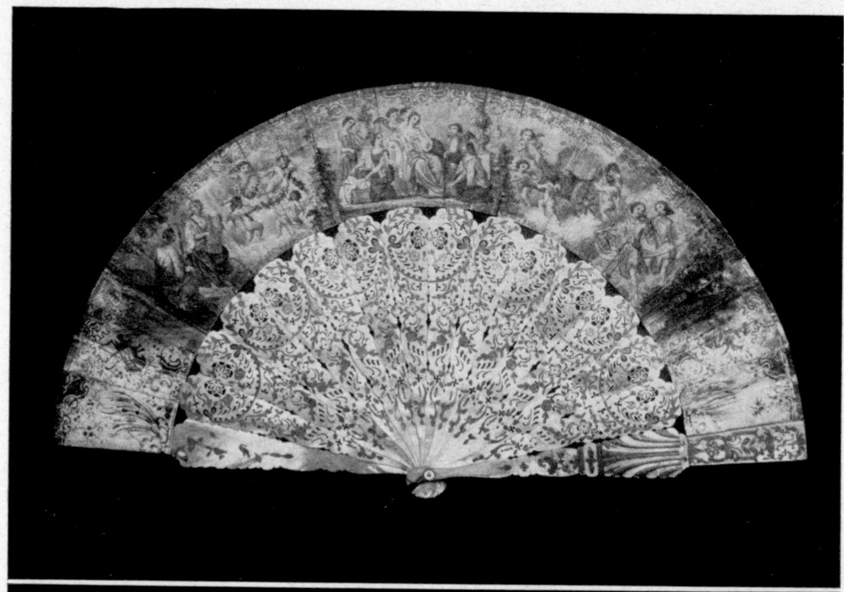

46. Two notable fans. The wedding fan is painted with a bride dressed for the ceremony, a winged cupid arranging her veil and others bringing the bridal car. The finely pierced sticks are mother of pearl embossed with gold and silver foil. The cabriolet fan with a second, narrower mount, is painted with a scene showing a catastrophe involving this popular little vehicle and its lady driver.

47. Fans with rich pictorial ornament on the mounts. *Upper left:* "Maternal Amusements" after Adam Buck, a stipple engraving in the Regency classic mood yet not wholly free of the fan painter's flower sprays. *Upper right:* romantic country house scene above superbly carved pearl sticks. *Lower left:* Interesting example of a marriage fan, made for the Princess Anne, daughter of George II, 1733; the sticks are carved to show the princess receiving her betrothed as a classic hero. *Lower right:* lovers in a harvest field, a medallion bridal fan with emblematic reference to peace, industry, patience, constancy and other virtues; the sticks are notable for their individualistic carving of marriage emblems. Mid-1770s.

48a. All-white 19th-century fan with carved ivory sticks and guards unobtrusively harmonising with the rich lace mount.

48b. Ivory carving at its most intricate in a ribbon-bound brisé fan. The uncarved medallions are richly painted, the central figures pledging their troth representing Mrs. Fitzherbert and the Prince of Wales.

fills four pages with sweet-water recipes at a time when double distilled lavender water was selling at three shillings a pint. For perfumed water she recommended "three handfuls of the tops of young lavender and as much of the flowers of woodbine full ripe and plucked from the stalks, then take as much orice roots as two walnuts and a half, one orange peel dried, and as much calamas as one walnut, and beat them all together". Rosewater and orange flower water figure importantly in these recipes. Distilling might be left to the enthusiast but infusions with such garden scents were comparatively cheap and easy to prepare. More were for sale in the shops: by 1800 London alone boasted forty manufacturing perfumers and Paris twice that number. As many as thirty different odours might be listed by a perfumer of the 1830s and Victorian days saw a vast development in their trade, but associated with chemical laboratory rather than with stillroom and herb garden.

Perfumed water discreetly introduced filled a room with delicate fragrance: the visitor looked for exotic out-of-season flowers and found instead a vase or bowl supporting tulip, carnation, rose, of finely tinted porcelain, superbly made petal by petal and "brought to life" with perfumed water sprinkled from the small rose of a watering pot equally decorative and charming. Perhaps the earliest of these little scent sprinklers were in the late-18th-century's fine matt-surfaced stonewares, the caneware and relief-ornamented jaspers that many potters adapted from those of Josiah Wedgwood. But the majority so eagerly collected today date from the beginning of the 19th century onwards when translucent bone china, fine textured, brilliantly white and far stronger than the previous century's porcelains, offered new opportunities to English potters to create exquisite flowers in full relief and also the perfumed water pots that completed the make-believe.

It is difficult to exaggerate the charm of these Regency, late Georgian and early Victorian china flowers, the ribbon-tied standing bouquets made by Derby, the flower-encrusted baskets of Coalport, the bowls of rich blooms from Spode and Rockingham. Bright-eyed narcissus and auricula, anemone, marguerite, even full-blown roses, were meticulously copied and coloured by hand, petal by petal, as individual creations. The more formal, artificial-looking flowers respond best to such representation, perhaps, such as glossy tulip and papery everlasting, but all are completely matched in mood by the manufacturers' china watering cans.

The early bone china can is baluster-shaped, its gaudy colour scheme caught from the japanned iron "tin" pots and kettles and cans then in their heyday. It has a straight, up-tilted spout with some nine holes in the wide rose. It lacks the bail handle and half hood of the metal can, however, and has instead a close-fitting lid to minimise oxidisation, sunk well into the vessel's mouth lest it fall when tilted or the finial receive a knock. To complete it there should be a tiny saucer to catch any staining drips: some of Spode's finest cans have saucers with boldly convex rims.

Spode introduced effective gilding of handles, knobs and spouts in matt-surfaced, unburnished gold in 1802 but many of the specimens found today are conspicuous for the bright gold on handle and spout, often as a band covering only part of a spout that may otherwise be plain white in contrast to the rich japan patterning that became a delightful feature of these cans from about 1810. Josiah Spode developed his own japan style as early as 1804 and Derby soon after. These bright, crowded all-over patterns in garish colours and gold were based on the Japanese Imari style. They effectively cover flaws in the china and perfectly suit the style of the vessels. Spode might introduce delicately pencilled birds and flowers and his japan patterns show considerable Chinese influence. Bloor of Derby in 1817 advertised for "twenty good enamel painters who can paint different Japan patterns". The Bloor colours are applied in haphazard, incoherent gaiety of red and blue with solid gilding that has a brassy tone, but on unmarked work it is often difficult to distinguish Derby's japan patterns from Spode's.

Chamberlain of Worcester was using japan patterns by 1806. He made these little cans with such ornament and more with heavily gilded grounds displaying flowers and foliage in high relief decorated in natural colours. Coloured grounds on watering cans date from about 1830 onwards, a new process of ground-laying being invented by Henry

Daniell in 1826 which for the first time made it possible to produce a smooth glassy surface of colour unaffected by the subsequent firings required for the enamelled ornament. There may be a mark in red script *Chamberlain Worcester* but many are unmarked.

Rockingham cans are a delight sought by every collector, with their particularly brilliant colours including the characteristic thick opaque apple green, their rustic handles and their lavish gilding, now showing a tinge of copper. Some are in japan patterns, the reds ranging from deep pink to maroon; others have flower sprays in high relief, the flowers in colour, the leaves in sparkling gold: these bear the puce-coloured griffin mark. More of these relief-ornamented cans were made by Coalport in a vulnerable design with a six-inch long spout, all too liable to lose its gilded rose. Until the early 1830s Coalport grounds might be in heavy gold and thereafter in colours.

The problem of the projecting spout was tackled by the practical potter John Davenport of Longport, whose cans are in a strong stone china, and who copied the coppersmith by giving the spout a sharp upward angle and linking it with a strut to the shoulder. His cylindrical little cans may be recognised by their small animals and similar motifs supporting the finials of their domed lids, and by their high curving handles, but most conspicuously by their spout design with half a dozen small tubes protruding from the rose, intended to ensure that the perfumed water would trickle exactly where required. Davenport applied Daniell's new process of ground-laying to his watering cans, leaving white reserves for his enamellers to paint with colourful little flower posies. His mark may be found on cans from 1830, *Davenport's Stone China* in a circle with a foul anchor.

Obviously these small cans might be used for watering the violets and mignonette and other treasures of hall and conservatory but one may find, too, an occasional pot made specially for the conservatory in rustic terra cotta, glazed only inside. William Baddeley, Normancott Road, Longton, began such work in 1862, making also the crocus pots and fern stands, the flower baskets and mignonette boxes required to hold the plants, all in the same rustic styles. His watering cans are designed to represent sections of bark-covered tree trunk with branch spouts.

Perfect accompaniment to the collection of china watering cans is a miniature specimen. Queen Mary, who delighted in diminutive toys, possessed several, two to four inches tall, in the old japan patterns, blue and red and gold. Here the design more exactly copies the japanned iron can of the conservatory, cylindrical, with a straight, wide-rosed spout, a half hood, an arching bail handle of flat or semi-circular section, as well as the plain curved handle at the rear and three tiny pointed feet, often all heavily gilded. Spode japan specimens may be marked *Spode* in red with the early-19th-century japan pattern number 967 which was used on cans until 1827 and long continued on different wares.

Not all these miniature cans bear japan patterns: some are ringed with tiny flower posies. Spode issued some with rose sprays in the style associated with William Billingsley's Swansea work. Even Swansea's own elegant duck egg porcelain has occasionally survived in such a tiny can, but some Swansea marks may be noted on delightful flower-painted cans made in the 1840s, long after the factory had closed, these being issued by a former Swansea decorator Henry Morris. Bloor's Derby potters made miniatures too, and here again the style was continued by successive potters: Stevenson and Hancock, of King Street, Derby, marked theirs from 1862 with the Derby crowned crossed swords over a script *D* flanked by the letters *S* and *H*, and Sampson Hancock continued the issue of miniature china from this "Old Crown Derby China Works" even until the present century.

Chapter Fifteen

PIECRUST WARES

HOME cooks today, it seems, seldom "raise a pie". The massive pastry confection that stands unsupported on the platter tends to be left to the expert. Some cookery books fail even to mention such "hot water pastry". Instead we buy magnificent ceramic representations of these golden-brown creations. Many of these are modern, but the collector with a love of the bygones from English kitchen and pastry-room seeks out the "pies" of the 18th and 19th centuries before it is too late to save any of these extravagantly fine pieces of ceramic make-believe.

For centuries the raised pie was a vital item on the menu of every big establishment in the country, and at every back door, too, since these were the thick, gravy-rich crusts that were given to the poor. Among guild records of feasts one notes the vintners buying flour for venison pies in 1510, the pewterers and the ironmongers listing their pewter pie plates and pastry plates in the 1640s, the blacksmiths feasting their wives and families with mutton pies, poultry and codling tarts in 1657. It is only necessary to go through any old household records to realise the endless struggle to feed the family and staff on food both fresh and palatable. Compared with the incredible numbers of small birds slaughtered and the barrels of salt fish broached in lean times, the items of game included in the menu represented luxury indeed, a delight to be prolonged to the utmost and shared with friends near and far. Hence the splendour of the game pie.

A peck of flour worked up with three pounds of butter was recommended in 1740 by Edward Kidder who kept a pastry school in Little Lincoln's Inn Fields; 24 lbs. of flour,

6 lbs. of butter and ½ lb. of suet by John Farley in *The London Art of Cookery*, 1789. The enduring case of flour and butter or lard was filled with pieces of game (venison, say, when snow drove the deer down from the hills) laid on suet and covered with butter, seasoned and spiced. Pastry lid and walls were brushed with egg yolk and enriched with ornament cut out in thin pastry. An ambitious cook would thus indicate the contents of the pie: Kidder illustrates wild boar pie with rope-work around the sides and a boar's head on top. But an easier alternative could be cut with pastry moulds, such as the fruiting vines suggested by Farley.

Then came a baking of four to six hours and finally and importantly a "lear" or seal made from two pounds of butter in a rich hot gravy was poured in through a hole in the crust, the hole sealed and the pie put away to set for at least eight to ten days before use. Such short-term preserving gave time for distribution: in the Naworth accounts of January 1618, for instance, it is possible to catch a glimpse of the whole important procedure in the small detail of two new padlocks bought for "the 2 hampers with dear pyes".

On the home dinner table the pie would take its place among an array of dishes far more numerous and ample than would be required for family and guests: the early-18th-century *Complete Housewife*, for example, illustrates a "second course" upon the table with a 20-egg baked tansy in the centre surrounded by woodcocks on toast, hare with savoury pudding, roast turkey and hot buttered apple pie. This tradition of massive display continued throughout the 18th century. Sophie von la Roche in 1786 commented on the large dishes for sale in pewter, china and crockery "because a quarter of a calf, half a lamb and monstrous pieces of other meats are dished up and everyone receives almost an entire fish", although she realised that the servants benefited by the custom.

By then, however, new problems were looming for the ambitious cook. The flour tax levied during the Napoleonic wars banished massive pies from the table: even the Royal Household ruled that rice was to be used instead of pastry. Such a decorative item as a raised pie, such a useful vessel in days when only metal ware could go in the oven, was too valuable for such banishment, however. Josiah Wedgwood turned from his classic vases and massive dinner services to meet the cook's need with splendid substitutes in a smooth-surfaced, fine-textured golden-brown stoneware known as cane-ware.

These are the earliest of such collectable items, representing the pie at its most elaborate, with richly decorated sides and a shapely finial to the lid. The ware is a fine-grained stoneware ranging in tone from pale cream to piecrust brown and was perfected by Wedgwood in the early 1780s, being described by him in 1787 as "bamboo or cane coloured bisque porcelain". It was coloured throughout its body and required no more than occasional tinting to achieve the variable tones of pie-crust. Glaze was applied only on the inside where it was in contact with the hot cooked meats and is thin and meagre at that, with none inside the lid. Such a pie would stand up to the kitchen heat though it could not be placed in the oven. Some merely contributed to the table display but more were intended to hold hot foods, though not always perhaps the game or pork or other delicacy which their ornament suggested. Open tarts were made too, their lattice "crusts" probably covering nothing more ambitious than stewed fruit.

Crock pies was the contemporary name for these deceptive creations: even that tremendous trencherman Parson Woodforde, whose diaries catalogue the multitudinous dishes laid out before him each day, had to suffer them, as recorded on September 1st, 1801: "Crock, alias Cottage Pie, and a fine Leveret roasted with stuffing" although I suspect that his opinion of such shams would be no better than that of Lucinda-and-Jane's two bad mice.

Lord Cockburn in *Memorials of his Times* recalls that in the year 1795–96 "there was a greater dearth than has ever since visited the British islands" and it is from this date onwards that the substitute pies can be noted in bills and records of the Wedgwood firm: in June 1801, for instance, 12*s*. 6*d*. was paid for a "Raised Pie"; by 1869 a Wedgwood tart and dish found a place in a sale at Christies, going for 10*s*. Wedgwood made each pattern in four sizes.

These early caneware pies are oval—round pies are comparatively rare in caneware—the sides sloping slightly inwards, the base encircled with rope work. Relief ornament was sprigged to the sides, that is, attached with thinner caneware slip before the pie was fired. The motifs were those of the pastry-cook—dead game in a mixture of flesh and fowl, or conventional flowers or fruiting vine, separately shaped with metal moulds in similar caneware. As on the real pie the most ambitious ornament appears on the lid, which the pastry-cook was advised to sink well below the level of the rim so that his extravagant motifs would not be scorched. Collectors of caneware pies look for Wedgwood's cauliflower finial, aware that there is a world of difference between the clear-cut, finely shaped early specimen and the mid-19th-century version. Often this motif is a dead bird, such as pheasant or duck.

A find for the collector is a pie impressed *TURNER*. The Staffordshire potters John and William Turner of Lane End made some of the finest in a close-textured caneware that shows hard and glassy when chipped. This firm was celebrated for its pies until 1804. Other marks to watch for include Samuel Hollins of Shelton (*S. HOLLINS*) and *E. Mayer*, or *E. Mayer & Son*, from the Hanley firm of Elijah Mayer, not to be confused with Charles Meigh (1835–60), another notable caneware pie-maker. But these are only a few among the many, including even such important firms as Mintons where caneware pies were made towards the mid 19th century. The firm of Lakin & Poole, Burslem, even distinguish on their invoices, 1792–96, between English pies and the richer-crusted French pies, and as late as the 1840s contemporary comment marvelled at the continuing demand for these "dishes resembling baked pastry".

A simpler method of decorating the sides was developed in the mid-1830s, John and William Ridgway evolving a caneware which could be moulded in relief. Two examples have been noted with the mark "Published by / W. Ridgway & Co / Hanley / Oct 1st 1835". This was the date when the pattern was registered at Stationers' Hall to give it copyright protection for fourteen years. The result lacks the sharp undercut outlines of the applied ornament, however, and is a step further from the pastry original.

It must be stressed that none of these early pies could be placed in the oven: the filling was cooked in a pan, and served in its rich casing. It was in Derbyshire that the first ovenware was evolved, an ironstone caneware developed for cheap fireproof oven dishes. The piecrust vessels in this ware lack the rich, crisp finish of earlier work and the moulding on top and sides is weak, but they were intended for a cheaper market, and they were so strong that they really could take the place of pastry as their meaty contents simmered in the oven. Among these vessels it is rare to find a maker's mark, but a few have been noted. Many of the most attractive came from the Woodville or Wooden Box Pottery and these might be marked *H & D* (Hall and Davenport) until 1858. The name *THOMAS SHARPE* marks some ironstone pies from Swadlincote; after about 1860 the mark changed to a monogram *S B & Co.* The Hartshorne Potteries marked some with the name *J. THOMPSON*, and the Rawdon Pottery some with the name *BRUNT*.

Wedgwood's early pies appear far richer and more attractive, but this cheaper fireproof ware offered a challenge he could not ignore. The result is a series of Wedgwood pies in a cheaper, lighter material than the caneware, a buff-toned terra cotta, the sides and top shaped with moulds. One finds groups of hanging dead game moulded in relief around the sides, linked by swags of fruiting vine and on top a hare or duck moulded in deep relief. But such details as the crimping around the edges entirely lack the earlier meticulous precision. This was a cheap answer to the Derbyshire potters, but the terra cotta was not fireproof, and to compete Wedgwood introduced glazed ovenware dishes of ironstone stoneware so that the meat or poultry could be oven-cooked and placed, vessel and all, inside the pie crust to come to table. These too are to be found in four sizes and in the 1850s were supplied in quantity to university colleges.

The fashion for piecrust wares has never entirely left us. In the third quarter of the 19th century the Denby,

Derbyshire, firm of Bourne & Son were still making pork pie crusts. These were in their renowned Brampton cane stoneware, and might still serve to hold a couple of dozen birds for a rook pie, but they were a far cry indeed from the original inspiration of this homely ware, the giant pies of a more raucous, lustier age such as launched that most famous dwarf Jeffrey Hudson on to the dinner table and into the service of Queen Henrietta Maria.

Chapter Sixteen

LOCKETS

VICTORIANA is becoming ever rarer and therefore more appreciated, yet almost every home in the country, surely, still possesses the half-forgotten treasure of a locket. What is more, this most perfect representative of those beloved and encumbering chattels, this scrap of sentiment unabashed and endearing, is still easily acquired and, to the comprehending collector, immensely rewarding. Here is Victorian design, simple or fussily elaborate, elegant or frankly pretty, and Victorian craftsmanship of an age when even costume jewellery was subjected to close examination and lasting use. And here is a range of materials including every jewel and gemstone in the Victorian galaxy, and metals from the richest golds, bloomed and tinted, to economical "rolled gold" and the cheapest of gilt-metal.

Lockets were introduced centuries ago when well-to-do Tudors and Elizabethans wore miniature paintings of their loved ones. These were flamboyantly boxed to protect their fleeting colours and to establish their wearers' grandeur. The oval case was of jewelled or enamelled gold bearing perhaps a relief representation of the sitter portrayed within, or set with a precious stone or a gem such as agate or onyx. Sometimes the case was of carved ivory or the jet of bereavement. Inside it was elaborately engraved and inscribed with the sitter's name, opposite the painted miniature, revealed by opening the case on a hinge at the bottom and secured at the top beneath the hanging loop by a tiny latch known as a loquet.

Obviously this suggested the name locket, but at the time these handsome pieces of jewellery were known to their owners as picture boxes. A locket to them was a jeweller's term for a pattern in small jewels such as the "locket of diamonds" Samuel Pepys made his wife refuse as a gift, although "worth about forty pounds"; the same year, 1668, he paid £38 3*s*. 4*d*. for a "most rare" miniature of his wife, including its "crystal and case, and gold case" costing £8 3*s*. 4*d*. An advertisement of 1704 announced the loss of a gold case for a watch "set on the outside with nine Lockets and little diamonds between".

By the 19th century, brooches, pendants, even bracelet clasps, were designed to permit the inclusion of tiny personal mementoes. But the term locket is now usually reserved for the ornament opening with a hinge and clasp. This makes it easier for the collector bewildered by the wealth of Victorian ornament, although by the time the term had acquired its present-day meaning the hinge had moved from the base to the top and then to the side and workmanship was too perfect to require any elaborate clasp or loquet.

Few early picture boxes remain but the National Museum of Antiquities in Scotland contains the Penicuik locket dating to the 1570s with portraits of Mary Queen of Scots and her son James VI. In the Victoria and Albert Museum, London, is the "Armada jewel", its enamelled gold case set with diamonds and rubies and a gold portrait bust of Elizabeth I as indication of the painted miniature within. This locket was given to Sir Thomas Heneage by the queen when she visited Tilbury Camp in 1588 for his services as Treasurer at War at the time of the Armada, its authenticated history making it particularly valuable to study.

The fashion persisted through the 17th century for wearing these large oval locket pendants, smooth-backed in gold plate and fronted with patterns in coloured stones rimmed with pearls, ladies suspending them from matching jewelled brooches. Elaborate mourning lockets were evolved too, with richly worked ornament in black and white enamel. Occasionally transparent mica protected the portrait.

Ladies continued to favour lockets throughout the first half of the 18th century, the cases now hinged at the top and latched on the lower rim. The poet John Gay noted the style in 1720 referring to their inscribed verses:

> Some by a snip of woven hair.
> In posied lockets bribe the fair.

Later in the century hinge and fastening might be placed to the sides of the locket and the miniature might be displayed, glazed and framed in gold. The hinged cover was then relegated to the back, lifting to disclose a lock of the sitter's hair suitably worked into an ornamental design at a period when patterns in hair were popular as the main decorative theme in countless items of adornment.

For anyone fortunate enough to possess one of these valuable early lockets the miniature itself offers the obvious declaration of period, painted perhaps on vellum or the smooth back of a playing card, although from about 1720 there was a preference for an oval slip of ivory set in a thin rim of gold, perhaps engraved with the sitter's name. Flint-glass to display and protect the miniature was introduced in the 18th century, but perhaps not until the fifties or later when the glass was well enough annealed to suffer atmospheric changes with little risk of a sudden fracture.

More lockets remain from the sentimental years of the late 18th century, small and often circular. The typical design opens like a book from right to left to disclose a miniature portrait and opposite it, on the reverse of the front panel, an inscription, lock of hair or other memento. The outside, front and back, may be splendidly jewelled, with step-cut diamonds on the front and a coronet or cypher of diamonds on the back.

The late years of the 18th century, and on into the Regency, with their anxieties and threatened calamities, prompted an intense indulgence in sentimental keepsakes, an urge to stress the bonds linking loved ones together. Every embroiderer, it would seem, worked her own version of Charlotte weeping at the tomb of Werther, from Goethe's novel, and surely wore a locket displaying a funerary urn or similar enjoyably lugubrious detail, even a willow tree weeping seed pearl tears.

Hair mementoes, finely plaited or shaped into simple patterns of plume or flower knot by specialist craftsmen in "human hair jewellery", were entirely in the mood. These have always been associated with lockets but at this period might be displayed under glass as a background, perhaps, to a diamond-sparkling monogram or framing an enamelled weeping willow, or a cypher engraved on opalescent glass. At the beginning of Victoria's reign hair ornaments were entirely out of favour but were back in the forties and fifties and in 1879 Yapp could declare that hair work "doubtless will always be in demand". Other memorial pieces may be found from the Regency, too, but more from Victorian days. Many are simply patterned in gold inlaid on black enamel, both sides identical.

Convex clusters of jewels, whether diamonds, pearls or coloured gemstones, are found on the small lockets of the Regency, George IV's reign and on into the 1840s. One costly series included a coronet in the design: a locket rich with diamonds and pearls would bear an initial surmounted by a coronet studded with diamonds.

George IV asked to be buried wearing "the locketed portrait of Mrs. Fitzherbert" but many tiny lockets of the early 19th century are children's treasures. Such a piece may enclose a lock of hair and an inscription, within covers prettily patterned in the close-detailed, naturalistic manner of their day. One may find the clasp shaped as a hand. A heart-shape of this period is often delightfully clustered with tiny diamonds, rubies and pearls, or perhaps with rose diamond points on a six-pointed star in seed pearls. Much the same attractive shape but with an arching loop above was used throughout the locket's era of popularity to suggest a padlock guarding the hidden memento. This may be in gold edged with pearls, or mounted with a star of tiny diamonds. Occasionally, still, there is a small panel of glass revealing the plait of hair within.

Daytime costume in the 1840s banished the low lacy neckline that set off the small locket and chain, and its charm was never quite recaptured in the larger specimens that remain to us in such profusion. These date from the second half of the century and more especially from about 1867 onwards when day-time fashion relented a little and the neckline permitted the display of a locket on a gold or silver-gilt chain or velvet ribbon in the more dominant style of its period.

The 1870s saw big, heavy lockets spectacularly fashionable, two important factors contributing to their success. More heavily alloyed gold might be used—the law was modified in 1854—and the costly miniature could be replaced by tiny photographs of husband, parents, children, usually secured by inner frames of cheaper metal. Here, then, was the opportunity for wide sale among a less critical, moneyed public who would accept really good machine tooling for the earlier delicate hand craftsmanship in hinge and snap fastening and surface ornament. Low relief patterns could be produced by a single stamping operation; high relief work with three stampings, the metal being annealed between each to prevent splitting. Even the Regency's delicate rims of cut steel facets could be imitated by the Victorians with long ribbons of die-stamped impressed work, suggesting at a glance the earlier individually riveted heads. The many lockets remaining in attractive condition today demonstrate the care given by English craftsmen to even the least conspicuous details of inexpensive trifles, far superior in this to much Continental work.

Mid-Victorian lockets show the use of enamels combined with small diamonds or pearls. Dress was heavy and colours strident: a locket matched by earrings could be in a bold design without losing its essentially personal note. To our Victorian great-grandmothers there was no sense of garish disharmony in an assembly, for example, of ruby, emerald, garnet, amethyst, ruby, diamond, since together their initial letters would spell the word REGARD. The association of pearls and brilliants in such jewellery reflects the period's love of surface contrasts in all media, noted too in blendings of matt or "bloomed" and polished gold, of pearl and ruby, of translucent amethyst and opaque turquoise towards the century's end.

Among substantial jewelled lockets one finds settings of half pearls and half turquoises and similar effects in black onyx for memorial lockets, an English notion taken up by the jewellers of Paris. This delight in jewels and gems resulted in a device of the mid-1860s whereby the locket could be altered to suit different occasions. Its jewelled frame might display a monogram in relief or an engraved crest during the day that could be removed in the evening for the insertion of a diamond star, perhaps, with such further alternatives as patterns in pearl and coral, or turquoises and diamonds, or emeralds and opals, as the wearer's costume might indicate. A special slide could be obtained for inserting with mourning wear, bearing black enamelled monogram or cross. This colour-violent period also enjoyed ornaments composed of small diamonds, emeralds, rubies set into another stone such as an oval amethyst.

Less flamboyantly, one finds small diamonds associated with coloured enamels inlaid in gold lockets which are plain-backed, save for engraved crest, cypher or inscription. The diamonds may form a star or crescent in the blue enamel or an enamel wreath may frame a pearl. Sometimes emeralds and pearls are set in a diagonal band across the gold. But the larger style permissible with the open-necked day costume suggested other more ingenious designs in jewelled lockets, too, such as a gold book with hinged leaves shaped to take four photographs. The front cover may be studded with the "regard" jewels or richly chased. A jewelled crown on the book-cover indicates the Bible of a memorial locket.

An effectively simple jewelled locket may be plainly mounted with amethyst and rock crystal forming the front and back panels. Clear rock crystal for the front panel, oval or navette-shaped, was being imitated by the 1870s in flint-glass, however, displaying the treasured lock of hair or perhaps merely a luck symbol such as a four-leaved shamrock. With so much heavy jewellery in fashion to suit the heavy costume styles it is not surprising to find other lockets consisting of cairngorm, agate, onyx or other pebbles, oval or square, finely worked and polished and set in hinged frames of gold. Carbuncles, that is, garnets roundly cut *en cabochon*, may be found too. A hinged frame of gold or gilded silver may be mounted with carbuncles back and front, the front encircled with small pearls. A more ingenious design has the pebble itself hollowed at the back where a gold or silver cover protects the photograph.

These pebbles continued popular into the 1880s, contrasting with the deeply carved jet that was greatly sought after, made fashionable by Adelina Patti. These are on jet chains of faceted links, less coldly hard than the imitative facet-cut black glass invisibly mounted on metal plate. By the 1890s the locket gems were such subdued beauties as opal, turquoise and gentle moonstone, as jewellers responded to the enthusiasm of the aesthetic movement and colours were softened, jewels polished instead of faceted and even the sparkle of the emerald subdued by mounting *en cabochon*. Around this period one notes a revival of an earlier custom with engaged couples exchanging miniature portraits, the man wearing his fiancée's on his watch chain and the girl wearing a richly jewelled locket.

Among the less costly costume-jewellery lockets some strange notions remain from the strident 1860s and 1870s, when contemporary comment, such as *The Englishwoman's Domestic Magazine*, was reporting (1870) that the locket was "becoming quite *de rigueur* with bodices open *en chale* and seems an indispensable finish to the toilet". There are sporting lockets, for example, bearing the enamelled portrait heads of horses and dogs for the "outdoor girl" of the sixties and all manner of other minor motifs engraved or enamelled—flower bouquets, pairs of hearts linked by ribbons, cupids, horseshoes, pairs of butterflies, beetles, stars, crosses, urns, for this was a period extraordinarily rich in "fancy jewellery" with every kind of insect and animal motif, the "insect mania" reaching its peak in the 1880s.

Some of the most intricate effects were achieved by shaping the ornament separately and applying it to the locket's front panel. For evening wear and with a low neckline the back of the locket was, of course, plainly smooth. This motif may be as extravagant a notion as a black enamelled serpent with diamond-studded head and *cabochon* ruby eyes. One may find an idealised cameo "portrait" cut in very low relief in rosy tinted shell, a tiny skull in the design sometimes indicating a memorial locket. Cheaper effects in the 1870s were achieved with small panels of painted bone china, a posy of flowers perhaps or a Watteau-esque scene. A locket and pair of ear-rings—a demi-parure—of about 1880 in the Victoria and Albert Museum are set with enamelled plaques.

A considerable amount of mid-Victorian jewellery is composed mainly of gold with little resort to other media, and another long-favourite locket design is an enamelled gold Garter inscribed with the wearer's Christian name. There was always a market, too, for the heart, star or escutcheon, flower bordered and engraved with crest or cypher. Innumerable hearts, padlocks, shields, remain from this period, even the oval design being elaborated with loops and bows for hanging. Many are inexpensively made from paper-thin gold or from a gold-plated pinchbeck alloy. Hearts bound in chains may date to the 1890s.

Massive silver lockets were in favour by the 1880s on silver chains that impress us today both for their elaborate detail and for their delicate lightness in the hand. But the mood of the 1880s was becoming less tolerant of extravagant lockets. *The Queen* in 1880 mentioned "brooches were given this season in preference to lockets". Many of the small specimens that remain are enriched back and front with the self-effacing line ornament known as engine-turning and the still simpler line work called flat stitch. Or one may find radiating lines cut in the plain gold centring on a pearl or diamond. The monogrammed birthday locket was acceptable at this period, its back engraved with the dates of the birthday and presentation.

A locket that can be dated is always interesting. Occasionally one turns up in a design registered at the Patent Office to protect it from copying by rival firms. The diamond-shaped mark with a central *Rd* was discontinued in 1883 (see page 34).

The gold itself often suggests a locket's date. Until 1798 hallmarked gold had to be of at least 22 carat fineness: then a lower quality, 18 carat, was permitted, hallmarked with the numerals 18 as well as the crown or the Scottish thistle. In 1854 still lower standards were authorised, of 15, 12 and 9 carat, and these numerals had to be included in the mark, used until 1932 when 14 carat replaced the 15 and 12 carat standards. Most collectors are familiar with the changing silver hallmarks, although these might be omitted if they would ruin an intricate design.

Victorians found immense pleasure in the tones and surface textures of their metals and especially in tinted gold and the "bloomed" surface achieved by treating the gold with an acid mixture that removed the alloy from the outermost film and left pure gold full of minute holes. When fashion demanded open settings for diamonds in all their magnificence the solid, almost plain, little locket maintained the English craftsman's reputation for fine metalwork. Many lockets are not even in 9 carat gold, however, but are of gold fused on to base metal, termed rolled gold. The cheapest are no more than base metal brightly gilded by electro-plating, so cheap that a popular locket of 1863, opening on a hinge to display two diminutive photographs of the Prince of Wales and his bride Alexandra, could be sold wholesale for a halfpenny.

Chapter Seventeen

PIQUÉ WORK

TORTOISESHELL and ivory are of the very essence of elegant ornament. They call to mind the snuff-box and fan, the étui and bonbonnière, all the sophisticated galanteries of late Stuart and Georgian social gaiety and fashionable good taste. But that such subtly decorative materials should be lit up with touches of gold—that, surely, was a notion only an Italian artist could conceive, just as only an Italian craftsman would have created the scintillating effect of piercing the shell or ivory with tiny metal rods until the surface appeared to be dusted with gold spangles.

Yet today the Neapolitan originator Laurentini is forgotten, and the whole delightful notion is frequently attributed to Charles André Boulle (1642–1732) who did not begin at the Louvre until 1672, considerably after Paris had discovered the beauty of this work. Indeed, France adopted the craft with such skill and enthusiasm that it is known today in England also by its French name of piqué. There is no English name for this exotic work, and there is quite a possibility that it might never have developed at all among England's skilled tortoiseshell craftsmen had not this country offered religious tolerance to the Protestant Huguenots after the revocation of the Edict of Nantes in 1685, and received in return not only the familiar flamboyant glories of Huguenot silver but the delicate loveliness of shadowy gleaming tortoiseshell pricked with patterns in bright pure gold. Yet England made considerable contributions to the craft in its later, less exclusive phases.

Some of the earliest English piqué was applied to the handles of the knife, fork and spoon sets carried by wealthy 17th-century travellers, to cane heads, to boxes in both tortoiseshell and ivory, and to extremely delicate watch cases. The piqué that collectors seek today includes all manner of snuff-boxes, tortoiseshell making the perfect vessels for this astonishingly popular powdered tobacco leaf, preserving its varying delicate aromas more perfectly than any metal except gold, seldom warping or cracking to spill in the pocket or fail to open in the hand, and offering in texture and translucent variable tones, yellow and brown and honey gold, a constant and enduring delight to finger and eye.

Among snuff-boxes alone a collector can gather a wonderful range of work, including various shaped outlines, many suggesting the shells that also figure considerably among the birds and insects, the scrolls and vines and more formal arabesques in early piqué and inlay ornament. Some boxes are silver-mounted instead of in gold. An early box may open with a small drop hinge but the projecting pin hinge came into use early in the 18th century, its high quality being a feature of English piqué.

For the same reasons the shell—untarnishable, flavour-free—was ideal for the tiny, strongly-perfumed breath-sweetening cashews known as comfits, although today comfit boxes are more often presumed to be for patches. But the list of possibilities for a determined collector is far wider, including étuis, bodkin and needle cases, small drinking cups, scent flasks, trays, fan sticks, netting shuttles and their boxes, playing card boxes, and the jewellery trinkets made early and late in the 19th century.

Early piqué of the late 17th century is particularly delightful but all too rare, in the style that gave the craft its name piqué d'or. Insects, exotic birds, formal scrolling arabesques, vine patterns, coroneted monograms, the piqué worker's peculiarly elaborate scallop shells, all were created with points of gold or silver closely clustered and in varying sizes, cut off level with the shell's silken glossy surface and polished with it into glowing loveliness. Even the plainest repetition of these points of light distributed evenly over the surface of the shell creates an effect of shimmering, restrained beauty.

It is possible to find piqué d'or fan sticks, or a delicate

snuff-box with minor flower borders around a splendid peacock, outlined in the smallest size of gold points or studs and with six or more sizes of point upon its tail. Patterns in large points were given the name cloute d'or or nailhead piqué. The term piqué is also applied today, however, to the style more exactly known by its old name of inlay or posé d'or. In this the ornament is more emphatic, being formed with inlays of strip gold or, more rarely, silver, sometimes still with the piqué patterns for background diapers, trellis work and leaf outlines among the heavier solid scrolls.

Occasionally a really elaborate box may be inset with solid little panels of gold, closely chased with shells or similar detailed relief work, set off by delicate many-pointed scrolls of gold inlay surrounding exquisite diapers in different sizes of gold piqué, so that the whole gold-lined box, lid and sides and even base, possesses a mellow golden glow far richer and lovelier than solid tool-worked gold.

By early Georgian days, however, posé d'or was being used alone, and this work offers far more possibilities for today's collectors, reflecting the changing moods of French ornament that dominated 18th-century Europe. Some specimens may appear almost overladen with gold in the Louis XV manner of chinoiserie scenes and figures among pillared ruins, of pastorals and hunting groups, of pavilioned garden tea parties and music parties and cloud-borne cupids in a wealth of scroll and leaf borders. Even the Paris balloon ascent of 1773 has been commemorated on snuff-boxes of blonde tortoiseshell suggesting cloud-wracked skies. The elaborate outlines of many snuff-boxes well suit this extravagant ornament, and often the gold itself is chased, a refinement that adds greatly to the delicacy of the effect.

Perhaps as an escape from such flamboyance the English piqué workers developed what is known as hairline posé d'or in the early 18th century. Landscapes, seascapes and other pictorial scenes were achieved in lines of gold or silver as delicate as pen drawing, the subjects becoming more elaborate in the early 19th century. But such work is now comparatively rare. More specimens found today reflect the change to more formal patterns in the second half of the

18th century. One or two pseudo-classical motifs may be developed with exquisite delicacy—an oval patera, perhaps, with a graceful swag of husks on a plain, oval box, or a conventional anthemion flower or the inevitable urn flanked by loops of drapery.

The ellipse or oval with pointed ends was popular in the last years of the 18th century and the first twenty of the 19th, and at no other period—the shape of the netting and tatting shuttles popular through a century when many a great lady mitigated the tedium of coach journeys by "knotting threads". Many of the boxes are factory made and some magnificent piqué shuttles were made to gratify the same whim. Piqué étuis might serve those who preferred the destructive occupation of drizzling—snipping the gold thread from uniform and waistcoat and winding it on a reel to sell for its gold and thus make some pin money. But étuis may be found to meet many personal needs, the general style being a slightly tapering, flattened cylinder opening on a narrow hinge about a third of the way from the top and compartmented within to take scissors, snuff spoon, tweezers, memo tablet and the like. Other possible finds are long narrow bodkin cases, small boxes for needles and thimbles, small comfit and patch boxes, tobacco boxes, scent flasks, even an occasional tea caddy.

A particular joy of this gold and silver inlay is the perfect clarity of the shell under the metal: no cement or glue was introduced that would show on the underside. Instead the shell—mostly the brilliant, transparent shell of the hawk's-bill turtle found on the coasts of Brazil—was heated over fine quality smokeless charcoal and the metal cut to shape and pressed upon it. As the shell cooled it contracted and held the metal firmly. The gold or silver was entirely pure, without any alloy at all, so that it could be rolled and beaten paper-thin: with the inlay in position shell and metal could be polished and burnished together to a perfect smooth gloss. Only when the shell was embossed was adhesive used, and in work of such high quality the shell might be lined with gold.

This embossed work is another form of early Georgian piqué. The shell was softened by boiling in salted water so that patterns could be tool-impressed upon it, the motifs appearing in relief. The soft metal foil was laid on the embossments and cemented into position. But the rub of use soon wore holes in the thin metal, and indeed even the flat-surfaced inlay is easily polished to destruction. In the hand and pocket the shell retains its silken gloss but the collector's display cabinet may render it dull and lack-lustre. The cure then is a finger-tip application of non-acid gun oil followed by rubbing with cotton wool or the palm of the hand until the shell feels warm and all the oil has disappeared.

On the Continent piqué soon deteriorated when the flamboyant rococo phase was over, being reduced to background detail of stars and flowers often subservient to a painted miniature. In England the same change of taste, expressed in simple pseudo-classical motifs, put the creation of tortoiseshell ornament within range of factory accomplishment. Such pioneers as Matthew Boulton of Birmingham included tortoiseshell among their factories' contributions to less exclusive but extremely elegant society ornament. In a letter to James Adam in 1770 Boulton confirmed that production was in progress, and ten years later he acquired the business of the well-known tortoiseshell craftsman John Gimblett.

Boulton made his snuff-boxes, including large boxes for table and mantel shelf, of sheet tortoiseshell. This was rarely more than a thin plate one-sixteenth of an inch thick, pieces of shell being welded together by the application of a smokeless heat so that seams are invisible: even ornamental motifs in relief could be punched in the softened shell, and saw-cut separately by hand to be welded into position, giving three-dimensional ornament to a box lid comparable with the period's embossed silver, and to the base an all-over pattern in low relief to please the fingers and ensure a firm grip. Only when held against the light can this welding be detected as irregularities of shell colouring fail to correspond with surface markings.

All-over incised ornament on the thin tortoiseshell was introduced by Boulton, too, who made and sold lathes for this delicate engine-turning, suitable for several media. The favourite basket-work pattern, for instance, may surround an inlaid motif and show a nailhead point at each intersection. Boulton work is well designed, richly mounted, with a craftsman's pride in every detail of fit and finish: only the ornament tended to become stylised and uninspired in its endless repetition of swags and husks and similar neo-classic notions.

Substantial gold inlay continued as a successful branch of the Birmingham and Sheffield factory trade in tortoise-shell well into the 19th century. One result was that the hand craftsman in piqué turned to ivory, and the loveliest gold stud work of piqué d'or was developed much more extensively than before on this almost equally inviting surface, not only in its own subtle colours but often vividly stained. Pale or blonde tortoiseshell came into favour in the last years of the 18th century, but in ivory the points of gold or silver could be set off by green, red, blue or black.

This work continued throughout the late 18th and early 19th centuries, on comfit boxes, dance cards, bodkin cases and innumerable cane and parasol heads. The blades of an ivory fan, for example, may have gold piqué d'or piercing the ivory to appear in identical patterns on both sides. Snuff-boxes are rare. Some heavy nailhead or clouté d'or piqué suggests Boulton craftsmanship, the stud head facets shaped by hand: in Victorian specimens they are machine worked. Posé d'or on ivory seldom goes beyond line work.

By the 1820s, however, when lavish hand-craftsmanship was briefly reasserting itself, tortoiseshell piqué achieved something of its old brilliance in the same flamboyant inlay or posé work. Sometimes the piqué on a snuff-box serves as a vivid frame to a delicate portrait miniature painted on ivory or an enamel plaque painted with classical figures, cupids or other gay, conventional nonsense. As might be expected at this period, a special delight is the use of gold in a number of different shades to achieve greater variety, for example, in the petals of a flower design. Jewellery may be found—butterfly brooches, crosses, pendants, necklets, pins for the chignon, dangling ear-rings—beautifully made if somewhat ponderous. But even here the machine triumphed in the end. Machine-made piqué jewellery, trinkets and crosses appeared in the 1870s, their patterns of wavy lines and geometrical motifs hailed as far superior to the flower and foliage elaborations they superseded. As proof of their popularity it is even possible to find imitations, with gilt stars and points cemented to celluloid. But soon the whole lovely piqué craft was dead.

Some collectors include the application of piqué work to a surface covered in shagreen and others allow the insertion of major features cut from mother-of-pearl in tortoiseshell or ivory among their specimens of piqué. This is not generally accepted as legitimate use of this widely abused term, but the work is often so lovely that it is a joy to collect under any name. Tortoiseshell and mother-of-pearl go magnificently together, as was discovered by many a Victorian maker of those immensely decorative little flat cases in which everyone of any consequence whatsoever carried visiting cards. The warm-toned irregular mottling of the tortoiseshell contrasts with the deliberate, almost laboured designs of flowers, birds, chinoiserie scenes cut out in the cool, shimmering pearl-shell, the two surfaces being levelled and polished together to a wonderful smooth finish. A small cabinet in such work, for instance, usually dating to the first half of the 19th century, or an inkstand set of pots and tray, is a strikingly handsome possession. Sometimes the pearl-shell is found accompanying silver piqué or inlay work so that metallic shine as well as nacreous lustre may contrast with the natural bold patternings of the tortoiseshell.

Chapter Eighteen

POTTERY MONEY BOXES

THE early weeks of the new year must have been a lean time for Elizabethan and Georgian apprentice and houseboy. But one small ritual had to be observed. His "Christmas box" or "rattling box", noisy with the small coins freely given to ill-paid servants around Christmas, would have been smashed to obtain the contents, and now he must acquire a new one for another year's accumulation of savings.

Whether in white tin-enamelled delft ware or plain red or buff clay, the money pot he chose would be cheap and plain enough for its Boxing Day disintegration to cause no anguish: only today do collectors regret the narrow slits in those early vessels that did indeed defy the pilferer but led to their almost inevitable destruction when their contents were required. Only today does the vessel itself appeal for the very homeliness of its design and fabric, and for its suggestion of cloud-castle dreams committed to the care of jar or beehive or saucy hen.

It is extremely difficult today to find one of the countless money boxes abounding in Elizabethan times, such as Higins described (1585): "A money box made of potter's clay wherein boyes put their mony to keepe, such as they have in shops &c towards Christmas", or even of the Stuart boxes mentioned by Cotgrave in 1611 as commonly used by "butlers and prentices". Mason in his *Handful of Essays*, 1621, wrote: "Like a swine, he never doth good till his death; as an apprentice's box of earth, apt he is to take all, but to restore none till he be broken". In this particular small byway of collecting, however, the later specimens tend to appear more interesting, and the collector can still find an assortment of late-Georgian and Victorian notions for fostering the virtue of thrift.

The early tradition, harking back to Roman times, was for the money pot to be a pot indeed, swiftly turned on the wheel and thus more or less spherical or bottle-shaped, like the Roman cistal, cylindrical with a cone-shaped top, and this form continued into the 19th century while gradually acquiring more decoration. Rectangular boxes were far less common. An Elizabethan specimen may be plainly bottle-shaped, three or four inches high, wide at the shoulders below the small neck with its plain, immovable stopper, and sloping inwards to a flat base. The fabric may be a coarse yellowish or buff earthenware covered only on neck and shoulders where it is splashed with mottled green glaze. The slit is small and thin, cut vertically down the shoulder.

Stuart specimens remain, sometimes with an almost globular body on a small foot ring, and short-necked with the slot cut vertically near a small button finial. Occasionally the outline suggests a minaret with a tall spire neck and finial above the rounded money holder. Or there may be two or more near-spheres as separate vessels for different coins one on top of the other on a stemmed, circular foot, the spheres linked together and to the pointed finial by primitive scrolls or loops. This more complicated design, which suggests Continental inspiration, appears more at home when found in the Dutch-inspired English delft ware that I describe later.

A rare specimen may be noted in red earthenware as well as the more usual buff: it may be blotchily green-glazed like earlier work or possibly covered down to the base with a wash of clay slip in a deep chocolate brown. After the mid 17th century the slit might be placed diagonally, but the horizontal placement is to be noted as a post-Restoration, late 17th century return to the oldest known slot arrangement.

Money boxes lost in the great fire of London, 1666, have been excavated and indicate how the formal designs continued, but in the last quarter of the century another type became popular, with a horizontal barrel body, perhaps five inches long, handled at each end and resting on absurd little legs with their period's bun feet.

This was the beginning of more intriguing designs: the collector of 18th-century primitives experiences the delight of discovering markedly naïve imitations of the period's more sophisticated decorative ideas. The most crude of hand-modelling is set off with casual dots and daubs of runny colour; clay slip is applied in contrasting streaks of white on dark brown and sprigging—the application of moulded clay shapes in relief—has the easy irregularity of child's play, and more likely than not was in fact the work of children too little skilled to be set to more costly craftsmanship.

Basically the material is usually earthenware, red or buff still according to the quality of available clay, covered with a wash of thinner clay slip so that it is drab-white beneath its glowing yellowish glaze formed from powdered lead oxide. Small one-man potteries continued the primitive style long into the 19th century, the advantage being that a single firing in the kiln hardened the clay and glazed the surface.

An alternative, highly desirable but liable to be a modern reproduction, is the money pot in the earthenware known as English delft ware. This was first made at Lambeth in 1671 and soon afterwards at Bristol, Liverpool, Wincanton and elsewhere. A red or buff earthenware was dipped into a white tin oxide enamel, dried and fired in the kiln. The white surface, faintly tinged by the underlying earthenware, was then decorated, mostly in cobalt blue, perhaps with a little purple and yellow and occasionally other colours too, such as green, puce, brownish red and black. A second kiln firing was then required to fix the clear glaze that protected this ornament, making this altogether a more elaborate proceeding which sought to suggest the lovely blue and white porcelains of China. It may be differentiated from the Dutch delft ware that was its immediate inspiration by its denser, more vitreous texture: in comparison the Dutch is light in weight, porous and so soft that a knife will mark it.

An occasional specimen in English delft is known bearing a late-17th-century date. Some are cube shape with a slot cut in one face. Others are more or less globular, but here too there may be two or three spheres on top of each other, smallest to the top, mounted on a domed foot to make an imposing little vessel topped by a spire finial.

Among the simplest developments introduced in the plain earthenware money pots of the 18th century is the squat pineapple or pine cone suggested, perhaps, by the warm tones of the red earthenware under the yellowish glaze and represented by rows of small undulations quickly "pinched out" by the potter. With very little difference the dome becomes a beehive. But to judge from those that have escaped destruction the prime favourite was the hen and chickens. Or perhaps an unduly large proportion of this design remain simply because the potters forsook their original intention and created money pots too appealing, too positively ornamental, to be smashed without regret.

The usual design, some five and a half inches high and four in diameter, has the hen and her brood on the flattish top of a nearly round pot—egg-shaped in some later specimens—the hen in the middle and the chicks, facing her, perched precariously on the sloping shoulder, all roughly shaped by hand but alertly bright-eyed to guard the "nest egg" inside the pot.

Even the tiered pot with two or three slotted containers one on top of the next may have its hen on top and its chicks around the vertical slots. In the 19th century the pottery at Gorsty Hill, Worcestershire, was still making hen and chick pots, but bigger, almost eight inches across by six and three-quarters inches high, and often splashed with manganese brown under the yellow glaze. Sometimes the pot itself is found shaped as the hen, some five inches high, with a slot along her back for coins. Although it is composed of a single piece of hollow earthenware, when well designed the bird appears to be brooding comfortably on a nest raised on a stemmed foot, nest and foot being rimmed with an ornamental bead. Such a hen is at her best, perhaps coloured a rich brown under haphazard white slip decoration mellowed by the yellowish glaze. But an attractive alternative is a glaze of vivid green, the blotchy effects round tail and comb and wattles only adding a sense of texture.

The Sussex piggy bank associated with 18th-century Brede and Rye potteries and less commonly with Chailey, Cadborough and Dicker, is in a similar mood, slotted along its back, and brown-mottled or brilliant green or yellowish and speckled with dots. Some are found in the tough brown salt-glazed stoneware I describe in greater detail in Chapter 20. Occasionally these are impressed with potters' names. Pigs continued to be made in many places through the 19th century: when they are Rockingham-glazed they date from the 1790s onwards. Brede hen-and-chicks pots are known too, and other simple 18th-century designs such as one five and a half inches high, with rosettes applied to the surface under the yellowish glaze.

The splendidly rich looking chocolate-brown Rockingham glaze with a purplish bloom is a lead glaze stained with manganese oxide: it was evolved at Rockingham by Thomas Bingley in the 1790s but used by potters everywhere. At first it tended to run in the glazing oven so that the colour is deeper towards the base, but as the century advanced it became more uniform as well as more brilliant.

Most of the more elaborate money boxes date from the 19th century when cheap pottery ornaments were hawked round the streets and offered as gaudy little fairings. It is among these that it is possible to find the more ambitious designs, for sale to folk with an eye for a usable "chimney toy" and no intention of smashing it to reach its contents. Castles and cottages, beehives, cows, lions, dogs, cats, cocked hats and top hats, globes, chests of drawers, amusing heads and heads of celebrities; all the gay nonsense of 19th-century earthenware figures usually classed as chimney ornaments is found suitably slotted for the coins of its period.

Cottages alone make an interesting collection, the earliest pre-dating the early-19th-century vogue for cottage pastille burner and night light holder in more delicate bone china (see Chapter 5), although bone china money boxes were made too in the mid 19th century—spick and span villas rather than cottages, on square mound bases that lack the abundant flower encrustations associated with the diffusion of fragrance.

Among earthenware cottages design was often crude, with a slot high at the back of the roof. One design suggests two semi-detached cottages with the gothic windows of the early 19th century and a shared central chimney stack. The collector looks, too, for the circular toll house with a central chimney or the late cottage with *SAVINGS BANK* printed in black or painted in gold across the façade. Colouring is often brilliant, although here again some are to be found in Doulton's homely brown salt-glazed stoneware, including a collectable design by Mark Marshall impressed *M.V.M.*

A noteworthy find is the earthenware cottage guarded by roughly-shaped figures of a boy and a girl. Figure busts as money boxes may be found too. These may be in bone china, shaped in moulds, slotted across the crown of the head, and quickly painted—familiar characters of their day, whether popular hero or merry negro. But this was a period of limitless ingenuity, and designs range from the top hat and tricorn inverted to receive largess to the small bracket clock intended to take two shillings in copper coin and numbered accordingly into twenty-four hours and half-hours, with a movable metal pointer to record each contribution.

Pairs of money boxes offer many challenges to the collector. A boy with a cow may require a girl with a cow to match; they may be decorated with underglaze sponged colours or with bright overglaze enamels, or with the rich all-over brown bloom of the so-called Rockingham glaze. There are pairs of lions, too, coloured or Rockingham-glazed, and reputed to be copied from the celebrated marble lions in Florence. Thomas Rathbone of Portobello, Scotland, is thought to have started the fashion for these among potters in 1820. John Walton of Burslem made them too. There may be a recess behind the pedestal intended for the china seller to paint in the purchaser's name, a common enough detail expected of him as late as the 1840s.

Perhaps the collector's most important guide in dating a money box, however, is the size of the slot. Gold and silver coins were almost paper-thin, and even a shilling of James I measured scarcely more than an inch across and was

D. Fan painted with figures in a country setting. The carved and fretted pearl guards and sticks are heavily enriched with gilding. Nineteenth century.

facing page 160

reduced under William III. The silver twopenny-piece or half-groat—a more likely saving—measured only three quarters of an inch across; the last issue of silver pennies, 1763–86, resembled this century's silver threepenny bits. Silver was augmented by copper farthings in 1649 but even copper half-pennies date no earlier than a five-year period from 1770. The real flood of copper coins—and hence the abundance of larger boxes for storing this weighty wealth—came at the end of the 18th century. The cartwheel two-penny-piece, almost a quarter of an inch thick and over an inch and a half across, was first minted on behalf of the Royal Mint by Matthew Boulton of Birmingham in 1797, and copper pennies and more half-pennies followed in 1806. The obvious result is the typical 19th-century specimens, maybe seven inches or more in height, two inches across the slot and assuredly the grandest, gaudiest money boxes in the collector's cabinet.

Chapter Nineteen

PAPIER MÂCHÉ

"TEA-BOARD, waiter, bread basket, snuffer tray and four little stands, all alike; a black ground with a silver pattern. . . ." Thus, as early as 1783, did Mrs. Papendiek record "Mr. Clay's elegant present". Fifty years later she noted in her diary: "The tea-board is only just worn out". Yet even by then papier mâché in the innumerable styles that make it loved today was only just becoming widely established among the manufacturers of Wolverhampton and Birmingham who won it renown, and the very name as now accepted was not yet in use.

Clay himself was by no means the first in the field either. "Papier machie" was in production in London in the mid 18th century, noted by Mrs. Delany in 1755. An improved composition was patented by Obadiah Westwood of Birmingham in 1786, the patent referring not only to tea trays but to dressing boxes, bottle stands, picture frames. By the 1820s this particular variety was in demand for wall brackets, ceiling ornaments and other interior decorations. But Clay's is the ware that is sought by collectors today because, as Mrs. Papendiek proved, it was tough, resistant to heat and moisture and prepared and finished with a care and thoroughness that resulted in much extremely attractive work, the brilliant, smooth surface never quite being equalled in the wealth of specimens that coloured the early Victorian home.

Clay prospered and retired in 1802 but it was only in the 1820s that many other manufacturers took up the story. By the 1830s some twenty firms were at work and for another forty years, perhaps, the trade flourished. Every early Victorian drawing room had its trays and folios, its workbox and firescreen of lustrous papier mâché, black, vermilion, green, yellow, scintillating confidently in paint and pearl and metal powders, helping our romantic great-great-grandmothers to forget the narrow confines of their convention-bound world and pursue their dreams within their north-facing rooms shaded by layers of Nottingham curtain lace.

The history of English home decoration tells of continual questing after vivid colour. When Oriental lacquer cabinets appeared here in the 17th century the country was swept by a craze for imitations. This "japanning" was practised first on wood and then on iron, but wood tended to warp and crack and iron was heavy. Papier mâché became enormously successful because it was light, reasonably tough and smooth of surface.

Today collectors look for papier mâché trays painted with coaching scenes or vividly natural flowers, or ceremonious little Orientals in shaded gilding. They look for letter racks and the like, incongruously adorned with views of abbey and cloister aglow with light streaming from gothic windows. They may find a writing desk, perhaps, or a polescreen decorated with a famous building, every detail depicted in metallic bronzes or in wisps of pearly shell.

Boxes, trays, blotters, vases, inkstands, hand mirrors and trifling ornaments constitute the majority of today's finds. Their prices largely depend upon their state of preservation, for repairs are practically impossible. An 18th-century tray may cost fifty pounds, but a tea caddy may sometimes be obtained for four or five, and the small vases and boxes of the Victorian whatnot for half a guinea. In its heyday chairs, stools, footstools and tea tables were made with thick scrolling legs and the unstable style of tea chest mounted like a firescreen on a stem and plinth peculiar to the early 19th century when it acquired the name of teapoy. It is important to realise, however, that right through the period of papier mâché manufacture there was the widest possible range of quality, not only in the decoration but in the basic material.

The development that led to its establishment among valuable furnishing and decorative media was made by the

Birmingham japanner Henry Clay who took out a patent in 1772 for what was long called Clay's ware or paper ware. Not until the following century was the misnomer papier mâché applied to this superior material which the French themselves called *carton pierre*. Clay became Japanner in Ordinary to George III and the Prince of Wales, but left it to his successors to develop the potentialities of his material beyond the making of simple flat panels. These were used for trays—tea boards—and as decorative mounts for screens, boxes and the like, and in the sides of coaches and sedan chairs where their lightness was an immense advantage.

The success of Clay's process depended simply on hard manual work, and it is important to consider the amount of work required for even the smallest ornament. The ware consists of sheets of paper, rather thicker and tougher than good quality blotting paper. About ten of these sheets, saturated with adhesive, were gradually built up into a panel of the shape required. Careful smoothing and pressing, interspersed by repeated dryings under heat, made it so tough that it could be planed, filed and even carved.

The base colour was applied in a tar-varnish mixture, and then followed a succession of stove dryings and varnishings and scrupulously thorough rubbings with wet pumice and rotten-stone. After receiving its decoration the panel was stoved yet again, both before and after a final protective coating of clear copal varnish. Last of all came yet more polishing, women's bare hands giving it the silken lustre that was the hallmark of English work.

The best of Clay's early pieces are notably well painted, the successive styles of ornament being most easily traced on the ever-popular trays. In shape these trays are quickly recognised: plain vertical rims were screwed to flat panels. When the ware was more widely developed in Birmingham and Wolverhampton in the 1820s trays were made in a range of standard designs.

Decoration on paper ware resembled that on contemporaneous japanned iron, the all-over geometric designs being superseded by masses of colourful flower heads and leaves extending to the edges of the rims and soon mingled with bamboo fronds, pampas grass and butterflies. Most important among Clay's tray decorations, however, were the oil paintings by established artists in the styles of popular engravings and these were continued in varying quality by his successors. Coaching scenes were followed by innumerable landscapes, hunting groups and pictures of exotic birds. Borders became popular in the 1800s, in gold at first and after 1815 often in bronze. These tend to be twining patterns of flowers and leaves but after about 1835 geometrical line patterns became popular alternatives. Sprigs of heather are associated with the 1850s.

Such tray decoration continued in favour throughout the early 19th century and as the period progressed pictures were painted on all kinds of papier mâché articles. There were the Nash engravings of interior views, for example, laboriously copied by such specialists as Beattie Lucas who also met the period's demand for paintings of luxurious mansions in country settings. After 1842 such favourite artists as Landseer were given protection by the Registration of Designs Act from free pirating of their works, but earlier paintings were still copied.

Some interesting painting is found on table snuff boxes from the 1820s, as papier mâché proved a splendid material for keeping the powder in good condition, neither warping nor cracking to spoil the fit of the lid and suitable for every kind of ornament. Samuel Raven, for example, is remembered for his careful copies of paintings by Wilkie and others from about 1818 to the 1840s. An early snuff box lid has no rim, the painting extending to the edge, but after about 1830 a narrow convex strengthening rim was used, often gilded or bronzed. On a larger scale a tip-up table may have a top measuring nearly four feet by two and showing three different painted views, such as Edinburgh Castle and Holyrood Palace separated by a scrolling medallion containing a view of Melrose Abbey. Such a table was typical of the larger work in what was indeed papier mâché as distinct from the earlier paper ware.

Paper-ware, made from sheets of porous paper, was subject to a paper duty. The papier mâché patented by Richard Brindley of Birmingham in 1836 was made of untaxed rag pulp, the patent covering a process for shaping large, thick panels which could be carved, planed and in every way treated like wood for furniture units, further improvement in texture dating to 1847. It is easy to see the pleasure manufacturers found in taking liberties with this strong, grainless material, giving the legs of their little chairs and stools exaggerated curves expensive if not impossible with wood, and small work such as hand screen and letter rack wildly serrated edges, clear-cut as metal yet rigid and wonderfully light in the hands. Nevertheless this cheaper ware never quite reached the standards of near-perfection that had made Clay renowned. Compared with the paper ware, pressed papier mâché is somewhat brittle and its surface very slightly undulating.

Long before this development, however, other important decorative styles were being evolved. As early as 1812 Thomas Hubball, a japanner of Clerkenwell, introduced the technique of constructing whole pictures in scintillating metallic powders. These were developed in a range of eighteen shades obtained from brass, copper, zinc, Dutch metal and other coloured alloys, some stained, and were applied over gold size. Even landscapes and the heroic scenes then fashionable could be reproduced. Other decorations were carried out entirely in gold, especially by Clay's successors, the firm of Small & Son, Guest, Chopping & Bill. The gold lent itself particularly to Oriental fantasies. These were made immensely popular in the 1820s by Joseph Booth, an employee of the notable Birmingham firm of Jennens & Bettridge, who copied Oriental lacquer imports. Gold at its most splendid against black backgrounds appeared from 1831 onwards, in the various shades of gold produced by the use of different alloys, then popular in several crafts. Some wonderfully brilliant effects were achieved on flower petal, butterfly and bird with pure gold and silver leaf.

From about 1825 Booth made his pagodas and mandarins even more like Oriental lacquer work by shaping them in low relief under the gilding. At the same time his brother Edwin developed a delicate Indian style of ornament for the Wolverhampton firm of Walton, and a little later this firm evolved what became known as the Wolverhampton style of decoration in a combination of oil paint and bronze powders. This achieved particularly vivid representations of sunrays and moonlight, often shining through stained glass (oil painted) gothic windows. From about 1860 the soft silvery bronze of aluminium was used for moonlit scenes and as edging to sombre cloud masses.

The great decorative development of the 1830s, however, was the use of pearly shell, prompted by one of the period's outstanding manufacturers, Sir Edward Thomason of Birmingham, who was interested in the Oriental method and had long been alive to the potentialities of paper ware and papier mâché, using it at least as early as 1803. From 1825 when the method was devised by their employee, George Souter, to 1839, the firm of Jennens & Bettridge had the monopoly of what was called inlay but in fact consisted of sticking little slabs of shell to the papier mâché and then adding further background varnish until the shell and background could be polished together.

The tones of the shell suggest mother-of-pearl, but in fact the shells used were a greenish flat shell and the pink aurora or giant sea snail. After 1840 the preparation of "japanners' ground pearl" became a specialist industry: the wafers of shell were ground paper-thin and the earlier hand cutting replaced by more intricate shaping and etching with acid. The period's favourite applications of the shell included ambitious views of historic buildings, thus vying with silver embossments on card case and snuff box with their views of Windsor, Warwick and other castles, the method reaching its ultimate brilliance in such scenes as the Houses of Parliament across the Thames by moonlight. Notable combinations of colour and iridescence are to be noted when transparent colour has been painted over the shell, as in some quickly worked flower patterns dating from about 1842. After 1842 ornament on the shell itself might be etched with acid.

Before 1850 a further development was the introduction of glass panels mounted in papier mâché: the glass might be painted with a picture in oil colours and a few conspicuous features enriched with pieces of shell fastened to the underside of the glass. An alternative was to introduce various gemstones, enamels, foil-backed cut glass and the like to the back of the glass, unadorned areas being covered with reflective metal foil and the glass sometimes diapered with gold. This was known as gem inlay.

In contrast to such exotic treatments, another Jennens & Bettridge employee created a vogue for a particularly appealing type of flower painting. This was George Neville, remembered today for his blue convolvulus or morning glory flowers. We tend to associate papier mâché with glossy black grounds but it was only when Neville tackled the problem of fading that these became popular. Thereupon he and other notable flower painters made full use of the brilliant effects of clear bright colours on the glossy black. All too soon, however, in the 1850s, the flower painting deteriorated, becoming coarse and gaudy.

On some cream-toned papier mâché boxes of 1845 and later transfer printing was applied. Intricate line work was thus easily introduced and could be coloured and gilded by hand and finally varnished. After about 1860, however, it was usual merely to paste a paper engraving to the box lid. Another notion of the 1850s and 1860s was to colour papier mâché in mingled tones to suggest marble, green malachite and blue john and this unwelcome trend is to be noted too in grained effects on trays, boxes and the like, copying veneers of such popular woods as walnut and maple. Small desk items and other minor articles with shell ornament showing a general grey or mauve tone may be dated fairly exactly to 1861 as they may be numbered among the mementoes issued after the death of the Prince Consort.

Occasionally the collector finds a named piece of papier mâché and others may be attributed with some confidence such as the many views of Oxford, its colleges, public buildings, gardens and the like decorated by the Oxford firm of Spiers & Son who obtained their paper ware, undecorated—firescreens, workboxes, inkstands and the rest—from Birmingham and carton pierre from Jackson & Sons, London, for panels to be introduced in interior decoration.

Birmingham makers who impressed their names on their best work include Jennens & Bettridge on paper-ware from the 1820s: from early in the 1830s the mark was "Jennens & Bettridge London and Birmingham" and from 1840 a crown was added above and "Makers to the Queen" below. The letters "McH" were used by McCullum and Hodgson.

Wolverhampton firms whose marks have been noticed include Shoolbred and Loveridge (marked *LOVERIDGE*); Alderman & Illidge (*ILLIDGE*); Frederick Walton & Co (*WALTON* or *F. WALTON & Co*); Edward Perry (*PERRY*); A. Morton & Co. (*MORTON*). The mark *CLAY & Co* on a piece of paper ware is no certain indication of work pre-dating Clay's retirement in 1802 for although he sold his factory, which employed six hundred, to the firm of Small & Son, Guest, Chopping & Bill the showrooms in King Street, Covent Garden, London, remained in the family until after 1860.

Marked specimens have their own value, but in this material the condition of a piece is more important than its age, for even cleaning may prove somewhat hazardous: the best method is a soft rub with a paste of wheat flour and olive oil, avoiding all use of hot water. Every piece, therefore, must be judged by its own particular qualities of design and execution—and these are matters of personal taste in which a happy knack of arrangement or display may be more important than any amount of collector's lore.

Chapter Twenty

BROWN STONEWARE

VICTORIANS are too easily condemned for a preoccupation with over-decorated prettiness. A noteworthy development among 19th-century ceramics was the creation of attractive table ware, vases, even figures, plaques and other mantel ornaments in the plain, heavy ceramic known as brown salt-glazed stoneware. Nor was this merely a cult among a few aesthetes: Queen Victoria herself in 1871 ordered vases for Windsor Castle.

The ware tends to be massive, pitted under the glaze like orange skin, brown toned unevenly in a score of walnut and honey tints. Centuries of traditional skill are revealed in the potters' superb handling of this uncouth material, fashioning bottles and mugs and jars, figure flasks and pictorial jugs that splendidly outlived Victorian knick-knackery and are perfectly absorbed by the furnishings of today. As its name suggests it is magnificently strong, and many specimens are still available for today's collectors, but the more surprising fact, perhaps, is that some pieces are now becoming valuable rarities which only last century must have been turned out by the thousand.

English manufacture of brown stoneware dates back to John Dwight's pioneer work at Fulham in the 1670s when much more was imported from the Rhineland. Extremely intense heat vitrified the mixture of an ordinary single plastic clay with felspar and quartz in the form of sand or crushed flint, transforming it into vessels that are non-porous and wholly opaque but with a glassy texture when fractured that suggests hard porcelain. Such vessels are impervious to liquids and even endure boiling water without cracking, and the simple, cheap composition proved sufficiently fine and dense-textured to take incised and relief-moulded ornament, pleasing to those who still looked to the silversmith for inspiration rather than to the porcelain painter. The colour brought out by the salt glaze in the extreme heat of the single kiln firing depended upon the chance quality of the unrefined clay used by each individual pottery, many vessels being partially covered with a wash of semi-liquid clay that burned to a different, deeper tone.

The rich matt-surface glow from the light film of translucent glaze was acquired in the same kiln firing. This non-poisonous glassy effect was created by shovelling salt into the kiln when the heat was at its most intense so that the salt was volatised and the fumes filtered among the vessels, depositing a fine film of what, when cold, became intensely hard soda glass fused to the stoneware and strong enough to withstand food acids and knife-ware. As early as 1702 the Pewterers' Company was complaining at the "great increase of mugs made of earth and a mark impressed thereon in imitation of sealed measures to sell liquid commodities" and doubtless also shellfish and the like.

The characteristic granular surface of this brown ware gives an attractive matt reflection of the light and varies even in different parts of a single vessel. But it was recognised at the time that this effect was ill-suited to drinking vessels which may be found rimmed with silver. It could be overcome by smearing the vessels with red lead before firing but this thicker, smoother glaze was quickly scarred by table use.

Mortimer's London directory listed "brown stone porters" in Lambeth and Fulham in 1763 but even by then many potters were forsaking this cheapest, simplest and most serviceable ware for the white stonewares that sought to imitate Oriental porcelain, stoneware being in fact half-way between hard porcelain and hard earthenware and considerably harder than either. White stonewares were more refined, more elaborate and costly, but they lack the warm, earthy glow of the brown ware.

Bristol, too, is associated with some 18th-century pieces but the great period for this rugged ware came in the 19th century when the main producers were at Lambeth and in

Derbyshire. Construction of a coach-road from Derby to Alfreton led to the discovery of extremely fine clay deposits in 1806 and these prompted the launching of the Denby pottery by William Bourne, a potter of nearby Belper. Bourne and his son Joseph are associated with many fine brown stoneware domestic vessels.

Other potteries followed, working the same bed of clay and producing a vast output of brown stoneware. The makers whose names are most often noted stamped into the more decorative pieces include Bourne & Son, Denby (*BOURNE* or *BELPER & DENBY | BOURNE'S POTTERIES | DERBYSHIRE*); William Briddon, Brampton (*BRIDDON*); William Burton, Codnor Park until 1833 (*BURTON*); Welshpool and Payne Potteries, Brampton (*KNOWLES*); John Oldfield & Co., Brampton, from 1838 (*OLDFIELD*); Doulton & Watts, Lambeth (*DOULTON & WATTS* until 1854 and then *DOULTON*). Nineteenth-century Brampton ware is often mistaken for the now rare Nottingham ware made before 1799. The firm of Oldfield, for example, made innumerable sauce jugs, butter pots, pudding moulds, figured stands for Stilton cheese, tea and coffee pots, strikingly handsome tobacco jars, watch stands, fruit trays and puzzle jugs.

In the 1820s technical advances resulted in finer quality stoneware and further improvements were made in the 1850s. But at this time Henry Doulton of Lambeth was still more interested in revolutionising men's ideas on urban public health with his brown stoneware, and his triumphant development of the ware to its artistic limits dates no earlier than the 1870s.

When John Doulton and John Watts began their own small pot works at Vauxhall Walk, Lambeth, in 1815, they concentrated on useful wares—pitchers, tobacco jars, phials, gallypots, anchovy jars selling at two shillings a dozen and six-gallon cans at seven shillings each. But an account book dated 1818–19 shows that they were meeting a demand too for "fine jugs" and figured mugs and jugs, making more decorative use of this cheap and sturdy ware. Goblets, tumblers and cups were turned out in great quantities and inkstands, candlesticks and other similar work.

Perhaps the most notable brown stoneware vessels at this time, however, were grouped under the account book heading of hunting pots. These are fascinating and some fine specimens remain from the 18th century. Some are huge, heat-retaining vessels for serving hot toddy, with two, three or even four handles, so that the collector seeks for a series in decreasing sizes, no two alike in ornament but all harmonising in their buff-brown colour range.

The decoration that gave them their name appears in high relief: animated little men and animals rushing around the full curving body of the heavy vessel against backgrounds that may include windmills, bee hives, trees, more men taking their leisure, smoking, chatting. Often the main theme is a hunting scene with stag or hare pursued by hounds, the happy-go-lucky medley of motifs, which in early work were shaped separately and applied to the ware, their representational style and solid rounded contours all suggesting a 17th-century picture in raised stumpwork embroidery. Modelled hounds may form the jug handles and its spout may have a mask below the lip.

Such hunting jugs continued in popular demand to the end of the 19th century. Straight-sided flat-based mugs known as cans were made too, and hunting jugs in this cylindrical outline known awkwardly as canettes. The same kind of scenic ornament in relief may be found occasionally on a wall plaque made for a cheap, uncritical market, shaped by pressing the clay into a mould, and sometimes crudely coloured with unfired paint.

Toby jugs figuring Toby Fillpot, usually associated with glazed earthenware, may be found, too, in the brown stoneware of Brampton and the greybeard jug with an aged rascal's face below the lip. This popular jug is sometimes known as a bellarmine but the term is more exactly reserved for the wide-bodied stoneware bottle with the mask below the rim, originally a derisive caricature of Cardinal Bellarmine. From the greybeard developed many a 19th-century character jug, with the whole body of the vessel forming a man's head or bust, whether celebrity or grotesque.

As with so many of the 19th century's inexpensive ornaments, celebrities appear importantly among the collector's pieces. A splendid Nelson head may be found impressed *TRAFALGAR 1805*, made by Doulton, but in about 1830, or a simpler version with a handle resembling a twist of rope. Mantel shelf figures of celebrities were made too. There is a charming Doulton & Watts figure of Queen Caroline, consort of George IV, crowned, although in fact she never was, and holding a scroll with her famous declaration, "My Hope is in the People". This was probably the firm's earliest figure piece, and was followed by the Dukes of York and Cumberland, William IV and Queen Adelaide, Sir Robert Peel, Sir Walter Scott, and others.

Finer clay and better modelling may be noted in these figures from the mid-1830s, their subjects including Victoria and Albert who is wearing the Order of the Garter, indicating a date in the 1840s. Still finer modelling was introduced in the mid-1840s while specimens dating from late in the century are meticulous indeed, such as the best known characters from Dickens. Small animal figures are delightful finds—stags, various breeds of dogs, cats, horses, cows and inevitably dubious-looking lions. They were made by the Brampton potters but never, it seems, considered worth marking. From the 1860s Doulton made stone ware figures in brown, blue, green and claret red.

Some particularly interesting figures are the head-and-shoulder flasks or bottles especially characteristic of the 1830s–40s, intended for shelf display in taverns. Perhaps the earliest were the flask shapes with bas-relief medallions on both sides, unambitious reflections of the craze for cameo portraits. Here the distracting change from brown to buff on the flask body at shoulder level occurs at forehead height. Dante may find himself surprisingly paired with Napoleon, and the fashion continued long enough for Victoria to appear with the Duchess of Kent. But these are less interesting than the figure flasks shaped in the round to about waist level. Early specimens are individualistic portraits, frequently with a political slant reflecting the public excitement associated with parliamentary reform. Such a flask, seven to eleven inches tall, may have a slogan on the plain lower body such as "Bread for the Millions" or "Irish Reform Cordial": Lord Brougham may declare THE SECOND MAGNA CHARTA (sic) and Earl Grey advocate THE PEOPLE'S RIGHTS, or Lord John Russell, sponsor of the Reform Bill, THE TRUE SPIRIT OF REFORM.

More ambitious flasks with figures in the round appeared from the beginning of Victoria's reign, including Bourne's "Queen Alexandrina Victoria" with "May Peace and Prosperity Prevail" on the reverse and sometimes a handle, and Oldfield's "Queen Victoria 1st". Bourne's flask of Sir Robert Peel shows him full length, standing on a plinth. Later came such figures as Samuel Johnson, John Bull, Mr. Punch announcing THE TRIUMPH OF THE PEN, and, one of the last, Jim Crow, issued about 1860. The stoppers of these flasks might be ground uniformly by machine instead of individually by hand after 1833 when John Wisker of the Vauxhall pottery patented a suitable machine.

Other flasks are found in all manner of imitative shapes—pigs, powder horns, grandfather clocks as well as the conventional figures made by several firms. Several versions are to be found of such stock favourites as a jolly sailor seated on a barrel above the name of the contents, such as "Old Tom" on an Oldfield flask. Figures of "Smoking" and "Snuffing" came from the Vauxhall pottery, and Doulton made a popular night watchman with a lantern and truncheon. Doulton kept twenty men working on these cordial bottles. Stephen Green of Lambeth even introduced a mermaid, and one fish design as much as fifteen inches long. Green made popular flasks shaped as pistols, too, and as tipstaves in the early 1840s, often bearing the arms of the City of London in relief. Some fifteen-inch examples show the letters *V R* in relief on one side and the insignia of the Order of the Garter on the other.

An occasional find in brown salt-glazed stoneware is a straight-necked bulbous-bodied puzzle jug, also known by their other name of teasing pitchers. All are made in much the same way. There is no mystery about drinking from such a many-spouted vessel, but only a need for deftness in covering the unwanted outlets that give the unwary a drenching. Puzzle jugs are associated with the 18th century but the later brown stoneware piece can be distinguished by the position of the several small spouts half way down the perforated neck instead of round the rim.

Sometimes inscriptions and dates are incised to suggest 18th-century origin, but this is a characteristic of many Victorian notions, and in brown stoneware the same pitfall may be found, for example, among the two-handled posset pots and loving cups made until the 1880s. The *Art Journal*, 1869, illustrated one made at that time at Brampton but incised with the date 1750. The Prices at the Temple Works, Bristol, were reported to be producing "excellent imitations of the antique, of very fine body, of faultless glaze and elegant form", from the mid-1840s, these being described as "admirable copies, perfect in shape and firing".

Nor are dates the only hazards. The whole delightful style of many pieces harks back to the previous century yet their manufacture dates to 1850–90. There are reposeful classic candlesticks such as Wedgwood already had copied in fine stoneware and other potters in earthenware from the silversmiths of the 1770s, and adaptations of these smiths' tea-kettles. There are grotesque tobacco pipes to hang on the wall, and candle-socketed tobacco jars bearing relief ornament—figure scenes or ugly dead game—like the hunting jugs. Such relief effects were created with no small skill by pouring liquid clay into absorbent plaster moulds cast from the original carved models, a method still in use for many simple earthenwares, the mould being kept revolving until enough of the wet clay is evenly distributed around its walls where the plaster quickly absorbs the moisture, allowing the wetter clay towards the centre of the mould to be poured away. In this manner exact facsimiles of the hollow, complicated shapes could be produced in unlimited numbers.

The most ambitious effects date from the 1870s when Henry Doulton was persuaded to participate in a quest for more attractive decorated pottery than the tawdry over-ornamented wares then all too popular. With the eager co-operation of the Lambeth School of Art much splendid brown stoneware was produced, still treated with the old respect for its qualities and limitations, still salt-glazed, still achieved with a single kiln firing, but expressing the ideas of a new generation of artist-craftsmen whose names are known and whose initials frequently mark their creations.

Chapter Twenty One

CRYSTAL CAMEOS

CAMEOS are as old as civilisation itself. The goddess brooch that secured a Roman toga may have become a treasured pendant for an Elizabethan lady. In the 18th century it might lie hidden in a collector's cabinet, but by the 19th century equally gracious little replicas, frequently carved in shell, would be fastening cloak and shawl for our Victorian forebears. These small heads of gods and goddesses and allegorical groups carved in low relief were revered by the ancient Greeks, were collected—and faked—by Renaissance nobility, and have reappeared time and time again in precisely similar designs but in many materials.

Ancient cameos have been found carved in sardonyx with no fewer than nine variously coloured layers, each devoted to different details in a portrait or scene perhaps less than an inch in diameter and a fraction of an inch deep. The famous Cheapside Hoard, now in the London Museum, includes cameos of Romano-Egyptian, Byzantine and 16th-century Italian origin, some in their Elizabethan settings. This collection is believed to be the stock of a very ordinary jeweller of about 1600.

Periods of great material advance, however, have always been associated with a renewed desire for the peace, the unchanging, idealised loveliness of classic art. Cameos proved particularly agreeable to the Regency's self-conscious admirers of the classic tradition, such portraits showing a cool serenity, an aloof austerity that delights when romantic prettiness tends to cloy. The Greek styles that spread through Europe after the Directoire (1795–99) required plentiful but plain jewellery to recreate the pomp of the Caesars—massive earrings, necklaces, as many as three bracelets on each wrist, rings even on the toes. The *Journal des Dames* in 1805 reported that a woman of fashion would wear cameos at her waist, cameos on her necklace, a cameo on each of her bracelets, a cameo on her diadem, and declared that "antique stones or in default of these carved shells are more in vogue than ever".

Much of the cameo work that remains today is carved in shell, carving in the whitish outer layer appearing silhouetted against richly coloured linings: this was the persuasive material of the Italian Renaissance jeweller and of England's 19th-century itinerant cameo cutter who fashioned tiny portraits—of Apollo and Venus and Juno rather than of living men and women—and thus spread the liking for this work among ordinary folk remote from classic scholarship. These cameos were frail enough, however, and only a little less vulnerable than their fragile rivals in wax or flimsy silhouettes.

Once the particular delights of such contrasts in extremely low relief had come to be appreciated there were innumerable attempts to achieve the same results in less exacting materials, in horn, enamel, ivory, semi-precious stones and Wedgwood jasper wares. For the cameo portrait at its most delightful in this rôle, as a fascinating trinket for desk and dressing table or mounted on a vessel to grace the dining table, it is necessary to explore an intriguing byway familiar to comparatively few collectors of old glass and find the cameo held within sparkling crystal, known by its creator as *crystallo ceramie* and today as the portrait crystal cameo.

It is difficult to realise today the value Georgian men and women attached to portraits—of royalty, of celebrities, of fashionable belles, of themselves—before the camera took the excitement out of "catching a likeness". Cameos, expressing each detail of feature and character with the slightly three-dimensional effect of extremely low relief carving, are among the most appealing styles of portraiture they have left us. When, in 1819, Apsley Pellatt introduced these exquisite cameo portraits, gleaming like silver within the solid thickness of brilliantly clear glass, he found an eager market for paperweights, plaques, lustre-hung candlesticks and candelabra, decanters, goblets, tumblers, tea caddy basins, trinket boxes, scent bottles, even small pieces of jewellery such as pendants and rings and earrings, sometimes commissioned in quantity as gifts by the subject of the cameo portrait. Cameos with religious subjects were made for reliquaries, church candlesticks and the like.

Portraits of fashionable celebrities preserved in this way, usually profiles, could be bought from the glass sellers—George III, say, or his heir, naïvely represented as a Roman emperor, or the Duke of York or the Duke of Sussex in a cushion-shaped paperweight or on the side of a square decanter, or Princess Charlotte on a flattened oval scent bottle and her fiancé Prince Leopold on a sugar basin. In some examples George IV is presented in coronation regalia with obvious souvenir purpose, and sometimes a cup shows the heads of both George III and the Regent. Princess Charlotte, the Prince Regent's daughter, figures frequently in these austere settings, which were considered fit vehicles for expressing the nation's distress at her death in 1817.

Much of the joy of these cameos, however, lies in the fact that wealthy folk commissioned their own portraits. With glorious arrogance a client might have decanters and drinking glasses made by the set, every vessel bearing on one side his coat of arms, possibly in full colour, and on the other his cameo profile, with his crest gleaming in every decanter finial. The actual technical achievement in wholly surrounding the tiny cameo in clear glass delighted the easily mystified, and if it no longer appears phenomenal at least it is still recognised today as a small triumph of glass craft.

The crystal cameo in perfection was the English achievement of Apsley Pellatt, M.P. (1791–1863), an interesting and forceful Londoner who was responsible, incidentally, for the glass lenses of deck lights and for the fact that a crossed cheque is only payable through a bank. The idea for his cameos came from Bohemia: in the late 18th century poor quality specimens were produced, the bas relief crazed with tiny cracks through unequal response to atmospheric changes, the glass itself mediocre. French glassmen achieved somewhat better results but these still tended to show flaws.

Many crystal cameos of Napoleon taken from Dumarest's coin and from Andrieu's medal were issued and with the return of the Bourbons came cameos of Louis XVIII modelled from Andrieu's medal of 1817. French glassmen have been credited, too, with some fairly commonplace models of George IV and the Duke of Wellington among others who aided the restoration, just as English glassmen included cameos of Louis XVIII among their stock made from available coins and medals. A charming little heart-shaped crystal may be found occasionally, commemorating Marie Antoinette's daughter, the Duchess of Angoulême, from the Sèvres 1817 model in biscuit porcelain, but later, it appears, the French work deteriorated into cheap little knick-knacks used for political propaganda through the uneasy years of the 1830s to 1850s.

Pellatt's work was far above this mediocre level; by 1819 he was in a position to take out a patent, and for six years produced cameo portraits at his father's Falcon Glassworks, Southwark, so perfect, in glass so magnificently clear, that no imitator could rival him for a quarter of a century. The cameo itself, despite its silver sheen when viewed through the brilliant glass, is made of greyish, vitreous fine stoneware, the composition, mainly of china clay and purified barium sulphate, being fine enough to reproduce every delicacy of detail from a plaster of paris mould yet hard enough not to warp or crack in the red hot glass. Coins and medals supplied the models for some moulds, but other sitters' profiles were carved specially in wax and suitably reduced, so that the enthusiastic collector searches with a magnifying glass for the wax artist's signature reproduced in the mould-shaped stoneware.

Armorial pieces may be found—great rarities these—painted with bright metallic oxide colours. Pellatt discusses his colour work in his book on *Curiosities of Glassmaking* (1849) and his Birmingham selling agents, Mary Rollason & Sons, advertised in 1822 "ornamented incrustations called Crystallo Ceramie by the improved process, ornaments of any description, Arms, Crests, Portraits, Landscapes of any variety of colour may be introduced into the glass so as to become perfectly imperishable". I have seen a scent bottle inset with a coat of arms in all its magnificence of full-colour painting bought unrecognised for a few shillings.

The cameo—known to collectors as a sulphide—was oven-baked and hand-finished with tooling and under-cutting, then enclosed in the finest possible flint-glass made with pure sand from Sydney and lead oxide from Derbyshire prepared by a new process that removed all trace of blue tone. This superb glass, worked always in small quantities, is a notable feature of the early crystal cameo. The workman blew into a gather of the hot glass on the end of his blowing rod, forming a long glass bubble. This was cut open for the cameo to be inserted by another workman, then reheated to seal the cut, and finally collapsed around the cameo by withdrawing the hot air up the blowing rod. Even for glassmen accustomed to the intense heat such a delicate operation was a severe test of skill.

One of the taken-for-granted marvels of glass is the fact that under heat it will fuse so that a cut can be sealed and more glass can be added without its clarity being marred by any trace of the join. Once the cameo was safely enclosed the paperweight or plaque could be built up into any required shape. The same attribute made it comparatively easy, too, to apply a cameo to a hollow vessel. A blob of viscous glass dropped over the cameo when it was placed in position on the side of a vessel could be smoothed and levelled until the fusion was undetectable. The glass would certainly appear thicker, but this could be masked by elaborate diamond-cutting.

This was a great period for cutting in deep relief, and the brilliant points and lines of light are characteristic of Pellatt paperweights and plaques. Cross-cut diamonds on the back of a flat, vertical cushion weight or star radii on the base of a mushroom dome enhance the refractive effect of the light brilliantly illuminating the cameo. A dome of glass over the cameo not only emphasises the three-dimensional quality of the portrait but also magnifies the diamond-cutting on the reverse. Facets or points may rim a medallion pendant, and in a decanter or scent bottle every part of the vessel may show rich diamonds, horizontal lines and similar patterns lighting up the cameo and enhancing its simplicity, with its glass polished, even burnished, to perfect glowing smoothness.

Pellatt ceased manufacture after six years and comparable work did not appear again until the late-1860s when the maker was John Ford of Edinburgh, his glass as richly clear but more lavishly cut.

Pellatt himself developed a less hazardous, costly method of embedding his cameos, patented in 1831. Plaques may be found, and plates for dessert and substantial tea caddy basins, mugs and other vessels. Here again Pellatt was shrewdly alert to the trends of the period, and he shaped his glass by the new and soon commercially triumphant method known as pressing. The viscous glass acquired its outline and even its well-defined patterns from a mould, being forced into shape by a plunger (see Chapter 22). The cameo was inserted through a slide cut in the mould and the glass reheated and re-pressed. But the glass itself in remaining specimens is not of the splendid quality Pellatt used in the 1820s—a fault associated with pressed glass. As a result the cameo itself loses something of its delicate silver sheen.

A variant found occasionally introduces coloured glass for the first layer—blue, amber, ruby or black—and this hint at a change in public demand is reflected in a more conspicuous break with the cameo tradition when a cameo-mounted ornament is further decorated with a small trinket such as a flower or bird modelled in the round and painted in brilliant metallic, kiln-fired colours and inserted into the glass.

Glass manufacture leapt ahead in England after 1845 when the century-old glass tax was abolished, and in particular the small frivolities previously uneconomic appeared in abundance; but there was the reduction in quality inevitably associated with keen price-cutting for a wider and less discriminating public. Cameo incrustations, or medallion inlays as they were called by then, appeared in greater numbers, but these lack something of their earlier charm. Even the small cameos themselves are less finely finished, and the glass, though richly glossy, is too heavily leaded to give them their sheen of silver. Paperweights may be found, and plaques, their subjects frequently celebrities of their day. A detail to search for is the name *Pellatt & Co.* in tiny script which distinguishes these later works of the originator from those of his rivals. But within ten years cameo portraits were out of fashion.

The revival by John Ford of Edinburgh in the late 1860s was marked by the reintroduction of brilliantly clear glass. More than seventy subjects have been listed. It is still possible to find, for example, a cameo portrait of Victoria embedded in a cube of glass for a paperweight made to commemorate her 1887 jubilee, but it is liable to show a slight flaw in the sulphide itself.

Since the work dates to the days of Victorian ingenuity, some glassmen produced paperweights cleverly suggesting the effect of the cameo without the labour of fashioning the sulphide or introducing it into the glass. These were known at the time as medallion paperweights, and portraits may be found of all the leading celebrities of the period, from the church, from politics, the services and stage. Viewed from above the flat block of clear flint-glass, round or hexagonal, appears to contain a silver sulphide, but in the hand it is found that the portrait consists of a hollow impressed into the flat base. This is not even wheel-engraved but shaped by an intaglio mould. Dipping into hydrofluoric acid clouded the base and when this was polished from the flat surfaces the hollow portrait retained its delicate opacity. William Kidd of London made some of the finest, and the Birmingham firms of Lloyd & Somerfield and F. & C. Osler. The Birmingham firms gave their weights elaborately cut borders, but none of these substitutes possesses the dignified beauty of Pellatt's *crystallo ceramie*.

Chapter Twenty Two

TUMBLERS AND BEAKERS

THE most successful collectors of antiques today, I find, are those who delight in the small everyday articles of yesterday. Such necessities tend to be found in some quantity and a range of materials, their design functional and lastingly pleasing, their ornament direct, but often with just that extra charm that tells of some unimportant artisan's joy in the making. Drinking vessels are typical of such pieces: here the collector will discover fine silver to set the style, no less decorative glass, bone china calling for the admiration due to display-cabinet specimens, and a fascinating assembly of less pretentious materials, earthenware, pewter, horn, and silver-rimmed treen.

The vessels considered here are the simplest of all, lacking even handles, stems and feet: only the naming of them may introduce slight complications. "Nests of small drinking bowls" or "quaffing cups" are noted among early Tudor records of good living. English silversmiths met a considerable demand among travellers with a peculiarly attractive vessel, small enough to slip into pocket or travelling chest, with a heavy rounded base that would maintain its equilibrium despite rutted roads and stormy seas, or at worst, spill only a tiny quantity of liquor. At home it served for a short drink quaffed without pause, the drinker returning it to the sideboard upside down.

This was the tumbler properly so named, shaped from a single flat piece of silver plate by prolonged, skilful hammering. The silversmith used the term beaker when he met an equally simple need for a table vessel that would stand firmly without rocking at all, its substantial inserted base forming a sharp angle with sides that tended to be a little concave for easy gripping in contrast to the tumbler's continuations of the base. Such an obvious distinction was confused, however, by glassmakers who applied the term tumbler to the beaker outline—justified by the argument that at least it could fall more safely than a stemmed glass—and contributed a further term, tun, which they applied to the wide-based beaker with a pronounced waist.

Glass tuns are now comparative rarities and never, it seems, were considered important enough to appear in trade catalogues: silver tumblers are rare too, as they seldom date later than the mid 18th century. But the most useful beaker design, flat-based and more or less straight-sided, may be traced in silver, glass and other media through a succession of minor variations in shape and ornament calculated to beguile any collector with an eye for detail and an interest in the original surroundings and purposes of everyday antiques.

A pair of silver tumblers in a leather case saved the traveller from the ills associated with tavern vessels of base metal and porous wood, and they could be packed inside each other for easy carrying. Fashion-loving Samuel Pepys recorded his purchase of a pair in 1664 when coach travel was becoming established as a spartan form of entertainment. The usual style has straight sides rounding into the heavy base and is wider across than its depth of about two to three inches. Many tumbler cups bear a coat of arms for identification, or a crest or cypher or, for lack of such distinction, its owner's name and a date engraved below the rim. Some of the most attractive are decorated on the rounded base to show when placed rim-downward on the side table.

A pocket travelling set of late Stuart or early Georgian days may include richly decorated tumblers along with knife, fork, spoon, nutmeg grater, marrow scoop and other essentials to good dining. Patterns include scrolled flowers and foliage, and the hunting scenes common to ornament of their period with their endless frieze of huntsman, hound and deer. Only among purely ornamental specimens made for 19th-century romantics, however, does one find tumblers worked in high relief repoussé, rendering the inside rough and hard to clean, and these may be traps indeed for the unwary with their Latin inscriptions and bogus 16th-century dates.

By those early Victorian days silver tumblers were long outmoded, though more were made in late-18th-century Sheffield plate. But the beaker remained in constant use throughout the 18th and early 19th centuries. By Elizabethan days silver beakers were made in four sizes, great, middle, small and children's, the middle size being some six inches tall. Construction consisted of shaping a flat strip of metal into a more or less cylindrical tube and inserting a flat base. In practice this base is rarely quite flat, soon acquiring the bumps and bulges of use and cleaning, but these are raised slightly above the table top by three or four rings of strengthening moulding so that the vessel stands firm and is difficult to upset.

Lively pictorial ornament may be flat-chased around the vessel, strapwork and scrolling flowers extend downwards from the rim, and a coat of arms perhaps or an owner's name and a date be engraved upon the base, reminder of days when the rich boy went to boarding school equipped with a linen sheet and a silver beaker and spoon.

Most beakers, however, even when gilded within, depend upon good proportions and workmanship for their attraction, their ornament being limited to handsome moulding around the base. Beakers of Charles II's reign include the rare double beaker with a half-depth vessel acting as foot ring, corded moulding marking the vessel's shared base. Some collectors include also a type of beaker shaped for nesting like the tumbler cup, but this has a short stem and foot and is better given its contemporaneous name and classification of goblet. Silver beakers of this period tend to be wide, three or four inches tall, the sides chased with flowers and foliage and the base closely banded with reeded moulding. In a late-17th-century example a band of relief ornament may ring the vessel, which has a less spreading rim than formerly.

Already by then the everyday silver beaker for milord's cyder and the rich child's spiced ale was beginning to go out of fashion, giving place to costly Chinese porcelain and the first clear and sonorous English flint-glass; but presentation beakers were in demand, some with ornate covers, some in gold.

Beakers for everyday use by the fastidious man of means were wide and shallow throughout the 18th century, and many specimens dating to the last twenty years of the century bear simple patterns in the silversmith's sparkling technique of bright-cutting with tiny cut-away facets forming the pattern. Contrasting matted backgrounds are associated with this period too, which produced some attractive little beakers scarcely more than two inches tall for potent spirits: these fit closely into each other, and a "nest" is a find indeed. Certainly it is far more attractive than the so-called Elizabethan designs evolved around the mid 19th century, their hand-raised repoussé work executed in rolled silver plate that could be shaped without distortion of the pattern but would lack the gradual thickening that strengthened the rim of the real Elizabethan beaker.

Nowadays, depending as we do upon ceramics for every kind of vessel from coffee pot to egg cup, it is difficult to realise what poor earthenware drinking vessels were available even as late as the mid 18th century, the glaze tending to be porous and quickly stained, the rim harsh to the lips, and the cracks and crazings of use rendering it thoroughly unhygienic, as some 16th-century doctors pointed out.

For everyone who could face the cost the far preferable alternative to the rich man's silver and gold was a drinking vessel of glass. This, until after 1674, meant fragile soda-glass. The drinking vessel known as a tun was described as early as 1551, concave-sided and with "both ends lyke bigge". Mid-17th-century records of Magdalen College, Oxford, refer to tuns holding a third of a pint. By the 18th century the rim was considerably wider than the base but the vessel remained difficult to upset, and some mid-century specimens are found with extra heavy bases, like ships' decanters: small specimens, two to three inches tall, were called dram glasses. Until the 1770s the waist was low and thereafter about mid-way between rim and base, but the shape was never particularly pleasing.

The vessel finds no place in trade lists of distinctive glasses, but is mentioned from time to time as a safe, companionable piece to stand by bed and chair. Lord Shaftesbury (1621–83) wrote of his friend Henry Hastings that "he has always a tun glass without feet standing by him holding a pint of small beer which he often stirs with a great sprig of rosemary". In the 19th century Robert Southey wrote in his *Commonplace Book* that there was always a tun glass standing by him. It may be enamelled or gilded or bear a mid-19th-century engraved inscription, but I have never heard of cut ornament on a tun.

Among glass tumblers, however, the collector finds a far wider range of possibilities, though rare indeed is the glass vessel following the silversmith's notion of a tumbler—the round-based nesting cup such as the London dealer John Greene ordered from Venetian glassmen in Charles II's reign. These he specified were to include plain, ribbed and speckled glasses for beer, claret and sack, and in a smaller size for brandy. Nests of such low, round-based tumblers, six or twelve together, saved space and protected each other during their journey to the wholesaler, provided, as Greene insisted, they were "well fitting".

This is the earliest reference to glass tumblers in England, and imports continued even after George Ravenscroft in the 1670s established the superiority of his flint-glass for sturdy drinking vessels. Not until about 1700, some twenty years after Ravenscroft's death, was flint-glass blown into the Venetian tumbler shapes known as quaffing glasses. A detail of such early flint-glass is the kick or hollow in the base that contributed to the annealing or toughening process applied to table glass, and incidentally raised the vessel's rough punty scar clear of the table surface. Technical improvements soon rendered the kick unnecessary and produced thinner, less massive little tumblers, mainly three to five inches high, their rims only a little wider than their rounded-off bases, to sell, unornamented, at sixpence a pound in the 1730s.

When Greene had ordered tall narrow vessels from Venice, sharp angled where base joined side, he termed them beakers, but by the 1750s the tumbler in English flint-glass tended to acquire the squared-off base—ground flat on a horizontal stone—and straight, outward-slanting sides while retaining its familiar name. Beaker-shaped and tumbler-named these vessels have remained ever since, their strength and usefulness ensuring their popularity, the very simplicity of their outline resulting in delightfully varied ornament.

Plain, these vessels were selling by weight at 9*d.* a pound by 1769 and 1*s.* 9*d.* by 1819, challenging the collector to distinguish subtle changes of quality in the glass fabric. A few at least are distinguished by rich gilding, remnant of the many once rimmed in burnished gold above gold-touched engraving of crest or cypher. Gold borders became wider after 1750, but unfortunately 18th-century gilding quickly vanished in use. One finds little trace today of such delicate work as the gilding on wheel-engraved flower borders mentioned in the *Bristol Journal*, 1773, as "new fashion'd tumblers neatly burned with gold flowers".

Engraving, the glassman's most obvious enrichment, was restricted until the late 1730s to coats of arms, crests and rim inscriptions in light, tentative wheel-engraving or, a rare find today, in diamond point. But the better annealed tumblers of the 1740s were tough enough to take richer engraving. Regimental messes have specimens from as early as the 1750s, when it was fashionable to flourish the regimental badge.

Many advertisements of the 1740s–80s refer to "flower'd pint, half pint and quarter pint tumblers". In these one finds naturalistic flowers suggesting the painting on the porcelain of the time. An early example may show a single sprig—rose, carnation, daisy—perhaps with a crest or cypher on the opposite side, but specimens from the 1750s show sunflowers or still more exotic passion flowers, and on the opposite side often a bird or butterfly. Wide bands of flowers below the rim, some petals polished, date especially between the 1750s and the late 1770s, but among tumblers made from about 1670 onwards to the mid 19th century the most splendid are gift vessels engraved all over with pictorial subjects.

Here collectors with a bent for social history are in their

element, though one suspects that there is a tendency today to read more into the Georgians' casual ornament than ever its creators dreamed. Most themes are merely decorative, reflecting chance vogues for queer Chinese pastorals or picturesque English views, like blue transfer-printed earthenwares. Some are classical or allegorical, others touch lightly on social extravagances or commemorate historical events. Many of the most handsome bear ships in full sail, vastly popular until the 1820s and, as one expects of sailors' trophies, often fully inscribed and dated.

Huntsmen, too, liked factual ornament, much being dated to the 1770s and 1780s and more to the early years of the 19th century. Indeed, in late Georgian days glassman, silversmith and potter all looked to the sportsman for custom and had little to fear from artistic criticism. In picture and inscription these tumblers and beakers baldly commemorate great races and steeplechases, salute triumphant individual horses and hounds, wish success to a hunt, or proclaim the delights of a country pastime.

Engravings of men at work are comparatively rare on tumblers but their trade guilds, London and provincial, are remembered in many coats of arms. The most desirable addition on the reverse of such a tumbler is the owner's name and the date of his admission to the company. A simpler version for more general sale merely wishes "Success" to the guild. Records indicate the popularity of beakers and tumblers as gifts from guild members—ideal for use at the many feasts that enlivened the duties undertaken by the livery. Marriages, christenings and other important personal occasions may be commemorated on tumblers too, offering endless speculation to the imaginative.

Less personal but most decorative ornament consists of cutting, shallow in the early 18th century, but becoming somewhat bolder from the late 1750s, the early diamond-shaped facets and triangles augmented, for example, by finger flutes around the lower half of the vessel, becoming deeper and narrower later in the century—"cut bottoms" to the glassmen, such as the "2 doz $\frac{1}{2}$ pint Tumb^{ls} cut Bott^{ms}" that cost the Sitwell family of Renishaw sixteen shillings in 1791. Flutings with the crestings between them notched may date from the 1790s but more often from about 1815. A specimen made after about 1805 may show a radial star cut into the base.

By then glass-making technique permitted of the deep cutting associated with the Regency dinner table, when glass vessels in their hundreds would wink and sparkle as if set with diamonds. The thick glass of these hand-cut tumblers was clearer than ever before. It shows off to perfection the high relief diamond shapes of the 1790s variously crosscut and notched to achieve all possible glitter, the circular hollows known as printies preferred in the early 1820s, and the bands of prisms widely introduced from about 1825, all variously combined with fluted "cut bottoms" and the series of vertical and slanting cuts known as blazes.

Some tumblers are found shaped to suggest tiny barrels, incurved at rim and base and cut to suggest staves and hoops: these follow a late-18th-century fashion in decanters and other vessels, but in tumblers the serviceable shape may be noted too with no barrel markings. Some are engraved.

Collectors with an eye for quality seek their specimens among free-blown glasses, cut entirely by hand, but blown-moulded glassware is often attractive and possesses the interest of any commodity created to reproduce more cheaply the most coveted features of the rich man's table. The simplest development from the 1750s was the blown-moulded tumbler shaped and patterned by blowing the glass into a one-piece gunmetal mould. Many are plain, but from the 1760s ridges might be cut low in the mould to give the tumbler simple fluted ornament, and these could be given a spiral slant by a deft-handed glassman twisting the vessel immediately he withdrew it from the mould. One may even find these flutes Gothic pointed, a fashion developed from about 1820.

More elaborate patterning was achieved in the early 19th century with open-and-shut moulds, that is, moulds in two or three pieces that opened out to release the shaped vessel so that it could receive diagonal and horizontal relief work. Diamond moulding and the horizontal ridges known as Norwich rings may date from the 1770s. At a glance some of this ornament may even suggest the sharp clarity of hand-cut glass when it has been skilfully finished on the cutting wheel, but the vessel's interior is slightly rippled, and one may detect extremely inconspicuous breaks in the pattern, either two or three according to the number of pieces composing the mould. The presence of three faint ridges left by a three-piece mould dates a vessel to the 1820s or later.

These patterns are a study in themselves, the variants amounting to many hundreds and ranging from diamonds and flutes to high relief arching designs and scroll and fan motifs. The vertical convexities known as Roman pillar moulding date from 1835 when patented by James Green. Even the base could be patterned with a star or a circle of petals, printies or diamonds—any of thirty or forty designs —for an additional cost of 2*d*. a pound weight. Coloured blown-moulded tumblers date from the 1840s in delicate tones of amethyst, ultramarine, purple, amber and green, but within ten years pressed glass tumblers in translucent colour were coming into vogue, restrained, sparkling, and wholly delightful.

Many of the tumblers found today come into this equally collectable group, shaped by the glass press that dates in England from the mid-1830s onwards. Here again the intention was to imitate free-blown, hand-cut glass in a cheap mass-production manner, and at a glance the press-shaped tumbler is a good imitation, copying the rich deep-relief cutting that is the very essence of early-19th-century glass. Strawberry diamonds and other geometrical designs are found, swags, stars, wheatsheaves, hearts, oakleaves, fleurs-de-lys and most especially the oval printies known as bulls' eyes.

The press could force the glass into far sharper relief than the glass blower making blown-moulded tumblers, an obvious improvement but one that results in tiny fins of glass upon the surface of the tumbler to betray where the hot glass has been forced between the sections of the mould. On an early pressed tumbler one looks too at the base for a shallow, rough-edged fissure caused by the cutting shears, and inside for concentric ripple marks, often perceptible only to the fingers; one notes too the duller tone inside the glass. In about 1840 the pressed glass men found that fire-polishing gave their tumblers a rich sheen and they developed a wide range of low relief patterns, floral, Gothic, classic, even the Indian "Paisley shawl" design, all tending to become crowded and ill-balanced by the mid 19th century.

A deep star impressed on the base may date a tumbler to about 1850 or later. Vertical ribbed patterns are associated with the 1850s and 1860s and many designs of flowers and wavy stems, ivy leaves and fruiting vines, a return to higher relief work being noted after 1860.

Tumblers must not be confused with water glasses, those tall cylindrical glasses used for rinsing the mouth after a meal, a custom decried by some later 18th-century commentators such as Tobias Smollett who complained in his *Travels*, 1766, that he knew of "no custom more beastly". By then the water glass might be blown-moulded in an all-over trellis pattern and was weighted with a wide foot rim, until the rim was abandoned in the 1780s, the base itself being made thicker and heavier. There may be engraved ornament towards the rim of a late-18th-century water glass, which is clear below, and early-19th-century specimens sometimes turn up richly cut with diamonds in deep relief around reserves intended for engraved coats of arms.

Because glass broke too easily and silver quickly became too hot to hold, ceramic vessels were developed for hot drinks, with the obvious refinement of handles, such as mugs and cups and cans. Some mid-18th-century porcelain vessels do indeed lack handles but remain unmistakably cups. Nevertheless the collector may assemble a gay, perhaps somewhat gaudy, collection of beakers that record the major 18th- and 19th-century developments in the tough earthenwares, stonewares, so-called semi-porcelains and radiant bone china, evolved for hard work and too easily dismissed as useful wares.

Until well into the second half of the 18th century the choice for the potter was limited. The fundamental lead-glazed earthenware continued to be produced on traditional lines, dark-burning clays ornamented with blobby patterns of paler, more fluid clay slip. This lacked the decorative possibilities of the tin-enamelled delft ware developed in 17th-century London and Bristol and later in Liverpool, vigorously painted in green, yellow, manganese purple and especially in blue, but here again the ware is thick and rough to the lips. Brown salt-glazed stoneware was intensely hard and impervious to liquids but for pleasant drinking a mug or beaker still required a silver rim, and by the 1740s those who longed for the prohibitively expensive Chinese porcelains were welcoming the comparatively light, delicate white stoneware of Staffordshire. This could be painted with enamel colours and may be regarded as the first step towards the cream-coloured earthenware, to Wedgwood's cream-toned queen's ware of the 1770s and his whiter pearlware that revolutionised men's ideas about drinking pots.

In shape the late-18th-century beaker is usually straight-sided, slanting outwards considerably from base to rim, its height more or less equalling its rim diameter. Ornament is usually transfer-printed, sometimes with hand-applied colour over the printed outlines, crude, homely work that is very much to the modern taste. An example from the Herculaneum Pottery, Liverpool, of about 1800 in the Victoria and Albert Museum is painted in red, yellow, purple and green over black transfer printing to show a sailing ship in a bay with a fisherman and his boy on the headland, all within rough rococo scrolling, and on the other side a compass under a scroll with the popular words of many a jug and mug "Come Box the Compass". This specimen bears the name of I. Johnson.

Gaudiest specimens in such a collection may be painted in bright blue, green, grey, thick brownish-yellow under a clear glaze, colours that could pass unscathed through the heat of the kiln and by some are too narrowly attributed to the 1790s and to the potter Felix Pratt of Fenton. The moulding technique associated with much of this ware lent itself to particularly companionable beakers. An attractive find is a bell-shaped vessel, moulded on each side with a double face so that when filled with liquor it shows the horned head of the devil and when empty and inverted the

Pope under his triple crown. An elaborate specimen may be inscribed, "When Pope absolves : the devil smiles".

The majority of common earthenware beakers were, of course, no more than useful, and a collector has good reason to be pleased with the most casual sponged or marbled ornament—the terms are self-explanatory—or the queer "moss" or "seaweed" or "trees" dotted round a beaker of mocha ware. In a more important category come the tough little beakers of the early 19th century that occasionally turn up in Spode's blue-grey stone china, in production from 1805, gaily enamelled in remotely Chinese patterns, and in the less significant wares of his imitators quickly transfer-printed. But stone china was soon overtaken by a range of felspathic earthenwares which the mid-19th-century potters termed opaque-porcelain, semi-porcelain and impressive-sounding granite ware. The wares have a pleasant ring when struck and lack only the translucency of the cabinet specimen in the finest bone china.

Decoration is brilliant, preserved by clear glaze, skilled artists being required for the specialised techniques which permitted no correction of an error. Obviously the beaker shape offered great possibilities for balanced designs unimpaired by the handle, spout or other excrescence associated with most hollow ware.

In beakers of bone china and all these high quality 19th-century "porcelains" one looks for a mark upon the base, denoting such Worcester firms as Chamberlains or Barr, Flight & Barr, perhaps, or a Minton *M*. Patterns range from naturalistic hand-painted flowers to the delicate transfers known as bat printing, from formalistic arabesques in the rich japan colours to personal overglaze initials, and in a well-loved specimen one's eye notes appreciatively the heavily gilded rim. Only in the most ornate pictorial specimen, the cabinet piece delicately and laboriously painted, colour by colour, by the master enameller, is one suddenly aware that homely shape and proportions claim the beaker not for the cabinet but for the kitchen dresser.

Chapter Twenty Three

ENGLISH FANS

FASCINATION is a word most collectors like to avoid, but the lure of the fan is undeniable and today's collector may still assemble a rich array for no very great outlay. Queen Mary demonstrated how magnificently they could be displayed, mounted in screens, but gone is the chance to *use* them: we can only imagine how once they played their part in the elaborate conversational codes of fan movements that for centuries intrigued their convention-bound owners.

Perfect symbol of happiness and repose three thousand years ago in ancient Egypt, and fashioned of pearly sea shells by the Phoenicians, the fan has a long history of religious ceremony and regal splendour. A passage in Euripides mentions round feather fans—peacock feathers for greatest magnificence after their introduction about 500 B.C. Roman ladies fanned themselves with thin tablets of wood, and by the uneasy years of the Renaissance Italian fans, like the Japanese, might conceal daggers in handles exquisitely jewelled.

In England fans were never more splendid than in Elizabethan days when their long handles were of gold or silver or wood, carved, inlaid, overlaid and with "figures of divers beasts set in diamonds and rubies" and their mounts were ostrich plumes and scintillating peacock feathers at a time when luxurious, vulnerable textures figured high among status symbols, such as Elizabeth's aprons of dyed swansdown. The queen's possessions, inventoried in 1603, included twenty-seven standing fans. Some of these were so long in the handle as to suggest forerunners of the parasol—their use recommended "to prevent sunburn and to be refreshing to the complexion"—rather than of the "fan with pleated leaves" that was soon to become the darling of all Europe.

Japanese fans, symbols of authority probably introduced from China, included folding designs by the seventh century, but at the end of the 16th century Thomas Coryat, describing the fashion of Italy, could still observe: "These fannes both men and women of the countrie doe carry . . . the fanne consisteth of a painted piece of paper and a little wooden handle, the paper which is fastened into the top is on both sides most curiously adorned with excellent pictures". These standing fans are interesting as obviously leading directly to the earliest European folding fans, made of parchment. As far as England is concerned these only became important socially when Charles II and his retinue brought flamboyant, costly Continental notions to England in 1660, and Huguenot refugee craftsmen became available in the 1680s to meet the growing demand with the first English fan manufacture.

Material, subject matter, treatment, shape and size all guide today's collector in dating specimens, but it must be realised that the sticks of a fan may be much older than the mount. As regards definitions, the terms sticks and mount or leaf are self-explanatory. The upper part of the stick which holds the mount is the blade, and the lower, exposed part is the brin. The end sticks are the guards. These terms cover the majority of folding fans, but some of the loveliest specimens do not carry mounts: the sticks alone, richly decorated throughout their length, compose the fan, riveted at the base like all folding fans but at the perimeter elaborately linked with ribbons. These are the brisé fans, most usually found in superbly fretted ivory, sometimes decorated in burnished gold. Unperforated brisé fans are found too, however, with painted ornament: these include the many-bladed puzzle fan opening so that only half of each blade is revealed and the right manipulation produces a succession of four painted scenes.

The folding fan novelties that Elizabeth I sent by foreign envoys as tokens of her friendship were expansive creations cut in vellum, parchment, taffeta, only less exquisite than their edgings of needlepoint lace. Until about the middle of the 17th century the fan opened to no more than about a third of a circle, on fewer than a dozen sticks, but late in the century it might spread to the full half circle, the mount so rich and massive that it extended down the sticks to cover two-thirds of their length, and the sticks themselves numbered as many as twenty-four.

Here then was the English folding fan in all its early magnificence. A fan made to the order of Charles II for the Duchess of Portsmouth was described as having a "skin mount, finely painted and finished, representing Ulysses before Deidamia with figures, slaves and camels, foliage and buildings. Sticks and guards of mother-of-pearl, carved with emblematic subjects, inset with gold ornaments; the whole buttoned with a paste rivet. On the reverse a landscape minutely detailed, attributed to Hollar. . . ."

Collectors today, however, rarely pursue their quest into an earlier reign than Anne's (1702–14) or George I's (1714–27). (American collectors find the craft well established in Boston by the 1730s). By Anne's reign painted mounts were at their exuberant loveliest, the finest being of vellum or the wonderfully supple kid or goat skin known as chicken-skin. These are painted in strong bright colours with gouache consisting of water colour paints given body and opacity with white and rendered supple with a little glue, too elastic to crack, and imparting to the work a fine velvety sheen. Subjects belonging to the first half of the 18th century cover the full range associated with the tapestry weavers. Gorgeous classical themes spread over the whole sweep of the mount in elaborate, lively scenes, or huntsmen gleam brightly against shady backgrounds and indulge in tremendous feasting.

Soon, however, many fans caught the rococo mood with fantastic scrolling borders and particular delight in lavish gilding that crowds in upon the painted scenes. Contending with this was the chinoiserie vogue, although English fan-makers of George II's day never achieved the international fame of Etienne Martin and his four sons, who developed a varnish imitating Oriental lacquer and introduced many European-Oriental designs. By the 1730s the Martins were using brilliant pigments on a gold lacquer ground and covering the full range of subjects required for export not only to England but to all quarters of Europe.

By the 18th century the fan sticks and guards, painted and jewelled in the previous century, became lightened by more adventurous piercing and carving in the same rococo mood and soon lost their early shouldered outline. There was a gradual change, too, from narrow sticks each bearing an identical pattern to designs that were wide and overlapping until eventually on the sticks as on the mount the fan would carry a single pattern or scene. The spread of the early Georgian fan was a little less than the half-circle but the whole fan had become huge by the 1740s, drawing the comment from the *London Magazine*, 1744, that they were "wonderfully increased in size from three-quarters of a foot to a foot and three-quarters or two feet". The *Universal Spectator* called them "monstrously large and monstrously strong". The exposed brins of the sticks were lengthened to display the full beauty of material and workmanship in mother-of-pearl, tortoiseshell or sweetly scented sandalwood, gilded, carved, spangled.

Madame de Pompadour fostered the use of ivory, obtaining specimens from the Orient to stimulate Parisian carvers. English fans may have carved ivory guards encrusted with gold ribbons and bows and studded with diamonds. When mount and sticks were made for each other the scene on the sticks may charmingly re-echo that upon the mount.

This is seen to perfection on some of the particularly lovely marriage fans that contributed to the brilliance of early Georgian days. These are a collector's byway of their own, but it is difficult to assemble a collection, despite the fact that innumerable bridegrooms gave such presents to their brides between about 1720 and 1800. In George II's reign the true bridal fan was created specially by a master fan-maker on finest vellum or chicken-skin with guards and sticks of carved ivory or mother-of-pearl or even lapis lazuli or coral.

Souvenir copies of this masterpiece were given to maids of honour and important guests, while still less significant fans, with hand-coloured printed mounts, were distributed to a wider circle, many of whom would already possess the betrothal fans distributed by the bride to announce her engagement, copied from the fan she had received from her fiancé. A betrothal fan may show the couple at the statue of Hymen, their portraits in miniature worked into the design, and the bridal fan, perhaps, more exquisite miniature portraits painted on ivory and framed into the jewelled guards, preserved by a case of shagreen. Painted on the mount itself may be bride and groom at the altar, an endlessly favoured subject, or in the guise of mythical deities, a notion even more frequently found carved into the brins, such as Venus receiving the homage of Mars.

Such a theme lent itself to the introduction of gay marriage emblems such as altars, doves, true lovers' knots, nuptial torches, festive masks and music trophies. Sometimes the wedding theme of the painting is more general, such as the marriage of Neptune and Amphitrite among marriage motifs surrounding interlaced initials worked in gold, or there may be a somewhat vague painting of lovers in a landscape among emblems of fidelity and constancy. The French artist Boucher himself was commissioned to paint the bridal fan for Louis XV to give his bride, and Boucher's work was copied extensively in England.

In the style of the artist Lancret a magnificent fan records the marriage of Anne, Crown Princess of England, daughter of George II, to Prince William IV of Orange in 1734. Anne is shown seated in a landscape attended by cupids and graces among trophies of love and war. George II ordered fifty copies from a leading London fan-maker. But many more souvenir and propaganda fans are associated with this betrothal and marriage, such as "Venus and Adonis" issued by M. Gamble, at the Sign of the Golden Fan, St. Martin's Court, London, and his subsequent "Orange Tree". Brisé marriage fans may be noted too, the ivory carved with suitable motifs, those of Oriental origin containing shields to be completed by English carvers or painters.

The marriage fan of the 1770s had lost some of its exclusive status, and London and Birmingham fan-makers produced a range of standard designs in tens of thousands—many for export—surrounding blank spaces to be filled by local artists or letterers. One firm under the name of Sarah Ashton printed fan mounts showing views of parish churches and their surroundings. Those found today are usually coloured and bear inscriptions directly related to specific occasions and individuals that bring them vividly to life. The prolific M. Gamble issued printed mounts on satin as well as paper for marriage fans, some painted in soft pastel colours with costume borders outlined in gold.

Throughout most of the 18th century, however, fan-makers like jewellers and dressmakers were devising designs to meet every possible contingency. It is fascinating to attempt distinction between fans for dancing, for walking, for baptism or bereavement. A white kid betrothal fan may show its rivet set with a pure white sapphire, while lush scenes of weeping willow, urn and marble slab in grey and black overlaid with white, on sticks of dark-stained ivory and silver mounted guards, permitted fashion to participate in the mourning for a royal death. Black fans were supplied to women mourners attending a funeral.

Church-goers were supplied with softly coloured mounts bearing Biblical and Apocryphal themes such as Solomon and the Queen of Sheba after a writer in the *Gentleman's Magazine* (1753) had complained of observing Hogarth's *Rake's Progress* and similar distractions among the congregation. Before the end of the century still less disturbing themes were offered "with the approbation of the Lord Bishop of London", and other fan mounts for chapel-goers.

At the other extreme a bold woman might feign modesty behind a lorgnette or quizzing fan from about 1755, peeping through transparent holes introduced inconspicuously in mount or sticks, or into tiny mirrors in the guards or even a spyglass above the rivet. A brief Parisian fashion note in the *Woman's Magazine* in 1806 mentions that "circular fans [parasol fans of the mid-Victorian Englishwoman] are too complicated, and fan very indifferently; but in their centre they conceal a perspective glass, which occasions the preference to be given to them".

By the third quarter of the 18th century a fan might extend

slightly beyond the half circle and include a more elaborate but less elegant design which has two, or more often three, narrow leaves across the sticks instead of the usual broad mount, the uppermost leaf being twice as deep as the others. This fan, too, reflected a passing whim and is known as the cabriolet fan, because one of these fashionable little carriages is to be found in the decoration, the equivalent, I imagine, of today's flashiest sports model and introduced into England in 1755 by Josiah Child.

By then, however, the fan was gradually losing its exuberance. The sticks became narrower and more widely spaced again. The painted scenes tended to be simplified into Watteau-esque pastorals that might be despised as mechanical were it not for their lovely colouring and the neo-classic mood may be noted in the ornamental motifs perfectly expressed in tiny Wedgwood bas reliefs among their carving. Collectors have long discarded the old notion that many artists of renown painted fans, and accept the skilled copying of work by Reynolds, West, Kauffmann, Watteau and the rest, occasionally with their signatures too. Angelica Kauffmann's picture of Sterne's Maria was immensely popular throughout Europe, and is found again and again on fans, plaques, jewellery.

On many of these later 18th-century fans the artist is restricted to tiny portraits or scenes in round or oval medallions set among musical trophies, flowers and ribbons or delicate formal tracery. Some medallions are painted on silk and applied to white silk mounts with spangles in gold or silver or, from about 1770, in burnished steel. These crescents, hearts, discs, stars were in and out of fashion on fans as often as on dresses throughout the century, and twinkled to every flutter of vellum, silk or satin, outlining designs in tambour stitch within guards of spangled ivory. There was even a brief vogue for covering silk fans with tiny painted motifs cut from vellum and vellum fans with scraps of silk in imitation, perhaps of the rare early mandarin fan peopled with queer little unreal figures, their faces cut from wisps of ivory and their dress from brilliant silks.

Among the finest medallion fans are those with solid

reserves set among the lovely fret designs of the brisé style: these may be painted with individual portraits by skilled miniaturists although subjects are often presented as classical figures, for this period was rediscovering such classical delights as the portrait cameo.

The Fan-makers' Guild, active from 1709, succeeded in stopping the import of painted fans from 1773, but by then a vast proportion of the trade had been transferred long ago to inexpensive printed work. Here, too, is a wonderful hunting ground for the enthusiast with a mind for the 18th century's political and social moods, and the patience for much crude, ugly, verbiose work among the charming and amusingly absurd. Here especially collectors follow their own interests: theatrical and political subjects are often among the least beautiful but most valuable.

Always, of course, paper must have the texture and quality of hand manufacture, although some collectors do now accept the 19th-century printing processes of lithography and aquatinting as well as the earlier line and line-and-stipple and mezzotint engraving on a base of vellum, silk or paper. Colouring may appear to be hasty but as often is delightful, such as the late-18th-century favourite of a brown-printed design with blue for the field and silver and white for added detail. Some printed fans were perfumed, a treatment that might have destroyed a painted specimen.

Here was a chance for endless topical themes, the paper quickly ripped from the sticks when a new idea caught the popular fancy. Royalty was feted, politicians were derided, plays were advertised, songs were plugged, victories celebrated, dance steps taught. One day the popular choice was a crude design showing the King's Champion challenging the world on behalf of his monarch at George II's coronation banquet; another day every fan was celebrating the peace of Aix la Chapelle. When Swift's *Gulliver's Travels* caught the public imagination in 1726 every woman had her Lilliputian fan, but equally welcome was, say, such an event as the ascent of Biaggini's air balloon—and "The Fall of ye Balloon". Tens of thousands of printed fans were issued by such fan-makers as M. Gamble. Collectors soon come to look for his name and, after 1749, for some reference to the fact that the publishing of the fan complied with the Act of that year—the Act, not the fan, being of that date.

Early printed fans tend to be crude and it is vain to look for much artistic quality, but after about 1760 they improved, and some of the leading engravers of the day contributed classical and mythological designs, printed in black or sanguin, often over-painted by hand. The use of lithography, invented in 1798, is sometimes hard to detect under hand painting. Subjects of these later fans may be intriguing still, such as a vivid representation of a Napoleonic invasion, the ships supported by balloon air cover and a channel tunnel prepared for arms and infantry. "The Ladies Conversation Fan" appeared in 1797 and a "New Gipsey Fan" for fortune-telling about the same time. Others require to be read rather than looked at, such as "England Since the Conquest", dated 1793, with plain bone guards and sticks and scarcely a trace of ornament among the closely spaced script.

By then the fan's most aristocratic phase was coming to an end. *The Ladies' Magazine*, devoting page after page to the dress worn by the highest in the land on splendid royal occasions, scarcely once mentions a fan in the years 1806–08, save in a brief fashion note from Paris which offers a clue to the situation: "The fans are constantly very small and the bouquets very large". Not only were they small but also comparatively inconspicuous, often of thin silk or cobweb net or muslin with no ornament save a little wispy painting or a scattering of spangles, a style that reappeared late in the century when it, too, was an expression of nostalgia—for the lost "Empire" days.

The loop on the fan for a ribbon to hang on the arm, while the wearer coped also with bouquet, smelling bottle or ornamental handkerchief, is a 19th-century addition, and fan chains figure among the delicate details of Victorian dress, some being of hair. Even in the brisé fan, however, the finely fretted ivory and mother-of-pearl tended to be replaced by bone, sometimes lightly painted, laburnum wood and cut steel. Even horn was in use by the 1830s. Medallions on the brisé fan blades were covered with engravings hastily coloured. Only nine names of London fan-makers appear in Pigot's directory of 1822–23, and by 1839 only two.

Revival came early in Victoria's reign, of course, but little that was new. Wide vellum or paper mounts painted with idyllic—but fundamentally Victorian—figures and pastoral scenes, mother-of-pearl sticks carved in elaborate scrolling patterns, all these were retained throughout the reign; sometimes they are very large, but all remember the 18th century's discovery of such splendour, and in any case few are of English manufacture. More general use of smaller and less splendid fans returned in the 1850s–60s, many with somewhat coarsely pierced sticks and muslin mounts spangled with cut steel stars and flowers, or of flower-painted silk, or in a brisé style of sandalwood painted with the horsy, doggy motifs that characterised the trimmings of the mid-Victorian outdoor girl. Some were the work of amateurs.

By the 1870s fans were considered essential once more and feather fans of this period, for example, are a subject in themselves for all who love the rare quality of their colours and textures; these were followed later in the century by ostrich plumes, black or white, and mounted accordingly on tortoiseshell or mother-of-pearl. A curious offshoot of this vogue for feathers was the fan with ivory sticks each mounted with a separate feather-shape cut in silk and merely edged at the top with an inch or so of real feather to soften the outline. If means allowed, however, the later Victorian flaunted a fan of exquisite hand-made lace or the nearest approximation she could afford at a time when machine-made net supported a variety of needle and bobbin work. Here at last was the perfect declaration of wealth and good taste, with no trace of vulgar ostentation, to be comprehended only by those with an equally keen eye for quality and technique, making a further contribution to the age-old language of the fan.

Index